D1565549

CALLED to SERVE

Stories of Men and Women Confronted by the Vietnam War Draft

Tom Weiner

For Ed,
In honor of your
extraordinary story that deserves
a book! And with hopes that.
these testimonies further illuminate
those turbulent times!
Fondly,
Tom Weiner

Printed and published by
Levellers Press
Amherst & Florence, Massachusetts

ISBN 978-0-9819820-4-5

To the memory of George Williams, crusader for justice, artist, writer, humanitarian and a veteran for peace who died in September, 2010. He wholeheartedly supported this work.

To all who gave so freely of their time, energy and memory to promote the long overdue healing that still needs to occur almost forty years after the end of the Vietnam War.

TABLE OF CONTENTS

PREFACE

Charlie Clements attended the Air Force Academy and went on to fly cargo planes during the Vietnam War. After the experience of extricating himself from his role in the Vietnam War, which he delineates below, he became a physician combining his medical skills with human rights activism in Central America. He spent the early 1980s treating victims of the civil war in El Salvador, some wounded by the same U.S. military aircraft in which he once trained. He wrote about his experiences there in Witness to War *(Bantam, 1984). He led the first fact-finding mission of Vietnam veterans to Central America, which included many of the early activists of Veterans for Peace. In 1997 as president of Physicians for Human Rights he represented that organization at both the treaty signing and Nobel Prize ceremonies for the International Campaign to Ban Landmines. Now, at 65, he is executive director of the Carr Center for Human Rights Policy at the Harvard Kennedy School. The Center's mission statement reads in part: "Our research, teaching and writing are guided by a commitment to make human rights principles central to the formulation of good public policy in the United States and throughout the world." Charlie is a tireless advocate for peace and justice.*

Millions of men's and women's lives in the 1960s and each of our subsequent life's directions were profoundly affected by the war in Vietnam. If we supported the war, we may have stopped whatever we were doing at the time to enlist. If we did not believe in participating in the fighting, we faced the moral dilemma: Will I just wait to see what my draft number turns out to be, taking the risk of being sent to Vietnam, or will I choose among alternative strategies, some legal, some not, some straightforward, some not, some of which included military service but avoided the risk of a combat tour in Vietnam? And some of us simply responded to the draft or volunteered out of a sense of duty without knowing anything about Vietnam. Our opinions on the war evolved with our experience.

Whether we fought in Vietnam, served in the military outside the theater of war, provided alternative community service, sought a real or crafted medical exemption, went to Canada or Sweden, burned our draft card and went to jail, or were the friend, partner, spouse, or parent of someone in one of those categories, our life choices and directions for our futures surely were powerfully impacted by the existence of the draft.

Over the decades, I have waited for someone to recognize and write about the profound fork in the road facing those of us affected by military conscription in the 1960s and '70s. Assuredly, there have been a lot of books that looked at the lives of men (and women) who followed the path of serving in Vietnam. Now, *finally,* there is a book exploring both that decision as well as the lives of some who chose the other fork in the road. Could the latter be said to be the "road less traveled?" I think not: it's only the road less written about.

I, too, faced the fork in the road, which would forever change my life. As a fairly new pilot and recent Distinguished Graduate of the U.S. Air Force Academy, I chose to fly a cargo plane, so I wouldn't have to kill anyone. I felt an obligation to be there, but I wanted a role in which I considered myself a non-combatant. After nine months of flying fresh troops from the large bases where they would land, out to firebases, and then picking them up – when they left for R&R, when they were wounded or had died, or as their one-year tours of duty were ending – I began to feel very differently about the war. I watched on Armed Forces Television one day as President Nixon looked the American public in the eye and lied to them about the U.S. not being engaged in a combat role in Laos.

Gradually I began to see the deception every place I turned and I was being asked to participate in it. I knew we had many not-so-secret bases where American pilots in civilian clothes, who did not carry military identification, flew unmarked aircraft in support of U.S. covert military operations in Laos. In January of 1970, I flew a top-secret mission into Phnom Penh, Cambodia for what I was told was a State Department delegation. Later I was told that it had been a CIA mission, that in six weeks Prince Sihanouk would be toppled in a coup when he went to Paris for a medical consultation, and that the U.S. would be 'invited' to invade Cambodia. I didn't believe it. Six weeks later Lon Nol took power in a coup.

And suddenly I was facing a dilemma very much like the dilemma facing my classmates from graduate school who had been morally opposed to the war. Would I continue to participate in something I had come to understand was morally wrong? Would I just go along for another few months until my tour of duty was completed? Would I stand on principle and risk a court martial to make a statement?

On April 30, 1970 I flew a dozen sorties from Long Binh Army Base near Saigon to a firebase in the "Parrot's Beak", a small protrusion of Vietnam into Cambodia. On each flight we ferried about eighty combat-ready American soldiers, who I came to understand were preparing to invade Cambodia. At the end of the day I refused to fly further missions, a decision which would land me in an Air Force psychiatric ward. As difficult and lonely as that experience was at the time, that decision was the first step of a discernment process that would forever change my life.

So in some ways I was part of both the world of those who served, and those who refused to serve in the war. I saw that most in each group felt they were serving their country; those who protested the war felt themselves to be as patriotic as those who served.

Today, North Vietnamese and Viet Cong soldiers who once fought fiercely against American soldiers are engaged in reunions with those they once attempted to kill. The Vietnamese military works hand-in-glove with American military teams trying to find those designated as Missing in Action. American organizations such as Vietnam Veterans of America have asked their members to return memorabilia they may have taken from dead Viet Cong or North Vietnamese soldiers, so they can help the families of their former enemies have closure. American veterans as well, as some who actively opposed the war, return to Vietnam to assist families damaged by Agent Orange.

Unfortunately, those who fought each other in Southeast Asia have done far more reconciliation work than those of us who stood on opposite sides of the war here at home. It's my hope that *Called to Serve* will be read' and shared by those who supported the war as well as those who opposed it, because a great deal of unexpressed grief, unresolved anger, and probably many unspoken misunderstandings, still divide us.

Reading these poignant stories can encourage all of us to bring our truths, our experiences, out into the open. After all, how can we heal from the divisiveness of war if we don't even speak and listen to each another?

Aeschylus, the Greek playwright, understood the power of these emotions when more than three thousand years ago he wrote: "He who learns must suffer. And even in our sleep pain that cannot forget falls drop by drop upon the heart, and in our own despair, against our will, comes wisdom to us by the awful grace of God."

  May these personal reflections, which Tom Weiner has so carefully and so respectfully gathered, help us both individually and collectively find wisdom and healing from the many ways we looked this moral dilemma in the eye and the very personal choices we made in response.

INTRODUCTION

I'VE BEEN ON A QUEST — FOR *FORTY* YEARS AND MORE. It began with the Vietnam War era draft lottery in December of 1969. The war was not going well, in Asia or at home, and in an attempt to blunt the anti-war movement and provide additional soldiers more democratically, the Nixon administration in its first year inaugurated a lottery. I will never forget the night, December 1, 1969, when the first drawing occurred. Several fellow Trinity College students and I didn't want to be just sitting in a room when we got our numbers, so we were listening to the radio as we drove around Hartford. As the capsules containing slips of paper with all of our birth dates on them were drawn from a water-cooler-size glass bowl, we held our collective breath hoping we'd be chosen in the latter half of the pool and thereby avoid the draft and all it betokened.

I still remember the nervous energy with which each number and accompanying birthday was greeted. One of my friends received a number in the 30s, and we offered sympathy along with a good measure of gallows humor. However, I had to wait a bit longer before my birthday, October 22, received #117. I knew full well that unless the war miraculously ended before I graduated in May of 1971 and lost my 2-S student deferment, a number like 117 meant I'd be receiving my draft notification even before graduation.

I stared out the windshield at the surreal sight of people walking calmly through downtown Hartford. Didn't they know our lives were at stake? Didn't the announcer realize he was sending some of us to a terrible fate? Wasn't there something very wrong with how this was unfolding? How could driving around in a car lead to finding out whether you'd go to war? Were my parents listening? Did they fully realize what my number meant? I thought of my friend, Michael, who so desperately wanted to avoid the draft, he'd enlisted in the Marine Reserves. What number would he have received? Would he have been able to avoid the *six*-year commitment to the military already affecting his psyche?

I couldn't participate in the joking and silliness with which we defended ourselves. I sat in silence for several minutes. Now I knew my future. At the same time, all over the country, other men twenty to twenty-five years old were also learning their fates, so I knew I was not alone.

It wasn't that I hadn't been thinking about the draft already. The war and all it meant for our country and for me personally had been on my mind and the minds of virtually everyone I knew at Trinity College. It didn't matter whether it was hearing the latest horror stories, or witnessing the shell of a man who came back to school after a clearly traumatic stint in 'Nam; whether it was participating in yet another demonstration or having an argument with an ROTC student about whether the war was legitimate, let alone effective, the late '60s was about Vietnam. Without a doubt, it was more in our minds than any and everything else – school, civil rights, rock music, drugs and, that previous summer, Woodstock and a man on the moon.

Since I so completely opposed what the U.S. military was doing in Vietnam, I had to make serious preparations for what was more and more clearly going to happen as graduation approached. I filed a CO (conscientious objector) application with the support of a draft counselor. Fortunately, I was in the privileged position of being able to see all the doctors I needed to see to arrive with documentation of my back injury, allergies, mental health issues, and the calcium deposits on my feet. I, like many of my peers, both listened to and then watched, *Alice's Restaurant,* in which Arlo Guthrie tells the story of a man resorting to temporary insanity to flunk his physical. The film was, in other words, deep into American youth culture by the time I was ordered to report to my draft board in Newark, New Jersey, less than a week after graduation.

I arrived in Newark feeling as anxious as I had ever felt about anything in my life. Although I had numerous possible causes for failing the physical, I was completely unprepared for being one of the only white people in the room, knowing at that moment beyond doubt's shadow that if I was successful in avoiding serving my country in a war I believed was unjust, then someone else, someone who was very likely to be black, was going instead of me. My succeeding in not going did not mean one less person was required. It simply meant that someone else would take my place. I remembered studying the Civil War and learning how those who could afford it were able to pay someone to take their place. Was this different? I was troubled and very confused.

And then there was the actual examination. It turned out that none of my physical ailments, though well documented, were sufficient to have me fail. Then I got to see an Army shrink, since I had a letter from the school counselor at Trinity documenting my need for therapy while a student there. What happened next, though etched in my memory, must be one of the briefest interviews in draft board history.

A man sitting behind a desk asked me two questions. First – "Have you ever smoked marijuana?" to which I answered in the affirmative. Second – "Have you ever had any suicidal fantasies?" to which I again responded yes.

That was it. He leaned over the paper I brought in to him, wrote very few words, called me over to the desk, and handed it to me. I glanced down, and to my great relief I saw the designation 1-Y, which I knew meant I was out. However, right beside it I saw the words "Drug Abuse." It was 1971 and, with the well-documented information about drug abuse in the military that has been revealed since that time, it is retrospectively much less surprising that those two very brief responses were sufficient to result in my new status. More cannon fodder waited outside his door.

An article by Peter Beinart in *The New Republic* of May 10, 2004, entitled "Two Countries" discusses this reality from the perspective of both then and now:

> In 1975, James Fallows wrote a famous essay for *The Washington Monthly* titled, "What Did You Do in the Class War, Daddy?" In it, he recounted taking a bus to the Boston Navy Yard with other Harvard students drafted to serve in Vietnam. Soon after, another bus pulled up, this one filled with draftees from the working-class town of Chelsea. The Harvard students brought medical records carefully manipulated to show they were unfit to serve – and roughly 80 percent returned to campus "as free individuals, liberated and victorious." The draftees from Chelsea, by contrast, "walked through the examination lines like so many cattle off to the slaughter." Fallows remembers the moment the military doctor wrote "unqualified" on his folder. "I was overcome by a wave of relief, which for the first time revealed to me how great my terror had been, and by the beginning of the sense of shame which remains with me to this day."
>
> Fallows's essay is a withering indictment of the generational elite to which he belonged. His peers, he argues, took the easy way out – neither serving nor accepting jail as a consequence of their refusal to serve – and thus never applied the political pressure that might have forced an earlier end to the war. But, harsh as the essay is, it still feels, by current journalistic standards, a

little quaint. Shame? In the elite America in which I grew up, the military was a distant, self-contained world – populated by other Americans – with no conceivable claim on me. And now those other Americans, some my age, are dying halfway across the globe. I may feel sad, even angry, but how can I feel shame when no one ever suggested it should be any different? What did you do in the terror war, daddy? I fear my own answer, in its way, will be even worse.

So I was out, which was clearly my goal. However, I was conscious not only of my place being taken by another, most likely an African American given the location of my draft board in Newark, but also of the damage I might have caused myself with this new designation as a drug abuser. Would it negatively affect my future prospects for further schooling and/or employment? Was this an acceptable way to have "beaten the draft?" It surely was not one of the ways I had anticipated or planned for when developing my multi-pronged strategy, but I was definitely willing to employ any means necessary. I was most confused and anxious.

When I got back home to Teaneck, New Jersey, my parents were supportive and relieved. I called my draft counselor and told him the story, sharing my concerns about having the words "Drug Abuse" follow me. Then I received his reassuring words, "Don't worry. You'll be a hero someday soon." Though I never felt like a hero, he was correct. I didn't need to worry. As the war continued, and it became ever clearer that our country would never succeed in either selling the war to its people or winning, what it said on my draft card became a non-issue and has remained so until this day.

From the start, I was aware of the incredible lengths my age-mates were willing to go to avoid the war. There were those who feigned mental illness, who took strange combinations of drugs to flunk the urine test, who chose to attempt to starve themselves or to accentuate and document physical or mental ailments that did not actually affect their daily lives. One friend pretended he was gay. Each of these "performances" had risks attached and led to great anxiety, as did the decision to leave the country or face jail. After hearing many of these stories at the time they were unfolding, I became convinced that somehow, some day, I would do what I could to bring them to light.

Now it feels especially important to tell the story. As those of us who were directly affected have begun to hit and pass through middle age, it's clear that if nobody ever writes these memories down, the tales will not only be lost to our fellow Americans in general, but perhaps more importantly, they will be unavailable to the generation coming of age during the current controversial wars in Iraq and Afghanistan who could make use of their lessons.

In preserving these stories, I first thought to focus exclusively on the lottery's impact. However, as I dug deeper, it became clear that the draft itself, before and after the lottery, had changed the lives of every person it touched. For some, facing the draft meant exploring alternatives to serving, which included conscientious objection, a jail sentence, or leaving the country. For others, the possibility of the draft, or of receiving a low number, caused them to enlist or to participate in ROTC (Reserve Officer Training Corps), OCS (Officer Candidate School) or the reserves. Consequently, it seemed clearly important to include these stories as well.

The personal narratives in this book reveal in their complexity, their intensity, and their humanity, the deep emotional significance these pivotal moments had in the lives of those who experienced them. Yes, the war is about casualties, politics, strategies, victories and losses, but as the enormous outpouring of accounts of the Vietnam War convey, this particular war is also about what happened to a generation of men and women who were required to make life-changing decisions at too young an age, when their values, circumstances and lives were still in flux. These decisions would have effects ranging from having military and selective service records that could follow and haunt a person throughout one's life, to alienation from one's family, to serving time in jail, to expatriation, to risking one's life.

It is still not a simple matter. When a newspaper article was written about my book project, I asked the reporter to keep the answer to the questions I was asked about my marijuana use "off the record." I teach a unit entitled Human Growth and Change with two weeks devoted to drug education. Would the parents of my students have concerns about my having used "drugs" – even thirty-nine years ago? Would that compromise my teaching? The material was still loaded for me. But telling my story here is oddly freeing.

In virtually every interview I undertook, the subjects voiced the realization that the choices faced and the decisions made had an enormous impact on their subsequent lives. The chance to remember themselves with as much power and vividness as memory can supply has also offered them help in coming to terms these many years later with whatever actions they ended up taking. Reflecting upon who they were, how their families influenced them, how the times – the music, the drugs, the protest movements, the politics – shaped them provided an opportunity to look back with the advantage of age and perspective. My only regret is this book has to have an end, because it's my belief there are countless other tales, equally compelling, that deserve to be remembered, told, and honored.

But why this particular book at this point in time? There are numerous other Vietnam oral histories, and I commend them all. In books like *We Won't Go: Personal Accounts of War Objectors* (1968) collected by Alice Lynd, and *Hell No, We Won't Go: Resisting the Draft During the Vietnam War* (1991) by Sherry Gershon Gottlieb, draft resisters speak their truth and tell their stories. So do African American men in *Bloods* (1984) by Wallace Terry. *Chance and Circumstance* (1978) seeks to be comprehensive in its examination of the Vietnam generation and covers much ground, but uses research and data, rather than first person accounts of those who experienced the draft, to bring the reality to the reader. Also, the fact that it was published in 1978 allowed little time and distance for reflection.

Individual memoirs by people like Ron Kovics and, of course, the great works of fiction that illuminate the Vietnam War – Tim O'Brien's *Going After Cacciatore* (1979) and *The Things They Carried* (1990); Larry Heinemann's *Close Quarters* (1977); Denis Johnson's recent *Tree of Smoke* (2007) – allow the reader access to all levels of an individual's experience. A recent memoir by Doug Anderson, who is a subject of this project, entitled *Keep Your Head Down* (2009), enables the reader to get to know him even more multi-dimensionally than his interview allowed.

What this book does, which has not been attempted either in the immediate aftermath of the war or since, is bring to bear the wide range of possible outcomes of facing the draft and, in the case of the women interviewed, the war itself, into one volume. Given the full range of experiences detailed here, the reader is able to recapture the fullness of the war's effects on those who did and did not serve. In addition, instead of simply recounting what happened at a physical or during basic training or even while in jail, the interview subjects contextualized their experiences, making it easier for the reader to more fully understand "where they were coming from" as the draft landed on them.

The stories clearly indicate more healing needs to occur for our country to learn Vietnam's lessons. Inevitably there were painful disagreements between the various groups who felt strongly about whichever of the various approaches they took in response to the draft. Having their stories collected together makes it possible for veterans to see what the resisters were thinking and how their choices played out, while those who sought and received conscientious objector status can better appreciate the choice made by those who found ways to "beat the draft." Creating a broader understanding can go a long way to help the Vietnam generation stop reliving the war or seeking someone to blame for its outcome.

As for my methodology, the process of creating the book was organic. As I've said, it began with my interest in the draft lottery. However, as the word spread via announcements I put up, the news story about the book in the local paper, and the various networks I was able to tap into in my community, men not only came to ask if they could tell their story about the draft, but also often told me about a man or woman they knew who had a powerful story I should include in the book. Some of these stories were about men who served after being drafted. Their experiences were compelling in different ways and also important to chronicle.

In terms of the interview process itself, I would usually begin by explaining, by phone or an e-mail, the purposes of the book: to allow for a re-examination of a critical time in the subject's life and to have a repository for a wide range of experiences, so others could benefit from them. Then the initial interview generally began with a series of questions regarding the subject's circumstances prior to the draft, and the effects of the draft on his or her life. Once the interviewee became comfortable, however, my asking further questions that pointed in a certain direction, e.g. "What did your parents think about your response to the draft?" or "What was your position on the war?" seemed to actually limit the completeness of the subject's narrative. As a result, the process became one of close listening, allowing the subject to tell his or her story without being nudged or prodded. I recorded the interviews and gave assurances to the subject that he or she would have final say over what was published.

The editing process proved very challenging as every story contained parts that were difficult to eliminate, and some of the sixty-one stories I received could not be included at all due to space constraints in the current volume. I know there are many people across the country who could have been included, but I had to limit myself geographically due primarily to financial and temporal constraints. Not surprisingly, given our mobile society, many of those featured in the book who now live in western Massachusetts, grew up all over the country, so their draft boards represent very different communities throughout the U.S. It is my contention that similar books could have been written from many states and regions. Had I been living in a different part of the country there might have been more divergent views about whether the war was worthwhile, or whether it was fought with the right strategy, but its effects would have been no less profound for those who faced the draft.

When it came time to move towards publication, each subject was able to revisit his or her interview. Many had been transcribed by students at nearby Smith College where I am employed, through a program called STRIDE, which matches students with faculty members working on projects leading to research study and/or book publication. Interestingly, though not surprisingly, these students found the interviews to be fascinating and most educational, given their awareness of the Vietnam War was minimal. They had many questions, since the references made were remote and required explanation in order for them to make sense of what they were typing. Their ignorance of this major historical event, the Vietnam era draft, is another reason such a book is necessary.

What I am left with, as my quest finally comes to a close, is a feeling of gratitude to all of those who so willingly told me their stories. I am very thankful I was able to participate in a process by which the subjects got to know themselves better. For them, and for me, there is now a clearer sense of closure to this harrowing chapter of our lives, and to the repercussions it had both at the time and since. The men and women who shared what I have come to call their "testimonies" with me deserve recognition for their honesty, their courage in facing their past regardless of what it contained, and their support for this project.

That's the why and how of the project. The what, the stories themselves, will take you back to a different time and place, a time when the hopes of a generation striving to transform the cultural landscape in a myriad of ways never seen before ran up against the realities of the Vietnam War. Regardless of how they felt about this war, young men between the ages of nineteen and twenty-five were forced to confront it. The very existence of the draft necessitated taking a stand. Was it the draft itself that helped bring the war to a close? Would we still be fighting wars in Iraq and Afghanistan if there were such a draft now? These stories will provide a look into what was motivating young men and women during those turbulent times, and perhaps shed some light on what is happening, and not happening, now.

CHAPTER ONE

THE DRAFT IN AMERICA: A BRIEF HISTORY

WHETHER THE CAUSE FOR WHICH THEY WERE DRAFTED WAS POPULAR or reviled, and whether their opposition was religious, moral, legal, or otherwise, since our country's beginnings men have objected to being seized by the federal government and made to fight. So that the reader can better understand the testimonies that are about to unfold, and place them in the proper historical context, here is a brief review of the causes and effects of the various drafts that have occurred since the country's inception.

America's earliest settlers came predominantly from Great Britain, so it is important to understand the impact of the British culture on our military procedures. The British Army was a microcosm of the larger British society, and as such, reflected its class structure. Most of the officers were members of the moneyed classes, the aristocracy and the landed gentry. Officers were obliged to purchase their commissions and promotions. Some were highly motivated by the ideals of service, honor, and duty. Some went into battle to burnish their images, make names for themselves, and increase their prestige. The best among them believed that workingmen, who made up the bulk of common soldiers, were under their protection. But others exhibited behaviors in the field and in battle that were motivated by money and status and sometimes by sadism. Officers rode on horseback while the rank and file marched, and they were used to lavish accommodations (for the battlefield), complete with tents, cots, servants, and claret.

The common soldier typically came from the lowest classes. The army was a reprieve from starvation, unemployment, poverty, boredom and legal problems. Recruits were bribed with alcohol and small amounts of money, along with false promises of high wages, fine living conditions, opportunities for promotion, and, of course, adventure. Once they had accepted their shillings and drams, however, soldiers were often mistreated, faced with harsh discipline, poor pay and food, and unhealthy accommodations.[1] And officers, in general, looked down on them.

During the Napoleonic Wars, Field Marshal Arthur Wellesley, First Duke of Wellington, famously referred to his soldiers as "the scum of the earth."[2] Here is a description of the 18th century British army that George Washington belonged to and then challenged, both militarily and culturally:

> Since Parliament was consistently reluctant to sponsor a substantial standing army (they feared such a body would be unduly influenced by the crown) the British infantry was an elastic collective of uneducated British peasants between [the ages of] 17 and 50, Scots, Irishmen, many thousands of foreign troops (most often Hessian mercenaries), aggressively recruited in times of war, and unsupported and neglected during intervals of peace.[3]

This is a characterization of the individual soldier, as printed between 1698 and 1700 in *The London Spy,* a tabloid clearly critical of the British army:

> A Foot Soldier is commonly a Man, who for the sake of wearing a Sword, and the Honour of being term'd a Gentleman, is coax'd from a Handicraft Trade, whereby he might Live comfortably, to bear Arms for his King and Country, whereby he has the hopes of nothing but to Live Starvingly...The best end he can expect to make, is to Die in the Bed of Honour; and the greatest Living Marks of his Bravery, to recommend him at once to the World's Praise and Pity, are Crippled Limbs, with which I shall leave him to beg a better Lively Hood.[4]

This military tradition bred some of the customs followed by the fledgling American forces, but also explains the antagonism to that tradition that developed.

The story of the draft in America starts with the very beginnings of our country. Who had the right to raise troops in the first place? What were the circumstances that could demand such an action? When was it appropriate for the government to use conscription? And who was likeliest to be called?

The inhabitants of the original colonies, composed as they were largely of British settlers, adopted a system for the common defense with which they were familiar – the English militia system. All men between the ages of sixteen and sixty were required to own firearms and to defend their village or town from attack. The members of the militia convened once a week for drill, and, every evening, members stood guard, acting as town watchmen or town criers in case of trouble. When the Pequot Indians were perceived as a significant threat to the Massachusetts Bay Colony, the General Court of the Colony, by an order dated December 13, 1636, organized the individual militias into three regiments – the North, the South, and the East. This is now seen as the precursor of the National Guard.[5]

During the Revolutionary War, new state-based governments assumed the authority to draft men that the colonies had used for establishing these militias. This authority was then extended to include long-term state-specific military units in Washington's Continental Army, but the states denied Washington's request that the fledgling federal government be empowered to conscript directly; in essence, the men were seen to be on loan.

As volunteering for these military units subsided, most states increased their forces via enlistment bounties and the occasional draft, which produced more hired substitutes – predominantly the poor and unemployed – than actual draftees.[6]

Since that time, power, influence and money have played a predominant role in deciding who ends up doing the fighting. From the very beginning, a disproportionate number of poor men have been compelled to serve and a similarly disproportionate number of more affluent men have found ways to avoid combat or service altogether.

Several states recognized Quaker and other religious conscientious objectors, while some dissenters suffered. Perhaps not surprisingly, the short-term militia was largely middle class, while the long-term volunteers and substitutes of the Continental Army were mainly poor young men, white and black – indentured servants, laborers, unemployed drifters, recent immigrants, or the sons of marginal farmers. Not only were these men often poorly trained and led, but many also left service unpredictably to return home and maintain their farms.[7]

At best, conscription during the war produced mixed results, and success varied considerably on a state-by-state basis. The New England states and New Jersey filled their quotas most of the time; they did not have to rely on a draft, because the very possibility of conscription stimulated men to volunteer. On the other hand, Virginia, with an almost constant demand for troops, was much less successful. According to one chronicler, "Of the 3,250 men requested to be drafted by an act of the [Virginia] legislature in October 1780, only 773 draftees were delivered to the army."[8]

Resistance became widespread in Virginia. It sometimes took the form of physical rebellion. For example, "In Accomack County on the Eastern Shore, in May 1781, several hundred men armed with clubs, swords and pistols prevented the holding of a draft."[9] Draft records were often the targets of mobs. These protests were caused by a combination of frequent call-ups, hardships endured by families, and fears of the "horrors of the Southern climates."[10] They resulted in Governor Jefferson suspending the draft in thirty-seven counties.[11]

With the adoption of the Constitution in 1789, Congress (in Article I, Section 8) was given the power "To raise and support armies..." and " To provide and maintain a navy." Conscription was neither explicitly allowed nor prohibited, though the same Section 8 maintains that Congress has the right "To provide for calling forth the militia to execute the laws of the union, suppress insurrections and repel invasions..." and "To provide for organizing, arming, and disciplining the militia, and for governing such part of them as may be employed in the service of the United States...."[12]

As president, Washington proposed federal legislation to address his concern about the difficulties that would arise in mounting an armed force were there to be another war, but his efforts were futile. In his original proposal for a national Bill of Rights, James Madison included the following clause: "No person religiously scrupulous of bearing arms shall be compelled to render military service in person." It is not clear why this clause was not adopted, but the evidence suggests the framers favored leaving the question of military exemptions to the states.[13] For the most part, they believed that the United States, like Great Britain, would enlist, rather than conscript its men, and fund future wars through taxation. Only Rhode Island, at its 1790 ratifying convention, voiced concerns regarding the "potential oppression of national conscription."[14] Their delegates ended up presenting an unsuccessful amendment that "no person should be compelled to do military duty otherwise than by voluntary enlistment except in cases of general invasion."[15]

The Constitutional provision was not the end of the government's efforts to hold sway over America's military. The Militia Act of 1792 sought to strengthen the Constitutional clause regarding the government's power to call men to serve. Under its provisions the president could call state militia during an emergency. Those so called would have the same status as "regulars" and receive the same pay. The act was first put to use the same year it was created when militiamen from four states were called up to suppress the Whiskey Rebellion in western Pennsylvania. Once again, as during the Revolutionary War, the force of 12,500 men, mainly draftees, was comprised mostly of the very poor and destitute. Many refused to be drafted when they realized they would be expected to wage war against their countrymen. Violent protest to the draft occurred in several counties in Maryland and Virginia, but fortunately for the fledgling government, the rebellion itself quickly died down. This prevented further draft resistance, which would have been a stern test of the country's wherewithal to handle such actions.[16]

With only limited or sporadic threats to national security over the next hundred years, a two-army tradition was created. The small volunteer Regular Army was a "peacetime constabulary and wartime cadre."[17] From the Indian wars of the 1790's through the Spanish-American War of 1898, the wartime armies were comprised both of citizen-soldiers and volunteers who were locally raised and led but federally financed and directed. Volunteers were distinct from the U.S. Army and the militia, later called the National Guard.[18]

The War of 1812 saw some states use the draft. Daniel Webster, a Federalist opponent of the government, denounced the effort as an attempt at "Napoleonic despotism."[19] He was not alone. A significant number of congressman believed that the Constitution did not give the federal government the power to conscript. Jeremiah Mason put forth the argument that conscription was a direct refutation of the personal freedom the Constitution guaranteed.[20] Given the opposition, Madison's administration failed to enact national conscription.

As the war dragged on, recruitment efforts were undertaken including thirteen-month enlistment periods, a sixteen-dollar sign-up bonus, and a promise of three months' pay and one hundred sixty acres of land upon discharge. Even with these incentives, the government failed to attract the requisite number of recruits, so Congress authorized President James Monroe to call up one hundred thousand members of the state militia. With the central government still seeking to define its role and power, some states did not comply, and the soldiers who were compelled to serve were mostly untrained and "frequently unwilling to face the enemy."[21]

The outbreak of the Civil War, which created the need to sustain massive armies for years at a time, gave America its first experience of a national draft. The Confederacy adopted a draft in April 1862. It had a smaller population to draw upon for its military, and its conscription policy eventually included white males seventeen to thirty-five (later amended to fifty) years old. Twenty-one percent of the eventual one million Confederate soldiers were drafted, but many saw conscription as a violation of individual liberty and the states' rights that had been the battle cry of the Confederacy. Unpopular class-bound occupation exemptions (such as that of overseer on large plantations) only succeeded in fomenting more discontent and resistance. On top of whatever inequities were real or perceived, the draft policy also included a three-year term of service. In 1865, with defeat an increasing likelihood, the Confederate Army began to conscript slaves.[22]

In the North the need for a sustainable army, likely to be in existence at unparalleled numbers for several additional years, became clear. In 1863 the North inaugurated a selective conscription law as volunteers dwindled, casualties increased, and desertions soared. It applied to males from ages twenty to forty-five. Occupational exemptions analogous to those that had sparked unrest in the South were disallowed. Instead draftees were entitled to escape personal service by hiring a substitute or by paying the government a three hundred dollar commutation fee that resulted in exemption from the draft. This was equal to an average worker's annual wages, but it turned out to be less than the going rate for substitutes. At this point, Peace Democrats claimed it was a "rich man's war, but a poor man's fight."[23]

When military provost marshals began conscripting, thousands evaded or actively resisted the draft. In 1863 New York City's famous and bloody Draft Riots occurred. The causes of these riots were many and complex. There were deep social ills that had festered for decades before the war. In addition, there were economic upheavals resulting from the fact that one of the southernmost of northern cities derived much of its revenue from slave-dependent industries. Irish immigrants who participated in the riots had felt the double sting of losing jobs to free blacks willing to work for less (just as many of the Irish had been willing when first arriving in America during the Potato Famine in the 1840s) *and* being required to serve in a war that would, should the North emerge victorious, result in countless more free blacks. Arguably, the three hundred dollar exemption merely added salt to the wounds of the marginalized, whose list of injustices had been growing long before the National Conscription Act became law. On July 11, 1863, the York *Daily News* stated, "That the Conscription exempts the rich and fastens its iron hand upon the poor alone, is sufficient demonstration of its injustice."[24] New York was the epicenter of the nation's wealthiest and poorest citizens. To replenish the forces that had been severely tested and were now depleted, northern authorities increased enlistment bounties.

Southern blacks and immigrants were also actively recruited, making up ten percent and twenty-five percent of the Union Army respectively. In

1864, Congress, by law, did away with commutation, as additional men were required to maintain the advantage gained after Gettysburg. Nevertheless, the legislation did allow drafted religious pacifists to do alternative service or contribute to a hospital fund. Four federal drafts produced only forty-six thousand conscripts and one hundred and eighteen thousand substitutes (two percent and six percent, respectively, of the approximately two million Union troops). Regardless of this seemingly small contribution to the war effort, the draft was credited with encouraging the re-enlistment of battle-trained veterans and the enlistment of volunteers.[25]

The 1864 revision of the Civil War draft would have momentous implications for conscientious objection. For the first time in our history, federal law made specific provision for religious objectors to war by eliminating commutation for all but these men. The law provided further that objectors drafted into military service "be considered non-combatants." Lincoln made it governmental policy to assign such noncombatants to duty in hospitals or in the education of freed slaves. For the first time, thanks to these regulations, a *de facto* mode of alternate civilian service introduced civic content into conscientious objection. A watershed moment had occurred with respect to the meaning of national service in America.[26]

With the draft's questionable track record, it was not until the onset of World War I, when the likelihood of American involvement increased, that the United States developed a strategy for the armed forces that relied primarily upon conscription. This resulted in a growing debate between pro- and anti-conscription forces. As events became more critical in Europe, Leonard Wood (supported by Theodore Roosevelt) initiated a civilian-led "preparedness movement." Wood had been commander (1914–1917) of the Department of the East (Asia) and had advocated for the creation of civilian training camps. This brought him into conflict with the neutralist position of President Wilson and incurred the president's displeasure.

Meanwhile, the burgeoning anti-war movement encompassed a coalition of liberals, socialists, anarchists and progressive unionists. Emma Goldman used her magazine, *Mother Earth*, as a forum to oppose military preparations, and in the months before April 1917, she helped start the No-Conscription League. The intent of this organization was to encourage conscientious objection. Goldman spoke out against the draft repeatedly; her rallies drew as many as eight thousand people. The government retaliated by placing her and her associate, Alexander Berkman, under arrest on June 15, 1917. The charge was conspiring against the draft, for which they were subsequently convicted and sentenced to two years in prison. Goldman's magazine was banned, as were several other periodicals opposing war. Hundreds of foreign-born "agitators" were deported.[27]

The Selective Service Act of 1917 was adopted in large part because the "preparedness" movement, led by Theodore Roosevelt, had persuaded many Americans through speeches, writings and demonstrations, that "a selective national draft was the most equitable and efficient way for an industrial society to raise a wartime army."[28] In the end President Wilson had to overcome his own resistance, as well as the opposition of agrarian isolationists in the South and West, and ethnic and ideological opponents of the war in the North, to enact the temporary wartime draft.

The 1917 draft law reflected the lessons that had been learned during the Civil War. It "prohibited enlistment bounties and personal substitution, but authorized deferments on the grounds of dependency or essential work in industry or agriculture."[29] Religious conscientious objectors (CO's) could choose noncombatant service within the military. A Selective Service System was created, composed of a national headquarters, commanded by a major general, and some four thousand local draft boards, staffed by civilian volunteers who decided the fate of those to be drafted in their district. Under pressure from the American Friends Service Committee (AFSC), which had been founded in 1917 in response to World War I conscription, the military authorities eventually made some limited and local adjustments for those who sought alternative service, but no formal alternative-service program was developed. For those seeking this status and the alternatives it could have afforded, the Wilson administration's policies towards conscientious objection were a step backwards from the alternative service standards President Lincoln had permitted during the Civil War.[30]

In 1917 and 1918, the Selective Service registered and classified almost twenty-four million men, aged eighteen to forty-five. Two million eight hundred thousand of them were drafted. In all, seventy-two percent of the wartime army of three-and-a-half million troops was raised through conscription. In 1918, the U.S. Supreme Court unanimously held that national conscription was constitutional.[31]

Many places saw opposition to conscription, which occasionally became violent. In Arkansas a small religious sect believed the war betokened the end of the world and that anyone participating in it would spend the rest of eternity in hell. As a result they refused to honor the draft. Eight men soon found themselves surrounded by an armed force consisting of local men, law

enforcement officers, and the Arkansas National Guard. The group cited religion as their rationale for refusing to fight. Specifically, they believed in the
Russellite Doctrine, which was formulated by Charles Taze Russell, a founder
of the Adventist sect that preceded the Jehovah's Witnesses. Their position
was developed in *The Finished Mystery*, a book that labeled wars stemming
from patriotic or nationalistic fervor as narrow-minded hatred of other
people. Five members of the group were charged with desertion, sentenced
to five years of hard labor and given dishonorable discharges upon their
release.[32] The book itself was banned in 1917.

In spite of a few violent episodes such as these, and a number of anti-
draft demonstrations, there was no wide scale repetition of the Civil War
Draft Riots. Opposition was expressed mainly through criticism and
through evasion. Between two and three million men never registered, and
three hundred thirty-eight thousand (twelve percent of those drafted) failed
to report when called or deserted after arrival at training camp.

Those who sought status as conscientious objectors were required to
fulfill two criteria: (1) The objection had to apply to all wars in all forms;
and (2) The objection had to be based on "religious belief and training."
Sixty-four thousand seven hundred registrants sought CO status. Of the
twenty thousand nine hundred COs drafted into the army, four thousand
refused to participate in any military role, and four hundred fifty "absolutists" (largely Jehovah's Witnesses) were sent to prison.

The next major development in the movement to stop the draft and
to end war was the formation, in 1923, of the War Resister's League (WRL).
The WRL was organized by men and women who had opposed World War
I and saw very little had been gained from such massive losses of human
life. Many had been jailed for refusing to serve. Its founders, including
Jessie Wallace Hughan, a leading women's suffrage supporter, socialist, and
pacifist, believed that if enough people stood in total opposition to war,
governments would hesitate before plunging into another one.[33] Although
that may be so – and Vietnam began to test this theory – the next great war
was the famously "just war."

The fall of France in 1940 led Congress to adopt the nation's first pre-
war conscription act. Once again, it was through the efforts of the "old
preparedness" leaders that this procedure was enacted. Since the U.S. was
not at war, pacifists, isolationists, and others intensely opposed this seemingly unnecessary action on the part of the government. To make it seem
less onerous, the term of service for the draftees (aged twenty-one to thirty-

five) was only one year, with service initially restricted to the Western Hemisphere and U.S. territories. In August 1941, however, Congress, by a one-vote margin (203-202) in the House, voted to keep the one-year draftees in the Army beyond their term.[34]

After Pearl Harbor, lawmakers removed all remaining restrictions and extended the draft to men aged eighteen to thirty-eight (and briefly to forty-five) for the duration of the war. Approximately ten million men were drafted through the Selective Service System, and nearly six million enlisted, primarily in the U.S. Navy and Army Air Corps.

Whenever the U.S. declares war, there are those for whom it is unacceptable. Some seventy-two thousand registrants applied for CO status, twenty-five thousand of whom entered the army in non-combatant service. Twelve thousand went to civilian work camps. Twenty thousand had their claims rejected. Six thousand, the majority of them Jehovah's Witnesses, similar to their "absolutist" predecessors in World War I, were imprisoned when they wouldn't even accept noncombatant service.[35] Some anti-draft incidents occurred in Chicago and other cities. They were a direct result of protests by African Americans against discrimination and segregation in the armed forces. Draft evasion did not disappear. The Justice Department investigated 373,000 alleged evaders and obtained convictions of sixteen thousand.

Two contemporary filmmakers, Judith Ehrlich and Rick Tejada-Flores, in their PBS film, *The Good War and Those Who Refused to Fight,* have succeeded in capturing the enormous struggle faced by those whose love of country did not extend to killing others. A large part of their decision to create the film stemmed from their mutual realization that, if others were as unaware of these men's stories as they had been, the telling of them was long overdue. As described on the PBS website:

> The film sheds light on a previously ignored part of the World War II saga – the story of American conscientious objectors who refused to fight "the good war." It is a story of personal courage, idealism and non-conformity based on ethical and religious beliefs. Many were Quakers or others whose religious beliefs interpreted the commandment, "Thou Shalt Not Kill," to include war; others were passionate pacifists who felt morally incapable of co-operating with a violent conflict, no matter how worthy the cause.[36]

Many Americans considered such beliefs, and a position against serving based upon them, cowardly and unpatriotic. To prove their patriotism while adhering to their principles, many CO's risked their lives during the war as fire jumpers and medical guinea pigs who took part in government experiments. Thousands of others volunteered to work in mental institutions. Their efforts helped to transform those institutions, many of which were places of filth and degradation, to the more humane places they are today. All of these endeavors were conducted under the auspices of the Civilian Public Service, a national system of work camps funded by the three "peace" churches – the Quakers, the Mennonites and the Brethren. There were also many men who refused to cooperate and who spent the war years in prison where they employed hunger strikes to help racially integrate the federal prison system. All lived with the scorn of their nation and often that of their family and friends.[37]

Would the draft have ended after World War II had there not been a Cold War? Perhaps. The on-going draft did help maintain a sizable number of men in the armed forces (a mix of volunteers, conscripts, and draft-induced volunteers) during the periods when an active war was not taking place, but the will to maintain such a provision apparently waned, since there was a brief hiatus between 1947 and 1948.[38] In response to the return of the draft, another organization of resisters was created in 1948: The Central Committee for Conscientious Objectors (CCCO). Active to this day, it was and is dedicated to helping people avoid or escape military conscription. Their efforts continue during the current wars in Iraq and Afghanistan.[39]

During the Korean War one-and-a-half million men, aged eighteen to twenty-five, were drafted. One million three hundred thousand more volunteered, primarily for the Navy and Air Force. Discontent led to an increase in conscientious objection once draftees were inducted. During Korea, nearly one-and-a-half percent of inductees were granted exemptions, or ten times as many as were granted exemptions during each of the world wars.[40]

The Korean War ended in 1953. The official start of the Vietnam War remains the source of much controversy. Whether one selects the Congressional passage of the Gulf of Tonkin Resolution on August 7, 1964, which allowed President Lyndon Johnson "to take all necessary steps, including the use of armed force" to prevent further attacks against U.S. forces,[41] or whether one chooses the March 8, 1965, arrival of the first combat troops (33,500 Marines at China Beach to defend the American air base at Danang) the irrefutable fact is draft calls soon soared from one hundred thousand in 1964 to 400,000 in 1966, enabling U.S. forces there to climb from 23,000 "military advisers" in 1964 to 543,000 troops by 1968.[42]

Although draftees made up only sixteen percent of the American armed forces, by 1969, they accounted for eighty-eight percent of the infantry riflemen in Vietnam and accounted for more than half the Army's battle deaths. Because of student and other deferments, both the draft, and the casualties fell disproportionately upon working-class youths, black and white. African Americans made up only eleven percent of the U.S. population, but accounted for sixteen percent of the Army's casualties in Vietnam in 1967, and, overall for fifteen percent of its casualties for the entire war.[43]

During the Vietnam War conscription itself became one of the many casualties. As the draft calls and casualty rates rose, so too, did opposition. With strong support from a coalition of anti-war groups including, but not limited to students, pacifists, clergy, civil rights and feminist organizations, and many other liberal and radical groups, the draft resistance movement grew in strength and influence. Its tactics included demonstrations, draft-card burnings, sit-ins at induction centers, and break-ins and destruction of records at a dozen local draft boards.[44]

Between 1965 and 1975, 22,500 of the well over 100,000 apparent draft offenders were indicted. Almost nine thousand were convicted and four thousand imprisoned. In 1968 when the Supreme Court expanded the criteria for conscientious objection from religious to moral or ethical objections, CO exemptions grew in relation to actual inductions from eight percent in 1967 to forty-three percent in 1971, and an astonishing one hundred-thirty-one percent in 1972.[45]

Although evasion has always been one of the ways men expressed their feelings about war, it was undoubtedly the most common form of draft "protest" during the Vietnam War. Of the almost twenty-seven million young men who reached draft age between 1964 and 1973, sixteen million (sixty percent) did not serve in the military. Of those who avoided service, 15,400,000 received legal exemptions or deferments, and perhaps 570,000 evaded the draft illegally. Among illegal draft evaders, 360,000 were never caught. Another 198,000 had their cases dismissed. Nine thousand were convicted, and four thousand sent to prison. In addition, an estimated thirty to fifty thousand fled into exile, mainly to Canada, Britain, and Sweden.[46] The truth is there is no way to accurately determine this last figure, and estimates vary widely with numbers as high as 100,000 with Canada accepting at least ninety percent of those who fled. The *New York Times* estimates 25,000 still live in Canada.[47]

The three prongs of the anti-war movement – GI actions within the military, massive desertion, and draft resistance – are widely acknowledged as being essential elements in forcing the U.S. out of Vietnam. Steve Morse, a former U.S. Army soldier who was active in the anti-war movement among GI's during Vietnam, and today coordinates the GI Rights Program of the Central Committee of Conscientious Objectors, explains, "This was an unprecedented event in U.S. history. Underground newspapers, GI coffeehouses, petitions, demonstrations, black armbands, stockade revolts, the FTA shows, leaflets, discussion groups, civilian/veteran support and counseling, combat refusals of riot control training and duty, revolts on ships—these all occurred many times."[48] The truth of the matter is that it is very difficult to determine how many service members were prosecuted for acts that directly resulted from their opposition to the war. Rates of soldiers who deserted or went "away without leave" – known as "absence offenses" – reached proportionately all-time highs during Vietnam, with 1971 and 1972 being the peak years.

The draft became so controversial Congress was obliged either to change it or to eliminate it. General Lewis B. Hershey, the Director of Selective Service since 1941, supported by many Congressional conservatives and hawks, prevented any changes until 1969, resisting even the 1967 recommendations for equity and national uniformity. These recommendations emerged from a presidential commission under Johnson's administration, headed by former Assistant Attorney General Burke Marshall. President Richard M. Nixon, after criticizing the draft in his 1968 campaign, phased out occupational and dependency deferments and instituted an annual draft lottery among eighteen-year-olds (beginning in December 1969.) He also removed General Hershey and appointed a commission, headed by former Secretary of Defense Thomas Gates, which in 1970 recommended an All-Volunteer Armed Force (AVF) with a stand-by draft for emergency use.[49] Many of the testimonies documented in this book were the result of the changes Nixon wrought, along with the on-going draft and the increasingly disastrous war.

Over time Nixon reduced draft calls while gradually withdrawing U.S. troops, but his secret invasion of Cambodia in 1970 led to massive public protests. In the face of the enormous public outcry, Congress reluctantly extended the draft for two more years in 1971. Much to the distress of many, student deferments were eliminated and a massive ($2.4 billion) pay increase was instituted for the lower ranks, in the hope of achieving the goal of an all-volunteer force by mid-1973. In what most consider a political maneuver, during the 1972 election campaign, Nixon cut draft calls to fifty thousand and stopped forcing draftees to go to Vietnam. On January 27, 1973, the day a cease-fire was announced, the administration stopped drafting, six months before induction authority expired on July 1, 1973.

What followed is often the source of either inaccurate information or myth-making insofar as the fate of those who resisted the Vietnam draft is concerned. The conventional wisdom at the time assumed that:

on January 27, 1973 the war ended for the various sorts of resisters;

during the war only isolated numbers resisted and most of them were "draft dodgers";

all legal issues pertaining to resisters were resolved, and they eventually "got off";

refusal to serve only occurs when people face a draft.

Such false assumptions and related forms of presumed social knowledge, along with other "facts" about this war and wars in general, are designed to have a significant impact on future generations of enlistees and draftees; there is definitely a stake in putting them forth and perpetuating them. As already indicated, the truth about the Vietnam War is that significant numbers of men resisted military service in numerous ways, including draft refusal and resistance after enlisting.

Universal amnesty was never given to war resisters. The reality is that resisters who fled the U.S. over forty years ago who seek to return may still face punishment, either through criminal prosecution or a bad discharge. Every year some men are arrested when they return. Richard Allen Shields is an illustrative example. He went AWOL from an Alaskan Army base in 1972. Upon attempting to return to the U.S. from Canada in 2000, he was arrested on March 22, at the border in Metaline Falls, WA. He was trying to drive a lumber truck into the country and instead ended up at Fort Sill, Oklahoma, where he was finally discharged with an "other than honorable" discharge a month later.[50]

Over twenty-five years ago, during the administrations of two presidents, one Republican and one Democratic, two programs were created to come to terms with the unprecedented numbers of men who had resisted the war. Before examining why neither program provided relief to resisters, we must understand what each set out to accomplish.

First it is important to recognize that military resisters and draft evaders received different treatment in the Ford and Carter programs.[51] President Gerald Ford's program was initiated on September 16, 1974, and was intended to provide partial relief for war resisters and to begin to deal with the upheaval in the culture and in the lives of individuals. A month earlier he had told a gathering of the Veterans of Foreign Wars that he favored "throwing the weight of my Presidency into the scales of justice on the side of leniency and mercy."[52]

His plan encountered immediate opposition across the political spectrum. Those advocating amnesty for draft offenders saw the program as overly punitive and strongly believed that Ford sought to distract the American public, especially those most likely to protest, from his unpopular pardon of Richard Nixon for his role in the Watergate Affair. Moderates were troubled that the floodgates would be opened and many whom they felt undeserving of clemency would now be welcomed back.[53]

In any case, the Ford plan covered the following categories.

- convicted draft violators
- convicted military deserters and AWOLS
- draft violators who had never been tried
- veterans with less than honorable discharges for absence offenses

Inconsistencies in the granting of clemency by the different government agencies undermined the program's effectiveness from the outset. The Department of Defense was not seeking the reconciliation Ford promised. Their central goal, in fact, was to eliminate its deserters' file. The result was a confusing and arbitrary system that resulted in five thousand men receiving undesirable military discharges. Meanwhile, other deserters who did not avail themselves of the clemency program, but instead went through "normal military channels," received honorable discharges. The Justice Department and a nine-member clemency board handled other offenders, but failed to make a dent in the one hundred thirteen thousand cases up for review. Few draft violators applied for clemency since many were not listed for prosecution. In addition, there were inconsistent requirements for community service and poor, uneducated men, who were the majority of the offenders, lacked the knowledge and understanding, as well as the resources, needed to present their case to the board.

Not surprisingly, the Ford program did not provide the reconciliation the nation so desperately needed. The program was essentially a failure and even those who were responsible for implementing it agree with this perception. Lawrence Baskir and William Strauss, two staff members of the clemency board, wrote, "Its tone was too punitive, its conditions too unrealistic," and "the clemency it offered was not better, and in some ways worse, than the relief that was available through normal government channels."[54]

In exchange for clemency, an individual was required to perform up to twenty-four months of alternative service and sign a broad oath of allegiance to the U.S. These requirements were considered discriminatory and excessive by many of those who were eligible. Harold Jordan is convinced that, given how Ford had essentially relieved Nixon of any burden resulting from his illegal actions with his comprehensive pardon, having to swear an allegiance oath as a consequence for desertion during a deeply divisive war was particularly offensive to some of those eligible for the program. Nixon not only got his pardon, but he also received a generous pension and did not have to take any oath of allegiance despite his participation in a host of acts that undermined our nation's democratic principles. Since about 566,000 military "offenders" did not have their needs met for repatriation after the Ford program ended, its failure is evident.[55]

Military deserters received undesirable discharges.[56] They could apply to have them changed at a later date to "Clemency Discharges," considered "other than honorable," after performing their alternative service, but it was very difficult to obtain such a change. GI participants in the program would therefore automatically lose all veterans' benefits, which was not what happened to others who left the service with less than honorable discharges.[57]

Given these major limitations, not surprisingly, only 27,000 of the over 113,000 eligible men applied. 21,800 received clemency, but most already lived in the country and were not returning from exile; the total was almost equally divided between "draft offenders" and "military offenders." Those living in Sweden, Canada, England and France actually endorsed a boycott of the program because of its punitive aspects.[58]

With an estimated 566,000 military "offenders" not served by the Ford program, clearly something else was needed. In 1977 President Jimmy Carter established two programs to assist resisters. First, in January he declared unconditional amnesty for draft resisters – those already accused and those who could be. Next he set up a two-stage pardon process for those who had served and then resisted. Again draft evaders and military absentees were treated differently. If there were no other legal charges against them, evaders received universal amnesty and did not have a criminal record based on their evasion. No formal application was required. It was a blanket amnesty granted to all draft evaders regardless of their legal status.

Military resisters never received such consideration. There are no figures for the number of evaders who benefited from the Carter amnesty program, because they were never even required to let the government know of their actions. The only limitation on their being granted a full amnesty was that they not have other [non-draft evasion] charges they were facing. If a draft evader had criminal charges for participating in a protest demonstration, those charges would remain and only the evasion charges would be dropped.[59]

Under the Carter plan military deserters and AWOLS* could apply for a limited pardon if they faced no other charges, but they would automatically receive a less than honorable discharge and could apply for an upgrade later. This was quite similar to the Ford plan and the upgrade was far from automatic. In fact, few veterans secured one. They were also denied benefits that many other veterans with less than honorable discharges enjoyed. These men had only a five to six month window in 1977 during which to apply.

Here's what happened:

- 4200 were considered eligible for the program
- fewer than 25% were processed and received the less-than-honorable discharge
- 430,000 men with bad discharges were allowed to have a case-by-case review
- 16,277 benefited from this procedure.

Despite these obvious problems and the large number of men not served by the amnesty, the Carter program is considered more successful than the one Ford had attempted. Many resisters (especially military absentees) had tremendous difficulty surviving in other countries. As opposed to the earlier program, exile groups urged their members to take advantage of the Carter program and to seek a full amnesty upon their return. Still,

---

* AWOL refers to military personnel that were "Absent Without Leave"

many remained in exile because of poor advertising of the details of the relief program following what many had considered so discriminatory under Ford's clemency program. To make matters worse, Congress refused to fully fund Carter's program. Both programs had conditions many exiles found unacceptable and, even for those willing to accept the terms, the period of time during which application could be made was limited.[60] In addition, the program encountered major criticism from mainstream veterans' organizations and others who saw the blanket pardons as demeaning the obligations of those who served in the military.[61]

Estimates indicate that fewer than thirty thousand military resisters received any legal relief and many of those received bad discharges. Five hundred fifty thousand received nothing. This is a number, to gain a bit of perspective, roughly equal to the number who participated in the Gulf War of 1990–91.[62] This remains a major stain on our history and yet another way in which our country has not yet come to terms with the legacy of the war in Southeast Asia.

Could there have been an equitable draft during any time in our history? This chapter seeks to demonstrate the basic flaws in such a notion. As for the testimonies of those who the Vietnam War-era draft affected, it is most useful to see their choices, their actions, and the consequences they faced in the context of our historical challenge as a democratic country forcing men to serve, especially during times of war. Nevertheless, it is worth remembering the particular confluence of historical and social events that attended this particular war. The fact that "war" itself was never officially declared; the widely perceived notion that the philosophical underpinnings of the war were bankrupt; the social changes that occurred in the late '60s – the aftermath of the civil rights era; the sexual revolution; women's liberation; rock 'n' roll; widespread drug use – and a prevalent belief that authority was to be resisted and mistrusted combined to foster a volatile and ultimately incomparable time.

CHAPTER TWO

THOSE WHO SERVED

GOING TO WAR HAS BEEN A RITE OF PASSAGE FOR MEN since the dawn of civilization. Historically, in almost all circumstances, the decision to fight on the part of most men was neither seriously examined nor questioned. It was one's duty. In our country, the alternatives were largely unacceptable (with the exception of those during our own Civil War who were able to purchase their exemption or find a replacement.) Refusal to serve meant the derision of society, the risk of jail or the acceptance of exile. If you were lucky enough to have come of age during a time of peace, then you escaped the risks, which others inevitably faced. The same was true for those who had physical deferments, although there were certain wars and situations in which those deemed unable to serve felt humiliated and mistreated since serving was equated with both manliness and patriotism. Over time, especially during the two World Wars, being a conscientious objector became a less abhorrent option than in previous wars, but generally being called to arms meant serving.

As the Vietnam War progressed and the draft started to take larger and larger numbers of men into the ranks of the armed services, the war itself caused many to question the call to arms. Certainly there were still those who enlisted for a variety of reasons: love of country; a sense of duty; an acceptance of the reasons given by the government, such as combating the spread of Communism; a powerful belief in the jingoistic slogan, "My Country: Love It or Leave It" which adorned car bumpers during the heyday of the war; or a lack of other opportunity due to issues of race or class in the society from which they came. But increasingly, in order to have enough men "in country" to carry out the "mission," as interpreted by the administration and the generals, the draft was essential.

In this chapter you will meet men who, for a variety of reasons, ended up in the military. They are a very small cross-section of those with stories to tell, but their testimony illustrates what such a war can exact on the hearts, minds, and bodies of those it requires. Some of these men enlisted to avoid the likelihood of serving in Vietnam, since they had been told being drafted would require such service. Some did not have the "luxury" of being able to find a way out. A few even tried to believe in the war, at least at the beginning of their service. Some simply lost the fight to get out after trying a variety of methods.

Is there a just war? Perhaps. When people perceive a war to be just, they are more willing to risk being injured or killed. World War II comes close since many accepted that it was being waged to prevent despotic rulers from accomplishing their quest for world domination. Was Vietnam such a war? Except for those few remaining apologists and those in denial about what actually took place, there are no longer those who try to argue that what happened in Vietnam was necessary or just. Instead, even principal instigators like Robert McNamara (in the 2004 documentary *Fog of War*) seek to account for the error of their ways. MacNamara enumerates eleven lessons to be learned, but what they basically boil down to is his awareness that what occurred in Vietnam was a mistake. Each of the men in this chapter had to confront that mistake directly, and to consider, if obliquely, the questions John Kerry asked at the hearings he participated in upon his return from Vietnam: "How do you ask a man to be the last man to die in Vietnam? How do you ask a man to be the last man to die for a mistake?"

Those in this chapter, who attempted to see what they were doing as having some justification, struggled not only with being in the military, but also with the fact that there were Americans at home demanding through an historic protest movement that the president and Congress stop the war and bring them home. For many, their own eventual homecomings were difficult, and almost all had to deal with the toll their service took on their psyches and lives.

This chapter will focus on the factors that led to the decision to enlist or accept the decision of the draft board and become a member of the armed services. The testimonies feature aspects of the draft experience and what occurred as a result of the decision to serve, whether the experience included stateside or Vietnam service. These intense narratives will set the scene for the contrasting decisions to not participate in the military described in subsequent chapters.

Chuck Hommes

Chuck, fifty-eight, is originally from Whitensville, Massachusetts. He is a carpenter. He lives in Florence, Massachusetts with his wife, Vicki, whom he met and married upon returning from Vietnam. Their daughter, Ari, is twenty-three-years-old. Chuck has a passion for motorcycles and thoroughly enjoys working and riding on his Harley and his Triumph.

It was 1970. I had just graduated from high school. I'd gone to a trade school so there weren't really any college prospects and it was summer. I was looking for a job and just hanging out. I was living in Whittensville, MA, which is a little mill town south of Worcester, MA. My brother was in the Army in Germany at that time. The lottery was going on, but the year before, the number for my birthday was in the three hundreds so I just assumed I'd be safe.

My dad had been in the Coast Guard for four years on the USS Cambria. In World War II one of his jobs was to drive landing barges for some campaigns. He was sent into Nagasaki two weeks after the August 1945 atomic bomb was dropped. He supported Nixon and later Reagan so I knew if I were to go to Vietnam he would be proud of me, but I don't think he really wanted me to go, because he saw, first-hand, the dangers of war.

I hadn't really been following the Vietnam War that closely. We had some anti-war marches at my high school, which everybody would participate in, because either you believed in it or it got you out of school, but being a small mill town and somewhat conservative, there were a lot of people who were ready to go. For them there was no question. But I wasn't thinking about joining up at the time and hoped my number wouldn't be pulled.

To my surprise, my number in the second lottery was 26, and suddenly it was, "What I am going to do now?" I talked to a lot of friends who were in the service, but not stationed in Vietnam. I asked them, "How'd you get out of being stationed in 'Nam?" I'm thinking, "Well this might be good – go into the Army, go to Germany like my brother. Or maybe some other country and see the world just like the ad said. Just not go to Vietnam."

Soon after I got my number, I went to Springfield. A recruiting officer there told me, "If you enlist right now, you can go anywhere you want." That fit right in with my plans. I'm thinking, "Well, with my number, I'm in anyway, and they say I can pick where I go..." so I signed up. I was naïve back then.

Everyone I knew had stories about how to flunk your physical and I knew that if I flunked I wouldn't have to deal with the military at all. I had some crystal meth. I went down there pretty stoned. I didn't really get nervous until I was there and then it hit me. Oh, my God, this is real. Once I take this physical and pass, I'm on my way to Fort Dix, New Jersey. My heart was pounding like crazy. You just went in there, and they checked you out. They made sure you didn't have flat feet or any other medical problems. But some of us tried to flunk by doing things like being stoned. Maybe they saw right through what some of us were trying. Maybe they knew the symptoms were temporary. "His heart is pounding like crazy; he's obviously doing something." I passed with flying colors.

We were all so naïve about what was actually going to happen, of what it was like to be in a war. You kept thinking, "This war is going to be over." It was 1970 and it had been going on for a long time. The government kept saying, "It's going to end."

In a small town like mine, if you got drafted they threw a party for you, a going away party. So they had a party for me, too. You just go out with a bunch of friends and a bunch of beer and everyone gets drunk.

All through boot camp I thought I wasn't going to 'Nam. My brother was into small arms repair. He worked with rifles, pistols and other small arms in the supply room and to him it was an eight-hour a day job where he could go and do whatever he wanted to and the day was over. He got paid for it. He was traveling all over Germany and other parts of Europe, and so he was having a great time. That's what I expected – some version of that. I had enlisted and that was what I was told would happen

After boot camp I came home and I had thirty days before I had to go to my assignment in Aberdeen, Maryland. I got my orders saying I was going to be an aircraft armament subsystems repairman on helicopters. I kept hearing: "Nobody's going. Don't worry about it. Only the people they really need are going, and they don't need us." Even if that wasn't completely true, I was still thinking, maybe I'll go someplace cool...

I went to Maryland to school for twelve weeks of training. We had inspections, KP, physical and technical training, but other than that, our time was our own. Towards the end we got our orders, and to my great shock, I got orders for Vietnam! I had fifteen days between receiving my orders and going to Washington state. I came home and stayed for thirty. I was AWOL, but I didn't care because I felt, "If I'm going to 'Nam, I'm taking as much time as I want just to sort of regroup." I knew I was taking a risk. My parents knew. I told them, "I'm not ready to go. What are they going to do? Punish me by sending me to Vietnam?"

I figured if they want me to go, they'll just have to wait. In my own head I just wasn't ready. I thought, "What can I do? Where can I hide? If I left the country, I could never come back. At that time there was no amnesty. So, do I really want to go to Canada? I'm sort of a homebody. I wouldn't know anybody. I'd be in this country that I don't know anything about."

The truth was I didn't know how else to get myself out of the mess I was in except to leave the country. I think that was the only thing I considered. You could hurt yourself, and I didn't want to go that far. I certainly didn't go there in my head. I really *didn't* want to go to jail. I couldn't imagine spending five years there. I'd seen what happened in boot camp to a couple of kids who said that they were conscientious objectors. The drill sergeants just ripped them to pieces. They said, "I will not pick up a gun," and it was the worst thing you could say because, holy shit, I have never seen people get so verbally abusive. They can't touch you, but they are going to verbally abuse you. I just said to myself that I'm never going to say that. It was definitely fear.

When I finally reported after the thirty days, nothing happened to me. I went to Fort Lewis, Washington and they said that I was AWOL and they looked at my orders and saw that I was going to 'Nam. They said. "Okay, don't worry about it," but I still didn't know for sure if I was going. I was at Fort Lewis for fourteen days and I had five different sets of orders in that time. They would come down and tell us first that everybody's going, then that nobody's going, then that certain people were going. I would call my parents and tell them, "I don't think I'm going." Two days later I'd call again and say, "I think I'm going." It was the rumor mill, and it was really hard to tell. One fond memory of Fort Lewis was spending Thanksgiving with a local family that volunteered to take a few servicemen to dinner.

Since our orders kept changing and they had a large backlog of troops, they had us walking shoulder to should across the base picking up every bit of scrap that wasn't dirt or grass. Finally we all stood out there in formation, and they started reading off names of where you were going to go. "You're going to Fort Bragg," and they'd call fifty names. "You're going to Texas," and they'd call off another fifty. "Hawaii," another fifty.

When they said Vietnam and my name was called along with maybe fifteen others, I couldn't believe I was going. It was just like with the lottery. I lost all over again. That was when I started to think, "I'm not that far from Canada. If I'm going to do it, this is the time to do it." I was thinking, " If I just take off..." You're not rational. You're standing in formation and thinking, "If I can take off and I can thumb a ride fast enough, then I can be up there, and they'd never catch me." Of course, I really didn't think that would work, but that's when I almost bolted.

We flew from Tacoma, Washington to Anchorage, Alaska. We landed on an airstrip that was frozen, so the plane was fishtailing. I thought, "Well, O.K., I'll just die here. I'm never going to make it to 'Nam." I noticed that the farther away from the States we got, the stewardesses had more and more clothes on. Eventually, they were covered from their heads to their toes, pants-suits, nothing provocative. Part of me was thinking, "Oh, I see, they're just trying to break us. We're not going to see any American women for a long time." Strange the things you notice on your way to a war.

We flew into Japan at night and as far as you could see were the lights of the city. I was in Tokyo for about an hour. I watched John Wayne in Japanese on TV in the airport. Then on to Da Nang. We got off the plane and onto a bus. We went though a small village for my first real culture shock due to the living conditions compared to home and the sheer number of people.

I spent about four days as they say now "in country" getting briefed and waiting for orders. It was also monsoon season, dark grey and raining all the time. I think everything I had was wet. I was waiting for my orders, so I went into an enlisted men's club and I saw a familiar face. It was Ralph Schotanus from Whitinsville. He had left in eighth grade. He looked like he was still in eighth grade. "Oh, my God, it's Ralph!" It was a connection. He had three days left. He said, "How much time you got left." I said, "I just got here." He said, "Aw, man. I'm gone in three days." He sat me down, and we played cards for three days, and he just told me about what I'd need to do. He said, "Forget everything they told you in boot camp. Just follow the older guys. See what's going on." It felt good that I had someone familiar to connect with, but actually, even though I was there with all these people I'd never seen before, I really felt connected to them, too, because we were all dressed in green. We all looked alike. There were no cliques.

The next thing I remember is getting prepped and going through all these trainings. I then got orders for Vinh Long, which is about as far south as you could go. I'm thinking, "Yes, this is cool. Even Vung Tao, which is where everybody goes for rest and relaxation, is north of us." We got to fly down in a helicopter. There were no doors. Guys are sitting with their feet on the rails with harnesses on, and it's freezing because once you get up high enough, it's really cold. My suit is as green as green can be. Anywhere in Vietnam when you see somebody that's really green, that's an FNG, a "fucking new guy." Stay away from him. He's dangerous, because he doesn't know what to do. He could get you killed, which I didn't know. You learn that when you get there.

The scariest part of the trip was when we got off the helicopter. We were walking across the flight line and mortars were coming at us. I thought, "I'm dead. This is it. How am I going to make it a year? We're right on the airstrip." I was freaking out. A lot of people were just saying, "It's pretty normal." They got into their bunkers, or they ducked down behind sandbags. Then it stopped, and they got up and just started doing things. And I'm thinking, "You've got to be kidding me. This is nuts!" People told me, "They're going for the birds, not us. It's more important to hit the helicopters."

When I got to Vinh Long, it was still monsoon season. It just rained and rained. Everything was wet. Our clothes were wet – everything. I was an aircraft subsystem repairman. I worked in a shop. I worked on rocket launchers, grenade launchers, mini-guns and helicopters. I'd go out when the "birds" came in. I'd pull out all the armament and fix what had broken. Then after work I'd go to my hooch (a hut or simple dwelling, either military or civilian) and sometimes I'd go for beers with a bunch of the guys. You could go downtown and get a good meal or a hooker or...whatever. I felt, "All right, I can do this."

Then somebody got his throat slit downtown. After that they didn't let us go there anymore. This guy went down, stayed overnight, and obviously there was some kind of trap. He just never came back. You couldn't tell who was North Vietnamese and who was South Vietnamese. It was like who's from Kansas and who's from Nebraska. It was the same people. The infiltration – I mean there were North Vietnamese everywhere. That was a little scary.

Being around soldiers who had been there for months and months could also be scary. My first shift on guard duty, I'm feeling scared to death. I'm watching for people, and these guys next to me were sleeping. I was supposed to wake one of them up to watch with me. When I did, he said, "Forget it. Go to sleep. I'm not going to watch." Then I find out that in this particular place that I was guarding there was a path from outside the compound through all the barbed wire and the mines. Our guys would stay out late and come back along this path. Nobody told me. My first shift I saw someone coming towards me and I was about ready to blow him away. But he's waving and calling out to me. I'm thinking, "This has got to be a trap." Then this other guy wakes up and says," Hey, that guy is so and so, and he's just coming back from town." I'm thinking, "Oh, Jesus, and I nearly killed him!"

While I was in the southern part of 'Nam we had to go out into the rice paddies to check the Claymore mines,* which were seven hundred eighty ball bearings behind a plastic explosive. When you set them off, they just send balls across the field. When you're checking all the connections, you're up to your waist in water with both a machete and a .45, because more than anything else, you're worried about snakes. Checking out connections shouldn't have been dangerous in and of itself, because you disconnected the electrical charge first, but the scary part was that, unbeknownst to us, some of the mines had been turned around to face us. Snipers came in at night. They crawled through what seemed like impossible stuff and turned the mines around. Then, when we set off the explosives, all those balls would head *toward us*. Another bizarre aspect of checking the mines was that you had to try to see what was what at times when the rice grew too high for clear vision. To do so we'd pump J24 – jet engine fuel – out into those rice paddies and light it. This was people's food! We pumped the jet fuel out there and lit it. We'd been told, "Just burn it out. We don't care about those rice paddies." Everything burned, even those little houses out there, and the little stations people worked out of when they were picking rice. We're burning out this whole field around the base, and sometimes the little shacks the Vietnamese would sit in during the heat of the day would blow up like crazy, because they were full

---

*The Claymore mine is an explosive device. It's about the size of a Frisbee, but it's rectangular and concave, so when all the little pellets exploded out of it, they shot outwards. You would use it to clear away the enemy from in front of your foxhole. It had a wire attached, and all you had to do was squeeze the trigger.

of armaments. They're blowing up and it's like the Fourth of July. It was really wild, but you don't look at it as a scary thing. You just numb yourself out and do your thing and just wait for your time to be over.

Of course, drugs were part of it, too, part of the numbing out. I got quite heavily involved in drugs over there. Marijuana was just like smoking cigarettes. It was everywhere and there were all kinds – Big Bad Buddha and North Thai, which we dipped in opium. You had opium dens, which I really never saw, but guys used to talk about them. The other big drug over there was heroin and it was incredibly pure. I heard numbers like ninety-five to ninety-six percent, while at the time in New York City it was fourteen percent. What was happening was that soldiers who'd been doing heroin in the States were coming over. They'd just fire it up, unaware of its greater potency, and end up overdosing.

For me, drugs were an escape. Marijuana was okay, but the heroin was unbelievable. I basically couldn't deal with what was happening to me in 'Nam. With heroin, I wasn't there. I would get up in the morning. I would do my job. I'd function. What we used to do was put the heroin into cigarettes. Shooting it was just too potent. I could stay up all night long, just nodding out, and then be so rested that I could function all day again without sleep. The bottom line was that for me doing drugs was just an incredible escape.

I didn't go to extremes with heroin; I just maintained a level that worked. I didn't try to get crazy, but I still certainly ended up addicted. For many guys, doing drugs meant keeping your wits about you. You had to, because you could get busted.

Getting busted was another way to get med-evaced* out of 'Nam. A lot of people were doing that. They failed the urine tests on purpose. Towards the end we were being tested about once a month, supposedly "by surprise," but we always knew. You could prepare yourself by drinking tons of water. Then they'd come along: "Okay, piss test. Let's go." "Now?" "Yup, come on."

But, for me, there was a huge stigma in my head. "Oh, my God, I can't get med-evaced out for drugs and end up stuck in a hospital for ninety or a hundred twenty days near my hometown. It would destroy my parents. It would just destroy them. They're religious. They go to church.

---

*"Med-evac" refers to air transport of persons to a place where they can receive medical or surgical care; medical evacuation.

Different guys divided themselves up around the various substances they did. There were the drunks, and the guys that did the drugs, but there was also a real defining line of Black and Hispanic and Caucasian. The brothers, the black brothers, if there were only three or four in a group, would just meld in, but once it was a bigger group they definitely separated. They were all great guys. We were good friends. I worked with these guys and we were best buddies. We worked together in the shop, but once you were out and back into your living area it was, "You're not really welcome here."

After Vinh Long I got transferred. They were closing bases up. Since we didn't have identification numbers for specific machinery or helicopters, we just "disappeared" them. We'd dump them in a lake or bury them, because, if we couldn't identify a piece of equipment by showing its number, we shouldn't have it. We left tons and tons of stuff there.

They sent me to Quang Tri, which is about as far north as you can go. The second night there I had guard duty. I was assigned to the area where they kept all the fuel in these gigantic rubber bladders sitting in shallow graves just to hold them. Right when I was on watch, a mortar hit one. I'm thinking, "The world is ending." It was just flames and explosions. People all around me were running in panic. I thought, "Oh, shit, what the hell am I supposed to do now?" It didn't come out until later that it was *friendly* fire. Some guy was fooling around with a stupid grenade launcher and set one off that went straight up and happened to drift our way. But it was panic. It scared the hell out of me. I was on guard duty for a couple more nights and I kept thinking, "Hopefully, *that's* not going to happen again!"

Being in Nam was very weird in terms of the culture and the people. Women would come to the gate of the base, and all these guys would go down and pick one up for themselves. They would have sex with one of these women, bring her back to the gate, and she'd go home. It would be a line-up, O.K.'d by the officers in charge. The girls got younger and younger. Mothers would bring their daughters, because they could make so much money doing this.

All of us did the best we could to take care of ourselves. We used to equip our bunkers (underground fortifications) better than our hooches, because that's where we hung out a lot of nights. A lot of mortars would hit while we were trying to sleep in the barracks. The mortars weren't really a threat to us. Theoretically, the Vietnamese weren't trying to hit the barracks – they wanted to knock out the helicopters. But, of course, it didn't exactly make for restful sleep. The Vietcong were skilled at hiding and could get very close to us, and using little rocket launchers, they could send the mortars quite a distance. This mortar fire tended to be in the middle of the night, fairly late, around one or two. When that happened, we'd all get up, run into this giant hole in the ground covered by sandbags, and immediately reach for the six-packs we'd cleverly stashed in the fridge there.

Next I was transferred to Marble Mountain near Da Nang. Marble Mountain was a giant rock, *huge*, from which we'd get mortared every night, and every night and day we'd bomb that rock in return. The infantry would go up there and try to take out the Viet Cong (V.C.). However, the other side would put captured villagers in front of the line. This created a major moral dilemma. If you were going in there to do a dive with a helicopter and you saw a bunch of kids and women standing where the mortars might land, do you drop rockets on the place not knowing who these people are, what side they're on? Thankfully, I didn't have to deal with going out there and doing the actual firing. I know some of the officers, the warrant officers,* who had a lot to think about when they came back.

Meanwhile, sexual diseases were being transmitted big time. My third or fourth day on the base, this guy said to me, "Come on, we're going downtown." All of a sudden I was in a room where I had sex and ended up getting gonorrhea. A lot of guys had it.

You went into the bathroom, and there'd be people trying to pee and screaming at the same time. The process of getting better involved going to the first aid desk where they would hand out four big tubes of penicillin. A nurse said, "The warmer you get it, the less you feel it." You're waiting and you walk up, and you get these four shots in your butt. You are in so much pain you swear, "I will never do this again."

There were some nasty weapons. One was a rocket, which had six-penny-like nails with fins on them. It would just spray and the person hit would get nailed to whatever you were in. This guy came back from a reconnoitering trip, and told us there were bodies ripped to shreds and nailed to trees. I didn't see that, but we had a couple of snipers we killed, and you'd go look at them and it was really sad. There were also times we'd be driving down the highway going from one base to another getting supplies

---

*A military officer, usually a skilled technician or a helicopter pilot, intermediate in rank between a non-commissioned officer and a commissioned officer, having authority by virtue of a warrant.

or something, and we'd see dead Vietnamese on the side of the road who looked like they'd been left there forever.

One night I was walking flight line duty, which is out there at night looking for anybody, and I hear the crack of a rifle. Then I feel this, like this thwack, and I swear it almost hit my head, and it turns out to probably be a round from friendly fire. A lot of people died from friendly fire, from somebody just fooling around with his rifle.

In Da Nang they have these big trailers, which were air-conditioned and contained all the computers. I'm sitting on the steps and I'm thinking, "Ah, I think I'll go off and smoke a joint." I get off the steps. I walk around the sandbag wall, which is ten feet high, and a mortar hits the steps of the trailer. Another couple of minutes of sitting there and I wouldn't be here now.

While we were on Marble Mountain I used to really get into my work. I started to do woodworking. I said to myself, "Look I'm a carpenter." We had our own little shop, separate from the hanger. We put a roof on it, a white picket fence around it. It was our own space. I worked like an animal, because it was such a trip being able to do something that I enjoyed. I was sweating like crazy, it was so hot over there. I've never worked so hard in my life, but I'd think, "This is great. I'm finally getting to do something I like." That helped a lot.

I even backed down on the drugs at that point. The job was my high. It meant I wasn't out on the front line; I wasn't out in the jungle. Instead I was doing something interesting, and I really got into the mechanics of working. When I had a bunch of weapons to fix, I didn't look at it like I was fixing weapons. I looked at it like it was a mechanical task. I was very meticulous about what I did. Rewiring a rocket pod is a nightmare because there are hundreds of wires. But if you do it just right you can make it look nice, with the wires and the plate lined up just so. I took pride in that. It was a job. I wasn't out on the front line. I wasn't in the jungle...

Right before I left Marble Mountain and went to another place called Bien Hoa, I *was* out in the jungle. They just dropped us there. First they created a perimeter (the boundary of a defended position), and then they dropped in our guys. Sometimes it was the Marines ahead of us, and then we'd go. It was called a firebase. The helicopters came in and out, in and out. When they were in, we'd fix them and get them loaded and ready to go. We were closer to the action. We were out in the jungle, and there was nothing to do but wait until our job came in and then do it.

One night there was a sniper attack. Some of the Arvin Army (Army of the Republic of Vietnam) took off; they didn't want to fight. The Marines were there and there was another group, the Rock. They were a really hard-core part of the South Vietnamese Army; they held it together and kept everything safe. If we'd gotten overrun, that would have been it. It would have been all over. It was scary being out there, because we just never knew what might happen. We were just waiting. I was out there for two or three weeks. It was awful. Your rifle never left your side.

When I got transferred to Bien Hoa I only had a month left: I was really getting "short," the term we used for when a guy was close to going home. I'm thinking, "I really have to be careful. I can't get killed now." On one of my first weeks there a neighboring base had a large ammo dump hit by the V.C. All night it looked like the 4th of July as rockets, mortars, grenades and ammo went off – some heading our way. So for the rest of the night and the next day we were on high alert, shooting flairs all night to light up our perimeter looking for possible V.C.

Then, with only two weeks left, I got busted. Major Kennedy, yes, I remember his name, was a bastard. He just had it out for the guys who did the drugs. And I'm thinking, "What am I going to do?"

Fortunately I was able to pull off a real James Bond kind of a thing. Weeks before I was scheduled to leave, I had received my orders to go, but after the bust Kennedy had them. He also had my ID badge in his desk. I went up to the CQ (Change of Quarters) runner, which was the guy who took care of the desk at night. "Hey man, you mind if I just cut through here? I need to get something." "Yeah, yeah. Go ahead. Sure."

I broke into the major's office. I stole my ID. He had my orders in a file somewhere, and to this day I don't know how I found them. But I did, and I took them, and Kennedy didn't even have a clue. The next day I processed out. I went to every place you had to go. There'd be like five or six guys who had to sign you out. I'd throw down my orders. The first sergeant signs. Then I'd throw my orders down again, looking away, and get my orders signed by another one. Then the supply guy signs them, the guy in charge of weapons signs them, this guy signs them , that guy signs them. I figured, "Hey, I'm getting out of here."

I know some of the guys who are heading out. "Hey, we're going to Saigon. You need a ride?" I hop on their helicopter. I go to Saigon. I'm there. The guy's processing my orders, and he says, "Hey, you didn't get this signed. You can't go." "You've got to be kidding me. Come on. Please just let me go."

"We'll just make a phone call." He calls my company, and the warrant officer who was in charge of our shop answers the phone. "Not a problem," he tells the guy. "Just let him go." And, just like that, I was gone! Somehow, I don't know how I did it, but I got out of there. It just was, "Do whatever it takes…"

That's how I got back to the States, back to California. Everybody said, "Keep a low profile. A lot of people out there don't like you." You'd run into people and if you looked like a service guy there was hostility. My clothes were kind of out-dated and my hair was as short as can be. We were obviously coming from a base. People looked at us strangely. I never got accosted, but I just had this sense. I wish it had been better in California, because I would have stayed there, but my mindset was that I had to get somewhere safe. The only place I knew was my bedroom in my little town. It was just too scary to be anywhere else. My job was to get across the United States and just get home.

They wanted us to stay on the base for a couple of days, and I wanted to go home. This guy said, "Hey, look. Get your civvies on. Meet me here and I'll take you out to town." Four of us just left. We got ourselves to the airport. As long as you have orders you can fly for free. All we had to do there was walk up to the flight attendant and say, "Here are my orders. I'm processing out." They ask you where you're headed and then give you your ticket. It really wasn't like we were doing anything wrong.

Two of us fly into New York City. We've got to get to the Port Authority. A taxi driver picks us up and says he'll take us there. Then he drops us off in the middle of the city somewhere. We're looking for a subway stop, but it's like two o'clock in the morning. Finally we get on a train. We're just sitting there and a whole gang, maybe five or six guys, gets on… I'm thinking, "Fuck. I'm just trying to get home." One of them says, "What you got in the bag?" I say, "Here, take it! Take whatever you want! Go through it. I don't care." He rips both of our duffle bags apart, pulls out all our crap, and helps himself to miscellaneous stuff. I gave him a cigarette. I'm thinking, "I'm gonna get killed on the subway." But they were cool and they left us alone. They were just being tough guys.

We packed our stuff back up and got to the Port Authority. My traveling buddy lived in Albany, so I went to his house first. I don't think I was ready to be alone yet. When we got there, his parents drove us to get something to eat. Just being in an ordinary American restaurant put me into total culture shock.

I was also still strung out on drugs. I had just stopped. I know it seems impossible, because how can you "just stop"? I quit because it was either quit or don't go home. I couldn't have processed out with any drugs in me, because you've got to do urine tests on the way out. I knew when I was going to be leaving Vietnam, so I had to get clean. I just cut myself off the drugs. I got *so* sick. I would drink cold clear water, and I would vomit cold clear water. It wouldn't stay in my stomach. I felt so completely empty. At work, everyone knew what I was doing and why. I'd sit in the corner, shaking and having cold sweats. We had this bunker out back, and sometimes I'd go out there and sit for a while. Everyone would cover for me. Whatever I did, they'd cover for me. With them supporting me like that, I did it: I quit! My urine test came up clean and I was on my way out of Vietnam. In fact, I was still recovering on the way home.

Meanwhile, I'm now in Albany and I'm freaked out, so my buddy's father drives me to Lee, Massachusetts, where my family was now living, and he drops me off in the middle of town. I call my father and he asks, "Hey, where are you stationed?" I tell him, "I'm in town. Want to come get me?"

Most of my local friends weren't around any more. It was 1972, the summer of "going to California." The whole group kind of migrated to California in their VW vans. I just went home and slept for a week. I just slept and slept and slept. I felt safe, but it was very strange, because everyone around me was still doing the same things they did before I left. I had just gone through this mess of Vietnam. How could everyone else just be going about their business when so much stuff was still going on?

The other thing was, I had gotten home, but I wasn't out yet. I had orders to go to Fort Campbell, KY in thirty days, late in December. I decided to boycott. I just didn't go. What were they going to do? What I did was I hooked up with friends. I started drinking out at the bars, having beers, shooting darts. I don't know where the forty-five days went, but I just vegged out and dealt with my folks. They were thinking, "Who *is* this person?" I had an incredible attitude. "Don't ever tell me what to do again. If I leave, I leave. If I come home, I come home." I think I was pretty brutal to them. I sort of lost it at this point. I was just totally out there. I was trying to cope with what I was doing in this tiny little town of nothing. I was like, "God, I can't be living here."

Then there was an old friend of mine who was messed up. He had gotten wounded in 'Nam, and now he was a total alcoholic and drug addict. There was another guy, too, from a tiny little nearby town. This guy would sit in the bar, and all of a sudden, he'd climb under the table yelling, "Incoming!" at the top of his lungs. Everybody knew him so they'd tell him, "It's okay man. It's okay. Come on out." I wonder to this day how I can be as sane as I am. How can I be like this? I think, "Well, okay, it's a long time ago. It's history." But I do know that when I came out I was struggling.

After forty-five days, I went to Fort Campbell and checked in. The first words they spoke, of course, were, "Hey, you're AWOL man. What the hell's wrong with you?" I showed them my orders, and they said, "Look at that. You've been through hell, and you only have three months left to serve. I don't know why you're still here: when people have six months or less left, procedure is to let people out." I had three months so I'm thinking somewhere down the road someone knew something and said, "Well, if this guy's going to screw us..." because I kind of connected it with all the stuff I had pulled to get out of 'Nam. Someone probably said something like, "Look, his orders are messed up. Let's just make him stay when his tour is up. We're going to give him the full two years."

So there I was, in Fort Campbell and still in the service. It was freezing cold, and they said, "Well, we're going to play Army. You're in aircraft armament. We're going to put you out in a tent with a bunch of new guys, and you're going to train these guys, and you're going to sleep in the tent overnight, and then the helicopters are going to come in, and you're going to go out and fix them."

So, I'm out there. None of us want to get out of our sleeping bags to stoke the stove. It is so cold. We're all shaking in the morning. The officers are pissed off because the tent is not warm, because we didn't stoke the stove. I was out there for maybe two days, and they said, "Send him back. Maybe we can do something with him back in the barracks." I'm in the barracks thinking, "I'm not going to do this. I'm not going to do this." The colonel walks in, and I say to him, "What are you going to do? Fire me?" He responds with, "You're out of here!" and I say, "Great. Good. I want to go." But they didn't do anything. I guess maybe they said, "He's just come back. Give him a little slack."

There was something called an "early out." I called my father, and I said, "You've got to get me out of here." He talked to a carpenter in Pittsfield who wrote me a letter saying, "Yeah, I've been waiting for a guy to come work for me. If I don't get him pretty soon, I'm going to have to give the job away."

They let me out. I think I got out a month early, and I went to work for the guy. After four days he fired me, because I was useless, but I got what I wanted. I wanted to be back home, and finally I was really out. I got the honorable discharge, and was free to resume my life. Unfortunately, given my condition, what that meant was drinking a lot. I'd be down at the Men's Club, 10:30 or 11:00 in the morning, shooting darts, doing drafts and just hanging out with the guys. A soldier I met in basic training when I was at Fort Campbell even tempted me to try heroin again. I was in such a lost place, I actually agreed. While I never fell into doing that again, it's a sign of how much having been in Vietnam did to my head.

Telling this story has brought back many memories, some clear, some vague. I feel as if this story is just a piece of my experience. It brings back memories of more places; snapshots of so many faces, memories of laughter, sadness, friendships – both American and Vietnamese. I only wish I could see them again for a hug and a beer. I hope they made it.

George Williams

George passed away on September 2, 2010 as a result of a heart attack. At the time of his death he was a retired New York City firefighter and father of two children, ages thirty and thirty-four. His son was living with him in Northampton, Massachusetts, and his daughter lives in Brooklyn. He was active in two local veterans groups, the Veterans Education Project and Veterans for Peace. He visited area high schools as a representative of these groups to speak to students about his Vietnam War experience. Recently he had been asked to mediate a dispute between military recruiters and students on the campus of Holyoke Community College in Holyoke, Massachusetts where he had spoken numerous times in the past. George was also a visual artist. Called to Serve is dedicated to his memory.

I grew up in Brooklyn. I got my first real job while I was in high school working for Hayden, Stone and Co., a prominent securities firm, in 1965. My mother was very proud – there was a black man on Wall Street. I enjoyed the job, which involved working closely with the California office. I had an older brother, an older sister, a younger brother and two younger sisters. My mother was a single parent, and my money helped out the family. I was living a fairly good life and figured it would go on that way. Then I got drafted in 1966.

I had been aware of the war, because Martin Luther King was speaking out more and more against it. My father served in World War II, and my older brother was in the Air Force, so I felt a responsibility to do something. It was just my turn to go into the military. Sure I had choices. I could have gone underground. I could have gotten a phony ID and gone to Canada. I could have gone to jail. My response, though, was just to accept the fact I would be sent to fight.

The letter from the Selective Service told me to "Report to Whitehall Street" in downtown Manhattan. There even was a subway token taped to the top of it. I went down there, and they gave me a basic overall physical. During the exam you felt like you were part of a buffalo herd, and you just went along with it. There were a couple of people who probably took LSD or something, because they were bouncing off the walls. Some people were gay, and they pushed that issue right out in front. In all though, there was just a handful of people who seemed to be fighting what was happening. In fact, for me the physical was more like a reunion than anything else.

A lot of people from my high school, guys I hadn't seen in a couple of years, were there, and we were all going in together.

After my physical I started to hear more about the war, and I became more interested in it. However, despite what I was hearing, and even though all my folks, especially my sisters, were hesitant about me going, I just felt like it was something I had to do, like a rite of passage.

It took about six months before they told me to report. When I got the notice I went down to get all my gear, get sized up, jump on a bus and go get a haircut. Then they shuttled us back to our homes to say our good-byes. My father was home, and it was the first time he ever hugged me. I didn't even know how to react to that, because he was always very stand-offish, a disciplinarian. I thought it was just him doing what he needed to do, but I was surprised. I almost couldn't feel anything; it was such a foreign experience.

In basic training we were holed up in Georgia. The drill instructors were all white southerners. They hated New Yorkers, so they had us and the southerners in separate barracks. They were very harsh and not everyone was used to it. They told us, "We're going to break you guys from New York." They did things to us that were inhumane to say the least. There was one guy who couldn't do enough push-ups. They told him he was a monkey and needed to go climb a tree. They actually had this guy hugging a tree, humping a tree. One guy had a book with him, a paperback with a picture of his family tucked into it, and the drill sergeant took the book and ripped it in half. The guy broke down and cried.

There was a time when we were out in a field and we were looking at these rolling hills of Georgia. Everything was so green. I was just saying how beautiful the country was, when this southerner came up from behind where we were standing and said, "Hey, niggers, get off my property!" Back in New York, it wasn't that unusual to run into racist types, and usually we could just go our own way. Being in the military, though, we had to deal with it in other ways.

One way we dealt with it was to be the best that we could be, so they couldn't say anything to us. If we were faster than everyone else was, and did more push-ups and chin-ups, we were less likely to get mistreated. Or we could join one of the clubs. We could join the boxing club or something like that, because if you were in a club they treated you differently.

After basic training we went to advanced training in Fort Jackson, South Carolina. That's where the training got more intense. The rifle we learned on first was the M-14, which was before the M-16. It was actually a better weapon, because it had a wooden stock. It was a real down-to-earth weapon. You could drop it and pick it up, and it would still work. When they gave us the M-16 everyone used to call it a Mattel toy because it would jam up at the drop of a hat. You got one little grain of sand in it, and it would jam up. Everyone knew it wasn't made for Vietnam. A lot of guys, when they got to Vietnam, said, "Either you give me an AK-47 or you take me home!" We also had more specific training at Fort Jackson, learning about weapons like the Claymore mine in addition to the M-14.

In South Carolina we were put in barracks where, for the first time, instead of being with the whole group in one huge room, we were stuck in a dorm situation. There was one guy who had never been more than twenty-five miles from his house. He was the real country boy, the big guy, but we got along well because of our similar size. He was down to earth, and he was on the wrestling team, so we wound up wrestling. He kept offering to run down and get us some moonshine.

Some of us used to steal milk from the kitchen and bring it to a rural community near where he lived. Those people were mountain people, and they were really poor. They didn't know me, but they accepted me because I was in the military – it was automatic acceptance. The kids always got a kick out of me. I've always had a thing with kids.

When it was finally time to go to 'Nam, just stepping off the plane was a situation in itself. When the plane was coming in, there was mortar being fired. We made this really sharp turn, and the whole plane was shaking. All of a sudden it really hit home that I was in Vietnam and I could die. Then, when we opened the doors, we got this hit of air and it was like a hundred degrees. As we were walking along on the runway, the guys who were going home were passing us. They'd say things like, "You're going to go home with fewer guys than you got now," and "You've only got 364 more days to go!"

We jumped into a bus that was pitifully reinforced. It looked like somebody from a shop class just put some wire mesh on the outside. We went into the station where they told us where we were going. They just basically numbered us off and said, "All the one's are going there; all the two's are going there," and so on. I wound up going with the First Infantry Division, which was a rifle division that went into the jungles. We'd fly out on helicopters on some missions and try to spot any enemy going through the "boonies."

Fear was always a common denominator, no matter where you were, no matter what you were doing. Even when we were back at base camp, we weren't safe. We had been mortared there a couple of times, and one time somebody got blown up by a mortar round. That kept the fear with you. There were so many emotions, though; it's hard to pinpoint any one as the strongest. Sometimes we'd get into a firefight, and it would be so chaotic. We'd get mortared, and at one point a mortar landed behind me in a tree, and that's how I got some shrapnel in my buttocks. I was treated in the field and was seen by a battalion doctor when I got back to the base camp, but for some reason the Army neglected to include it in my records. To this day I'm still trying to get my Purple Heart. The Army says I have to find the medic who treated me, because even though the battalion doctor treated me, the battalion doctor says he doesn't know how I got the wound. I say, "I was in Vietnam. I got wounded. Where do you think it came from?"

But I think also at that time a lot of guys were wounding themselves, trying to get out. I mean I've seen guys cut themselves on the shoulder, so they wouldn't have to carry a backpack. One guy I know drank a bottle of booze, and then told another guy to smash his hand. The range in people's attitudes was unbelievable. There were people who loved being in combat; really to the point that I thought they were psychotic. They loved the act of killing. Then there were guys who wanted to get out so badly they would do anything.

I was somewhere in the middle. I was trying to do my job, despite the fear that was with me all the time. That fear was so powerful; it was almost like it was strangling me. I just wanted to get my time over with. There was a calendar with a Playboy-type model posing, and it was a line drawing with 365 little blocks in the woman's body. Each day you would shade in the block, and where the vagina was, that was home. Everybody had one of these calendars, marking the days off.

There were a lot of Vietnamese children there. One day I noticed that, no matter where you went, there were kids running all over the place. As a child I wasn't well off. My family was on welfare, but when I was in Vietnam what I had thought of as the poverty level was blown away. One little boy was holding his sister who was eating out of a sandbag that we threw our food away in. It was a really dirty sandbag, and he was feeding her out of it. His clothes were all tattered. More and more I saw kids like that. There was one ten-year-old boy, I remember; besides Vietnamese, he was able to speak German, French, English and Korean, and another dialect I didn't even understand. If you wanted any pot, he'd bring it to you. He would ride around on a little motor scooter, and if you wanted a girl, he would bring a girl. He was like a little pimp. I saw how war affected these children.

More and more I realized we weren't there for a legitimate reason. Even the way we fought the war showed how crazy it was. We would fight, take over certain areas and leave, and then they'd regain them, and we'd go back and have to take the same place over again. It just didn't make sense, strategically, militarily. It felt like we could have been there forever. It was like constantly taking one step forward and one step back. It didn't make sense to a lot of soldiers, to a lot of ground soldiers at least.

It didn't take long for us to realize we needed to be numbed out, to become "self-medicated," just to get through all the craziness and danger. We drank, and we smoked pot. Pot was probably the most used drug of choice, but there were some people who went to Saigon and got opium and heroin. They used to say, "If you're going into an opium den, don't go in alone," because some soldiers would go in and get killed. If you were going for a night out, you had to be wary, because the Viet Cong were all over the place.

I was really opposed to the way the war itself was being fought. There were the "zippo raids." I didn't like them at all. Even if the Viet Cong were around the area, why burn a whole village? If we got shot at, we used mortars until we could get an air strike, but a lot of the time we hit innocent villages. That's what the Viet Cong did. They hid behind the villages, but we took out the whole village killing many innocent people.

However, the more I was there, the more I understood the Viet Cong. I felt like they were doing a better job than we were, and some other soldiers felt that way, too. In fact, I just got a call from this guy who I was with in 'Nam. We talked about lots of things that happened, like how some guys always got separated after a firefight, and how our unit had to go look for them. Guys next to me got blown up, but I couldn't feel angry; I mean I understood all too well why the Viet Cong were fighting against us. In fact, I, and a handful of other soldiers, understood the whole war – they were fighting for their homeland and we were fighting to prevent them from winning it back. The officers, on the other hand, tried to have us dehumanize the Vietnamese, so we would be more likely to follow orders. We could be as brutal as we wanted to be and there were no consequences.

Fortunately for me, the neighborhood I was in when I was drafted was a blue-collar neighborhood. I had the support of the immediate neighborhood, even if there were some protestors. While I was in Vietnam, having good community and family support helped a lot, and we stayed in touch. Years later, in '85 or '86, I was on a T.V. show about the war with two other vets, one a paraplegic, the other a double amputee. While I was on the show, I started reading one of the letters I had written to my mother*:

Dear Ma,

How are things back in the World? I hope all is well! Things are pretty much the same. Vietnam has my feelings on a seesaw.

This country is so beautiful; when the sun is shining on the mountains, farmers in their rice paddies, with their water buffalo, palm trees, monkeys, birds and even the strange insects. For a fleeting moment I wasn't in a war zone at all, just on vacation, but still missing you and the family.

There are a few kids who hang around, some with no parents. I feel so sorry for them. I do things to make them laugh. And they call me "dinky dow." [crazy] But it makes me feel good. I hope that's one reason why we're here, to secure a future for them. It seems to be the only justification I can think of for the things that I have done!

Love to all.

Your son, George

All of a sudden, when I had gotten halfway through reading this letter, a wave of emotion came over me and I started crying. I was really surprised; I had no idea all this was pent up in me. It was reading what I wrote about the children that shook me up. We saw kids blown up, and they had nothing to do with the war. You were just ordered to bomb a village, and no one cared if kids lived there.

Something I didn't realize until I got back was the proportion of blacks on the front line. It felt like a good twenty-five percent, and everyone knew we weren't twenty-five percent of the U.S. population!† It's hard for me to prove that not receiving my Purple Heart, and not getting pro-

---

*The letter appeared in *Dear America: Letters Home from Vietnam*, ed. Bernard Edelman. W.W. Norton and Co., New York. 1985.

†88.4% of the men who actually served in Vietnam were Caucasian, 10.6% (275,000) were black, 1.0% belonged to other races. 86.3% of the men who died in Vietnam were Caucasian (including Hispanics). 12.5% (7,241) were black. 1.2% belonged to other races.

moted to sergeant, resulted from racism, but it sure looks like it. As to actual racial incidents, there was only one I saw personally. This black guy was test firing a rocket launcher. There's always a backfire behind, so the twelve feet behind you needs to be clear. But this time a white guy walked behind him. So of course he got hit by the backfire, and his response was, "Oh, you stupid nigger, I'm gonna get my gun. I'm gonna blow you up like you tried to blow me up." He was going for his weapon, so the black guy took out his bayonet and stabbed him. That was the only incident I saw.

Actually, it's hard to say which things that happened were products of racism. I know that while I was there, serving on the front line, being a black guy on the front line, I didn't always realize the effects racism had. It definitely felt like the only people promoted were white guys. I was an "acting jack," which meant that if a sergeant gets killed, promoted, or sent to another unit, they give you a band with sergeant stripes as a temporary promotion until a permanent replacement arrives. Usually when you get that, you get promoted, and I was waiting for my promotion, but it never came in. Instead, a white guy who got his "acting jack" stripes after me was the one who got promoted. After that I said, "Either promote me or take these stripes." I wasn't promoted.

The day before I was going to leave Vietnam some of the boys wanted me to have a bon voyage party. There was drinking, smoking and all of a sudden I realized that I had ten minutes to fly out. I missed my plane! Any delay in Vietnam was like walking on eggshells. You were just waiting for something to happen. Thankfully I got out the next day.

But getting out wasn't like it used to be before the protest movement against the war. When I came back home, it was September of '68. By then the protesting was in full bloom. There were hundreds of thousands of people protesting. I joined the Veterans Against the War. I was with them in Oakland, California, but when they wanted to blow up places and burn draft headquarters, I didn't want any part of that. I didn't want any more violence.

So I returned to Brooklyn with no place to go, and once again I self-medicated. A couple of vets stayed at the bar all day only to come out at night to smoke pot. I did that for a couple of years. One of my closest friends, John, had to go to Vietnam after I got back. He was convinced he wasn't going to come back, and I remember being at the bar and saying to him, "Listen if I can make it, you can make it." He ended up dying in Vietnam. His brother gave me one of his dog tags, and I gave him one of mine.

His brother and I have these dog tags that we always carry around with us. He was one of my best friends.

I know that when soldiers came back from World War II, the whole town came out to meet them and welcome them home. They got all these benefits. When we came home from Vietnam, we couldn't even get regular VA benefits. Nor would the VFW allow us to join. They said Vietnam wasn't a declared war, so we couldn't even have a beer in their hall! World War II vets were calling us drug dealers and baby killers. Only in 1985 did the VFW finally hold a Vietnam Veterans' Parade. It was the first parade, and it had taken *ten years* to happen! I don't think the white guys were treated any better. I don't think any of us got anything.

For me things didn't really start to change until 1998 when I got involved with the Veterans Education Project. I read about the Education Project in the newspaper, and it was the first veterans' group I wanted to be a part of. They were doing something positive, helping kids understand the realities of war instead of just glorifying it. I got to go to schools and tell my story to students, which felt important and meaningful. So I joined them, and through them, I joined another positive organization, Veterans for Peace.

It was about that time that I found out my records were messed up. As I said before, I had been injured by enemy mortar fire, and they owed me a Purple Heart. I had to have my aorta replaced and was in the VA hospital for three weeks and out of work for a month. Bills piled up. By the time I was back on my feet, I had to go to a credit company for help. I was on the edge and my PTSD (Post-Traumatic Stress Disorder) was intense. I finally went to the VA to see what was holding things up with my Purple Heart. I took with me the required paperwork: one sheet about where you've been, what your assignments were, and what your specialty was. So I gave them this sheet, and told them I was a combat Vietnam vet, and one of them said, "Oh, it states here (he pointed to some papers) you weren't in combat. We'll need to see your Army records."

When the records finally came three years later my separation papers (DD215) showed that I was in combat – I got the CIB (Combat Infantryman's Badge*) – that I had an honorable discharge, and that I re-

---

*U.S. Army combat service recognition decoration awarded to enlisted men and officers holding colonel rank or below, who *personally* fought in active ground combat while an assigned member of either an infantry or a Special Forces unit.

ceived an Army Service Bronze Star. When the VA saw that, and more of my records, they admitted I'd been in combat and was due a Good Conduct Medal and a couple of Vietnam Service ones as well. Then, unbelievably, they told me I would have to buy them myself! Not only that, but I wouldn't be getting a Purple Heart, which would have given me a full disability check every month and prevented me from having to face all of the bills that had occurred while I was in the hospital. According to them they claimed my form gave no proof I was wounded by shrapnel from a mortar in combat, despite the fact that an Army doctor had treated me! All these years later I am still trying to find the medic who treated me during that firefight as mortar rounds exploded upon us giving me my wound. The local newspaper wrote a front-page story about what happened to me and how unfair it is, but I'm still fighting the Army to get what I deserve.

Domenick Lasaponaro

Born in the Bronx, New York, Domenick became a Bridge and Tunnel officer and got injured on the job. He got the N.Y. State Medal of Honor for saving a man who was on fire as well as for rescuing three children who were in a runaway car. When he jumped in the car to save the children, he was dragged down the street and herniated two discs in his neck and back . As a result he retired with a disability eighteen years ago – one month before the birth of his daughter. He is currently separated from his wife and is raising three children (a daughter eighteen, a son sixteen, and a son eleven). He lives in Northampton, Massachusetts.

I come from a big family in the Bronx. I'm the thirteenth of fourteen kids, and my father died when I was three. My mom had already had five sons drafted by the time my letter came in 1970. I had gotten number 6 in the draft lottery. I said, "I won the lottery, Mom." The truth was, I was very oblivious. For one thing, I wasn't the type that would have said, "I'm going to Canada." I didn't even know about anything like that. I was just a silly, dumb kid. My family had a lot of boys who were in the service already, so I just thought it was my duty to go into the army.

For my mother it was different. She was the one who got the mail. Back then in New York City, when they gave you a draft notice, they included a subway token to make sure you got down to the draft board at Whitehall St. in Manhattan. All my mother had to do was feel the token to know I'd been drafted, too. At first she didn't tell me about what had come in the mail, so I didn't know anything about the letter.

My first physical had happened about six months earlier. I was in night school, so I would probably have had a deferment at least until I got out of school, but I didn't even know I'd been drafted. Other people knew somehow though. They were giving me shaving kits, and crying; my girlfriend was crying every time she saw me. I sure was wondering what was going on. Then, the night before I had to report, my mother gave me the letter. I figured it was just a notice for a second physical, but it was my induction notice. She just couldn't bear to have another son in the service, so she held onto the letter until the last possible moment.

I couldn't hold on to my girlfriend long enough that last night. I was just very sad that I had to go away and leave her. I had never fooled around with her. I was only nineteen and still believed you didn't fool around until you were married. Later on, when I was on the Army base, I got a letter from her saying, "I wish you were here." I came home for my birthday to see her, and she was in bed with another guy. I was very unhappy.

The reason you get a draft notice before your induction day is because they want you to get your affairs in order. I didn't get my affairs in order at all. I was just sitting in my room, and all of a sudden I was gone. I didn't pack my clothes. I didn't pack my records. When I came home after my time in the service, there were no more records. My clothes were gone, too. My cousins took everything. Everything was gone. I was in a state of shock.

The day I went into the Army, I didn't use the token they'd given me to go to the induction center. I just saved it. I guess part of me wanted a reminder of that day. I had my last physical, and was sworn in. Then they put me on a bus to Fort Dix, New Jersey. I didn't come home for ten weeks. I remember getting off the bus that first night. I was really nervous. It was all so new to me. They started right in getting us to be the same. The first thing they did was they made us pack up our clothes and everything we owned. They put it in a box and supposedly sent it home, but that box never made it to my house. Anyhow, so now we are walking around with the Army clothes on, the field jacket and things like that. Then they cut our hair. It was funny when they did that. When you went to get your hair cut, they showed you pictures of haircuts – like a guy with a little bit of hair left, a guy with a lot of hair off. They said, "Pick – which would you like." I picked the one with the most hair on, and then they just shaved my head.

Then they gave us all our shots and checked our teeth. In fact, they actually taught us how to brush our teeth but in a mean way. They gave us these little red pills to chew and, rather than make us spit in a cup, they put the cup under our chins and said, "Spit it out." The stuff would just drip down, making a big red stain on our faces. Everybody walking around had this big red stain down his face. It was really humiliating.

Every morning they woke us up at five o'clock. They made us clean the barracks and then they'd march us around. I was inducted in March. Normally they'd march us out early in the morning, but if it snowed in the middle of the night, they'd wake us up at two a.m., because they wanted us to "play" in the snow. They changed their whole routine for rain and snow. They made us crawl around in that stuff all the time. Not my idea of fun. But they did feed us well. The military always fed us.

They didn't give out guns until almost the end of basic training. If you had ten weeks, you didn't get a gun until probably your eighth week there. They were very careful about guys hurting themselves, especially because you're always tired in the military. They march you some place, and then they tell you to go to sleep. You just put your helmet down as a pillow, and you're so tired you go to sleep right there on your helmet.

They were very careful about teaching you how to put bullets in your gun. You see these movies where the guy has the gun, and he kills the sergeant. That can't happen, because they don't give out bullets until the end of training. During the time when you're going to use your gun on the firing range, they insert rods to make sure there's not a bullet in your gun, and they make sure you have no bullets with you. There's no way you're going to get a bullet for that gun. You carry that gun around with you all day long. You clean the gun. You make sure you take the gun apart. You do all kinds of things with the gun, but you don't have a bullet, so you're not going to shoot somebody.

After Fort Dix I was sent to Oklahoma for artillery. I ended up in Fort St. Louis and stayed there. Up to that point, Vietnam didn't matter to me at all. I had no opinion about the war. I thought I was going to be with the artillerymen, so I didn't think I was going to be close to the fighting. It didn't really bother me though, because I never thought I was going to die being in the service. I never thought *I* could die from that, even though a lot of my friends did. I grew up in a largely Puerto Rican and Black neighborhood and a lot of the guys went over. They didn't know how to fight to stay out, so they just went. Many of the ones who went in first died, and others came back with a missing arm or leg. They'd make us younger guys sing songs. Here's one I still remember: (Domenick sings)

> I wanna go to Vietnam,
> I wanna be a major.
> I wanna go to Vietnam airborne,
> I wanna be an airborne major.
> I wanna kill those Charlies
> with a knife or with a gun.
> Either way will be great fun!

Of course, when we got to Basic, the Army was building us up all the time so we would be ready to go to Vietnam, so we'd be able to kill people. They would have signs up like, "Be a Soldier, Go to Exotic Places, Meet

Exotic People and Kill Them!" They wanted to be sure we fully understood we would go and kill people *any way* we could – with knives or guns or ropes.

One thing that was funny was the Army organized soldiers by the first letter of their last names. When you get drafted, you're drafted by your birthday, but then, what they do to keep you together, is put you with guys whose last name begins with the same letter as yours. So here's a whole group of guys, a whole Charlie company, and they were all "L's" – Lavapool, Lavey, Ladet, Ladinsky. For the guys who were stationed in my barracks, they even narrowed it down to the same names – Dominic LaPaul and Dominic LaPuda. It was really weird. I had five Dominics in my unit.

On the one hand, the Army made you become buddies, because you *all* hated the military. On the other hand, they also did things to keep us from getting too close. For example, for guard duty they had something called "make the man." If they needed ten guards, they picked eleven, and one of them would get the day off. They'd go down the line and say to a guy, "You are the best-dressed guy" or "You're the cleanest looking guy" and he'd get the day off. This caused the guys to compete for the privilege; it was just a way to divide us.

When you get into basic training, they offer you a choice of where you want to be stationed, and what you want to be. The forms are called "dream sheets." They asked me, "Where do you want to be stationed?" and I said, "Fort Dix, New Jersey." They sent me to Fort Lewis in Washington state. Then they asked me, "What would you like to be in the Army?" I said, "Artillery." They said, "O.K., we'll make you a cook, since you've worked at a butchery and can obviously handle meat." I said, "But my brothers, *all five* of my brothers are in *artillery*. One brother is stationed in Germany in *artillery*. Another brother is in Oklahoma in *artillery*. A third brother is in Korea in *artillery*. My father was even in artillery in World War II. Why would you make me a cook?" I had a big fight with those people. I had to talk to them several times, and finally they said, "O.K., we'll put you in artillery."

Before I started my artillery training, they gave us two weeks off. I was able to go home to visit my family. This was right at the time of the 1971 "Concert for Bangladesh" in Manhattan, so I got to go to the concert and to be with my family. My girlfriend was totally changed. I'm away for ten weeks and all of a sudden I don't even know who she is anymore. She's going out with other guys. I was really depressed, because I was with her for four years, and suddenly I didn't have a girlfriend anymore. It's making me sad all over again just thinking about that. In fact, it still depresses me to think, if I had just not been drafted, we might have gotten married like we planned.

After my break, I went to artillery school in Oklahoma. The fort is on a big, windy flat surface and the temperature could go up to 120 degrees. I got trained on all kinds of artillery pieces: 1-05s, 1-55s, etc. Next I was transferred to Fort Lewis in Washington, and I still didn't know anything about my future. They didn't tell you anything. They just kept sending you places. They told me, "Here's where you're staying until we figure out what to do with you." At one point I was supposedly in Nuclear Demolitions. So what was I doing? I was doing base clean up. They gave me a Jeep, and I just walked or drove around the base, and picked up cigarette butts. They also gave me a lawnmower and told me to mow the lawn. The base is only ten miles, a straight line, and I had a lawnmower. I'd walk the lawnmower to breakfast, and after breakfast I would start to mow. At lunchtime, I stopped mowing and ate lunch. After lunch I just walked the lawnmower in a straight line, and then I stopped, turned around and walked the lawnmower back again until dinnertime. Then they'd send me home. The next day they'd send me back with the lawnmower to repeat the process. I did that for months at a time! A few times during the year we would have a month of artillery training to be sure we stayed ready, but other than that, they had nothing else for me to do. I'd lost my girl because I was drafted, so I could do this?

That was truly boring, but then came the burial detail, which I really hated. We used to carry the corpses and fold the flags for the guys coming back from Vietnam. They used to send me all over the place. They sent me to Montana. They sent me to Idaho and Bull Run. We'd interact with the families. Every once in a while a family member would catch your eye, or somebody would cry, and, even though you weren't supposed to, you'd comfort them and then you'd be in trouble. They made it perfectly clear that was *not* to happen again.

By this time I'd become a sergeant, which at least meant I had my own room. Then all of a sudden orders come down that I'm to report to Saigon. So I clean out the room I got because I was a sergeant, pack my bag, and get taken to an airplane. They put me on the plane, and I'm sitting there waiting to go, when they tell us that our orders have been rescinded and we should go back to the base.

I'm not going to Vietnam anymore, but my sergeant's room is gone. Until another one becomes available, I'm stuck in the deportation center with guys just returning from Vietnam. They'd come into our unit for a couple of days, and then all of a sudden they'd be gone. Before they could leave though, they had to go through a whole list of things. They had to go to the library to make sure they didn't owe any library books. They had to go to the dentist to make sure their teeth were okay. So guess what my next detail is? Being one of the folks to walk these guys through all these steps! Mowing the lawn, burial detail, and now this!

At least I think we served a purpose with these guys. When they came back, they had stories to tell, and we were there to listen to them. The guys coming back from 'Nam would tell us all kinds of stories. They would tell us about being in a tank and going through fences with giant spiders on them, or blowing up landmines and losing buddies. Some guys would stay with us for a week or two, and we'd talk with them, and hear their stories. They needed to tell stories. It helped them acclimate back to the States. We would listen to them, and they would cry, and that was a good thing. Later on, at the end of the war, Nixon gave everybody a six-month "early out" and guys like these, just back from Vietnam, were right out on the street. Nixon wasn't doing those guys any favor. They didn't have any time to cope with what they'd been through, and they didn't get the time to debrief. "Early out" just meant they didn't have any time to talk, to get that stuff out of their systems.

After this the Army decided to make me happier. They actually gave me a real job to do instead of things like mowing lawns all day. They made me the contact person for the drug program. They felt soldiers didn't want to talk to captains or lieutenants, but they'd talk to a sergeant, somebody on their level. If a guy had a problem he would say, "Oh, I got a problem with drugs. Could you help me out?" or "I'm having trouble with drinking. Could you help me out?" and they'd talk to me.

Guys would be made to get urine tests to see if they had any LSD or heroin or whatever in their system. The Army then gave me the right to look in their "big book," where all the test results would be recorded. That meant I knew which guys had been doing which drugs. When soldiers would come to me and ask, "Do you know where we could get some LSD?"

I'd just look in the book, and say, "Oh, yeah, Bill Smith in the third cabin has it. Go ask him."

Obviously, I found a way to get some things myself, but I didn't use any hardcore drugs. I only smoked marijuana. One time I was burning some incense in my room and the MP's kicked my door down. They came in with a sergeant and I told him, "You have no right kicking my door down." "Well, we thought you were smoking marijuana." I said, "If I was smoking marijuana, I wouldn't do it in my room." I was very annoyed and I told my major the sergeant who kicked my door down had an alcohol problem. I got my revenge when the major made him go to urine analysis for a whole month – once every week! That sergeant always had bloodshot eyes like he'd been drinking, so I told him, "Don't kick my door down again, because I'll make trouble for you."

It turned out I was almost sent to Vietnam twice more. The reason why they kept rescinding my orders was because I was in a training unit. I trained guys with the artillery pieces. They needed guys like us to do this training, so they couldn't send me away.

While I was still in the Army, I decided to go back to school. The Army drafted me out of high school, so I felt I had the right to get a GED while I was in. I was a good enough soldier, so they said okay. They let me go to school on their time after I finished work during the afternoons. That's when I found out about the GI Alliance, which was organized by anti-war soldiers at Fort Lewis. This was exactly the time when Jane Fonda was getting involved in protesting the war. At first I thought she was wrong, but I wanted to meet her. So I joined the GI Alliance, because she was coming to town and I figured I could meet her by being part of what she was doing. I thought, "Let me meet her, and see if she's as bad as they say she is." I went to a party she was at, and she asked me for beer money. We went to a big concert afterwards with Country Joe McDonald, and I got to be behind stage with them. I thought, "Well, this is fun."

After I'd joined, the GI Alliance folks gave me literature to hand out to fellow soldiers on base, which I did until the MP's broke into my locker and took all that literature from me. They told me I had no right to hand out anti-army literature. I thought, "Who are you to tell me I can't have anti-army literature?" That's when I started having problems with the Army. They wouldn't give me any more rank after that.

I got out of the Army just like I got in – a fluke really. I was on a detail escorting this black guy who'd been in Vietnam and had to be processed out. He'd been given a bad conduct discharge, a BCD, because he hit his lieutenant, a white guy. I was told to hold him at gunpoint and take him right up to the front of each line so there'd be no trouble. Even doing it that way, it still took two days for him to get through the library line and the dentist line and all that. Now this was happening when it was very close to the time I was to be discharged, and I wanted to get out just as fast as I could. I knew if I just went through the process on my own, I'd wait in all the lines just like everyone else. However, if I could figure out a way for the BCD guy to do for me what I'd just done for him, then *I'd* get to go to the front of the lines, too. So, what I did was, I took the bullets out of the gun and gave it to the black guy to bring me around.

The black guy had told me he thought he was getting a raw deal in receiving a bad conduct discharge. He felt his lieutenant had tried to make him do something that would cause his fellow soldiers to get killed, and he had to hit the guy to save his unit. He told me he was really angry, and me bringing him around at gun point made him angry, too. I felt bad for the guy, and it was neat to help him feel better. He said when I gave him the gun to escort me around it made him feel really good to be putting one over on the Army!

Amazingly, no one was suspicious, and I quickly got out in Oklahoma. I went on a date with a girl who brought me in a convertible to a drive-in movie. These guys pulled up next to me and hit me over the head with a beer can, and beat the living hell out of me, just because I was a soldier, because I had a short haircut! In fact, I saw places in Oklahoma where it said, "Dogs and soldiers not allowed in here." For me it was another lesson about the real world. Even this could happen.

The truth is I'd thought that when I came back, the world would say, "He just came back from the Army, let's treat him good." How wrong I was. Nobody cared. I could have come back from having terrible experiences in Vietnam and no one would have cared.

John Hoogstraten

John grew up in Michigan. He is fifty-seven years old and the father of two grown children, ages twenty-four and thirty. He has two grandchildren. He lives in Williamsburg, Massachusetts, with his partner, Eileen Keegan. He works as a building contractor.

While I was in high school, I have to admit my focus was elsewhere. I was an athlete, played basketball. Like a lot of teenagers, I was more concerned with my own life than what was going on in the world. We didn't have TV at home, so I never got plugged into those images of the war like a lot of people did. The high school I attended was in a small town outside of Kalamazoo, in southwestern Michigan, a pretty conservative area. There was a strong and very vocal anti-war group of kids at school who were definitely fringe hippie types. I knew most of them and considered them friends. Certainly I admired their boldness in coming out with their views.

At times I felt they were all just jumping on the same bandwagon, making the same noise, but I guess that's better than watching somebody jump on somebody else's wagon. I knew I was opposed to the war, though I'm not quite sure why. Somehow I came to the conclusion that what we were doing over there was a bad scene, but it didn't really sink in until I was a senior that it might actually affect me. That final year it started becoming very real for me, and I started joining the protests. I grew pretty concerned about what might happen to me.

I remember seeing the older brothers of some of my friends, older boys in the community, come back from Vietnam pretty messed up and emotionally troubled. That's what really started driving home to me the fact that this was a very different type of war than the one my dad had fought in. My dad fought in World War II and he was a flag-waving patriot: "Believe in your country, right or wrong. They call you and you go." Every male he knew had served in one fashion or another in World War II, and for them it was a source of pride. It was not just what they did, it was a lot of who they were. I think my mother had the typical maternal conflict. She agreed with my dad politically, but of course she didn't want any of her sons sent off to Vietnam. She felt caught in the middle. She was the peacemaker in the family, trying to keep everybody happy, resolving conflicts, keeping everybody away from each other. When I started making noises about resisting the draft, my dad actually loudly, publicly, threatened to disown me if I resisted in any way or didn't go. That put my mother in a tough position.

I remember talking about the war and the draft a lot with my friend, Ted Klinger. He proposed that we buy ourselves some Harley motorcycles, and, if we got low numbers, hit the road and take a big trip around the country. We'd see all the sights and go to all the places we'd dreamed about, and then go right over the border into Canada. At least he wanted to do that, but he got married shortly out of high school, and that nixed his plan to hit the road.

As for the day of the lottery itself, I got out of my summer job at the usual 3:30 in the afternoon and decided I couldn't go home. I wanted to be in a private place when I heard my number. I didn't want to get it in my parents' presence. I didn't want them influencing, or judging, or even seeing my reaction. If I had a high number, I wanted to scream and shout and jump around, but I didn't want to insult my father or anger him. I just wanted to react privately first, and then go home and deal with them. So I just stopped at a store in town, got a newspaper, sat in my car, smoked a joint, and finally opened it up. They had the entire listing of lottery numbers there with all the birth dates. There was mine: 56! I sat there stoned for a while, not knowing how to process it, what to think, where to go.

I ended up going home. I hadn't really lost it at that point, so I could still drive. My mother had baked a cake. She had gotten the news earlier in the day, and had baked a cake, all decorated with a big number 56 in the middle of it. She had it sitting right there on the table waiting for me. I was quite upset when I saw the cake. In fact, I was stunned. It made me realize right then that my parents didn't get it. They just didn't understand what this meant to me. For them it was a source of intrigue or almost humor, this whole lottery concept. They were there with big grins on their faces. They thought that this was...actually I don't know what they thought. I went and closed myself in my room and came out later on and put the cake away. I didn't want to see any part of it. I made it clear this was not a cause for celebration for me.

I had a couple of friends who got very high lottery numbers, and clearly they were relieved. However, they also felt the lottery system was unfair. They said, "Why is this? Somebody pulls numbers out of a hat, and *you* go to Vietnam, and *I* don't? *I* get to stay home? What's fair about that?"

Even though my lottery number was drawn in the summer of 1971, my initial assumption was I would be taken early in 1972, so I took a summer job. As it turned out, because they were winding down, focusing more on those volunteering to serve, I kept getting delayed and delayed. I quit one job in anticipation of being called soon and found myself sitting at home waiting. So I took another job and just kept hanging out. I didn't actually get called up until late in the summer of '72. It was only then, when I received my letter to go to what they refer to as a pre-induction physical, that it really sunk in on me: I could end up wherever the military chose to send me!

Some of those anti-war protester friends of mine from high school were doing things like starving themselves, trying to be too skinny to avoid having to go. I wasn't motivated enough to do anything like that. At that point, I wanted to play by the book, just find a legitimate way out. I let myself hope I wouldn't pass the physical because of my height. Six feet, eight inches was the limit and I was six feet, seven and three quarters – a quarter of an inch too short. I had had some problems with chronically sprained ankles playing basketball in high school, and I had really severe allergies as a kid, so I thought I might have some legitimate claim to exemption. I thought that between being too tall, having bad ankles and bad allergies, jeez, why would they bother with me?

I went to my doctor who was sympathetic but professional. He didn't fake anything for me, but he did send me to a specialist regarding my ankles. The specialist examined me and wrote a letter on my behalf. My doctor wrote another one about my allergies. The doctors did not make any judgments themselves on whether I was fit to serve or not; somebody else would make that decision. But I tried to play it straight thinking that surely there was something that would work. Maybe if I had really worked at it... I remember trying to lay down on the bus trying to stretch myself out to the fullest extent possible, on the way to the pre-induction physical. Once I got there, though, I was on my feet for a long time. I guess I compressed enough that, when I got measured, I was still six feet seven and three-quarters inches tall. The guy announced it loudly. Then they got me on the scale – I was pretty skinny then – one hundred and eighty pounds. Neither my height nor my weight seemed to matter. "Son, you're gonna make a fine soldier," he said, and set me up at the next station. None of my other attempts worked and I passed the physical.

After that, I started talking around. I got the name of a draft counselor in Kalamazoo. Some people I knew had met with him. When I got my induction letter, I went into a panic. That's when I started going to this counselor. His approach for the most part was to play the system and beat it, doing almost a level of civil disobedience to try to stay out of the draft. What he encouraged me to do, and then provided me with the materials to do, was make a scene when it came time to be called up for induction. He gave me two little vials. One was butyric acid and the other an acid that could be used to create a temporary tattoo. He said, "Look, it's too late to go back through the Selective Service Board. That ship has sailed. You're going to have to do something to make the military think you'll be more of a bother than an asset, so they'll just turn around and send you home." He suggested I temporarily tattoo myself with anti-war slogans before I went to the induction center in Detroit. So I did. I actually did it at the home of my good friend, Ted Klinger. He and his wife helped me with the tattoos. I put one right on my forehead. Ted tattooed "Fuck the army" on the back of my hands.

The other vial, the butyric acid, was this incredibly smelly stuff. The draft counselor said, "If all else fails, you're through the system and they're not turning you around and sending you out the door, just take a few drops of this and sprinkle it on your clothes. It will reek to high heaven, and at that point the whole place will be in turmoil, and they'll certainly just send you out the door."

I was still officially living at home, but I didn't spend a lot of time there. I wasn't talking with my dad much at that point, but my family did know I had gotten support from our family doctor, the one who had delivered me. It was when he saw me taking steps like this to try and stay out of the draft that he issued his proclamation about disowning me. I have this mental picture of him not even looking at me, but announcing that no son of his would ever be a draft dodger loudly enough for everybody to hear. I think those were the words he chose. At first I was stunned, but soon afterwards, I realized it was probably more bluster than truth. I think he was just trying to shame me into giving all this up and just be a man, be a patriot. Even if my father wouldn't come, my mother and my sister should have been the ones taking me to the bus the morning I was off to fight, the way families accompanied World War II soldiers to the train station as they set off for war. But I said, "No, I can't do this."

Instead, I went and spent the night with the Klingers, and that's when they did the tattooing. By doing it at the last minute like that, my family didn't even have to know. The next morning when I got on the bus everybody was staring at me. It was probably the most difficult day of my entire life. I remember being incredibly fearful, not knowing what was going to happen to me.

When I got to the induction center and they saw me with the tattoos, they definitely reacted, but instead of reacting as I'd hoped, identifying me as a trouble-maker or an unlikely prospect to be a good soldier, they seemed to take it on as a challenge. They saw me and their eyes lit up. I was like an element of excitement in their day of lines and lines of almost faceless individuals, and not only was I close to being six feet eight, but I had tattoos on my forehead to boot. You could almost see their juices start flowing.

At that point, I had gone through all the stages I had hoped would work for me, and I was still in the system, still going through lines. I went in the bathroom and put those drops of butyric acid on my pants. I came back out, and it was awful. People were gagging and retching. The other recruits were running to the bathrooms. The people that worked there, the military guys that ran the place, lost whatever sense of humor they might have had. I remember them yanking me out of line and marching me upstairs to another room. It was a very ornate room, an inner sanctum, all mahogany panels, carpeted, and very plush. This was the room where you stand in line and take your oath and step forward. It was the Cassius Clay* scene. If you don't step forward, you are refusing induction. They marched me up there by myself to read the oath to me and let me accept it or not. They usually take a group of thirty or forty guys, but this time it was just me all alone with them.

Part of me was just trembling with fright at what was about to happen. But another part thought, "I'm in this so deep. What have I got to lose?" Jail or Vietnam? It didn't matter at that point. Take your pick. I refused induction. They repeated the oath, and I was supposed to take a step forward and put my hand up. I knew the drill, but I refused. I did not step forward. There was this wall of military guys with their chests full of medals and ribbons. They all looked at me in disbelief. They almost didn't know

---

*On April 28, 1967 Muhammed Ali (formerly Cassius Clay) – he had taken this name in 1964 - refused induction into the United States Army. The State of N.Y. revoked his boxing license, as did many others.

what to do. None of them wanted to deal with me given how I reeked.

They finally steered me into a hallway, and one of them took me on. He was the stereotype: a tall, hard-muscled, square-jawed, crew cut guy. He had more hardware on him than I'd seen in some hardware stores. He took me into his office, and I remember him throwing the window wide open and sitting on the windowsill while he talked to me. He tried a combination of fatherly advice and stern warnings. He basically informed me that I would go to federal prison for five years. He told me what it would be like. He said, "Don't think you're going to talk your way out of this in court. It doesn't work."

Maybe he was telling the truth, or maybe he was trying to bluff me. In either case, even before I got on the bus for the induction center, I had decided that, if push came to shove, I would not take a position that could end me up in jail. It was the summer of '72 and I knew at that point the chances of my actually going to Vietnam were pretty slim. They were bringing troops home from Vietnam by then. Nixon was calling for the "Vietnamization"* of the war. The plan was that then the U.S. could gradually withdraw all its soldiers from Vietnam and begin moving toward an all-volunteer army. It just wouldn't have made sense to go to prison.

My goal was to stay out of the Army. I wasn't so much afraid of going to Vietnam as I just didn't want to waste a chunk of my life. At that age, two years seems like a huge amount of time and I didn't want to have to play a military game. I just didn't want to have to do the military thing, even if I was just stateside at some easy job. I didn't in any way, shape, or form want to seem like I was supporting the military in all of its flawed endeavors, not just Vietnam, but I wasn't willing to go to jail. So, at the end of the conversation, he said, "We're going to bring you back in the room and give you another chance." At that point, I accepted induction. I did step forward. I decided to go.

After the swearing in ceremony, they said, "Where's that smell coming from, buddy? We gotta deal with this." There was still a strong smell attached to me, and by that point, not surprisingly, I had gotten a nasty reputation amongst all the other inductees. They found somebody to run

*Soon after taking office in 1969 President Nixon introduced his policy of "Vietnamization." The plan was to encourage the South Vietnamese to take more responsibility for fighting the war. It was hoped that this policy would eventually enable the United States to gradually withdraw all their soldiers from Vietnam.

down the street to a store and buy me a pair of very ill-fitting jeans. It was late afternoon by then. They put us on a Greyhound bus. I got a seat to myself, and they drove us down to Fort Knox, Kentucky, for basic training. It was a processing center where you get dusted for lice and whatever else they decide to do to you. I still had these tattoos on me, and my reputation accompanied me there.

One of the first things you have to do, of course, is go to the barbershop. I refused to let them cut my hair. The barber steps up to the chair: "Sorry, I won't let you cut my hair." He said, "Get out of the chair." He sent me out. Whoever was marching us through all this instructed me to stand in the middle of the street and said somebody would pick me up. This is in Kentucky in August. It's 110 degrees in the middle of the street, and I just had to stand there and wait. I remember it was a long time, and I felt as if I were going to keel over. Finally a jeep came roaring up and took me to some commander's office.

The commander gave me the whole rap. "You are in the Army now. You're not trying to stay out of the Army. You're in. You took an oath of induction. You're a soldier. Whether you look like one or not, or feel like one or not, you are a soldier and there are certain legal requirements now. One of them is that you obey orders or face the consequences. The consequence of directly disobeying an order is a court martial – which can end you up in jail. It's pretty cut and dry when you are in the military. You just refused an order to get your hair cut. So consider the consequences here." Then he looked me over and said, "All those tattoos have got to go." He took me into a supply room adjacent to his office, gave me a can of Ajax scouring cleanser and a scrub brush, and said, "Go to work. Don't come out of that room until those things are gone." I had to scrub myself bloody to get them off. Then they took me back and they cut my hair.

At that point I realized I better play their game for a while. What I was doing obviously wasn't working. It clearly didn't keep me out of the Army, and they weren't going to send me home. One big mistake I made was my timing. If I had done the tattoos and the butyric acid at the pre-induction physical, they might have turned me around and sent me home. By the time it was the actual induction day, it was too late.

So I realized if I kept resisting, I was only going to make my situation unnecessarily difficult or even a lot worse. I got in line with everyone else and started playing by the rules. I decided just for the hell of it, since

I was there, to see how good a soldier I could become, to play the game to win it. At first I refused to let them issue me the M16 rifle. I said, "I'm sorry, I don't carry a weapon." I was shipped off to my new company commander and given the same lecture about facing a court martial and jail. I said, "Alright, I'll take the gun," and I did. I had never fired a gun in my life; we weren't even allowed to have bb guns when I was a kid. But I learned how to use the M-16 and even got a marksman medal for it. I found myself in incredible physical condition, thanks to all the physical training they put us through, and proceeded to become the best marcher in my platoon.

At the same time, I was always watching, learning, and seeing what was going on. At some point, they started talking about where we were going to go next, and I realized this was an opportunity to steer myself into a place in the Army that I could live with. It seemed to me that the officers were a little smarter in a lot of cases, a little better educated, a little more intellectual than the drill sergeants and that crowd, so I requested an audience with my company commander. He already knew my history and had been watching me, waiting to see what would go on. I remember having an interesting conversation with him about the military and how I fit into it, what he was going to do for me, how I might not waste my time and the government's money for two years. I told him I very much wanted to stay out of any combatant roles, and he arranged a meeting for me with a chaplain. The chaplain then wrote a supportive letter and arranged for me to get assigned to a medical base for advanced training in preventive medicine down in San Antonio. Relieved, I went down to San Antonio, got settled, and started going through the training.

It still gnawed at me, though, that I was in the military on their medical base. Even if I was just going to be testing water supplies for e coli, I was still supporting the military and everything they did. It just didn't feel right. Fortunately, there were several draft counselors who set themselves up outside the base. I hooked up with one of them who encouraged me to file for conscientious objector status. I knew it was possible to do that even when you were in the military. I'd heard of people in combat, who would freak out, desert, or apply for CO status because they couldn't handle the war scene, but it hadn't occurred to me it might be a possible option in my own situation.

I need to back up a little bit. I remember inquiring about applying for conscientious objector status before I got called in. I had just gotten my lottery number and was investigating all my options. I even remember going to the Selective Service Board in Kalamazoo a couple of times to inquire about the status of things. The wisdom around Kalamazoo was the local Selective Service Board only accepted conscientious objector claims that had a religious basis. They almost always, if not always, disallowed any claims that just had moral objections to war. My family was not religious, and I had no religious basis whatsoever. All I had were my own personal morals, so my chances would not be good. I had also been counseled, again in advance of being drafted, that if you applied for conscientious objector status and were refused, it would be very difficult to ever have that decision reversed. So, convinced it wouldn't work, I decided not to apply.

Now in San Antonio I was being counseled to apply on the basis that I'd spent several months in the military, had experienced it, knew what role I was going to play in it, and, even as a non-combatant, I couldn't conscientiously support the Army. So that, in fact, was what I did. I applied as a conscientious objector and got put in something of a holding pattern instead of being assigned. I had to go through what felt like a token set of hearings. Again I had to chat with a psychiatrist. I also had to solicit letters from back home. Several friends wrote incredibly detailed, supportive letters. I remember writing to my dad and asking if he would send one. I thought this would be a good chance to reach out to him and to accept whatever he had to say. I said, "Look, I don't expect you to agree or even understand what I am doing here. All I'm asking is for you to simply write a letter stating that you think I am doing this honestly, with honest conviction." I explained he didn't have to submit the letter to the board; he could just send it to me.

The counselor gave me a letter of instructions to send to everybody I was asking for letters of support. On it were details of how to address the letter, what kinds of things the letter should say, and what form it should be in. Everybody else followed that, sending me these very proper, formal letters, but I received nothing from my dad. Then on the morning of my hearing for my CO status, I went and grabbed my mail one last time, and in it was a little envelope from him! Inside was this little piece of blank stationary with the date. It read, "To Whom It May Concern. I don't agree with my son, but I do think he is an honest person." Signed Robert Hoogstraten. The fact that my dad would do that had an incredibly powerful effect on me. I knew just how wrenching it must have been for him to do anything that would support my getting conscientious objector status. And the timing… If that letter had come the next day it wouldn't have done me any good.

I have memories of the hearing. It was one-on-one, just a colonel and me. I remember him posing a lot of hypothetical questions such as, "Someday, when your son asks you what you did in the war, are you going to be able to look him in the eye and tell him you were a conscientious objector?" I said, "Oh, yeah!" Once I was able to convince them I was honest, and not just making all this up because I was too lazy to serve, they let me out with an Honorable Discharge.

When it was all over, a couple of high school buddies came and picked me up. We took a little road trip to Mexico and through the Southwest and hooked up with Ted Klinger, who had joined the Army Reserves to avoid active duty. He was going through basic training in Louisiana. We hung out with him for a weekend and then drove home. I can still see my mother's response when I walked into the house and told her what had happened. She didn't give me any hug or anything. All she said was, "Are you gonna be in any kind of trouble because you did this? Did you really get a discharge?" She was concerned I had placed myself in some disadvantageous position for the rest of my life by how I'd handle my relationship with the military. I assured her that most definitely was not the case: I could actually even get GI benefits if I wanted. In fact, a year or two later, I was even given a monetary bonus for what I'd done by the state of Michigan, which had decided to honor all who'd served in the military during the Vietnam era in this way. At first I thought, "How the hell should *I* be rewarded?" Then I thought to myself, "It's money," and sent in the form. Eventually I got sixty bucks, or whatever it was, based on length of service. Clearly there had been no need for my mom to worry!

In terms of my dad, I never really had a heart-to-heart talk with him. I don't know if I thought that wouldn't be possible, or if I just wasn't interested. I do remember thanking him for sending the letter. I told him his doing that meant a lot to me, but he just brushed it off. Even so, I was aware his feelings about the war had changed. By 1973, when I was discharged, he'd gotten a television and had been watching the news. He'd done some reading and talking with other people. Like a lot of Americans, he had seen what a disaster the whole scene over there had become. Even though he wasn't willing or able to come right out and say so, I got the sense my dad recognized I'd been right. He seemed to respect the fact that I'd understood what was actually going on in Vietnam better than he had. He now understood my position and came around.

I had no career or work to be impacted by what had happened. I was held in high esteem by most people in the community and friends. There were some older guys I had played basketball with who'd gone to Vietnam, and I took a little bit of quiet flack from them. I think they respected me as a person; they just didn't understand what I had done. I could see them biting their tongues when they were with me, probably to avoid getting into an argument. By 1973 and later, after the fall of South Vietnam, they didn't want to be defending any role they had played in the military action over there. At that point, anybody who had served over there just wanted to hide from the whole thing. There was definitely not a lot of honor to be had.

When I look back on my whole experience with the draft process, I think it was a formative experience for me. Up until that point, I had been pretty willing to just ride whatever wave came along. However, when it came time to decide how to respond to my draft notice, I had to stop and think and consider actions and consequences and possibilities; I actually had to make some decisions about how to manage my life. That definitely was good for me. As a middle-aged adult with some life experience and a wider worldview, I actually see some value in mandatory national service for young adults as long as serving in the military is *one* of the options, but not an *involuntary* one.

It's funny though. Now as an adult, with a greater awareness of how short a period of time two years really is, I find myself wondering if I should have stayed in the Army and broadened my range of experiences. To have gone places and seen how the Army works would have left me better informed as an adult. Certainly I would have had to wrestle with my conscience the whole time in terms of being a military player, but it certainly wouldn't have hurt me to stay in the Army

I've told these stories in pieces – at work, little snippets here and there. It's been quite a while. I don't think about it or talk about it all that much any more. As for sharing this with my children, they know I was a conscientious objector during the Vietnam era. It came up in the context of their school work, questions in a history class. I haven't given them all the details about the tattoos and all that. I haven't shared my feelings about that period of my life and how I felt then, but they know how I feel now: they know I'm a pacifist.

I think talking about my experiences in this interview has been valuable, because doing so does reawaken memories. It jogs my feelings about the draft, and the potential for my daughters to get caught up in something similar. I've always been of a mind that when I think my daughters are emotionally ready to make their own decisions about their life, I would let them. It's my responsibility to provide them with however much information and support they ask of me, but then I need to let them decide what to do for themselves. If either of my daughters told me she wanted my help making the decision about how to respond to a draft, or wanted to find some way to fight it or avoid it, I would certainly give it. I would try to make sure they knew everything I could possibly help them know, so they could make a smart decision. I would not just share practical information about what it might mean to be in the military; I would also be open about how it would be emotionally for me as their father. And of course, under no circumstances would I want to see my daughters drafted *against their will.*

I do have one more story. I had completely forgotten about this until this interview. When I got sent down to Kentucky for induction, the first night there, when we were still in civilian clothes and just milling about, they brought us to our barracks and said, "Here's what you can do tonight. You can do this, you can do that, or you can go to the movie showing back in this little theater over here." Guess what the movie was... "Alice's Restaurant!" No kidding, the Army was showing "Alice's Restaurant" on the first night after our induction! And I'm jumping up, saying, "'I wanna kill! I wanna kill!'" (When Arlo goes for his army physical in the film he pretends to be psychotic and says these words.) I remember not being able to understand how on earth did *this* film make it on to *this* screen? Is this some really twisted thinking on their part? I never found out the rest of the story.

Al Miller

Al grew up in Missouri and is sixty-one years old. He lives in Montague, Massachusetts, with his wife, Suzanne; they have a small farm, which is something they both wanted to do for many years. He also writes poetry and spoke of having had a really good two-year period of writing – "taking some of the images of memory and fitting them into the present. Pat Schneider is my mentor, the teacher we all needed when we were five years old." Al has also been very involved in the Veterans Education Project, which brings veterans into classrooms to tell their stories.

I was the tenth child born to a working class family in southern Missouri in 1947. My father was a truck driver. My parents had grown up in the Kansas Dust Bowl during the Depression. They didn't have high expectations or any sense of politics. They just did their jobs. When I was twelve we moved to southern New Mexico, to the largest oil-producing county in the country. There was no one where we lived who questioned the draft, or military service, or what was going on in Vietnam, either publicly or privately. By my junior year of high school, my brother Larry had already been drafted and was serving in Bien Hoa as an MP.

I can remember my American government teacher in my junior year talking about Vietnam – about how we were fighting the communists there, and how important it was that we stop the spread of communism to protect our democracy. It was the spring of '65, and I didn't think anything at the time about Vietnam affecting my life. At seventeen, it wasn't on my radar. I was much more concerned with social events and having friends. I just didn't give a damn.

After I graduated high school I went to New Mexico Junior College. I just couldn't bring myself to go to class. I took an Air Force physical with a group of friends and passed that. Some thought the Air Force was a better place to go. For me, I think the motivation was one of my friends said, "Hey, you want to join the Air Force with me?" It was a chance to go to El Paso and sneak across the river to Juarez and party.

So I took the Air Force exam and qualified to do anything I wanted to, but I couldn't decide, so I didn't do anything about enlisting. It was just a matter of a few months before I was drafted. A lot of the people I knew from high school got drafted at the same time. I was inducted in El Paso, and it just didn't occur to me to question any of it. You went along with it. Other people in my family had been drafted and served during the Korean War. A cousin was killed in World War II, and nobody ever said anything about it. These were people who didn't think they had any options. So I didn't consider any other possibilities.

I remember getting the notice, which had the famous quote about how my friends and neighbors would feel proud of me. There was a mild sense of pride that I had passed this masculine threshold. I saw it as a rite of passage, and it felt subliminally important to acquire those markers of manhood. At the physical I could probably have made a point of bringing up the knee injuries I had, but I didn't. I refused to make a conscious decision to try to get out. I was more afraid of prison than going to the military and that was the only other option I saw. It wasn't until I got orders to go to Vietnam and had only thirty days before shipping out that I really began to consider what I should do. I took eighteen extra days. Instead of reporting after the thirty days, I went AWOL for eighteen more, trying to decide whether to go to Canada or Vietnam. I had no idea how the system for getting to Canada worked – how I would live, how I would access support people. I didn't talk to my parents about it. I just took the extra time. Eventually I came to the decision that it was easier for me to go to Vietnam than to go to Canada.

I spent the eighteen days visiting my siblings. I was also newly married at the time to my high school/junior college sweetheart. We got married during Christmas vacation between basic and deployment. Neither of us felt that we could do anything about what was happening to me. We had no frame of reference to discuss it. As for going AWOL, I figured if they were already planning to send me to Vietnam, what could the punishment they might come up with really be?

I can remember getting to the induction center, spending three days there and taking a battery of tests. We were herded around in a quasi-military formation. Those days gave me a taste of it – the artificial structure of the military, the threats, the shame – understanding what that was all about in terms of the coercion and intimidation and putting everybody in the same green uniform, shaving all their heads, getting rid of everyone's individuality; understanding that there's a real thread of masculinity being called into question – "You pussy," and other derogatory feminizing words if you couldn't do something. I've thought about it a lot later in my life – about how it is that the threat of femininity was a motivation at that age for seventeen- and eighteen-year-olds because the identity is malleable. I believe they draft you at that age for a reason.

Of course, all of this was nothing compared to what was coming. We got loaded on a bus one day and were sent off to our basic training unit. We got to a parking lot and there were drill sergeants waiting. They got on the buses and started screaming, "You maggots..." There were kids there who had never done anything physical in their lives and it was torturous, the pressure that was put on people, and people broke. People sobbed and, of course, that caused even more humiliation. I could hide out in the middle real well and I was grateful for that – not to be the last or up front. Our company commander had had two tours of duty in Vietnam and was going back. I never saw an expression on the man in those eight weeks. He said, "This experience of basic training...when we bring you to Vietnam you'll think you've got it easy because of this." It was really severe. I recently found this poem I wrote about what it was like:

An Ungrateful Tool

That's what was made
wrapped, bent, and shaped
by a world and ideas
not of mine.
Each day told
kill them, kill them,
kill our enemies
our voices hoarse
we dance our shadows
already in the fire.*

Hearing the Vietnamese called "Gooks" constantly, I understood, from psych courses I took and from talking with my older brother who had served before me while I was in high school, that we were being conditioned. We're not talking about human beings. We're not talking about another nation or country. We're not talking about mothers, friends, children – we're talking about "Gooks." Understanding that and how it worked and at the same time being coerced to participate was very difficult. I have

---

*Al wrote the poem during basic training – Stillwell Hall, Fort Ord Reservation, August, 1968 – on a napkin in the beer hall.

heard people in veterans groups talk about this and many have said that they think basic training may be the thing that takes the most time to get over. You're so conditioned, brainwashed and imprinted on authority. I can distinctly remember being at the firing range with a loaded M-16 and wanting to turn around and execute my drill sergeant. I had never felt so ashamed and so angry with anyone in my life. And now I understand that their purpose was to instill just that kind of rage. Of course, the mechanism and structure of authority is that you can't turn the weapon around. If you instill that kind of rage the way it was done, you really don't have much control over it. You can't say that it is only going to come out at your target enemy. About twelve weeks into my tour in Vietnam, I could list a dozen incidents of violence or the threat of violence among Americans to Americans. Everybody was armed and dangerous.

By this point it was '69 and Nixon had decided that he was going to begin to remove troops and start the withdrawal, so you have layered on top of this craziness the whole issue of "who wants to be givin' it up for such a cause." The percentage of people who died in Vietnam who had been drafted jumped incredibly from '69 to '70 – something like sixty percent. People tend to disparage those who were drafted. I qualified to go to West Point Prep School and turned that down; and OCS [Officer Candidate School] and turned that down and went to NCO [non-commissioned officer] school. That may have been a mistake. It never was a position that was given respect.

This lack of respect ended up being justifiable because you were trained in Ft. Benning, Georgia. You got an OJT [on-the-job training] cycle of AIT [advanced infantry training] where you were a platoon sergeant. It wasn't like you came up the ranks and earned your stripes the hard way. The rate of injury to squad leaders in Vietnam was so great that they had to do something artificial like this to have more leaders to quickly replace the injured.

Soldiers who had been there for a long time didn't appreciate this accelerated process of training platoon sergeants. Plus it's harder to go uphill on the chain of command with your rage. With someone you're with everyday – in the foxhole, in the bunker – that's where the hostility goes. As a platoon sergeant, already resented for how you came to have the authority you have, you could become an outlet for someone else's rage.

People in my squad on three occasions said to me, "I could take you out." One of them shot himself in the foot to get out. In one situation a young man I had ordered to carry a dead body after a very long time just said, "I can't do it anymore." He had been under stress in combat and then in helping me take out dead and wounded for hours. We walked back to where the fighting had been and in the dark we found this body. I had orders to move them all. I was tired and knew we had to get more distance from this ambush site. He pulled his M-16 on me and I was too tired to get freaked out. I just moved his gun aside and we kept moving. Within a week's time I got shot and knocked down in a rice paddy and this same kid crawls out to me and throws a grenade so I can get out. I tried to let them know that my authority was going to be used to find a way to get us all out and home and there were twenty of them. I was afraid, but you have to put it all aside. I tried to carry extra ammo for the squad as a way to try to say I am the squad leader and I am taking care of you.

I quit learning people's names after a short period of time. The first person I got to know in Vietnam was killed in my first squad leader command. I had taken a group of people to look for an observation point. By the side of the trail was a hole that spooked the shit out of me. I didn't say anything to anyone else about it. I had this fear that my role as a new NCO was precarious enough that if I went around saying, "I'm afraid of that place, stay away from it," my squad would end up saying, "Who's this guy?"

I had gotten to know this fellow, Daniel, from Indiana. We spent part of a day under a poncho liner in the rain, a day off talking about girlfriends, wives and our lives back in the world. We gave him an M-16 machine gun for his birthday. It weighs about twenty-five pounds. He was behind me in the formation. I went up, looked at this area, looked back, passed the hole in the ground again and I didn't say anything to anyone. It was on a side hill and Daniel had this heavy gun and he was sliding off the trail in the direction of the hole. I turned around and looked at him.

We made eye contact for the first time that morning and then the hole blew up. There was a kid in front of him and a kid behind him and they were hit, too. Daniel was lying on the ground, but I didn't acknowledge him. I went to work on the kid behind him who had a sucking chest wound and seemed to me to be the worst. I put plastic over him, took out a bandage and unwrapped it and tied him off. The other man was hit with a little bitty pin prick, blood running down his back and he was really acting in pain, so I tried to do what I could to knock that down. Then the sergeant who had been there for almost a year came up and said, "There's someone else laying on the ground." And I said, "There's nobody else." I told him to fuck off. I called him an asshole and told him to get the fuck out of there. And he said, "I can't do that. You better look." And I looked down. I could see Daniel was dead.

After that point all you can do is go into shock. There was no way to process it. You just start your numbing out. One of my numbing out manifestations was to not learn their names. If they go quick, then you don't even have an identity to deal with. I had heard people talk about the "new guy syndrome." They weren't even going to learn your fuckin' name until you'd been there for three months. I totally get that. That was one of the ways to deal with what we were facing. I sat down after the sergeant came up and said, "It was my fault. I knew this was a bad place." He said, "You can't do that to yourself. You're not God. You're not responsible." I know now that was one of the greatest things someone ever said to me.

Six weeks after Daniel was killed, I walked into a hooch and there was an NVA [North Vietnamese Army] lieutenant asleep. I woke him up and tried to get him to come out. I assumed he had a side arm, but I didn't check. He moved, and I thought he was going for a weapon, so I fired. I shot him and I killed him. At the time I said, "This is for Daniel." But deep inside myself, I totally got that Daniel wouldn't give a shit. My action had just been one of revenge and an attempt to vindicate something. It definitely didn't justify what I did.

Black people played a major role in my time in the service. It began in basic training. I was in a squad that was mostly made up of African-American men from Houston, Texas. They taught us how to survive by teaching us how to laugh at the absurdity of it all. They could do that. They made jokes. Every day after we came in, two of them would get together and start making jokes about what happened that day and they'd have all of us laughing. The white guys got enraged at their own mistreatment by the drill sergeants, but incredibly these black men, who had faced racism their entire lives, had a mechanism for dealing with how they were being treated. In Vietnam the African-American people I was in the service with had catch phrases. "Just say no." "All this shit don't mean nothin'. And it still don't mean nothin'."

Fighting to survive was a tremendous equalizer, but, as soon as you were in the rear area, all the old racism came up again. The anger, the hostility was all still there, and it put an end to equality. The African Americans I served with in combat were the best people I served with under those conditions, because they could handle adversity. There was a guy named Spook who, if the fighting ever started between the races, was one of the first ones to confront it, even if he was on the other side of the base. But as soon as the fight was over, he was off duty. He hated to fight. Of course, they demoted him to private and busted him.

It was amazing how the military got away with its structural racism. It leaves you thinking that it's because of the structure, but at the same time they were teaching you racism against the Vietnamese. By teaching us how to cope, the African Americans just saved us.

Then there was the alcohol. After I had been in Vietnam for a couple of weeks we went for our first standdown; you got off the choppers and everything – your rifle, your pocket knife, your survival knife, your hand grenades – that can be turned into a weapon had to be turned in before you could leave the area. That first time I was, of course, wondering, what's this all about. The standard refrain was, "You'll figure it out." We went back to an area with a kitchen near the beach in Chu Loi and there were fifty cases of beer, hard liquor and nationals selling pot. Within three hours people are fighting each other who had been fighting *alongside* each other. We were there for three days. The alcohol just made it all that much more likely that there would be fighting.

They wanted to give me a Bronze Star for what happened that night, going back for those dead bodies. All it really was to me was being twenty years old in this hierarchical system of authority based on doing what you're told. So I made my men do it, go back for another body and I took the responsibility for making them do it. We got the body and pulled back, and on the radio all the other squad leaders said they were going in in the dark, getting a dead body and coming out. When we got back and we dropped them off where the other dead bodies were collected, ours was the only one collected during the daylight. I said to the lieutenant, "You gave me an order and I did it. I put all my people at risk to do it. Now they know the other squad leaders protected their men by having them retrieve the dead bodies under cover of darkness. Now my ass is on the line." He said, "That's all right. We'll do something for them." And I said, "You've got to do something now. Otherwise my ass...they're going to question me. Am I going to do this to them again?" He said, "Well, this is a Bronze Star for

---

*This second Bronze Star was to be given in recognition of the wound Al received in combat.

you." And I said, "That doesn't mean shit." Later on, when I was in the med-evac after I was hit, the same lieutenant came up to me and said, "O.K., Sergeant Miller, that's another Bronze Star* for you for today." And I said, "That doesn't mean anything to me."

Stress. That's what hit me when I finally got out. I knew that everything had changed for me when I was released from the hospital in El Paso. I knew you couldn't just pick up and walk out the door and go back to your life. I had a group of friends who came and picked me up when I got back home. They were still the people they were when I left, but I couldn't find a way to relate to them because I couldn't talk about what they were talking about – their loves, their jobs, their interests. Your framework - everything I had accepted and assumed – was off the table.

I was married and trying to go to school and have a job and I drank just to get numb. When I talk about this, I want to get a drink. For a long time I carried the firefights in my brain. I would relive them in broad daylight, in full consciousness and be right back there. If I tried to lie down and take a nap or be still or quiet, it would come right back. I had to stay active and I took medication for a while. I just couldn't stay married. I wasn't the person that woman married. I didn't know who I was. I said, "I have to excuse myself. I'm sorry, but I am going to go away."

What are the ways of describing what I had experienced? Having been lied to and knowing the lies? The lies like we weren't bringing a democracy; that was not our intention at all. We were not protecting these people. They didn't want us there. What the peace movement was saying was true…just on and on. We talked about it in Vietnam – who were our real enemies. And while I was recovering from my wound, we talked in the hospital for 5 months checking things out with each other. It was 1970.

It turned out that the whole framework of belief was a lie. You felt totally betrayed by everything - your family since they never told you the truth, your church, your teachers, your school, your education that said all these things about America and the nobility of it. There was no redeeming quality in any fucking way. It was a failure of every possibility of human creativity, of human relationships, and there is never a way to really survive this. To be able to kill another human being you have to already be dead. It is mandatory. There's no fucking way out of it, because if you're alive and a connected human being, you can't kill. So then you're left with the emptiness inside you. Medication doesn't work. It just numbs you and there are many who live that way.

I made the decision after a year away, a year of really being medicated, that I didn't want to be medicated any more. I knew people who were therapists who didn't know what the fuck to do with me. I didn't know what to do with me. I tried to come forward. I was living in western Massachusetts and studying furniture making and it all unraveled. I called the Veteran's Outreach Center and for the first time in my life after Vietnam someone said, "I understand what you're going through. Come right in." I told them what was going on and they said, "We got your back." There was a therapist there, he's dead now, who just pulled me in under his wing. I sat down with him and talked to him every week for two years. Then I spent a year with a group of men who were combat vets in a therapy group there. And that was just the first step.

You still are left with a damaged soul and the only way to repair a damaged soul is in doing things for other people. That's just something I figured out. No one ever said that to me. I tried to find it in Tolstoy's writings, in Merton's writings – what do you do for somebody who knows they have a deficit in their own soul for assuming they're doing the right thing under the authority of other people. When you pull the trigger that authority evaporates. It's you and no one else.

I saw something in Vietnam that most people would find unbelievable. It came after I set fire to a Vietnamese family's hooch. Circumstances sent me away briefly from that fire and circumstances brought me back. It was when I was standing at the site the second time that I saw the form of Buddha. There was a soldier standing to my left, and I immediately asked him, "Did you see that?" When he replied, "See what?" I said, "Never mind."

What I found at the site of the burnt home of this Vietnamese family, one of whom I had just killed, was this little watercourse they had set up. There was this station where the water was collected, and there in the jungle were vegetable plants growing around it. I went down this mountain to an abandoned aqueduct and it was incredibly beautiful.

I had tried to justify my killing this man and it didn't work. I had tried calling him a "Gook" and a communist. And all that just evaporated because it became so obvious to me in his death how human he was. I couldn't have imagined him being in the jungle and the way he lived before I saw what he had done. We destroyed the jungle and he could live in it. So who is living in the Creation of the Creator and who is not? There were photographs in his breast pocket of his family, his mother and his brothers and his extended family. His mother had this great look of concern on her face. I knew that fear. She'll never know where he's buried or what happened to him.

All of a sudden all of the projection about enemy is going away. Now you're the enemy. In fact, you're the non-Christian because everything you're doing is against the Creation. He was my brother and I was assigned to kill him. In a way that act of taking his life is a very intimate act and there is no room to run from it.

It's through the grace of indigenous people and indigenous culture that I can sit here and talk about this, through their ceremonies of rebirth and healing that I have been privileged to be part of. The Buddhist community has embraced me as well. For me Buddhism is very personal. It doesn't have anything to do with any external expressions such as going to some temple. It is a gift. For me it means having to remember what I was then and what I'd like to be. I used to wake up from dreams, for maybe fifteen years, in which I was being hunted as a murderer. I would realize I was dreaming and I'd say, "God, thank you, it was a dream." The dream went away, but I had to figure out how to live with myself. If I am going to be a person who advocates for peace, I had to be at peace with myself and that's the hardest.

The Veteran's Education Project came to me after I did some presentations for a history teacher. I was working on his house and telling him how my political philosophy had evolved and he invited me to come talk to his class about the history of Vietnam. The woman who was the director of VEP came and listened and then asked me to speak and everything matched up in my evolution to be ready to speak publicly. There's a level of being informed that doesn't come with the greater culture so I go into classrooms and tell these stories to kids. I give them one person's perspective on the truth. There was no one who ever told me this is what will happen to you if you go to war. I don't want to be that person. It re-traumatizes me, but I don't know anyone else who can go into a classroom and say what I have to say. I still feel the weight of the people's lives that I took and the people that I knew who were killed and the voiceless and their voicelessness.

Writing poetry has played a healing role in my life as well. There's this quality of life and death that I *know*, and the deep way in which I know it. If I just tell you about my experiences in a general conversation, how much do you take in and how long does it stay with you? But if I say it to you in a way that releases some of the nuance of experience, that would be a better way to experience it in your mind, body, heart and soul.

I want to emphasize the struggle to find a place to be an American after this experience and to be in this society and culture and how difficult it is. War is the mechanism of the culture. War-making is the principal economy of the country. The policy will always have to support the economy until it changes. I went down to D.C. in 1989, twenty years after I got out – I was shot on my twenty-first birthday – and there, twenty years later, I started a forty-day fast on the Capitol steps for reconciliation with Vietnam. I knew that there were people in Vietnam who were suffering because of our government's punitive policy and what we had done to that country – really genocide. Here I was in this country saying I would like to heal from my wounds, the emotional and spiritual ones, since the physical ones are easiest to heal from. Yet it didn't seem holistic to me that I should heal while others from this collective experience were unable to.

Remembering and re-telling these experiences is very hard for me. I want to withdraw. I want to be on the farm with Suzanne. She is a wonderful woman who allows me to do this healing work. If I didn't have her support, I couldn't do it. She'll take me under her wing and pull me back, and I need a relationship like that. She helps make me whole and sane again. She's an angel – forgiving and teaching me much. I understand the importance of grief, and of grieving, and fortunately I am able to share my grief with Suzanne and others uncontrollably,

Re-living the experience is not just hard, but very emotional for me, and I usually try to stay distant from those emotions. When I'm speaking in a classroom, or doing an interview, like this one with you, I sometimes just can't hold it off, and at those times I just take a minute and step aside. Even now, it's been a challenge to keep my voice at this modulation and to stay somewhat detached. I know if I don't, and go into the depths of what I'm saying, I'll get in touch with some powerful emotions. In fact, if I didn't, I'd be one of the walking wounded still. So I consciously prepared myself for this interviewing experience. It doesn't always work, but it did this evening.

Doug Anderson

Doug Anderson's new memoir, Keep Your Head Down: Vietnam, The Sixties, And a Journey of Self-Discovery, *was published by W.W. Norton in 2009. His book of poetry,* "The Moon Reflected Fire," *won the Kate Tufts Discovery Award in 1995; and* "Blues for Unemployed Secret Police" *received a grant from the Eric Matthew King Fund of The Academy of American Poets. His work has appeared in many literary journals including* The Virginia Quarterly Review, Field, Ploughshares, The Southern Review *and* The Massachusetts Review. *He has received fellowships and grants from The National Endowment for the Arts, The Massachusetts Cultural Council and other funding organizations. In addition to poetry and creative nonfiction he has written plays, screenplays and worked as a journalist. He lives with his wife, Julie, in Hartford, Connecticut and teaches in the Pacific University of Oregon Low Residency MFA Program.*

It was 1963 and I had decided to try my hand at being a professional musician. I was a drummer and I played jazz. I was living in Tucson, Arizona. There was actually a pretty big jazz community there and I played at a place called the Sky Room. There were also comedians there. The drummer plays along with the comedian, anticipates the laugh line and uses rim shots to boost them. From this experience I decided that I wanted to be an actor. I enrolled in the drama department at the University of Arizona.

At that point in time, I had no idea what was going on in the world. There was this small war going on in Vietnam that we would hear about once in a while. I knew that there were Green Berets there and American advisors, but I figured it was not a very big war. It was just Americans trying to help stop Communism in Southeast Asia or so the rhetoric went.

But the truth is I didn't know anything about it. I had begun to party more than study and my grades began to suffer. A couple of years after I started in the Theater Department the war had intensified and they started sending over more troops. People around me were getting drafted – people with bad grades like me. I decided I would join the Naval Reserve unit to get out of the draft. They had a special deal where if you went to an eighty-day boot camp, you'd get a couple of months off your enlistment at the end of your two-year obligation.

I had no one to advise me. My mother had joined the State Department and was living overseas. I hadn't seen her since my graduation from high school. My father had been out of my life since I was seven, so there was no parental participation in my decisions at all. I did have one uncle who had been in the Army and advised me not to join the National Guard because the commitment to meetings was too long. So I was definitely on my own, just flailing around making bad choices, one after another. In my ignorance, I imagined that, by enlisting, I would have more say about where I went than if I were drafted.

I decided to go for the eighty-day boot camp and to get my two years active duty over with. When I was in boot camp, I was trying to figure out what to do. As a two-year enlistee you're eligible for certain schools, so I figured, "What could I learn that would enable me to work in the real world?" I decided to become a hospital corpsman so I could maybe be an ambulance driver afterwards. These were just idiotic, impulsive decisions that were not thought out at all and this was the worst one, because in wartime they take the corpsmen out of the Navy and put them in the Marines.

At the time I made this decision, the boot camp drill instructor called me an idiot for going that route. He said, "They're killing them like flies over there." Unfortunately at that time in my life I didn't believe anything anyone told me, which was a big problem. I didn't even ask him enough to learn that, in wartime, corpsmen are taken out of the Navy and put into the Marines, because the Marines had no capacity to train medics. They just ran the Navy guys through something called "field medical service," in which you do an abbreviated version of Marine infantry training – *very* abbreviated – and learn how to crawl around under fire. They give you a green uniform and then assign you to a unit.

I went to the Naval base at Great Lakes, Illinois for my hospital corps training. It was four months long. Then I was sent to Bethesda, Maryland where I was put on the thoracic ward. I did my apprenticeship there and learned how to do patient care. Then I was sent to Camp Lejune in North Carolina for field medical service school. After that I was put on a huge propeller-driven transport and taken to Camp Pendleton in California where I was sent to a little place called Las Pulgas, which means "the fleas" in Spanish. Ironically, Las Pulgas was one of the areas where the government would later on set up housing for Vietnamese refugees after the fall of Saigon. From there I was sent to San Francisco and finally to the First

Marine division in Vietnam. All the way over we were lying to each other about the cushy duty stations we were going to get. "Oh, I'll probably get a hospital shift," or "I'll probably get a nice air-conditioned hospital in Danang."

It was still not yet real to me. I had a program going in my mind that I grew up with that was born from my parents' participation in World War II and what a big deal that was. Essentially what it said was, "This is what all the men did." Of course, only one member of my family actually saw any fighting, but I was carrying some of that mystique with me.

We got to Danang and we were all hanging around, and this guy came out of this air-conditioned building with a clipboard and assigned us to various units. They put me in a truck with a bunch of other guys, and we drove down Highway 1 past the MACV* headquarters, past the Naval hospital on the right, past the Special Forces Compound and the Australian Special Forces Compound. We passed the Marble Mountains, which were five mountains – one for each of the Chinese elements: metal, wood, fire, air, and water. Below the Marble Mountains was a village named Nui Kimson, which was the last civilized area before the combat zone. Nui means "mountain," so it's Kimson Mountain. About two kilometers south of there along Highway 1 was the triangular berm that enclosed the Third Battalion, First Marines. I ended up in Lima Company, third platoon, first squad. By the way, my company is the one that's implicated in the Haditha massacre† in Iraq - my old unit. So there it began.

The reality started setting in very quickly. I was given a Unit One and a .45 Colt service revolver, a flak jacket and helmet, two canteens and a web belt and some extra battle dressings in my thigh pockets and was sent out with the patrol. Unit One has several different battle dressings; large, medium and small metal battle dressings, a scalpel blade, an airway, and nitropheroson for burns. It had atropine for nerve gas, which we never saw,

---

*U.S. Military Assistance Command, Vietnam, MACV, (*mack vee*), was the United States' unified command structure for all of its military forces in South Vietnam during the Vietnam War.

†Haditha killings (also called the Haditha incident or the Haditha massacre) refers to the incident where 24 Iraqi men, women and children were killed by a group of United States Marines on November 19, 2005 in Haditha, a city in the western Iraq province of Al Anbar. At least 15 of those killed were noncombatant civilians. It has been alleged that the killings were retribution for the attack on a convoy of Marines with an improvised explosive device that killed Lance Corporal Miguel Terrazas.

and copper sulfate pads in case white phosphorus burned somebody. There was Desenex for foot fungus and Bacitracin ointment, malaria pills, and the usual, including a tourniquet.

I was sent out on a patrol my first day. It was hot, unbelievably hot, and it wasn't even the really hot season yet. On that first patrol we got ambushed. I wasn't used to the idea that you would get shot at from two to three directions in an ambush – the enemy is usually in an "L" shape; they sometimes had a heavy machine gun up front and along the flank they'd have snipers. There were five VC [Vietcong] firing and I didn't know where the rounds were coming from. I could hear them going by and I knew they were intended for the others and me, but then somebody called, "Corpsman, up!" This was in the sandy area between Highway 1 and the ocean. I started running to where I heard the shout come for the corpsman, but I went in the wrong direction. One of the Marines grabbed me by the collar, turned me around and sent me up the hill. All the time I was going up the hill, I was quite aware that the VC were trying to kill me. I heard the rounds going through the branches and the scrub pine. I was running like hell. My heart felt like it weighed eight hundred pounds, and my legs felt like rubber.

I got to the top of the hill and there was another corpsman – the corpsman I was going to be replacing. A guy had been hit in the lower right back, right below the kidney and the bullet had come out his front. The exit wound had taken some intestine out with it. We could hear the rounds coming through the trees and pieces of trees coming down on us, but this guy was screaming and we were trying to keep him quiet, because they can use the screams to sight in their mortars. We gave him some morphine and got him out of there, took him down to the base of the hill in a poncho liner. Some other Marines had thrown a yellow smoke grenade to direct the chopper in. At that time we didn't have the HUEY'S.* The Army had the HUEY'S. We had those old things that looked like a flying cardboard box. They were really slow. They were out of the Korean War. We pulled the guy on board and tried to get out of there and I heard this "whack whack"

---

*Bell UH-1 Iroquois is a military helicopter powered by a single, turbo-shaft engine, with a two-bladed main rotor and tail rotor. The helicopter was developed by Bell Helicopter to meet the United States Army's requirement for a medical evacuation and utility helicopter in 1952, and first flew on 20 October 1956. first combat operation of the UH-1 was in the service of the U.S. Army during the Vietnam War. The original designation of HU-1 led to the helicopter's nickname of Huey. Approximately 7,000 UH-1 aircraft saw service in Vietnam.

of a couple of rounds hitting the side of the chopper. The chopper lifted off into the wind and banked back toward Danang. The ambushes only lasted a few minutes and usually by the time we were able to direct mortar fire or artillery or air they were gone. It was quiet by then. That was my first day "in country."

I somehow managed to live through that first patrol. It turned out to be fairly typical. Sometimes we'd go maybe a week or two without anything but an occasional sniper and somebody stepping on a booby-trap. Actually there were a lot of "improvised explosive devices." The Vietcong were really good at it. They could make a booby-trap out of bat dung that would somehow work. They would drive a bunch of nails through a board and then file them so they had hooks on the end and they'd smear human shit on that and put them down in a depression in the ground and cover them with leaves. Some American comes along and it's nice and hot so he's taken the aluminum sole insert out of his boot because he hates walking on it and he steps down in this disguised hole and gets nails through his foot. By the time he gets to the hospital, of course, it's infected in that heat. That one little, simple action cost the U.S. hundreds of thousands of dollars – the cost of the helicopter needed to fly out and pick him up, the cost of the surgery. It was little stuff like this that just ground everybody down.

By this point the Marines had given up any romantic ideas they might have had about helping the Vietnamese people against the evil communists from the North. They just distrusted Vietnamese – all of them! When you're walking down a trail, day after day, and you've got a group of American teenagers, mostly, walking down the trail with a lot of weaponry, and somebody steps on a booby-trap, and then they notice that in the Vietnamese village right next to the trail nobody has stepped on the booby-trap, elementary deductive reasoning leads to the conclusion that those villagers must know about the booby-trap. Why didn't they tell us? Our officers say, "They must all be enemies," so we must go in and beat the shit out of them or rape their daughters or shoot one or two of them or burn their hooches at least. The level of hatred of the Vietnamese at this time was extreme.

If you start a war in a culture you don't know anything about, which was certainly the case in Vietnam, and you go in with a very poor understanding either strategically or geographically and then things begin to fall apart, what's the big surprise? These things are going to happen. There were people that I liked very much in the platoon. I was raised in the South so I know how to speak redneck and get along just fine. There was funny humor – Southern whites and blacks and Northern blacks, this incredible heteroglot community. The culture of the war was fascinating during the downtime when we weren't getting hit. When you're getting hit a lot you will bond. You become very simple in the Darwinian sense.

Drugs were not a factor in my unit. Ours was a highly disciplined unit and the men were not draftees; they were people who wanted to be there. They believed in being Marines and they were patriotic. Drugs started to happen in the Army units that came over afterwards, in the late '60s and early '70s when the anti-war movement had penetrated the service. By that point you'd have people coming over with peace symbols on their helmets and on their flak jackets. The big Army units that were close to any large village or city would have access to just about anything. You could buy fists full of joints soaked in opium for a dollar. There was one guy who was a supply officer and he had some grass. I smoked some with him one day, but it did not become a habit. Getting stoned activates my fear in a stressful situation so I didn't find that a very pleasant thing to do.

I did drink a lot. We had an EM [Enlisted Men's Club] in the battalion that was up on stilts. We had this Philippino beer, San Miguel, which was preserved with formaldehyde. The joke was that if we got killed we were pre-embalmed. I would drink to unconsciousness and wake up to find that I had pissed in my cot. I became a falling down drunk. I wanted to lose consciousness after a big infantry operation; just become unconscious as quickly as possible.

I was an alcoholic for many years after the war and I didn't begin to recover until 1987. Now it's been almost nineteen years of solid recovery. I had also gotten into some other drugs in the '60s, but the truth is I went through a lot of stuff and ultimately I came back to drinking and barbiturates, because those are the great drugs to become unconscious with. I would follow these experiences with some speed to get over the hangover. There was a lot of self-destruction going on in those years.

I had tried to keep a journal while I was "in country," but reality became intrusive. That part of my mind just shut off. I was interested in when we were going to eat, when we were going to get some more water and when we were going to sleep. That was about as deep as I got, and all the time I hoped to God next time we would get shot at nobody would scream,

"Corpsman up." That was always my biggest fear. If you stay in an ambush, everybody else is going to go down on their bellies to return fire and if somebody gets wounded, who's the guy up and running? That was me. It was pretty scary. I never knew you could get shot at so much without getting hit.

I got…no, I didn't get hit, I got burnt. What happened was the guy in front of me was sliding down a ravine and the Vietcong had the booby-trap set up so, if you slid down the ravine, you'd hit the wire and it blew part of his left leg off. When I started to work on him I saw that there was a yellow smoke grenade on his belt. It had been set off and this yellow smoke was getting in my eyes and the grenade, the smoke grenade, was right next to an M26 grenade, which is a fragmentation grenade.* I realized I had to get that belt off of him and get rid of it, so I yanked off his web belt and threw it down the ravine. In the process of doing that, I blistered my hand. I managed to get a Purple Heart for that, which is one of the easier ways to get a Purple Heart. I was treated in the field and returned to duty.

I have memories of people who died under my care. There was really nothing I could do about it. There was one guy whose name was George Custer. I'm not kidding you, that was his name. He had joined the Marines at seventeen with his parents' permission. Can you imagine anybody naming their son that – building that suicidal script into their child? He was walking point and the front of the platoon, the point part of the squad, had dipped over a sandy rise and down into some trees where we were ambushed. He was hit; the pointman was hit right away. They called me down to get him, so I crawled towards him. He apparently had been dropping to his hands and knees when he was hit and the round went right between his clavicle and his trapezius muscle, straight down. It probably took out the sub-clavian artery so he was bleeding to death very quickly. He said to me, "Doc, am I going to be alright?" And, of course, I responded, "Yeah, we're going to get you out of here." The next thing I hear are death rattles. There was nothing I could do.

I had already decided very early in my experience in Vietnam that this war was a bunch of bullshit. I realized a big wrong was going on, and I was not that smart in those days, but I knew I had to keep this to myself. We had two lieutenants, and the second lieutenant was someone I thought I could

---

*A grenade that scatters shrapnel over a wide area upon explosion.

talk to. I had had enough with watching them brutalize Vietnamese civilians so I just went to the guy and I told him what I thought and felt and he said, "Yeah, I know, I know, but you gotta watch your back over here."

I remember one time I talked to my lieutenant commander who was actually a rather remarkable guy. He was a very decent human being and he said, "You know all these people ever wanted was their independence." He was intensely religious and he was a schoolteacher, a very good man in a traditional, wholesome sense. For him to say this showed much about him and his level of sensitivity to the people he was supposed to be protecting, but so often were the victims. He had pictures of all of his men. He remembered all of our names. He remembered who got killed and he had stories to tell about all of them. You could tell that there was deep, deep grief in this man.

Except for isolated moments like those where someone speaks the truth, there was nobody really to communicate with for me. I corresponded with my friend, Ellen, back in San Francisco. She was a stoner and was into "flower power," stringing beads, smoking hash and taking acid and wearing tie-dye shirts and running around buck-naked. She would send me these apologetic letters saying, "You and I are probably not going to agree about this war..." and I'm thinking, you have no idea how much you can hate war. You have no idea.

There had been a rumor going around for quite some time that the battalion was going to be sent back to Okinawa and refitted and re-staffed and sent out to the DMZ as a battalion landing team, so anybody who had two or three months left in their enlistment or in their tour was sent somewhere else. They wanted fresh meat. They wanted people who had at least a year to go, so I got sent to 1st Hospital Company in Chu Lai, which was on top of a hill overlooking the ocean.

There I got into some serious drinking. There was a club there and since there were no separate clubs for officers and enlisted men, we were all mixed together, so we'd all get drunk together. The truth is I had had a number of people tell me that I had a drinking problem even when I was still in the combat zone. I had gotten in a fight with somebody and I can't even remember why. I got my ear split open and it had to be sewed up. Another time I got drunk and wandered into the battalion area. There were a bunch of officers sitting around watching a movie. We used to urinate in these things called piss tubes. They were just like pipes driven into the ground. It was mainly to make sure everybody pissed in one place. I thought I was pissing in a piss tube, and I ended up pissing on an officer. I would occasionally get lectures about my drinking as well, but I was always able to do my work, except for when I was really drunk. Those times were during off hours.

I wasn't ready to listen to anybody at this point. By the end of my time I was...you might say I was *not* having a good time. I was sent to Danang to go home and had to spend the night in a hospital ward. They had these huts on the hill up above the airstrip called First Med and I was going to sleep in the hospital ward, but at three o'clock in the morning I woke up, and since there were always casualties coming up, here's the image I woke up to: there's all this moaning and screaming and I look across from me, and there's this guy and he's got both legs up in the air. These two doctors are giving him shots of adrenaline in the groin. It was the strangest thing. I didn't know if I was watching a film or what, since that was during Tet and we were getting hit all the time. I was just glad to get out of there the next day.

I was discharged March 20, 1968. In a way I was lucky because I got to Vietnam after the worst of the fighting, and I left before the fighting got really bad again. After I got out, my battalion went back to Okinawa, came north, did a landing and swept to shore. They didn't meet any resistance at all. Then they moved inland a ways and came to this area that Bernard Fall wrote about. He called it "the street without joy." He said they walked into a certain village and met a huge division-sized ambush. Within a few minutes my platoon ceased to exist. That was December, right before Christmas.

There's Thompson, there's Plunkett, there's all these guys dead. My therapist tells me that there's survival guilt in it for me. It was an operation called Badger Tooth and I am very glad I missed it. Lima Company was almost completely wiped out. Kilo Company did better because they could hide behind the tanks. Somebody told me a story of this one guy I knew who dragged a wounded guy behind a tank for cover so he could work on him and the tank backed up over both of them. It was all just insane.

After Vietnam, I came back to Tucson, Arizona to go to college and stayed with some friends. The psychedelic and sexual revolution was really picking up. Everyone was running around naked and stoned, and I just fell in with it. Being naked and stoned was much superior to what I had been doing. I was interested in having as much sex and staying as stoned as I possibly could.

I didn't talk about Vietnam the first year. It just seemed so odd to be talking about it. I had some very bad flashbacks. I remembered something about a time that I had blocked out involving the murder of a civilian. The word about me was, "Doug is lots of fun until a certain point," and "When is he going to get weird on us." I didn't get crazy and violent. I just became stricken. I would start sobbing. Nobody had a clue about how to respond. Not enough people had come back into that community from the war, and they probably wouldn't, because there was a class thing going on. Most combat veterans wouldn't be going to college.

I didn't know anything about politics and here I was with all of these middle class kids who knew a lot and were very organized. I was embarrassed; I didn't even know who my state senator was. I became fairly active in the anti-war movement until I became too dysfunctional to carry on those activities. No one ever asked me to speak about what happened to me. It was still too early for that.

There were moments when the memories would come to the surface. I had really bad depressions. I was unable to keep a job or keep a relationship. I just sort of floundered from one place to another, traveled all over the country. I'd meet a girl I liked and move in with her and that was how I lived my life. Through it all I was an addict, and addicts treat people like they do drugs. You enjoy the initial hallucinatory, highly eroticized stage, but you don't know what to do afterwards. Either I would leave or she would leave. A couple of the women I was involved with actually loved me, but I was just not able to receive it. Intelligence is required in a relationship and I was just not using it. The only thing I understood was the rush. Sex was just another thing to be addicted to.

Occasionally I would do some theater and get back into that. I did theater in Chicago and New York. and finally wrote a play in 1981 about Vietnam called "Short-timers." It was performed at Theater for a New City. The play was a flashback of a guy with no arms or legs or face or genitals – basically a vegetable – who lived in one of the wards where they never let you go. We used to call those places with the impossibly fucked up people "the pumpkin patch." The play was about his memory. It was disparate; a combination of styles and it had a pretty authentic core to it: the dismemberment of this one person was representative of the dismemberment of the collective psyche. After that, I went back to Tucson and got a master's degree. I needed to have some way to make a living.

I lived in New York for a while and in 1986 I moved out of the city. I went up to Northampton, Massachusetts. I have a friend from high school there, Leland Johnson. By the end of the first year I was in trouble in terms of drinking. I had a relationship that went bad, and I had left a lot of damage. Some of it was because I tried to stop drinking. This woman wanted me to stop drinking and, I said, "Of course," but when you do that without any kind of recovery program you become stark raving sober.

Ultimately I was "brought to my knees," I think, is the expression. I had to accept help. That was a hard time, because the first couple of years of somebody's sobriety is all about feeling the feelings you've been avoiding. In the program I entered there were some other vets and we had lots of conversations. I was just unaware of how much rage there was inside me. Other people were aware of it. When I became sober, I realized I couldn't continue with this level of rage. I had a feeling of having been completely violated and disrespected, of having had my suffering ignored. It was, of course, a very self-centered position, but it was there to feel. There was a lot to unravel.

I had always written. There's something about writing that when you put your pen down on paper and you start to write you begin to discover things. It's not the same as talking. It's not even being a raconteur. There's something about writing that is multi-leveled and allows you to discover. I would write a poem based on something that actually happened. I found that I could do it. That coincided with me getting into a group with Jack Gilbert and several formidable writers. It was in Jim and Susan Finnegan's living room. Susan is a painter and poet and Jim is a poet and an insurance salesman in the tradition of Wallace Stevens. I found Jack Gilbert in particular to be a great mentor. He began to shepherd me through the process of turning my war experiences into poems and the result is the poems in *Moon Reflected Fire.* I was very lucky with that kind of synchronicity. With my next book I tried to get completely away from Vietnam. Now I am writing a memoir.

About fifteen years ago I became involved with the Joiner Center for the Study of War and Social Consequences at UMASS Boston. A vet named William Joyner was the founder. He brought together a group of vets who were also writers. There are now a few branches of it including the summer Creative Writing Workshop in Boston where I teach a class. The Workshop developed a relationship with former [Vietnamese] enemies who had also become fiction writers and poets. We have brought them here and they have invited us back to Vietnam.

It was on one of these trips that I met these incredible people. We traveled from Hanoi to Saigon and surrounding villages in the company of these people and were treated wonderfully – taken into their homes and fed, introduced to their wives and children. Everybody drank together and they thought I was somewhat of a curiosity because I didn't drink. It was the incredible warmth of people who used to be trying to kill each other and who had suffered.

The Vietnamese suffered terribly from that war. They lost three million people. It destroyed forty million acres of prime rice land. You think of Americans being there for one or two tours of duty at the most. The Vietnamese were there, some of them, for as long as fifteen years in the jungle. They suffered terribly from the defoliants, from not having proper medical care. Their teeth are all screwed up. There is a lot of drinking in Vietnam and a lot of severe PTSD.

Some of the Vietnamese writers we were scheduled to meet I had already read. I had read Bao Ninh who wrote *The Sorrow of War*. There was a woman poet, Lam Thi Nida, who was a combat engineer on the Ho Chi Minh Trail and later an intelligence operative in the South. And there were others. I had done the forgiveness long before getting there and I had curiosity long before getting there.

On my trip to Vietnam, between Hong Kong and the Noibay Airport in Hanoi, I began to feel very anxious. I began to sweat. It was ice cold on the airplane, but I began sweating. I was sitting there next to Bruce Weigl who wrote *The Song of Napalm*, and he was taking back his adopted Vietnamese daughter to meet her birth mother for the first time. She and I were both sweating profusely, but nobody else was. Then we landed, and as soon as the doors of the plane swung open, I smelled Vietnam! Smell is so powerful. I caught a whiff of everything from rice paddies to the incredible pollution of the city.

Next we went down to customs and there were these young customs agents with green uniforms with red epaulettes and red collar tabs. They looked just like the guys you'd see in the newsreels parading the captured American pilots through the streets of Hanoi. That gave me kind of a chill.

We went to speak at the Vietnamese Writer's Association. I had prepared a formal lecture. About a third of the way through the lecture everyone was sweating profusely and the Vietnamese were fanning themselves and the translator was droning on so I just stopped reading and winged it. Afterwards, after all of the long-winded stuff about American poetry, Liam Duc Mau made a comment on poetry. It was eight words. "Life is the rice, poetry is the liquor." That was his minimalist response to all of the long-windedness that had gone on, and I thought that was the best definition of poetry I've ever heard in my life.

I had wanted to go to the area where my battalion was stationed. The program wanted to send me down alone on the train and I refused to do that. They decided to take a side trip and they took me to Danang. We ate lunch on a floating houseboat on the Danang River. A poet named Ving came down. He had been a platoon commander with an NVA division that was in the area where we were. I am sure we had been within a few kilometers of each other or maybe fighting with one another. We had a great conversation and it was a great feeling. Then we drove down to a village where my battalion had been. At one point I went to the end of the village and I looked out over this fallow rice paddy where the battalion used to be and, of course, there was nothing there. They'd bulldozed it down. It was amazing.

When I came back to the States I was flying. I can't even say why. Something had been completed. I couldn't stop talking about the trip. I became the cocktail party bore at the college where I was teaching. Someone would ask me how my trip to Vietnam was and they'd be there for an hour. I was feeling that something really incredible had happened. Something had shifted deep down. I now knew something about myself and other people I had never known before. I was quite high for some time after that.

After my trip, I started a Ph.D. program in English Literature at the University of Connecticut. They allowed me to write a memoir for my dissertation and I got it all done and had my degree in just three years. So much of the impetus for the memoir and the doctorate came from my wanting to write about the experience of returning to Vietnam; a good third of the memoir is about that trip. I knew immediately that it had been life-changing. How often do we have an opportunity to do that kind of healing?

Lidon Don Chevannes

Don Chevannes, fifty-nine years old, grew up in New York City. He has two daughters, ages thirty-four and twenty-four and one granddaughter, who is eight-years-old. He is currently living in Easthampton, Massachusetts, where he continues his efforts to recover from drug addiction. He has been clean since 2005. He attends meetings and participates in workshops with Veteran Services in support of disabled veterans. Don sits on the Veteran Advisory Board at the V.A. clinic in Leeds, Massachusetts which deals with issues ranging from starting new support groups to fixing the sidewalks so veterans wouldn't be re-injured.

He also participates in an organization called "Soldier On," which deals with homeless veterans with addiction and mental health issues. It tries to equip them with the necessary knowledge and skills so they can re-enter their communities as productive citizens. He provides information to assist those who have received housing vouchers to enable them to access the resources they need.

As a result of his work with "Soldier On," he was selected to pose for a statue that is used to honor the contributions of those who have aided and advocated on behalf of homeless veterans throughout the country. The first person selected to receive the award in 2009 was the Chairman of the Joint Chiefs of Staff, Mike Mullen. Don spoke at the ceremony and expressed his gratitude for the opportunity to, at long last, welcome Vietnam veterans home.

My last name is Chevannes, which is a French name. My mother and father were Jamaican. They came to this country and moved to New York. I was born and raised in Harlem. One of my teachers told me, "If you're going to go to a school, go to a school that's well integrated." That's what I did when I went to Seward Park High School. It was an area where you have Italians, people of Jewish faith, Chinese, Spanish...that area was just a melting pot. I really learned a lot there. Going to Seward Park I got a different outlook and aspect of what it is to deal with people of different cultures. I believe that helped me to deal with some of the challenges I faced, like going to Vietnam.

I did fairly well in school until the eleventh grade. Then I got a wild crush on a girl and my grades went downhill. It was '68 and I ended up going to Queensborough Community College in Queens. I figured I'd try to take the easiest classes that I could and just get all A's, but that wasn't the case. When I hit chemistry that was it. Chemistry was like talking another language to me. At this time the war in Vietnam had been going on for two or three years. I thought being at Queensborough Community I would be totally out of the realm of the draft board getting me, but what I didn't realize was that if I didn't keep up a certain grade average my number would be coming up in the lottery.

My father was very strict and very straight-laced – a bow tie, cigar-kind-of-guy – who kept himself well-dressed. He was a very well-organized person. I found out after he died that he was a bandleader. It shocked me to find out he played the banjo. My father had his idea of being a man – that the man had the right to go out, do whatever he wanted to do as long as he came home. The woman should stay at home – kind of old-world thinking.

My mother was like an angel. She was so nice you wouldn't know that a person like that had strength. She basically supported us. It wasn't that my father wasn't working, but what he provided was the house and the food. Everything else we needed my mother was struggling to maintain. She was a domestic worker plus she was a professional seamstress. The jobs she had paid her a dollar an hour. She saved all that money to pay for whatever else we needed, but it was thanks to my father that we stayed in the same home at 127th Street in Harlem for the first twelve years of my life.

By this point though it was 1969 and we were living in upper Manhattan, Ft. Washington, at 614 West 152nd Street. When we moved there, my dad was still with us, but he was never home. He'd come in, the rent would be paid, he'd sleep a couple hours and then he'd get up and go to work. He did this for many years. As I got older I realized that my father was just doing things like some men do. They'd have more than one place to stay. He had more than one woman. He had more than the four kids in our family, too. We counted at least eighteen kids and we stopped counting. My mother was not oblivious to it, but she knew that her priority was *her* kids.

My mother was not politically oriented. She was smart enough to give us other gifts. Her gift was her insight into people. She had insight into her kids, but also into other people. My father's gift was that I learned to be organized. Those file cabinets that my father had in the house were records of him paying rent, records of any expenses that he made.

So that was the family that I was living with in Washington Heights and into the middle of it all came this letter. I opened it up and read that I had to report to Whitehall Street in Lower Manhattan. I was devastated when I got that. I was like, "Oh, my god, I'm being drafted." I don't remember any forewarning, but looking back now, I'm pretty sure there probably was. I know I had a lottery number, but I don't remember what it was. My birthday is May 25, 1951.*

I'd been hearing stories about guys – how they'd get out of it. There were guys I knew that ate part of a bar of soap and when they went in for their physical examination their stomach was bloated and their blood pressure was high. The ones that didn't look well, they got exempt. There were drug addicts who went down there and you took one look at them and you could tell they were not draft material.

What happened was I got down to the induction center and I was really afraid. There were a lot of threats going on that the protestors – especially the draft resisters – would blow it up. When I got into the induction center I didn't get the physical right away. The swear-in was first and I swore in. Then I went and took the test. While I was taking the test I had this brilliant idea. I was doing the best I could for the first twenty minutes of the test and I realized, wait a minute, I don't really want to go. Why don't I just give the *wrong* answers on the test? I started revamping my answers. All the correct ones I'm now marking wrong ones and from that point on I started marking all wrong answers.

Then it came time for the physical test and what they did was they gave me a colorblind test. "Gee," I said to myself, "this is going to be a cinch." They would put up a green dot, ask what color is this and I would say blue. They put up a white dot, and I would say it was orange. When they started calculating the scores, they probably realized that there's nobody that illiterate or ignorant joining the army or being drafted. I was then approached and told that if I didn't take the test over I would go to jail. I had recently read a book called *Soul on Ice* by the Black Panther Eldridge Cleaver. I remembered him writing about his experiences in jail. I thought about what the Army guy had said, and what Eldridge had said, and figured I didn't want to go into the jail environment. So I ended up going along and taking the test over again. I ended up at Fort Dix in New Jersey.

You know, it's a funny thing. I was for the war, but when it came to them selecting me to go, I was against it. I think the reason why is because I felt that I had so much going for me. I hadn't started using drugs. I was

*Don's lottery number from the second draft lottery held on July 1, 1970, was 26, which guaranteed his being called to serve.

having a good time. Now all of a sudden, I felt like I could be going over to Vietnam and the picture the media painted of Vietnam at the time was of guys in firefights and guys carrying bodies and that really bothered me.

Before this time, I think what the government was doing was trying to get the sentiment of the country to be for the war. I think that's what the press was doing, too, but then because of the hippies and the Black Power movement protesting the war, the Establishment realized that they had to open up and tell us the truth more. That was when you saw more body bags and heard about some of the atrocities. Before this change I had gotten the feeling that I was being given one side of the war story, but after I was exposed to these movements, I started seeing things a little bit differently. By that time I was already in the Army.

So I went to Fort Dix. I got a communications job. I would be climbing poles and fixing telephone wires. I said to myself, "Gee, man, that's not so bad," but you still had to learn how to shoot. You still had to learn how to throw a grenade. This was when the movie M*A*S*H* came out. It gave us a comic view of the service. It made us look at service life a little differently. I felt that if Vietnam was anything close to the Korea in the movie, then it wouldn't be so bad.

During basic training there was racism. I wouldn't call it overt racism, but to give an example, there was a guy called Bean from Boston. He was white, short, a sturdy, all-American kind of guy. He did everything right. And there was me. In the platoon, they have a series of things that you do, physical training and mental training. What happened was, near the time of our graduation, they have to select the best person who fits all the ideals, physically and mentally. It has to be shown that he has proven himself in his scores. We worked with these different tests. Bean was such a stand-out kind of guy that when he went to the firing range if he made "marksman," they'd write him in as "expert." This happened with each test.

Of course, I was also taking these tests and doing very well on each of them, but everyone was focused on Bean. We went through all these tests and it just so happened that I went into the room where they were calculating the scores – the highest you can get is 500 – and when they got to Bean's card, he got 465. The captain and lieutenant, of course, jumped for joy. "That's it! Bean got the highest score!" and they put the card on the desk and kept saying things like, "This is it! That's 465! That's the highest one." The rest of the officers were calculating the rest of the scores and they came up to my card. They finished adding up all my points and one of them said, "485." They were stunned and there was also disappointment. Here was somebody who came in and beat Bean.

That was the first time I really felt good about my experience at Fort Dix, because there were guys coming up to me and congratulating me. The African-American guys were proud of me. I could see that it was an up-lift for them, but the officers were trying to downplay it, because for them it was disappointing. They had Bean as being the model soldier and it didn't happen. For me it really felt good. I realized that one person doing something right *can* affect a lot of other people. That was my first lesson. I didn't know that. I had always thought that if *I* do something right it's only going to affect me and it's only going to benefit *me*. I learned that in the Army, in that instance.

The next thing I remember that had a big effect was when they told us, "We got three places we're going to be sending some of you guys. Some of you are going to Vietnam, some of you are going to Germany, and some are going to Korea." There were about two hundred of us and we all stood outside and they said, "We're going to read off the names. They read off that one guy was going to Korea, two guys were going to Germany and the rest of us were going to Vietnam.

At that point my stomach dropped. I was like, "Oh, my God!" I didn't know what to think. I didn't know what to do. All I could think of was death – that I might get shot up, I might get blown up. I was nineteen. If you got a guy that was twenty-three, he was old. The average was nine-teen-years-old.

We had to go to Washington State to complete our training. We never really did any jungle training. The only folks who did were in Louisiana at Fort Polk, which was the closest thing to the environment in Vietnam. The guys who got trained there got a feel for the jungle, but we just went to Fort Lewis to get shots and learn about foreign diseases and what pre-ventive measures we should take. We then boarded the airplane that was taking us over to Vietnam. It was a sixteen-hour trip.

I was scared, but the truth is I'd been even more scared thinking about leaving the country for Canada when I got drafted. I didn't think I had the resources. I wasn't that brave. I admire those who could do that, and to this day I really appreciate the ones who actually decided, "Hell, I'm not doing it. I'm leaving the country." It took a strong person to do that. When I got to Vietnam I found out that there were guys who had started their service "in country" and deserted – just left. I'd go into some of the whorehouses there and see a couple of the guys who had deserted. I couldn't do that either. I didn't have enough heart.

I remember being on the plane and I'm the only one that's awake. Everybody else was asleep. The stewardess asks me, "Why aren't you asleep?" Everybody else is relaxing because they give you a pillow. It didn't affect me that way. I wanted them all to wake up and tell them, "You know where we're going?" But I felt maybe there was something wrong with me – that I was the only one awake and everybody else was asleep.

It took us sixteen hours to get from California to Vietnam. We flew into Cam Ranh, which is about two-thirds of the way down from North Vietnam. I have never been to a place as hot as Cam Ranh Bay. I was wearing combat boots and you could walk on the sand and feel the heat coming right *through* your boots, right onto your feet. One of the things that immediately struck me was that we were coming to this camp right near the airport and there was this cargo plane and they were loading body bags. Somebody said, "Those were the guys that you are replacing."

I went to a place called Camp Eagle. I was stationed at the headquarters company. Basically, I operated switchboards at night. I would repair wires if there was a broken switchboard a mile or two away. We used to communicate, not by radio, but by telephone. A lot of times because of the weather or whatever reason, wires would break. Right away I was really practicing what I learned from my advanced infantry training.

They would have me fix communications between two areas. They sent me out by myself. I was following the broken wire. The method was we would go in the middle between two points, point A and B, the place that I just left and the place that I'm going to. I'd go to the middle spot between A and B and cut the wire. Then I would call back to point A. If I reached point A, I would have to work on from the middle to point B. That's how we would learn where I'd have to fix it because a lot of times the breakages occurred underneath sand, dirt, trees, and rocks.

This particular time, I walked across this little valley and suddenly I was sinking. I walked right into this quicksand and I didn't have enough strength to pull my leg out. When I had sunk in a little past my knees I realized the quicksand was going to pull me completely under. If it wasn't for this low-lying tree that I managed to grab onto, I don't know if I'd be even talking here, because I realized once you're in quicksand it's like being in concrete that's on the verge of drying. I somehow made it out of there and realized that I was going to have to be more careful. I began to notice that it wasn't just the idea of being shot at that was going to be a problem, but there were other little things, environmental things that I would have to be aware of and I really wasn't.

Then came my first experience with drugs. I had already started smoking marijuana when I left Cam Ranh Bay and ended up in Bien Hoa. It was plentiful there. You could buy it with nickels and dimes, which would get you like two kilos of marijuana. There were little kids on scooters, and they would sell to us. It was their way of getting money.

My first bout with drugs was with a friend of mine, a Caucasian named Panther. He actually gave me scag. It was called scag, but it was heroin. It was sixty percent pure and they had to dilute it, because if you were given that drug at the percentage that they made it and took it out of the fields – it was something like eight percent pure – it would kill you. It was the only time I saw where you put it in a cigarette. It was odorless and tasteless. You wouldn't even know you were smoking it until the effects hit you.

We were in a thing we called a hooch, which was considered a cabin. He said, "Why don't you try this?" When he handed it to me, it was in a little valve, a little plastic valve. I'll never forget it. I opened it up and he was telling me just to smoke a little bit and I thought, "This can't be that good," and I didn't listen to him. Instead I ingested it through my nose and all I can remember was, when I opened my eyes my head was between my legs. We were sitting down. I was like, "God, this is too much; I don't believe it." He had warned me that it was strong, but I ignored him because the quantity was so small. I thought, "What harm could this do." He was just sitting there watching me, seemingly unaffected, because of having built up a tolerance.

Then there was the feeling of wanting to throw up, but not quite. I didn't get to that point, but believe it or not it was the best sleep I ever had. I didn't dream, but what happened was, when I woke up, I realized that so many hours had gone by. As soon as I stood, the effects of it came at me as though I had just started doing it all over again and I couldn't believe it. You would have thought I was drunk off of alcohol. But it wasn't that. Next thing I knew a missile had attacked and I fell into some kind of foxhole or something and I got hit on the top of my head where my hair is still missing. It was no big deal - not enough for me to leave the country or be considered for disability – but at that time I still felt the effects of the drug. They stayed with me for a good three or four days. I soon realized that when I was under the influence of this drug I was totally oblivious to a lot of things around me and much less scared. So I felt like maybe this was my way out.

One night me and my friend decided to go over to the Air Force base because they lived so much better there. Their facilities were great and there were no "grunts"* over there. While we were en route, we ran across some kids selling some marijuana. I gave one kid ten dollars. The kid came back with two huge bags of marijuana. They looked like laundry bags. You could see through them. They were huge, but we decided, "Hell, if we can get this in the Jeep, we'll take it," and we did. We stuffed it under the Jeep's dashboard.

By that time it was night and we were on this road when we heard firing. All of a sudden, this shooting started going down and we both jumped out of the Jeep. We ran separate ways. I could hear the bullets coming past us, because they were hitting the bushes. You can *hear* bullets when they're near. All I can remember is running down a gulley and landing in sewage, but I was so scared I stayed in that sewage for forty-five minutes. Finally somebody must have realized we were missing. When the military police found the abandoned Jeep they began searching the area. By that time, since the firing and shooting had subsided, I started walking towards the road and ran right into the military police.

That was my first jail experience because they found all the marijuana. Since we were in Vietnam and we weren't in a regular court of law, they threw us into this little pen for a few hours until our first sergeant came and got us. I had by that point decided that if I could get out of this mess, I would just be more careful about how I did my drugs. I never thought then about quitting.

So I kept using. I stopped the marijuana and I stayed with the heroin. They always say when you have a problem the hardest thing is admitting that you have it. I didn't admit that I had a problem because I felt like I was a "weekend warrior." I could use and then stop when I needed to so I could be a soldier. But what I didn't understand when I was in Vietnam and doing drugs, me being so young, was that I *thought* I was all right. I *thought* I had it under control.

---

*During the Vietnam War, infantrymen, the foot soldiers of the war, were often referred to as "grunts."

Little did I know that heroin would be a crutch for me later on. It was the only drug that I used and it made me feel relaxed. It made me feel like I was really good at what I was doing, that I had no problems and no pain. As a matter of fact, when I was on drugs, I never even really caught a cold.

The closest thing to knowing what Vietnam was like was watching the Oliver Stone movie, *Platoon*. That's about as close as you're going to get outside of seeing a documentary movie. Guys did come together. The movie showed men dancing, black men and white men and they're playing Motown music, and that is exactly the scene that I was in. We were all together, black and white, dancing to Motown music. We just were relieved that we were together and everybody was OK and we were listening to music. Oliver Stone was a vet himself and his film really said it.

My sentiments about the war didn't change that much until I saw more people getting hurt. My friends were getting wounded constantly. Guys were being flown into the firebase having been hit, but I still didn't get the anti-war thing. I was starting to realize that we went over there not to defend the Vietnamese, but to defend ourselves. I finally got to the point where after all that I'd been through – being shot at, being hurt, going through the drugs – I thought that going home was going to be the biggest relief for me. I finally got there in April of '72.

It was at the airport where I remember somebody spitting at me. It didn't get on me, but I saw the spit land near me.* There was a bunch of people on the side yelling and throwing stuff. I didn't understand why they were doing this to us. Yes, I knew they were against the war and thought we were a willing part of it. And it was true, we'd been over there, and maybe some guys really went to "defend the country" or whatever, but lots of us were only over there because we were drafted!

I remember coming back to New York. I took a cab from Kennedy Airport. Prior to getting to where I was living, I told the cab driver to slow down so I could think. I was afraid to get out of the cab. I just sat there in the back in my uniform and told the cab driver, "Relax because I'm paying: the meter's on. Don't worry about it. I'm paying it." I had my pay from leaving the service, but I just couldn't figure out how the hell I was going

---

*Though this was clearly Don's experience, the generalized notion that this was a common occurrence has been challenged by Jerry Lembcke in his book *Spitting Image: Myth, Memory, and the Legacy of Vietnam (NYU Press, 2000).* His thesis is that these allegations of hostile behaviors towards veterans have been used to discredit subsequent anti-war movements.

to get out of the cab, given people had already thrown rocks at us, spit at us, and called us names.

God must have answered my prayers, because all of a sudden it just started raining hard out of nowhere. At first it looked like there was not a cloud in the sky and the next minute all this rain is coming down and everybody started running towards their houses, running indoors. When I saw that I was like, "Wow, here's my move!" I paid the cab driver and jumped out of the cab and ran home. I ran upstairs. The very first thing I did was take off my uniform and put some regular clothes on. Little did I know that my problem was just beginning with the drugs.

For the first six months of being at home, every time I heard a firecracker I was jumping. I couldn't understand what the hell was going on with me. I would duck. I would look around. Things were happening to me that didn't used to bother me or affect me. It seemed like my personality had changed. I didn't know that until coming home. All the people saw it, but I didn't see it. I started using heroin again. I never shot drugs. I just did it by sniffing and because I continuously would do that and use it as a crutch everything that I was doing was affected – my family, my jobs. I'm a good worker, a hard worker, but because I was doing drugs it was causing me problems at work.

By this point I was living in Bloomfield, Connecticut. Although I never got married I started spending a lot of time with the girl I had taken to her senior prom before I'd gotten drafted. We had been living together in New York and had a daughter before moving to Connecticut, but I had never stopped using drugs. It was no surprise really, when one evening she told me she wouldn't give me any more money. As I walked out the door she said, "All I want you to do is just lead." What she meant was for me to lead the family into a better life. I walked away. I was mad that she didn't give me any money so I could buy more drugs.

I decided right then that I would stay in a shelter. I went down to the shelter and one of the guys there who knew me said, "Yo, Don, aren't you a veteran?" I said I was. He said, "You know, you should talk to that guy right there." I looked over a few feet and there was a guy leaning against the wall and I went over to him. I said, "What's up?" and he said, "I work for the United Veterans of America at the Veterans Hospital in Leeds, MA. If you don't have a place to stay or if you have any problems with drugs, you can come on up there and get things going. You can get your ID and start to get your life in order."

I said no because I wasn't going to leave Connecticut where I was living at the time. I walked away. Ten seconds later I thought, "Don, what are you doing? You're not doing anything. Your life is at a standstill. Wake up!" And in just that minute, I decided to go. That was probably the best decision I ever made. I'm just sorry it took me so long.

Since I've been up at the VA in Leeds, I've been clean. That was 2005. I'm grateful for both being part of the Veteran's Administration and being at "Soldier On," which was formerly the United Veterans of America. I've been able to get involved in programs where I can talk to kids about the war and my situation, and in the long run it's helped me a great deal. When I go into a school knowing the situation that those kids are in, I try to relate to them. I went to one place and instead of preaching to them, I talked to them about my experience and how I learned about the effects of war. I look at their faces and I know when I have a young person who's listening. First you see this stargazing look in their faces, and then all of a sudden they get this look like they're getting what I'm saying about my life, about war, and about getting hooked on drugs. They're starting to think, "That's happening to me; your story is similar to mine." I can see that in their faces. I say, "But you got a head start. If I knew twenty years ago what I know now, maybe my situation would have been different." I tell them, "You all got it now, and all you have to do is just take advantage of it." That's probably as much preaching as I would do.

Being here, being at the VA and around the kind of people who have given me a whole lot of support and hope, has made all the difference. I don't think any clinic or psychiatrist could give me what I have gotten. I've just gotten so much from my fellow soldiers and the people who care about us. I don't blame the war for what happened to me. I blame the fact that I was always pleasure-seeking with the drugs. True, it started over there. I used drugs to numb out, but after that it was all about pleasure-seeking. I thought addiction had to be physical and that's why you had to go through withdrawal, but even with mental addiction you go through withdrawal.

I was addicted to heroin. I didn't feel I was for a very long time, but now I realize it. I also realize now that I can live like a normal person and do things without having to get high. I'm not a stupid person. I'm a fairly intelligent person, but drugs can twist your mind and that's what happened to me in Vietnam. The heroin I started using because I was over there twisted my mind.

CHAPTER 3

THOSE WHO LEFT

PERHAPS NONE OF THE CHOICES CONFRONTING DRAFT-ELIGIBLE MEN was more fraught with anxiety than voluntary exile. This decision had far-reaching consequences, since it required young men not only to become fugitives from American justice, but also to leave behind their family and friends and the community within which they had become men. With the war raging and many Americans viewing those who left as traitors, deserters, or cowards, the likelihood of returning home any time soon was very much in doubt.

In his wrenching short story "On the Rainy River," from *The Things They Carried*, Tim O'Brien dramatizes the experience of a man who comes within twelve feet of making the choice to leave the country for Canada. At the moment of decision, his entire past rises up to confront him:

> I saw my parents calling to me from the far shoreline. I saw my brother and sister, all the townsfolk, the mayor and the entire Chamber of Commerce and all my old teachers and girlfriends and high school buddies. Like some weird sporting event: everybody screaming from the sidelines, rooting me on – a loud stadium roar. Hotdogs and popcorn – stadium smells and stadium heat. A squad of cheerleaders did cartwheels along the banks of the Rainy River; they had megaphones and pompoms and smooth brown thighs. The crowd swayed left and right. A marching band played fight songs. All my aunts and uncles were there, and Abraham Lincoln, and Saint George...and LBJ, and Huck Finn and Abbie Hoffman, and all the dead soldiers back from the grave, and the many thousands who were later to die...."[1]

O'Brien brilliantly presents the two strains of the discourse – the voices telling him to go and the ones urging him to stay – and he lets us understand how complex and textured the decision was, involving not only those who were being left behind, but an entire national history and literature and an entire established social fabric. His character turns back, not because of a failure to see the choice clearly, but rather, as he sees it, because of a failure of courage – that choosing to fight in a war he totally disdained was less difficult than abandoning all he loved and the esteem of those he knew.

> All those eyes on me – the town, the universe – and I couldn't risk the embarrassment. It was as if there were an audience to my life, that swirl of faces along the river, and in my head I could hear people screaming at me. Traitor! they yelled. Turncoat! Pussy! I felt myself blush. I couldn't tolerate it. I couldn't tolerate the mockery, or the disgrace, or the patriotic ridicule....I was a coward. I went to the war.[2]

In addition to making the decision to leave, once those who fled to Canada had gained landed immigrant status, many had to make other difficult choices, such as renouncing American citizenship and becoming full citizens of Canada. These decisions would obviously reverberate throughout their lives. At a desperate time for many, there was also the question of whether they would be accepted and welcomed by the Canadians into whose community they had moved. Would there be enough jobs for the new immigrants so they would not be perceived as taking employment from the locals? Would Canadians' attitudes toward the war and toward America result in hostility? Yes, there was safety across the border, but there were enormous trade-offs, not the least of which was never knowing if return would be possible.

There is some controversy as to whether those who left the country as a means of dealing with the draft should be classified as expatriates or exiles. The connotative difference has to do with choice – expatriates are individuals who have chosen to live in another country and exiles are those who have been forced to leave their homeland. During Vietnam these differences were obscured and became a function of one's perception of the level of threat as well as one's personal moral code. Is a man an expatriate or an exile if what drives his decision to leave America is an understanding that to stay would not only put his life at risk, but would require him to kill others? Such a conundrum is obviously far more philosophically complicated than the decision to leave the country for economic or social considerations. In the case of members of the armed forces who deserted, these alternatives – serving and killing, or fleeing – had already been faced.

Regardless of how they are classified, those who left the country to avoid the draft, largely middle class youth, chose to settle in either Canada or Scandinavia. More than 50,000 draft-age American men and women migrated to Canada alone during the Vietnam War, the largest political exodus from the United States since the United Empire Loyalists traveled north during the Revolutionary War. Their reasons were legion. Nevertheless, it was the draft and its demand for more and more men that drove the great majority to cross the border. Deserters, on the other hand, mostly sought refuge in Europe. A community was established in Sweden in 1967 when four disaffected servicemen off the aircraft carrier *Intrepid* were granted asylum. Military deserters in exile were far less likely to come from the middle class. Most of their number were lower class volunteers who had enlisted in the military for financial reasons, and who either left the ranks as transfer to Vietnam loomed or after having done time there.

Controversy continues as to what truly motivated those who chose to depart from America. John Hagan, in his well-received 2001 book, *Northern Passage: American War Resisters in Canada*, writes, "The evidence presented in this book indicates that the decision of American war resisters to come to Canada was, in political-process terms, a rational and productive response to the opportunity that immigration to Canada provided."[3] There is ample evidence to draw a more far-reaching conclusion, however. Many of the American war resisters who chose to give up the life they knew were acting out of a conviction that the Vietnam War was an illegal and immoral war. They felt that both their consciences and the provisions of the Nuremberg Tribunal prohibited their participation. Frank Kusch, in his book *All American Boys: Draft Dodgers in Canada from the Vietnam War* presents yet another view. He argues that:

> The draft dodgers who went to Canada during the Vietnam War were not always the anti-war radicals portrayed in popular culture. Many were the products of stable, conservative, middle class homes who were more interested in furthering their education and careers than fighting in Southeast Asia. The conflict in Vietnam was just one cause among many for their deep sense of disaffection from the land of their birth. These exiles remained quintessentially American, because evading the draft was, in their opinion, consistent with the very best American traditions of individualism and resistance to undue authority or state servitude.[5]

It was not until 1977, after many attempts by numerous peace groups, that amnesty was granted to resisters. It was never offered to deserters.

Craig Dreeszen

Craig was born and raised in Nebraska and now lives in Florence, Massachusetts with the woman who came to Canada to be with him in 1970. Diane's interview follows in Chapter Seven, "Those Who Loved, Supported and Counseled." He worked for the University of Massachusetts for seventeen years before retiring to set up his own consulting firm. He is a past president of the Board of Trustees at the Unitarian Society of Northampton and Florence.

In 1969 I was a senior at the University of Nebraska in Lincoln where I had grown up. I was also married. Everybody was anxious about the war, and I was active in the protest movement. I was student body president my last year, and I had been planning to go to graduate school. Academic life had suited me. I felt kind of sheltered from the storm of the war that was raging. Nebraska's a pretty conservative place, too. At the university there was a cluster of people who protested the war, but the surrounding state was very conservative.

I explored conscientious objector status, but a friend of mine had sought it and had been rejected. This guy had a lot more formal pacifist credentials than me. He had been active in a church that was anti-war and at that time, the draft board in Nebraska interpreted the classification of conscientious objector very narrowly. You had to be a lifetime Quaker or another religion where there was a creed that required pacifism, so I didn't even apply.

My parents were conservative Republicans and Nebraskans who don't talk about difficult things too much. When I decided to go to Canada and told them about it, they were incredulous. I'm sure there were lots of feelings going through their heads. Shame comes to mind. Perhaps they'd say they felt disappointed by my protesting, but then they probably also felt relief that I'd be safe. It was probably the only thing I had ever done that struck them as oppositional.

As for the lottery, it's funny. I don't remember the number at all. When I talk to people – most men can name their number – I can't remember that. I can remember that it was well within the range of what they were accepting. I've got real strong memories of getting the number, because I knew from that moment that there was no chance I wouldn't get called. I went into a kind of shock. I didn't sleep for a couple of nights, and

I didn't eat. I went into a precipitous physical decline, lost weight, and looked pretty haggard. In those days everyone had schemes, so I decided that I would pretend to be a drug addict. I poked a pin into my arm to make it look as if I had been shooting drugs. I also went to talk to a counselor at the University to tell him that I had a friend with a drug problem to try to figure out what some of the symptoms were of doing drugs.

So I went in for the physical. I hadn't been sleeping and hadn't been eating, so I probably looked like a drug addict. I claimed to be having a drug problem, but that didn't bother the doctors at all. From the moment I got to the physical I felt like a pawn in a system. They make you run around in your underwear and stand up and talk to people behind desks in a way that introduces you to the idea that you are about to become cannon fodder. I was very frightened and alarmed. It's hard to know whether my convictions about non-violence got mixed up with my own fears for personal safety. I like to think I was taking the high ground of a moral stand against violence, which is true, but then that's tempered by not only the fear for personal safety, but also the distaste for becoming part of what I understood to be a demeaning system. Every bit of it ran against my grain.

When I passed my physical, I made the decision to leave for Canada. Throughout this whole process, I had been investigating Canadian immigration. There was a network of people who could aid men to get to Canada. In those days there was no Internet, so it was telephone calls and letters. I called a number with information about leaving for Canada and got coached on what it would take to get accepted as a landed immigrant, and even the border passages that were the most supportive, the least likely to be confrontational. I quickly assembled as much cash as I could. I sold everything I owned, but I was a college student, so I didn't have any capital. I still wish I had my childhood coin collection, but I sold it along with my books and records.

My wife was very supportive. She followed me up to Canada. We decided that it would be a "back-to-the-land" move. I was reading about survival and organic gardening. We were acquiring camping gear and I was trying to get in better physical shape, walking around with a backpack full of books, the only heavy thing that I owned. Our stockpile was a couple thousand dollars, maybe three at the most. We began poring over Canadian maps. We picked out a remote fjord, although I don't think they call it that in British Columbia, which was our destination. There were months of preparation, which included getting a vehicle that would be fit to travel a good distance.

We went to Alberta to cross the border. The guards were very polite. They wanted to know that we wouldn't be taking welfare soon, but an English major doesn't have that many obvious job prospects. I talked about my hopes, and I didn't talk about the back-to-the-land idea.

There were six of us traveling. The others were just fed up with the country. They weren't evading the draft. They thought my departure would be an occasion for them to do something adventurous, too. We headed up to Bella Coola, British Columbia, which was a couple hundred miles north of Vancouver on the coast and it proved to be an absolutely beautiful place. But it was a long way from anywhere else, and I learned later that people didn't drive in. They took a boat in or flew in, but we drove in and left the muffler along the way, because it was several hundred miles of gravel road.

Of course, there was no land to be bought. It was expensive, and there was no work to be found. We had to go back down to Vancouver. We had this really naïve view of what it would take to get settled. My three thousand dollars was diminishing. We were living on peanut butter sandwiches and rice. We stopped at a campground – we camped all the time – and somebody said to us, "There's cheap land in northwestern Ontario."

So we headed to northwestern Ontario. It was summertime and fall was coming and we knew that we couldn't go into a Canadian winter unprepared. Coming from west to east, northwestern Ontario is lakes and forests, the Canadian Shield. It was very beautiful. We stopped in a town called Dryden. It's a pulp and paper town, really stinky. We stopped at a real estate agency to see if there was anything and found this little farm for sale. We had pretty high standards. The conventional wisdom there was that it took a dirt road off a dirt road to get isolated enough. With other realtors, we had looked at lots that were just bush and beaver swamps and just horrible places, but this time we found this farm that an elderly couple had to sell to move into a nursing home and the price was $3,000 for one hundred-forty acres with a river running through it. It was just perfect. We bought it with two of our friends. Our share was $1,500 and that brought our cash down to about two hundred dollars.

It was early September so it was getting a little bit cold and we had no firewood. The place was essentially a little shack. In addition to all the drama of trying to avoid the draft and trying to find a place to live, my first marriage was falling apart. It had started before we left for Canada, but in the middle of the summer, my wife decided to go back to the States. I didn't want to be there alone, so I called up a friend, Diane, to see if she would join me. To my amazement, she said yes. We hadn't known each other long. We have been together since.

It was a beautiful little farm, but there was no drinking water. The well had been filled in. There was no electricity. There was, of course, no phone. No firewood. We hauled water from a spring a couple of miles away.

Our friends who owned the only vehicle among us said they could only stay for another few weeks so we went to Winnipeg – two hundred miles away – to buy a vehicle. We got a fifty-dollar truck with a crank starter, drove it about a hundred yards and it died. The guy returned our money so we bought another little truck, a little more modern.

We went back to the farm and our friends went back to the States. Winter was coming on. We were now down to about fifty dollars. I had to get a job. I went into town looking for work and immediately got stopped by an Ontario Provincial Police officer. The car wasn't insured and the fine was fifty dollars. We were just eating rice and mixing dried soup mixes into it to give it flavor. That first winter it got down to forty below frequently.

There were a few weeks where we were destitute, but I finally got a job as a paper handler at a paper conversion factory. I did shift work for a year and saw a side of society I never would have seen: manual labor and tradesmen and shift work and working class people. None of these had been part of my life before. Diane took a job as a secretary in a clinic and then at the pulp and paper mill, and she had a steady salary as I tried other things. I think we still have a picture of our Christmas tree. We cut this straggly little tree and hung paper ornaments and popcorn on it. It was so cold we just lived in one room, as we didn't have enough firewood to heat the whole cabin. We had a little tin stove that had to be replenished with wood every few hours.

The neighbors were kind, but also very curious about us. We were likely the first people who hadn't been born there. People brought us some firewood, and we cut more with a handsaw, but it was green and wouldn't burn. We would struggle to get fires burning. Routinely the pail of water would freeze in the kitchen and the old truck wouldn't start because it was so cold. To start it, we had this elaborate ritual. On the very coldest days, I brought the truck battery in and put it under the woodstove to keep it warm. I would take a scoop shovel, put twigs on it, pour some kerosene, light it with the shovel underneath the truck's engine to heat the oil and then put the battery in.

It definitely was an adventure. There was a part of us that was excited about it, but it was just such hard work. I don't remember being discouraged. Diane got discouraged, and while I was going into town to work that first winter, she was just there in the one heated room in this little cabin. There was no electricity, no running water, and no phone. There was no way to call anybody, and no radio. I'd come back from shift work, hard physical work, just exhausted and we'd crawl into bed, and she'd want to talk. I'd say one word and fall asleep and that drove her nuts. She was very brave.

That first winter was the lowest point and then things got significantly better. We met other people our age and found close friends. They were mostly Canadians, but very sympathetic to our circumstances. In fact, I don't think we've had as close friends since that time. One family had converted a church into a house, so there was this big hall and we would put the tables together until we had enough for twenty or thirty friends.

The work that I did at the paper factory only lasted about a year and then I started doing carpentry work. We had given up the idea of subsistence farming, but we liked the idea of craftsmanship, and we decided we would be craftspeople, and that eventually became my career of ten years.

Since we lived on land divided by a river, we definitely needed either a bridge or a boat. We decided a boat would be more useful. There was an old man living nearby who made beautiful cedar boats. We heard he made canoes, so we decided we wanted to become canoe builders. I went to visit him to find out where I could get materials for building canoes. I was going to build a fiberglass-clad canoe, but he persuaded me that I should build a traditional canoe. I kept hanging around long enough that he handed me a hammer and said, "Well, help," and that ended up being about a four or five year apprenticeship relationship. Eventually he paid me.

I helped him build these traditional fishing boats, but I really wanted to learn how to build a canoe. I built one canoe under his supervision, but his methods were a little hybrid. Diane and I took apart an old canoe to learn more about how it was built in the traditional ways. She and I became canoe builders. First we worked with him, and then we had our own shop. For eight years we built cedar and canvas canoes.

Then two things happened. First, in the mid-'70s, there was a U.S. government offer of alternative service. I'd been indicted soon after we left, and now there was an offer that I could do some alternative service instead of prison time. I didn't take that seriously at all because we had a good life. We were happy, we had friends, and we had a home. When Carter was elected and offered amnesty, it sounded enticing, but even then we never seriously considered returning. We had every intention of being lifelong Canadians, although we never took the step of citizenship. We researched and learned that Canadian citizenship meant renouncing U.S. citizenship. We weren't prepared to take that step. I suppose it was because our families were in the States – our roots were there, too.

By 1981, Diane was getting restless. She said pretty strongly, "Well, I want to leave. Are you coming, too?" She kept asking, but for me there was the business. We made canoes and we made toys and she was a wood turner. The very best year we grossed $13,000 and with that you can just barely get by, but it was possible. So, I kept saying, "Well, next year we'll do better." And eventually she said, "There have been a lot of these years when we should have done better and I need more."

She wanted to go back to school, so we agreed, and in 1982 we went to Toronto. She went to school, and I worked at the Ontario Craft Council. That was my first professional job and that launched my arts management career. We worked there two years and in those two years, we asked, "What is it we want to do next?" Canadians are very accepting of Americans, but still there was that hint of resentment. Without citizenship and with our American heritage...Canadians are in the shadow of the United States, and our culture dominates, our politics dominate, our economy dominates. Some Canadians were very resentful of that. We had great friends, but there was always this sense that we weren't quite fitting in and again, Diane was thinking that she wanted to get home. She had gotten us off the farm and now she hoped to go back to the United States.

For a year we would talk about it over dinner and discuss what we should do next. She had a great draw to New Hampshire, because her family owns a summer cottage there, which had always felt more like home to her than any other place. She missed it a lot, and when we came to Toronto we would go down to visit. Before that time we had no money and until amnesty we couldn't legally go.

One time we did come back illegally. I borrowed somebody's library card as a proof of citizenship and snuck across the border to visit my family at Christmas time. The guard at the border looked at my ID and kind of smiled and handed it back to me. It could have been otherwise. When we got to Nebraska, my parents were so nervous. They didn't want me to leave the house while I was there. Diane wanting us to be in New England finally tipped the scale, and we moved back. That summer home in New Hampshire is such a beautiful place. It had a very strong magnetic pull for her, and eventually for me, and that's why we're in Massachusetts to be closer to it.

We sold off our belongings. I gave my notice at work in Toronto, and we went back to the farm. We had tenants, and we prepared the place to sell. We spent a few weeks getting organized. We packed up our belongings and sold a lot of stuff, which proved useful because that became our capital in getting established in the States.

We rented a truck, filled it up with what was left and drove back. At the border crossing they asked the usual things. They asked how long we'd been away, and I said thirteen years. The guard smiled, invited me into his office, and checked his computer screen. That was the first acknowledgement that I'd had that I actually was granted amnesty. The government doesn't send you a letter. I was a little nervous about whether the official record would be enforced, but the guard smiled and said, "Welcome back."

In that last year in Toronto, I had hired somebody who came from the Amherst, Massachusetts Arts Extension Service to teach a class for a conference I'd planned. She did a great job, and she also admired what I was doing. In that last year when we were debating about whether to leave, I corresponded with her and actually came down to the Amherst/Northampton area to visit. We made visits to Portland, Maine, Portsmouth and Concord, New Hampshire and here. We actually put a compass on a map and drew out fifty, one hundred, and one hundred-fifty mile circles around the little island in New Hampshire where the summerhouse was located.

When we arrived in Portland, it was a holiday and the town was deserted. Before its resurgence, it looked kind of gritty, and it wasn't nearly as attractive as it is now. Portsmouth we loved, but we couldn't figure out how to make a living there. Concord was too tiny. One reason we left the farm was because Diane wanted to get a degree. We decided we wanted a college town, and so the Amherst area was very attractive. When we visited the Amherst area, the woman I had hired up to Toronto toured us and had a party for us. It was very welcoming. When we decided we were going to leave, I called my contact here and said we're coming. I asked if she knew of any work possibilities, and her immediate reply was, "It's funny you should ask, because we just opened up a part-time job opportunity." It was actually a contract. We packed the truck, and decided to leave and then there was an offer, which included a two-day-a-week contract to do consulting, which gave us just enough to make moving to this area feasible.

The truth of the matter is I never would have done any of this had it not been for the draft. My life would certainly have been a whole lot different. I'm sure I would have gone to graduate school and then gotten an academic teaching post. That was the career I would have been most suited to. In a way I've hatched something like that anyway, but without the tenure track position. I found a university to work in, and I became a teacher. I did research. I published, but all from outside of the academic career. I worked in continuing education, so I was always trying to act like a professor. But it worked fine. I would have liked to have a cluster of students around me and the security of tenure. Instead I had a soft-money position. So it was much different than it would have otherwise been, but it's been very rewarding.

I have no regrets. For the first eleven years in Canada we were poor. We had no running water for the first nine years. We couldn't afford it. The last two years there, we were in transition, and the first years here we were in transition. We experienced a way of life we would never have lived, subsistence living, working in a factory. Those years in Canada had a lot of great things. We lived in the wilderness. We could hear wolves. We could see the northern lights at night. We could ski out of our backyard. We learned where water comes from: we had to dig the well by hand. We had to pull by hand to get electric poles up and cut down woods to make a path. We were aware of what it takes to survive in a way we never would have been. So that was good. The biggest impact on the negative side is that we had no savings. I was almost fifty years old before we started making retirement savings, and so that's been a scramble, trying to prepare.

As for me, the draft was the decisive event of my life. It made me do things I never would have done, but I don't have regrets. Whenever there was a rough period, we only had each other. We worked it all through.

When Diane wanted us to leave, she did ask if I would come, but I think she just put it in strong terms so I would know how serious she was about it. She did not want us to be apart. By that time, I had worn out my excuses of, "Next year things will be better." We love each other a lot and always have. She just was making it clear I'd run out of next years.

We continue to have periodic reunions with our Canadian friends. We've gone up there a few times. We're hoping this summer that some of our closest friends will join us again in New Hampshire.

Jay Holtzman

Jay grew up in Philadelphia. He was a psychiatrist who worked at the Cooley Dickinson Hospital in Northampton, Massachuesetts for twenty-seven years before retiring. He is married, and his wife is a psychiatric nurse with a doctorate in nursing. They have three children from former marriages, ranging in age from thirty-four to thirty-six. Jay lives in Belchertown. His ex-wife, Libby Holtzman, tells her story in Chapter Seven.

I am the middle of three kids and grew up in Philadelphia. My father was a dentist. During World War II he decided to enlist as a dentist in the Coast Guard. When I was three we lived in first North and then South Carolina; there are lots of pictures of my brother and me dressed in little Navy uniforms. My parents moved back to Philadelphia after my dad's years in the service and settled in a very blue collar, working class area of the city, where there were very few professionals and very few Jews.

Growing up, there was a tremendous focus on education. We just followed along and did what we were supposed to do. Our futures were essentially planned for us. We had a choice from the big three: doctor, lawyer or dentist. My brother became the dentist and I became the doctor.

My family was conservative in all ways. I was raised with the idea that teachers and principals were always right and above all, the president was always right. If the president were not really smart, he would not be the president. My parents generally voted Democratic as most Jews did. They did not have Gentile friends even though we lived in an entirely Gentile neighborhood. My friends at school were Gentiles, but I had this other set of friends through the synagogue, so I was living a split life even in those days.

One of my worlds was secret. My parents didn't know about my non-Jewish high school friends, and they particularly didn't know about the five-year love affair with the girl who sat next to me in class who came from an extremely rigid, fundamentalist Christian family. Outwardly, at least in terms of my parents, I did what I was supposed to do. I just ignored things, gave into my screaming mother, and went about my secret life.

I graduated from La Salle University in Philadelphia in '63. From there I went to medical school, following one of the Big Three choices my parents had scripted. Politics was still not an issue for me. My friend Herb, who identified himself as a pacifist, and I, had long arguments about pacifism. He introduced me to Bertrand Russell. His family was even more rigid than mine, but he was always rebelling. I was always the conservative. I would say, "Don't argue with your parents. Just go along with what they want for you." He was the radical.

Vietnam was starting to come up by then. Around my second year of medical school, there was a psychiatrist whom I had started seeing who was involved with a group that went on to become Physicians for Social Responsibility. I dated a woman in medical school who was very liberal as well, and for the first time I started asking questions.

In 1966 I went into my senior year of medical school and we were all looking towards internships. We were introduced to the Berry Plan,* which enabled people who were finishing medical school to get a deferment for the length of time they were doing their residency, with the proviso that, at the end, the person would go into the military as a specialist. In the meantime, interns and residents were actually getting drafted. One resident who was dating a very close friend of mine in medical school ended up going to Vietnam in his third year of residency. So people were being sent to Vietnam, but I was just not connecting. I was shallow. I was self-centered about what I was going to do next. I didn't even realize that by joining the Berry Plan I was really enlisting. I joined the Berry Plan and moved out to San Francisco to do my internship. I was actually sworn into the Air Force in the Bay Area, because there was a naval base near where I was working. It was the psychiatrist there who swore me into the military.

That was 1967. I was doing my internship. I was away from my family, living in the Bay Area, and having a wonderful time, paying no attention to politics. The plan was one year of internship, three years of residency in psychiatry and then I would go into the Air Force as a captain, just as my brother had done. He was stationed in Bermuda. I never saw myself as an Air Force person. I saw myself as an intern who was going to be a psychiatrist.

The peace movement was starting to grow at this point. Some of the other interns were far more active in it. It really started to make sense to me though. It was the Summer of Love and there was a split between me

*The Berry Plan was begun during the Korean War and allowed medical students to sign up for reserve commissions and defer their service until after they completed their residencies. The Plan provided the much-needed services of medical and surgical specialists until the end of the doctor draft in 1973.

and my family. When I broke loose, I broke loose! I really separated myself from all of my family's values. I went to Massachusetts General for my residency. I didn't want to leave the Bay Area, but I did.

It was no longer possible for me to ignore what was going on in Vietnam. I still didn't apply it to myself, but I started to become more active in protests. My first wife, Libby, who was a social worker from California, had a father who had been a conscientious objector during World War II. She had a younger half-brother who went to federal prison as a draft resister. Her family was very active. They had a bookstore in Palo Alto. Joan Baez was in their circle of friends as were several other very strong anti-war activists. Being exposed to this family caused me to be much more active in my protest.

When I got to my second year of residency we started talking about the fact that we were all on the Berry Plan, and all of a sudden it had a meaning for me. The meaning was not about my own safety. Psychiatrists are not going to be in the trenches. There was a good chance they would send me to Bermuda for all I knew, so it had to do with participating in something that was hideous, and it was getting worse and worse and impossible to ignore. A group of us all realized we were in the same boat. We explored the options we had in terms of becoming conscientious objectors and requesting discharges as CO's.

I didn't feel I wanted to apply as a CO on religious grounds as a Jew. I had had a very extensive Jewish education far beyond high school. Everything I knew about Judaism was pro-war, especially Zionism, and many of my family members were rabid Zionists. So I felt I could not do a religious CO. I did decide to apply for discharge as a conscientious objector who objected to war. I did not feel I was a pacifist, but as a matter of conscience I sought a discharge.

This began my odyssey. There were some lawyers who were extremely helpful. One guy by the name of Bill Homans was a wonderful man. He had a young attorney, Tom Shapiro, working with him, and they began guiding me through the process of applying for the CO.

The first hurdle in the application process was to meet a chaplain, which I cannot remember at all. The next was with a psychiatrist. I went to his office. It was private and not on a military base. I sat in his waiting room and looked at pictures. They were all the different models of warplanes. There were pictures of them dropping bombs and blowing things up. I thought, "This is going to be interesting." The only thing I can remember about the interview is that he was one of the stupidest men I had ever met in my life. He didn't know anything about psychiatry.

My final interview was with an adjutant general – essentially a lawyer – and for that I went up to Ft. Devens. This was the first time I was actually on a military base and it felt creepy. This guy was very smart, a very skilled lawyer, and he was grilling me. A lot of the questions I knew I would not be able to answer. I knew they were going to throw the Hitler question at me. I knew what my answer was going to be, and I knew it wasn't a great answer. It was, "I don't know what I would do." The only thing I felt I could tell him was that the Second World War didn't solve anything, because we then had a Korean War, and the First World War didn't solve anything because there was a Second World War. I didn't know how you dealt with dictators, but going to war hadn't changed anything. War just kills people. He looked at me and terminated the interview saying, "I think your request for a discharge is totally a matter of expediency. I think you just want to go on and become a psychiatrist and make your money and have a great life." That was his report, but that didn't end the CO effort.

I finished with my residency and applied for jobs. I knew I wasn't going into the service, so I was applying for jobs in California. It was 1971 and, of course, I didn't receive a lottery number in '69 because I was already in the military. I got my first set of orders, and they wanted to send me to this base off the coast of Japan. My wife, Libby, told her sister, who was married to a career Army optometrist, where I was going to be stationed, and she said it was the prize station in the entire Pacific. I got a stay of orders and we moved to central California. By that time Nixon was president. I then got another set of orders. My lawyer was in Boston and the job I had taken in Fresno didn't work out. We moved up to the Bay Area near my in-laws.

In the meantime I got a job, and I was in frequent contact with my lawyers. What happened next was that the adjutant general said no to my CO, the Air Force said no, and they continued sending me orders. Since I refused to obey the orders, I was told that I was going to have to go to federal court. Months went by before I heard anything and it was awful to be in this limbo. I felt like a sham working at the job. I couldn't commit to making friends. Libby didn't get a job, because we just didn't know what was going to happen.

I was aware that we were about a thousand miles south of the border of British Columbia. When we moved from the Fresno area up to San Francisco, we had talked about going to Canada as a possibility. As things started to snowball, and I became more entrenched in being a CO with the war getting worse and worse, we definitely were discussing leaving the county. We were in this strange state of waiting and feeling impotent, which is one of the government's major tools. I was also drinking a huge amount and hanging out with my father-in-law.

Meanwhile, back in Philadelphia... I had contact with my family. I had a phone conversation with my father, which was unusual since I usually talked to my mother when I called. He said, "You're crazy. I think you are absolutely crazy." My mother essentially said the same thing. They couldn't understand. My father had gone into the service and was a respected member of that community. My brother who had served in the front combat lines of Bermuda also had a wonderful life. They couldn't understand why I wouldn't want to be respected, be making money, and have a wonderful life. What was wrong with me that I wouldn't want that? They saw me as being under the influence of Libby, and they were right. Libby was an immense help to me in this. I wouldn't have done it without her and, after many years of divorce, I realized that was a major reason why I married Libby. She was the only one who could get me away from my family.

We had no money at that point. I was running up major legal bills. We needed money and at some point I said to Libby, "I am going to have to call my parents and ask them if they will lend me money." I hated to do it. I spoke to my father and asked him if I could borrow two thousand dollars. He said, "I will give you two thousand dollars to do anything you want to do, as long as it has nothing to do with going to Canada or not going into the military." I said, "I can't promise you that," and he said, "Then I am not going to lend it to you." This was meaningless in my family because my mother got on the phone and said, "What do you want?" I told her and she turned and said to my father, "We will send him the money." Then she said back to me, "I don't want you to do this, but if you need the money we will send it to you."

They sent me the money. Libby and I thought that two thousand would be sufficient, because if we chose to leave the country, I was a physician and I would be a valuable commodity in Canada. I knew that if I went to Canada and was not released from my service commitment, I would be a felon and that, if I ever set foot in this country, I would be arrested.

My lawyer filed a "habeas corpus" petition which enabled me to get a hearing before a judge who would then require the military to explain to the Court its justification for holding me against my will. I now had to get an additional lawyer in Denver because the Air Force headquarters are in Denver. I flew to Denver for the federal court hearing, but there was no decision from the judge.

Waiting for the judge to act didn't help. My hatred for Nixon, for the government, and for everything related to the government including the armed forces, was growing by leaps and bounds at that point. Four months went by and I hadn't heard anything. I called my lawyer and asked, "Can't you call the judge?" They said, "Absolutely not! You don't do that." I said, "Suppose it fell off his desk and is sitting under a desk somewhere?" They said, "No."

It was now November of 1971. Libby and I knew Nixon would be re-elected. We asked each other, "What do we want to do? Do we want to raise a family in a country under a president like Nixon?" We decided that, regardless of what happened, we were going to move to Canada. I applied and got a job at Riverview, the one state hospital in British Columbia, about twenty miles outside of Vancouver. It's called a provincial hospital. We packed up our dog, our houseplants and whatever other items we wanted to take with us and drove to Canada. I came into the country and applied for landed immigrant status. I had found out what I had to do and it was a very easy process, partly because I had a job offer.

Canada was wonderful to me. All Americans were able to get into Canada at that point. Soon after we arrived I began to look into what I had to do to get my licensure in Canada. About a month after we'd moved north, while we were living at Riverview, I got a call from my lawyer saying that the federal judge in Denver had turned down the petition. I belonged to the Air Force, and they would be issuing active duty orders. The lawyer said to me, "The only way I can get a stay of orders at this point is to go to the Supreme Court, which I have no problem doing." Money was clearly not a factor. This was a case that the young lawyer, Tom Shapiro, felt strongly about. He asked if I wanted him to do that, and I said, "I like the feeling of Canada. I like being here. I have taken a twenty thousand dollar drop in income (I was making eight thousand a year). I owe you eight thousand, but no, I don't want you to do any more. I'm done. I live in Canada. I will never go back to the United States."

That ended the legal issues. About three days later I got my orders to report to some place in North Dakota. I put them in a box with all of the other stuff I had from the military and didn't show up. I went about making a life for myself in Canada.

My parents would call from time to time. In one conversation I vividly remember my mother said, "A couple of men dropped by. They were very nice. They were from the Internal Security Branch of the Department of Defense. They really want to talk to you – very polite men. They wanted to know who your friends are. They were absolutely clear that if you came back to the country you would not have any problems whatsoever. I trust these people." I didn't bother telling her and my father what I thought of this. This was my parent's belief system. The government was good. These people are to be trusted.

About six months later, my father got slammed with an IRS audit that was one of the worst experiences of his life. My parents were honest people. They had to go through every receipt, everything that they had done. My father was a dentist. He collected money in cash in those days. They went through hell, yet they made no connection to what was going on with me. I made a connection.

My mother became involved with a group of Mothers Against the War. This was amazing. We never really talked about it, but I knew she was in it. Agnew's resignation followed by Nixon's were two of the happiest days of my life. We were absolutely glued to Watergate. It was as if everything I had told my family was being played out. I felt the exact opposite about the pardon. We pulled over while we were driving and listened to Ford's speech when he pardoned Nixon, and we were just devastated. Looking back on it with Ford's death just recently, I understand why he did it, and I think it was the right thing to do. The country was just racked. It didn't need that. Thirty years later I agree with it and I support it, but at the time we were in tears. Of course, with the pardon he announced the clemency program, which I had no interest in. I had no interest in going back to the United States...ever. I had no need to go back. I saw us making a life in Canada. I was happy in Canada. I loved Vancouver.

Libby, on the other hand, was very unhappy in Canada. She had gone to grad school at Smith College and wanted to go back to New England. She started on me about going through the clemency program, and I was extremely resistant. I did not want to do it. Finally she said, "I want to be able to go to the States and take the kids." I said, "You can. You're fine. You can go. The kids can go. I am the only one who can't go." And her reply was, "I don't want to go without you. I want you to go with us."

Some time after the visit from Internal Security and the audit, I received a letter from the State of California, a subpoena to appear in court. The State Attorney General was filing charges. What this subpoena said was he was filing papers with the Board of Registration of Medicine in California to revoke my license to practice medicine on the basis of moral turpitude, and I could not come into the country to defend myself. This was staggering. I contacted the ACLU (American Civil Liberties Union). If I were to lose my license to practice medicine in California, I couldn't apply in any other state, not if I had to put down that I'd had my license revoked in California on the basis of moral turpitude. I was licensed in Canada. I was certified as a specialist, but in the States there was no way I would ever be able to practice again.

Somehow the ACLU said yes and then dropped the ball. Nothing happened. My brother-in-law, Jonathan, Libby's half-brother, who spent a year in Lompoc Federal Prison in California as a war resister, had gotten out of prison very damaged in many ways. He had spent most of his time in solitary confinement. He had become a lawyer. He was Law Review, but decided not to take the bar exam, and was mainly doing draft resistance work. I called him and asked him to contact the ACLU. I had a month to go on the subpoena. He followed up on this and found out that the ACLU had lost my request. They picked up on it and fought the battle with the Board of Registration. They ultimately decided not to revoke my license, but to let it expire when it normally would. There would then be nothing on the record and so it expired and wasn't revoked. That was a relief, but it contributed to my feeling that the U.S. had declared a war against me. I saw them as trying to reach into Canada and grab me and hurt me in whatever way they could. Why in the world would I want to go back to a place that treated people like that?

But my wife did, and she finally got me to agree to repatriate. The base for deserters was Fort Benjamin Harrison in Indianapolis. I made the arrangement to fly to Indianapolis. Libby was going to stay with some close Canadian friends while I was gone. She didn't want to be alone. At the airports in Canada you went through American customs and immigration. I went to the immigration station along with everybody else, and I told an official I was going back under the Ford clemency program. One of them said, "You need to talk to this guy. Wait right here." They called this guy who was an American military type who said, "Come with me." He asked me a number of questions, and I was getting worried about missing my flight. He was quite unpleasant and refused to stop asking me questions. When we finally finished, he walked me back to the gate and...I missed the plane. I saw it taxiing away from the gate. I was getting very upset at that point. The airline said, "There's another flight to Seattle in a half hour. There are no regular seats. We'll put you in 1st class." I got on the next flight. When I got to Seattle I found out I had missed my connection to Indianapolis. I called Libby from Seattle and said, "I am coming home. I will not stay here." I got the first plane back to Vancouver. I was terrified that I was going to be picked up and put in prison. Having that guy talk to me and act the way he did and deliberately make me miss that plane...I was terrified.

I couldn't wait to get back to Vancouver. My friends picked me up. I kept saying, "I won't do this. I will not go back to that country." Everyone was trying to get me to calm down. Libby was hysterical because she saw her hopes for returning going down the drain. They all worked on me and argued that I was being paranoid and overreacting. They tried to convince me that since I had made the arrangements I should go back and try again. Finally I said, "I'll try again tomorrow." I rebooked the next day with no problem and made it to Indianapolis.

I had never spoken to another person who had left the U.S. in the five years I was living in Canada. I am at the Indianapolis Airport and it turns out there is a shuttle for deserters who are going for clemency. I go over to this shuttle and there were probably twenty-five guys and I thought, I am going to meet the others like me. I get on this shuttle expecting to have these political discussions, but not one of them was a political deserter. One was an Okie who was on leave from Vietnam. His father had fallen off a tractor and crushed his leg and he had to take care of the farm. Another one was a black guy from the Bronx. While he was gone, some pimp took all his girls, so he wasn't about to go back to Vietnam and let his source of income go so he killed the other pimp and got his girls back. It was amazing. I don't think there was anybody from Canada. These guys were from small towns in the south. They just didn't go back, and somehow they realized that here was an opportunity for them to get pardoned.

There was a part of me that thought this was wonderful, because I love when something brings me back to reality from my rarified ivory tower. Here I am thinking my thoughts about my circumstances, but this is not why one hundred thousand people deserted. There were real life reasons for why people did it. We get to the fort and we line up. There are two soldiers sitting there. You tell them the branch of the military you were in and what your rank was when you left. "Army private," "Army private," "Army private"...The guys sitting at the desk were fine. They weren't being rude. They were business-like. I got up there and said, "Air Force Captain." They both jumped up and saluted me. One said, "You're Captain Holtzman. You will not be bunking with the other returnees. You will be in the bachelor officer quarters." I said, "I don't want to be in the bachelor officer quarters. Can't I just go with them?" The other one said, "No, we have orders, sir." They separated me and threw me into this room and I am alone again. I was scared. Rationally I could think there's no reason for me to be scared. Underneath I was fuckin' terrified.

I got up the next morning and started getting processed, which took three days. Somewhere in the midst of it I was walking along going to the next station, and a Jeep pulled up. They said, "Captain Holtzman..." I now had been activated. I think they even paid me for three days of active duty. I was wearing civilian clothes, but they said, "The general wants to see you." I said, "What general?" And they looked at me like I was crazy and one of them said, "We have a three-star general who runs this base, and he wants to see you."

I got into the Jeep and again I was scared. They took me to the general's office and he said, "I have one question for you. Why did you do what you did?" I told him, "I did what I did because I thought this war was one of the most heinous crimes and it solved absolutely nothing. It just caused more death and destruction and was horrible." He looked at me and said, "That's all." I then said to him, "May I ask you a question?" He said yes and I asked, "Why have I been so important to you? Why did you track me down all over Canada?" He looked at me and said, "Do you realize you were the highest ranking officer to desert the Air Force? You are a source of staggering embarrassment to us."

I was shocked. I did all this in isolation. I wasn't related to the military. I had no concept of it. I didn't feel like a military officer. I wasn't a military officer. I don't know what it means to be a military officer. I was just me – one more dumb Joe not going to the war. The whole experience on that base was a view into the military mentality. I am a deserter, one of these horrible, treasonous criminals, and these two soldiers stand up and salute me. And this general calls me into his office and says, "You are one of the most important people we had in this entire war because you were such an embarrassment." It answered a huge number of questions, but it also underscored the absurdity of the whole military mission. It was insane.

Part of the repatriation process was you had to agree to do two years of public service. Bellingham, Washington was the nearest city to where I was living, so I went down to the mental health center to see if I could get a job, so we could continue to live outside Vancouver, and I could work in Bellingham. We didn't want to give up our home, which we really liked. Unfortunately the cost of living was so much higher in Canada. Washington State was somewhat depressed at that time and so the amount of money they were going to pay me would never have supported my family in Vancouver.

Eventually I said to Libby, "I made the move to California, and you didn't want to make that move and be that close to your family, so you pick this move." She decided she wanted to move to New England. I applied for jobs in New England and ultimately went to work at Baystate Medical Center in Springfield, Massachusetts. And here's one more little irony. Because I was doing something for the public good, it was an acceptable job for alternate service. I let the government know what I was doing. They gave me a discharge under less than honorable circumstances. When you complete the two years of service it is upgraded to a general discharge, which means you get veteran's benefits. The administrative assistant to the chair of the department at Baystate was a woman who was retired Army, married to a retired fighter pilot, both very conservative and ultra-hawks. This woman was obliged to hire me, and the ironic thing was that once a year over that two-year period, the Feds would come out to where I was working to make sure I was not being discriminated against because of my repatriation status

There is an epilogue. We were living in Amherst, Massachusetts, and I was working at Baystate, and I said to Libby, "We've got to stop living the way we live. We can no longer keep being these crazed socialist, activist, iconoclastic people who despise everything middle class, because we have children. We live in a neighborhood. Our kids can't be pariahs. So we need to disappear into middle America." She agreed and we tried to do that. It meant not being involved in any activist activities. My family was thrilled we were back. There were hard feelings for many years in my family about my total dismissal of their values and my on-going battle to stay separate. My family and I reconciled in ways, sometimes uncomfortably, but we reconciled.

I realized at some point, and I still feel, even thirty years after I repatriated, that what I did was the single best thing I have ever done in my life. More than anything else I have ever done, it made me feel like a man, a really valuable solid person, and there's nothing I have ever done that is as good as what I did. That's the reason I don't feel any guilt. The tears are not about being hurt, but about feeling proud of what I did. As I look back at this metamorphosis from this shallow, self-centered kid who really was a kid not taking any responsibility for anything, even in medical school when I was twenty-five, to what I became, I am just incredibly proud of that. I don't tell this story a lot. People who know me know it. In some ways, because I am so proud of it, it feels like hubris if I go out and tell it, but it doesn't feel that way this time, given what you are doing with it. So telling it feels like another step in integrating my life, especially getting to share this as I'm arriving at the doorstep of my retirement. I am grateful to have the time to do it at my leisure, and the timing couldn't have been better.

POSTCRIPT TO JAY'S INTERVIEW

While I was editing Jay's interview for publication, we had occasion to speak regarding a few of the details of which he had spoken. During our conversation he took the opportunity to tell me of the following development:

I don't think either Libby or I told you what happened soon after you interviewed her. I received a letter from her in which she told me of the impact of her interview and how badly she felt about having underestimated all I had done during that period of our marriage. [They have been divorced for many years.] She said she never appreciated all of the sacrifices I had made, and that if I hadn't been willing to do what I had done, we never would have made it through those very trying times. She wrote about how she was the one pushing us all of the time, struggling and expressing much resentment, and that I never complained. So I wrote back to her and said, "Yes, you pushed me, but that was the reason I married you, because you were forceful and I needed your strength."

Then you need to know about the inter-generational impact this has had. My daughter found out about Libby's letter, and she had lived through our complete cut-off from one another. She called me and said, "I can't believe Mom wrote you a letter." I responded, "Yes, she did, and it was wonderful, and I wrote her back." So there was a feeling of relief on her part – that her parents were no longer so estranged, that this interaction fueled by our interviews had resolved some of the enmity. I thought you'd want to know...

John Strickland

John was raised near Savannah, Georgia. He is a retired schoolteacher who taught middle and high school math, science, English and political science for over twenty-five years in Canada and the U.S. He now lives in Amherst, Massachusetts. He has two adult children, both of whom live in Canada. He has a list of about eighty-three articles and books he wants to write. They will be listed in the next yearbook of his Harvard class (1965).

I grew up outside of Savannah, Georgia, in a rural area. Neither of my parents had more than a seventh grade education. I have no idea why I started reading the things I did, science, math and philosophy in particular, but I just got interested. I had teachers who would mention things, and I would run off and read them. There was a group that conducted a talent search, and I got picked up along with a lot of other raw talent who'd taken the Westinghouse Science Exam they administered to find us. I got to take special seminars with all of the scientists in the area while I was still in high school.

I applied to Harvard and my high school principal said to me, "How can you do this, you have no money?" When I left Savannah on the train to Cambridge there was a brass rail down the middle - colored on one side, whites on the other. That's how I grew up. Occasionally I would talk with classmates at Harvard who would ask me, "Why aren't you prejudiced?" Maybe it was that I had grown up so poor. I didn't have the black color, but I had the same poverty. We didn't have indoor plumbing. Most of my relatives were relatively poor and some were even sharecroppers like those in *Let Us Now Praise Famous Men.** When I said I was going to Harvard, they didn't know what it was.

I knew about politics, but I was at times offended because people believed that since I was from the South, I couldn't possibly be "enlightened." I got tired of answering questions about why you people hate blacks. I went to hear Claude Weaver, a Harvard classmate, who talked about the Mississippi Summer Project. He described Mississippi in great detail and that got me interested in the Project. Then I went to a meeting in Roxbury and Fanny

---

*Let Us Now Praise Famous Men, text by James Agee, photographs by Walker Evans, was first published in 1941 by Houghton Mifflin. It lyrically and graphically depicts the conditions among white sharecropping families during the Great Depression.

Lou Hamer* was there. She still had her bruises from being beaten in the jail for "daring to vote." I was outraged. I understood what she was up against.

I went to Mississippi in the summer of '64. I was in Biloxi and later in Macomb. My family didn't know what I was doing with Freedom Summer. It was a tutoring program, which took place at Freedom Schools, and a voter registration program. I was ostracized. My father wouldn't talk to me for two years – no contact. When I came back to Harvard I took a leave of absence and then came back and finished in the spring of '66. When I left I got a draft notice, and I filed for a student deferment because I was on leave from school and was fully intending to go back. They granted me that. I didn't really want to go back to school after Mississippi. I wanted to go to New Orleans and be a writer.

I had mixed feelings about the military. I come from a military family. I still don't know what I would have done if I had been drafted at that point. If I had been asked to take a step forward, I might have done it and gone into the Army. In fact, I looked at Officer Candidate School. I took a test for it. I grew up wanting to go to West Point. I almost applied. I talked to the recruiter. I asked him about the philosophy department at the Point. He looked at me like I had crawled out from under a rock and that was it.

I took four-and-a-half years to graduate from Harvard, being granted an extra half year to read political philosophy for a senior thesis. After I graduated I wasn't sure what I wanted to do. My roommates pushed me to fill out an application to Harvard's Graduate School of Education, so I wouldn't get drafted. They actually filled it out for me and made me sign it. I was very ambivalent about the draft. I got accepted to Harvard with a fellowship and took courses required to receive a Master's in Teaching for Elementary Education, but I left before I finished. I didn't really want to teach. I've been a reluctant teacher all of my life.

I didn't want to be in the U.S. I didn't agree with the war. I knew what the problems were. People I knew were communists, and they offered me a chance to join the party. I said, "I can't do it. I don't believe in the historical inevitability of communism. I am very much more conservative." The first thing I did was sort of quixotic. I was going to go to Japan and send my draft board a letter from Nagasaki or Hiroshima, refusing to go. My friends were saying things like, "You can probably get a job as a

*Fannie Lou Hamer (1917-1977), field secretary of the Student Nonviolent Coordinating Committee, was an outspoken advocate for civil rights for African Americans.

westerner in Japanese movies." We had it all figured out until we got to the Japanese consulate in New York City. The woman there didn't understand what I was talking about. She said, "We don't have immigration."

I considered going in as a CO. I went to Atlanta to talk to a friend's husband. He had been in a MASH unit in Vietnam as a cardiologist. He showed me two hundred slides of Vietnam and explained to me why I couldn't go in as a CO, because you had to carry a gun to pick up the wounded – an M-16 in one hand and the wounded in the other.

I saw slides of Saigon, and of roadside fruit stands that were blown away the next day. I had had much the same experience in Mississippi. A place would look perfectly normal one day, and then it would be obliterated the next.

I did pass the test for OCS, and I would have gone to Officer Candidate School, but I would have been on the front lines. I had to believe in the war to do that. I could see from talking to the doctor in Atlanta that there was no way not to shoot people who weren't at all guilty of anything other than being in the wrong place. It was an unwinnable situation. I remember a Harvard mathematician who said, "No theorem is as complicated as this war. People who simplify it just don't get it."

So Canada made more sense, and Quebec in particular, because I wanted to be in a foreign culture, but I didn't want to be that far away from my family where they couldn't visit or I couldn't visit. My family and I had reconciled. My mother had come up north for my graduation. By that time my father and I had agreed to disagree, and we didn't talk about it. They drove me to the airport, and they knew I was going to Canada.

I flew to Montreal. I had gone earlier on a trip with a Swiss classmate from the School of Ed, Doris Winkler. She lived in Montreal. That's how I got to thinking about going there. She drove me with most of my belongings, but I returned to the States and flew in to get my landed immigrant status. I was prepared. I even had a signed, sealed chest x-ray from Harvard Medical Services. I arrived exactly at the stroke of midnight on June 30, 1967, as the fireworks were going off to celebrate Canada Day, which is July 1st. It took me about twenty minutes to go through immigration. All they wanted to know was whether I had the possibility of a job, and whether I would be a teacher or would need some more teacher training.

I had done everything possible. I was wearing – unusual for me – a jacket and tie. I even had a tiepin and a London Fog over my arm. I had a briefcase full of peanut butter and jelly sandwiches, but it was a new brief-case. I looked pretty spiffy for that crossing. A friend of mine figured I might have a headache, because I was prone to migraines, so he had given me some kind of headache tablets. I finally got through all of the hoops, and I am outside of the airport. I am clear. I'm across the border. It was like a scene from when Harriet Tubman takes that guy across the Canadian bor-der and he says, "Great God, almighty, I am free at last." I took out the vial of tablets to take one and I said, "What?" I was in shock. It was full of mari-juana. I had taken all of this incredible care in crossing the border, and this friend thought it would be funny to give me this vial of marijuana instead of the headache tablets! I immediately threw it in the garbage. I needed the aspirin more than I needed that.

There was a draft dodgers' hostel below the tracks run by Montreal Draft Resisters Counseling Center. It felt like the atmosphere from Eugene O'Neill's *The Iceman Cometh.* Everybody was waiting for landed immigrant status. They didn't trust me, because everything had happened too fast for me. I had done it in record time. I was dressed too well. They started spell-ing their names for me, thinking I would be reporting on them to Wash-ington, since I must be a CIA agent. Part of it was they were seeing me walking up and down outside the place listening to a radio. I was listen-ing to French stations, teaching myself French. It was a very paranoid en-vironment, so that's all it took.

I met a lot of interesting people, other draft dodgers. The most inter-esting was a guy who came with his wife. His lawyer had advised him to come to Montreal to stay. His wife was legally blind and pregnant. He was an art therapist on a psychiatric ward in New York City. He figured it would eventually work out to get landed immigrant status so he stayed with me and his wife delivered the baby prematurely. He would come back from the hospital each day and say, "She gained two more ounces today!" His wife's mother was a nurse and flew in from California to help them, and it eventually worked out. They were a great couple.

The most famous resister I encountered was a folk singer from Mem-phis. Jesse landed on the street with the shirt on his back and his electric guitar. As soon as he got his draft notice, he just hopped on a plane and headed straight to Montreal. He met these two guys who gave him a place to stay, and he eventually got an apartment. He had mixed feelings, because he had the same kind of southern family background I had, and the South was very pro-military. There was a wonderful song I heard him sing many times in nightclubs there entitled, "Jesus Christ Was a Teen-ager, Too." It was very funny, but he wouldn't record it, because it would offend his mother. He had a conservative streak. He had another song about twigs and seeds left at the bottom of a marijuana bag, which was really funny, too, and could have been a real best seller, another "Puff the Magic Dragon", but he wouldn't record that one either. He's stubborn that way. A lot of people, including Judy Collins and Joan Baez, sang his songs. He was a major figure in Montreal.

I helped out for a while with the counseling center. I helped one guy who was Canadian. I told him, "You just need to file for a student defer-ment. You're not even American. You're only subject to the draft if you're working in the U.S. You don't need to worry." I got him to fill his papers out and fly back. Another guy was a Marine who was probably the worst character I ever met in my life. He had a split personality with a sadistic streak. He would tell me stories about going to the zoo and tormenting the snakes. He had gotten a girl pregnant and taken the money her family had given them for an abortion and fled to Montreal. He was AWOL. One evening of talking to him was enough. I called him from outside my apart-ment where I had let him spend the night and said, "I am coming back to my apartment and I don't want to see you there anymore."

I ended up working in a school called Sir George Williams Univer-sity. It had started in a YMCA and become a university. They called it the Concrete Campus. It was an alternate to McGill. The French forced a mar-riage between Sir George and Loyola, which was run by Jesuits, and called it Concordia, because they didn't want to support two English universities. They share resources, but reluctantly. I worked in the library in the stacks, and they put me in government documents because of my background in political science at Harvard. I filed government documents during my first winter there, and it went down to thirty below.

There were a lot of draft dodgers who got employed in the university libraries. There was a kind of subterranean community. I was part of it for a time. I was very busy learning French. I ended up marrying a French Canadian, but she never spoke a word of French to me, except when she swore. I had to learn it on my own.

In my mind I was going to be a Canadian, which is why I gave up my citizenship. I wanted to go back to school, and I knew I needed a fellowship. The Canadian nationals weren't keen to give fellowships to people who were going to go back to the States, so one way of dealing with that was to give up my American citizenship, which you can do. That was another adventure. I had an argument with Arvid Holm, who was the U.S. Counsel General, who told me he would blacklist me forever, and I'd never be able to return to the U.S. I had gone to him to find out about renouncing my citizenship, and he was so offended by that, he got into this argument with me. I am not one to get into such confrontations. I was a little non-plussed. His argument was basically that I owed the country so much. I said, "Yes, but this war is totally unjust. I can't abide it and this is my protest."

It was shortly after the confrontation with Holm that I got my draft notice. I had to report to the Boston Army Base for the exam. I flew from Montreal back to Boston to take my exam. I went through the exam in Boston after having been in the clear in Canada. I had a piece of wire in my leg that I had gotten while in high school so technically I would have probably been rejected anyway. They tell you to waddle and I couldn't. The guy was checking off all of these tests, but he wasn't even looking. He wanted to get to his golf game. The wire didn't even come up. This guy was just processing us. Unless we were obviously crawling or paraplegic, we were O.K. I wasn't sure what I was going to do. If I didn't pass the exam, I wouldn't give up my citizenship. I might come back. It was part of the ambivalence.

When you pass, which I did, they give you a second form, a "moral exam," consisting mostly of questions about the Attorney General's List of Subversive Organizations. I balked. I refused to sign it. I didn't know about some of the organizations that I had to disavow. I was very polite. They were very polite, but they didn't know what to do with me so they sent me away. They rescheduled me for a week later, and I had to be interviewed by an Army Intelligence officer. I stayed in Cambridge for the week. He was a young officer, and we went over what I would and would not agree to. I still have a copy of the form in my file. "Would you agree to support the Constitution of the United States?" "Of course, it's a wonderful Constitution." "Would you say you had never been at any meetings where communists were present?" I said, "How do I know? I have been to any number of meetings." The funny thing was that, despite being young and relatively shy at the time, I guess I had a kind of confidence, because he asked me if

I wanted a lawyer, and I said, "No, but if you feel comfortable having one it's O.K. with me." I can't believe I said that. He was just very nervous.

I was very straightforward. I gave my reasons. I said, "I don't want to contribute to an Orwellian future for the United States of America." I wanted to know the national security relevance of every organization I was being asked about. "Cervantes Fraternal Society? Maybe it's a front, maybe not. Explain it to me." "I know the Ku Klux Klan. I can disagree with them. I don't want anything to do with them." "Chopin Cultural Society? He wrote the 'Revolutionary Etude', but…" So we agreed to that. I signed off on it, but left many organizations out. I have no idea what effect that had.

They next asked me about psychiatric records. I had lost a girlfriend freshman year and seen a Harvard psychiatrist. That tied them up for some time. Then I went back to Canada. I figured it would take quite a while for them to process everything, because I didn't do the ordinary things, and I was right. By the time they got back to me, I had renounced my citizenship. It was on July 11, 1967 that I became a stateless person, and I remained a stateless person for five years and four months, until becoming a Canadian citizen in 1972.

Eventually I heard from the draft board. I was re-classified. I had done everything by the letter and spirit of the law. Would I let them know if I changed my residence in Canada? I told them exactly where to find me – where I lived and where I worked. I told them I would inform them if I changed my residence. I told them I was planning to stay in Canada. I told them that I had given up my citizenship. My local draft board classified me 1-E, which I presume is still my classification, since I am still not a U.S. citizen. It's "alien not currently liable for military service." If I had come back, I would have been 1-A. I have always been in good standing with my draft board.

Once I had resolved the issue with the draft board, what I had was landed immigrant status in Canada, but I was a stateless person. I had a little white card, but I had no citizenship. I had to wait five years and four months, which was the soonest I could become a Canadian citizen. For those years I had no passport, so I could not travel outside Canada. I went to Toronto in '69 to graduate school. I taught political science and Canadian government while at Toronto, and while at York, which was essentially just up the street, I taught federal/provincial relationships.

Eventually I decided I wanted to return to the States. I have been back since '86. When I first came back, I wasn't sure about regaining my citizenship. I wanted to see where the country was. I felt at home and welcomed by some people, but I didn't know generally if there was acceptance. In 2005 even in Canada, when a group of draft dodgers got together, they got a lot of hostility from Canadians. It was another generation and they don't really understand what Vietnam was like. It's mind-boggling to me. They don't have an understanding of history.

So I waited. In 2000 I decided I would wait to see if Gore was elected in which case I would probably have tried for citizenship. I was eligible, because I'd been back in the States for well over the required five years. However, I continue to hesitate. I am not sure how people would feel about it. There's still a lot of anger around the Vietnam issues. Look what happened in '04 with Kerry's candidacy and his Vietnam record. Are there people who don't want me here, who don't want me to become an American citizen again, who want me to go back to Canada? I am not a confrontational person. I would go back.

I was even reluctant to do this interview. There's a question on the application for American citizenship that asks: "Did you ever seek to avoid military service by going overseas?" What's the answer to that for me? I would answer no. I don't know what they would think. I have this concern about how people would respond. There's been this reversion, under the Bush administration, regarding who the enemy is. I am an alien. Yes, I am white, but my status is still "other," and there has been much hostility directed at those who are "other." I continue to keep a low profile, invisible to everyone. It's a habit now. I still have my old habit of shyness, though I can speak easily to an audience of three hundred. The fact is – theoretically – I could still be hauled off to Guantanamo in the middle of the night, since I have no American citizenship. I am also subject to possible arbitrariness when it comes to my Social Security payments. It shouldn't happen, because there's a treaty between the U.S. and Canada vis a vis Social Security, but I worry about my Social Security payments, which sustain me in my retirement. It's a little nerve-wracking. Also, if you're a resident alien, you can't be out of the country for a year or you have to start all over again. You have to be here five years straight and I've been here since '86. In fact, I have been here longer than I was in Canada, but I feel more Canadian than I do American. How do you explain that? For one thing I was Canadian having been married to a French Canadian with whom I had two children who are Canadian.

I have never attempted to tell this story. It was painful, which I knew it would be, but in some ways I didn't expect. I didn't know the image of the photograph from Vietnam was going to be so painful for me to recall. The same is true of the civil rights movement memories. Thinking about seeing the bruised and battered Fannie Lee Hamer is difficult. There's a lot of emotionality attached to much of this. And then the Canada story... Americans just don't understand how different Canada is. I am glad that I came to know the country so well.

CHAPTER FOUR

THOSE WHO REFUSED

ONE GROUP OF MEN CHOSE TO REGISTER THEIR PROTEST in the most direct and immediate way possible – to stand their ground and say no - no to the draft on the home front, to fighting, to the irrational orders, and to the war effort itself on the battlefront. The price they paid for this was long-lasting, a record that would follow them throughout their lives, and often included conviction and incarceration. Though they might well have chosen another route, these men believed that they made a louder noise by raising their voices and allowing themselves to be singled out. They are often grouped with those who found a variety of other means to avoid service. Separating their response from that of other men who chose alternate approaches is an essential element of this book.

If these men were moved to act as they did by their consciences, should they be grouped with conscientious objectors? The fact of the matter is that though they, too, made a choice predicated on conscience, there *is* a difference. Those who refused to participate in the draft chose total non-cooperation with a system they believed to be corrupt, that denied everyone his right to choose his own battles. Total non-cooperation included not accepting the alternative service required of CO's. For those who were already serving, however, the choice stemmed from disillusionment with the war effort often combined with an intense desire not to be part of such an endeavor. The consequences of such a course of action were severe, so there had to be great conviction on the part of a soldier refusing to serve.

Thus, some men made their choice and took their position from the start; while for others, it took some time inside the military for them to reach a position of defiance and non-cooperation. Among the men I interviewed who made this difficult choice prior to being drafted, several found compelling and powerful inspiration in the civil rights movement. Each man engaged in work that fought social injustice, and it was that fight that fueled their willingness to go to jail to support their principles. They received encouragement and support from the examples of Martin Luther

King, who saw jail as a necessity in the face of the laws and actions he wholeheartedly opposed, and of Muhammed Ali who refused to serve and whose inability to obtain conscientious objector status as a Black Muslim resulted in his being sentenced to five years in prison. He remained out on bail while his appeal was pending and his case eventually went all the way to the Supreme Court. Its decision was that he, in fact, met the requirements for conscientious objection, thus reversing his conviction.

It is also important to recognize that there was so much opposition to the Vietnam War, and so much resentment towards those in authority who were waging it, that those who served time in prison were neither necessarily resented nor mistreated by their fellow inmates. They believed that the principal difficulty in going to jail was that it ended their efforts to pursue social justice and to be free.

There is a myth that those in the military who refused to follow orders or protested against the war were isolated from one another. The 2005 film produced and directed by David Zeiger about the anti-war movement within the military, entitled *Sir, No Sir* comprehensively explodes this distortion of history. Through a combination of archival footage of protests by servicemen and women, along with interviews with those who participated in the effort to stop the war, the film captures this extraordinary movement in all of its activism and bravery.

The reality of the Vietnam Era is that unprecedented numbers of people resisted military service in a variety of ways – before being drafted and while serving. Here is how the numbers break down:

DRAFT LAW VIOLATORS:
- 209,517 men were formally accused of violating draft laws.
- 360,000 more are estimated to have also violated the law, but were never formally accused
- 25,000 indictments were handed down
- 8,750 were convicted
- fewer than 4,000 served prison time

MILITARY RESISTERS:
- 1.5 million instances of AWOL and desertion documented by Pentagon
- 500,000–550,000 – official estimate by Pentagon and Ford Administration of AWOL and deserters

Adding other types of anti-war activities for which service members were prosecuted significantly increases these figures.

I have chosen to include just a few of the stories that could be told here. Others can be found in numerous outstanding books, including *Hell No, We Won't Go: Resisting the Draft During the Vietnam War* by Sherry Gottlieb. Thankfully, such books thoroughly illuminate these choices, since my resources in pursuing these stories were severely limited.

It is important to acknowledge, in terms of the timeliness of these testimonies, that in recent years several men accused of deserting forty years ago have been arrested, though their stories have not been widely publicized. Some theorize that this crackdown, undertaken by the Bush Administration's Justice Department, coincided with efforts to dissuade soldiers from deserting their posts at a time when manpower was an issue. It is also possible to see these arrests as evidence of our country's continuing difficulty with achieving any meaningful closure about the war in Vietnam. In either case, the testimonies in this chapter illuminate a time and an experience that resulted from responses, visceral and intense, to circumstances beyond the men's control.

Judson Brown

Judson's most recent gig was as a group quarters supervisor with the U.S. Census Bureau's 2010 Decennial operations with a home base in Pittsfield, Massachusetts and territory throughout western Massachusetts. His freelance writing career, developed after some twenty-five years as a community journalist covering everything from arts to education, is on a gentle simmer. He and his wife, an elementary school teacher, are parents of a twenty-nine and thirty-two year old. He is actively involved in St. John's Episcopal Church and in his small community of Laurel Park in Northampton, Massachusetts. He also sings with much enthusiasm in a local chorus.

I grew up at Phillips Academy Andover as a faculty brat. My Dad was an English teacher and I had a very protected childhood. The prep school campus was like a park. My parents got a place for next-to-nothing on the coast of Maine when I was a child, so in the summer months we went to this primitive, old island and lived a basic, wonderful, summer idyll. I was clearly very privileged, and all of this happened without my folks ever really having any serious money.

Politically I had no consciousness through high school. In 1965 I went to the University of Pennsylvania and had a huge awakening. I hit the streets of Philadelphia, and suddenly the whole civil rights movement was happening. The movement was in full flower, and I had hardly ever even seen a black person. I remember being almost intoxicated by the urban environment. My story with the war really begins with my awakening to some sense of social justice. I plunged into urban issues. Through that work my political consciousness was changed.

Right after I graduated I went to work for Philadelphia's *Evening Bulletin* and within six months I had been recruited to work for a black community organization in West Philadelphia. I left a remarkable career opportunity at the *Bulletin* and went to work for this charismatic black man, Herman Wrice, who had started a group called the Young Great Society. He needed a writer. Herman was very savvy, and he pulled me in when I went to interview him for a story. Before the interview was over, he had offered me a job. He wanted me to write a chronicle of the work he was doing with gangs. He was a former gang member who had almost died when he was caught in a crossfire. He was committed to turning gang kids around by exposing them to the business and university communities and giving them opportunities they never even dreamed of. My job was to chronicle these gang members going through the maze he had set up for them.

While I was in college I had a 2-S deferment, but in 1969 I drew the number twelve in the lottery. It scared the shit out of me. There is no heroism in my story. I got the number twelve, and I had gotten married by then. My wife, Sandy, and I had considered various possibilities. The Peace Corps was a possibility once the number hit. Our first apartment downtown had been occupied by Edward Rendell who had been the immediate past director of the Democratic National Committee, and is now governor of Pennsylvania. My first ploy was to duck into the Army Reserves, and somehow Ed got me into his unit. I joined the Reserves and started to go to monthly meetings. I had long hair, and I remember putting grease in my hair on Sundays to go to the Guard meetings.

Meanwhile I continued to work at the Young Great Society. I didn't want to have anything to do with the war, so I applied to be a CO. I wrote about my work in the ghetto community of West Philadelphia called Mantua. It was more intellectual than felt, but I put together a case for being a conscientious objector, presenting the work I was doing as a reflection of my social conscience. I also had partaken peripherally in the protest movement.

I remember a defining moment sitting around a kitchen table with a couple of high school friends in New Jersey. These guys were saying, "We're going to go for it. We're going to join the military. We're going to be soldiers, that's how we're dealing with this." I wasn't going with them. I didn't know my path. They knew theirs. They both went into the Marines. Then I remember my uncle saying, "This is the defining event of your generation, and you should go. You should be part of this." I heard him, but when the time came and the number came up I was scrambling. I knew I wasn't going, but I saw no clear path.

I didn't get the CO. They probably saw me as an opportunist. Drugs figure in the next chapter of this. I went up to Breadloaf (a renowned summer Writer's Conference affiliated with Middlebury College) with my writings from the Young Great Society. There was always this ambition to be a writer. It was a heady time for me, and it was enhanced by some heavy doses of hashish. By the time I came out of Breadloaf, I had decided, in the hashish euphoria I was in by then, that I was going to "Fuck 'em." I was going to go to basic training, but I was going to be a resister. Maybe it was hubris...

The basic training was for my service in the Reserves. My CO application had delayed things a bit, but after Breadloaf I was called and told to report to Fort Jackson in South Carolina. As I've said, I had decided I wasn't going to cooperate. I didn't know what the consequences would be and in a very immature way I felt invincible. My wife was terrified. She could tell you the story from the outside looking in. I was very young when I got married and I was hardly grown up at this point. Having grown up in the environment I did, and marrying early, I had a lot of immaturity to work out. But I was exuberant and invincible and on this "trip."

When I got to South Carolina I hooked up with this radical little "cell." There was a gay guy and there were lots of drugs in the house. I had a few days before I had to report. I didn't show up exactly when I was supposed to and I was befriended by this group and encouraged by them in the course of action I was about to embark upon. I decided to keep a diary. I showed up for basic training in the pouring rain and I tell the story in here (Judson reads from his almost forty-year-old account of his experience):

> *I was barefoot with hair looping down my neck, shirt open. Some friends left me off at the end of the Commanding General's driveway. I walked up, rang the doorbell. The general's wife answered. "Hello, Ma'am. I'm a friend of the General's, and I'd like to talk to him. Is the General in?" No, he wasn't, but would I like to come in? My toes sunk in the carpet, leaving little brown tracks.*
>
> *"You see, ma'am, I don't believe in war and I'd like to talk with the General and tell him what I intend to do. I've never actually met your husband, but..."*
>
> *She poured me a Coke. We talked. I explained that I had joined the Army Reserves a year and a half ago, had applied soon after for a discharge as a conscientious objector, but that had been refused and I had been considering other routes, including leaving the country, but had decided instead to report for duty and immediately refuse all orders.*
>
> *"To sort of 'test the System'?" she quizzed.*
>
> *"Not really for show, Ma'am. Just to state my case, that I can't remain in the Army in good conscience and take the consequences."*
> *She nodded dubiously.*

"Would you like a ham and cheese sandwich?" she asked, going into the kitchen. I accepted, drawing little circles of sweat and grime on the polished table while she cut big hunks of ham. She opened the icebox.

"You say you're opposed to war?" she called in. The icebox door shut.

"Yes, Ma'am. You see, I think the world's coming to an end, and..."

"Yes, well. It says that in the Bible, you know," she stated, placing the thick sandwich before me. We talked for about an hour. I told her I believed in non-violence the way Gandhi practiced it in India.

"Yes, but where do you think this country would be if..." I washed down a leaf of lettuce. "Would you like to live in India or China?"

"I don't really think that's the point." I swigged down the Coke. "Ah, do you have any cigarettes, Ma'am?"

She handed me a Parliament. We smoked and talked some more. We got along very well, and in a while, found that we agreed on many things, but that we just phrased things differently. After a while she drove me down to the Reception Station.

"Good luck," she said as I was getting out.

"Thank you, Mrs. Coleman." I started to walk up the sandy road.

"By the way," she called through the window, "keep to that non-violent thing." She smiled. I made a peace sign. She drove away.

I went to the Reception Station. I told them, "I am not going to get my hair cut." I was number 104. (Judson resumes reading from his diary):

"Hey, 104, you didn't bring no shoes or nothin'?" They laughed.

"You crazy." They sat around in their fresh fatigues drinking Cokes and eating Oreos, playing pinochle. Puerto Ricans, Chicanos, Blacks. A group of Arcadians from New Orleans. Some of them had finished high school; most hadn't. The Puerto Ricans couldn't speak English. One Chicano kept saying he wanted to kill a Jap.

Tuesday the Commanding Officer called me into his office and told me that at exactly 0900 he was going to give me an order to cut my hair and begin processing for training. Two hours later he called me in, issued me the direct order, and read the maximum sentence I could receive for refusing: five years hard labor. I refused. That afternoon I was ushered into the stockade.

I was looking at five years. I was still euphoric. I haven't looked at this since I wrote it and picking it up is strange. There are parts that are actually O.K., but a lot of it is immature. I was in a kind of fantasyland. I was living off this idea that I am this privileged guy; they can't do anything to me.

There were a bunch of losers in there – me among them. I was the only one there who was "politically motivated". Most of these guys were high school dropouts, working class from all over the South. Some of them had been to Vietnam and, in fact, Vietnam runs through here in the things I hear. Like on the golf course detail, I heard about mutilations, and it was all completely surreal. There was no pain involved for me. I was observing and listening to these guys who were much less privileged. What you find is this privileged, preppy guy who thinks he is invincible meeting these loser guys and, in some cases, war heroes.

While I was in there, I was keeping notes. I saw my time there as an opportunity to chronicle this experience. Sometimes I would get asked why I was there:

> *"How many times ya'll been AWOL, Brown?" I'd be asked.*
> *"None. I refused an order to go to basic training."*
> *"No shit, why?"*
> *"I'm, ah, well, I'm morally opposed to the Army."*
> *"Dig it. Fuck the Army."*

And I'd try to explain exactly how it was more complicated, but whatever I said came out sounding very contrived and ridiculously confused. I soon gave up my explanation altogether, realizing that if there was any difference between my "objecting" to the Army and merely resenting it like everybody else, it was a difference of erudition, not heart. It was fine to be "opposed to war" – I suppose I always shall be, and shall always feel compelled to explain myself – but I realized soon after I entered the stockade that that particular belief had nothing to do with being a prisoner, except perhaps by way of explaining why I became one. At one point in my diary I quote Dietrich Bonhoeffer:

> *In general a prisoner is no doubt inclined to make up, through an exaggerated sentimentality, for the soullessness and lack of warmth in his surroundings and perhaps he may react too strongly to anything sentimental that affects him personally.*

I think that is the dignified way of saying that that is how I was. It was a hyper-real moment for me, and I was taking it in aesthetically, emotionally and in terms of social learning. I was treated decently. I am above it all, of course. Everyone is a little bit caricatured in here. I keep going off on these lyrical passages, trying to evoke some kind of beauty out of the place – a surreal painting of the whole event. There are some places where I was able to capture what was really going on:

Alan Vencomo is a Puerto Rican dude (I'd gotten to calling everyone "dude" while I was working in Mantua with black people) *from the Bronx. He served in Vietnam for eleven months until he was wounded in both knees and got a "compassionate" leave, returning to a hospital in Florida to get a steel spring put in his right knee and a small rod in his left. When he was released, they ordered him back to 'Nam, to serve his last remaining month. He hauled ass. Got caught. Now he has sat for fifty-seven days in the stockade awaiting a General Court Martial and he hasn't yet had his charges read to him or had any word when his trial will be. His skin is brown and smooth; pupils dark, hard mahogany; hair black and wiry and parted down the middle. He talks in a rolling Bronx Spanish-English that sounds like marbles rolling down a board.*

"I'm a leader, man. Whenever we went out on patrols I'm in front. They thought I was a sergeant, man, and I told them, 'Man, I'm only an E-2' [private]. *But I was out front, so they thought I was a sergeant. Later they wanted to make me one, but I said, "Man, fuck you." And* when his knee was shot, they gave him a medal. Then his other knee was shot, and they gave him another.

"The medals don't mean shit, man. You can't buy a cup of coffee with 'em. I don't wear the damn medals, man."

He starts to talk to me about 'Nam, and about the hooch he built over there, and I tried to get poetic:

Alan was a leader. In the field he'd tell the new recruits, "Be cool, man. Don't try to be war lords." Alan concentrated on survival. Kept his medals in cans. He went about his business like a businessman and got thirty-one "kills." He went about his killing and survived.

Now he went out thirty days to the field. And back for ten. And out thirty. And he went out to the reeds and the quick knives that flashed in the mud. And he lay low in the reeds and hugged the bunkers. Then in thirty days back to the base and to his hooch, buried fourteen feet in the ground, which he built in three months with his hands, and in which he survived.

He dug a hole fourteen feet deep. Then he planted 9x9 beams and reinforced them with steel plates. Then he poured concrete for a floor and concrete for walls. Then he built a six-foot thick rocket-proof roof with the ramp he took off an old Marine amphibian landing craft, and a sheet of plastic they use for runways, and chicken wire and sandbags. Then he poured concrete over all this, like gravy, then bulldozed earth and worms and crushed grass over the works. Finally a friend drove a fifty-ton tank over the works, and the hooch held, the beams didn't splinter. As a last touch, he got an old submarine door to seal the entranceway, which made the hooch, at last, grenade-proof, bomb-proof, gook-proof, death-safe.

He lived there, in ten-day spells, for eleven months. Once, when there was an attack, and GI's were going crazy and running mad along the bunkers, Alan unlatched the sub door and yelled, "In here! In here!" They jumped off the bunkers, one hundred and fifteen GI's, scrambled and packed into the hooch and lay there, in piles and layers, breathing, until the pounding and yelling ceased above and, through seven feet of runway and ram and chicken-wire and worms, the world was still, and there were the dead and the Asians retreated to the trees. The hooch held. And all the little hooches in the ground lay quiet beneath a dark solitary mountain, called Nudy Bah Dinh, the Black Virgin, and a distance from which "you could spit into Cambodia."

I go on to talk about his love affair with a French Vietnamese girl. I am sure he was leading me on, but he talks about his hooch. "I love that place man. You know, when you build something with your own hands, you love it more." Then I asked him, "Were you changed by Vietnam, Alan?"

"Ain't got no more heart. Ain't got no feelings anymore. If you fell out that window and cracked your head, I wouldn't give a damn. I saw so many men cut down there, and there, and there." He points at imaginary corpses. "Gone. Dead. And you can't cry over every death. And it just don't mean nothin' anymore.

Alan, with his broken knees, head thumping with rockets, came home – one month short – to Florida to get his knees fixed. They fixed them. Then they said, "O.K., go on back, soldier." So he split and went to his wife and two kids in the Bronx. But he couldn't get into that anymore. That was gone. He was caught, put in the stockade. Here he is for 57 days. He laughs a lot and makes jokes and people think he's funny. He always got along. He's a leader.

But the prisoners don't see him at other times, wandering around the barracks with his mahogany eyes, all sad and dumb and dazed and shiny hard, talking about his hooch he made with his hands.

I was really listening. I had been doing this kind of writing in West Philadelphia, and so I was continuing this act of being the recorder of these lives that were very different from mine. Here's what I wrote when Alan left us:

"In Vietnam, man, we were all brothers. Black, white, Spanish. We had to stick together, man. And I..." He rubbed his arm showing his amber color. "I could go between black and white."

Everybody at the stockade loved Alan. Whites. Blacks. Puerto Ricans. Alan had all our blood in him. He was happy, or seemed so, and perhaps the prisoners were drawn to that. He was empty and lonely. Maybe it's that that drew us so. He was true. Of course, no one will miss him. It is as if one of the barbs has fallen with a clink off the wire...

Out on the golf course detail I heard some horrible stories:

Then he looked to the ground, and his spade sliced into the earth, and a brown weed shaped like an asterisk popped out. We went along, popping asterisks, as Carl told me how he lopped off Gook's ears after he killed 'em. Said he had a whole string of ears in his hooch, and for each set he had a medal. A tall, tanned sergeant, the greenskeeper as it turned out, was standing by us. "Yeah, man," he chuckled. "Guys used to slice off the gooks ears and penises and they'd sew the ears to their fatigues and wear the dicks on their belts." He burst out laughing. I looked at him stunned

"No shit," the sergeant winked.

"You're sick!" I shouted. "You're both sick!" We argued. Carl said Gooks weren't human beings and didn't have any feelings or values. I protested. They tried to tell me what war was like.

"*Can you describe pain?*" *the sergeant asked me. "I try to tell people what it was like, but how do you describe awful continuous pain? You can't." He said when he first got to Vietnam, his buddy was lost one night and found the next day, skinned alive. And Carl described decapitated GI's hanging from tree limbs.*

"*You learn to hate Gooks, man,*" *said Carl.*

The sergeant put a hand on my shoulder and asked, "Have you ever heard of revenge?"

Crushed, I told them if the Vietnamese weren't human, or didn't have morals or values, how were the Americans any different? Butchery was butchery. We moved down the fairway, squishing mushrooms under our boots. But soon the conversation had become intolerable for all three of us.

There was another character, a man named J. He was a musician. He played ten instruments, including drums, guitar, trombone, trumpet, and flute. He was drafted after a year and a half at Julliard. In Vietnam he minstrelled about with his guitar. He wrote ballads and here's one he sang for us:

I'd like to see the Prezident
In an Army hospital bed
With a broken arm and a fractured leg
And shrapnel in his head...

Then one day he fell off a forty-foot tower, busted his pelvis, and was shipped home. Spent five months in traction, and when he was released, flew the coop. Went back to the City and joined up with his band again. Played a few nightclubs. Trucked down to Ft. Lauderdale. Then he got picked up on the Gator Run (a weekly sweep of Florida for AWOL'S). When I got to the stockade, J. had been there forty-four days already, awaiting a Special Court Martial.

Sitting on the concrete steps of the barracks, J. was stoned on painkillers he took because his pelvis ached. He missed his instruments. He said at home he had millions of them. So he played himself, slapped his knees like bongos, made twanging noises imitating a guitar, blew air through the hole in his teeth as if he were a clarinet:

I'd like to give the Prezident
His very own M-16
Send him into the woods

The woods he's never seen.
Then I'm sure that he'll be back
To tell you what he saw.
He'll tell you that he's had enough
And that he wants no more....WAR!

I thought if I were going to title this next piece, I'd call it "Yentser's Hat."

This evening in line-up Sergeant Ace came up to Yentser and took the hat off Yentser's head, thumbed the rim back and forth, stuck his fingers through the moth holes and the cigarette burn holes.

"Burn it, Yentser," he barked.

Now Yentser's hat had become a weird symbolic diadem. He'd sliced the cloth up, the cloth of the brim, and worked the cardboard out through the scar, leaving the brim soft as flesh. And the brim flopped over his eyes and flapped in the breeze, and his red hair licked out like flames through the holes in the top. The hat seemed nearly organic and stood out in a row of trim caps like a vegetable.

Now the order came down from Ace. "Burn it!" In the barracks, Yentser emptied a butt can and put old cigarette packs in the bottom and lit them and dangled his hat in the flames. It caught with a sizzle, flamed and bubbled and began to melt and drip back down the sides of the can and the thick black smoke smelling terribly of roasted nylon, clouded up in the can. Finally the hat was just a large crusty ash with the texture of a meringue cookie. I got a matchbox and we broke the large crust down and filled the box with the little burnt, shriveled up pieces of hat and wrote on the side, "Yentser's hat died October 7, 1971." I'll carry the casket and keep it in my footlocker and remember Yentser, face filled with flames, gazing wild-eyed over the cremation.

I think it was a final example of juvenile revolt against the system – person against the machine. The environment was totally dehumanizing and these guys were trying to live their lives against this backdrop. We were all in it together. It was solidarity. To me there was something about all of it that was exotic. Coming out of my past there was the exoticism of the blacks' efforts in West Philadelphia and then this. I was drawn to something so other, something so beyond what I had known. I also saw this opportunity to use my descriptive abilities to try to capture this.

I applied for an "Undesirable Discharge" while I was in the stockade. My wife, Sandy had hustled around and found out information we needed to know about what I could do. My brother was a lawyer in D.C. and somehow he made an intervention. To this day we are not quite clear what he did. They wanted me out of there without a court martial – out of the stockade and out of the Reserves. I was branded "undesirable." I remember the feeling of being kicked out the door and being barefoot again. I went back to the little marijuana house and it was over. I was done with the military after five weeks.

I continue to this day to have enormous respect for those who went to Vietnam. My friend, Jim Munroe, recently described his experience including being seriously wounded in a grenade explosion. It changed his life entirely. He became a priest. I think back to my uncle saying, "This is the defining experience of your generation. You ought to be part of that." In a way I suppose I was. But I didn't suffer a loss. I got through it without injury. I got something from it – a rich encounter with folks I hadn't seen in my life. As a journalist, and in the work I do now, I try to break out of the class crap and try to be with folks who have other things to speak to you about – courage, character – and it is a privilege to take it in, to respect it and to honor it and magnify it. It was all a part of my process of coming of age.

In retrospect, if I had gone where my classmates from high school went, it would have been gut-wrenching. I don't have any sense of courage about what I did. This is how I took it on, and I was very lucky that I was able to avoid it. I just respect those who took it on and served in the war.

Steve Trudel

Steve works in a program called Moving Forward that intervenes in domestic violence. He is a senior counselor who predominantly works with men, but also women. His work takes him into the court system where he helps defendants who have been served restraining orders to understand the legal ramifications. He runs support groups and endeavors to change attitudes and behaviors. He also is an avid gardener and a cappella singer. He is fifty-nine-years old.

One of the things that influenced my decision to reject the draft was the idea of power and its effect in the world. Access to power is one of the carrots that is held out to boys as we're raised, and we find power either appealing or appalling. Most people find it appealing; to get things other people can't have through the use of power.

But it wasn't immediately appealing to me because my father was tyrannical and abusive to anyone who didn't go along with his ideas, and he was a captain in the military, a very powerful and influential person in his world. I was thrust into considerations of ambivalence around power. I knew I could have lots of things if I went for them, and yet, I was the object of power turned mean and it led me to have a really sharp awareness of social issues, social injustice in particular.

We had a very comfortable, upper-middle class life. My mother's family was affluent and I had the opportunity to see all the manifestations of the upper class life including domestic servants who were, for the most part, working-class and people of color. I certainly had a sense of guilt from an early age about money, because I could see that other people didn't have it. I was thrust into those considerations without really having a choice pretty early on. Everything was gray to me, and I was constantly thinking about the contingencies that I was making decisions about.

Because I had been the object of unfairness I had an intense need for fairness. I think there's something unique in someone who has been the object of power. In the work that I do now with men who are abusive, and in the domestic violence program, the people who usually get it quickest are people who have experienced abuse themselves. There's kind of a unique knowledge that comes to us and it really short-circuits that gratification, that thrill, that 0 to 60 rush that everybody likes to feel. God knows when you're a victim of abuse you're going to try to turn that around on someone else because you don't know what else to do, but it never worked for me.

Culturally speaking, I was definitely to the left. I was listening to Bob Dylan. I was listening to Phil Ochs. Like many of us, I knew the Country Joe and the Fish chant.* Anti-war songs just really stood out to me. I was predisposed to come to the conclusions that I later came to.

One of the pivotal sea changes for me was that I went from public to private high school when I was seventeen. At Williston Academy [in Easthampton, Massachusetts], I became very close friends with a fellow student whose father was pretty high up in the government. His father was involved in the secret wars in Laos and Cambodia and John told me one afternoon that the things we had spoken about, if told, would land him on the front page of *Newsweek*. It really blew my mind to realize that here I was talking to someone who had this knowledge and it could have that much of an impact. He was terrified and conflicted and obviously opposed to what was going on.

So I already knew that we were being lied to about Vietnam and I was then introduced to conscientious objection through Quakerism while I was at Williston. I was in school with the sons of Frances Crowe[†], and Barbara Gilbert, who were both Quakers and draft counselors. These women were mentors and very dear to me. I'd already been aware that there were options besides signing up for the draft, since one of my mentors from before I went to Williston was head of the draft board in Glens Falls [New York]. This was a man who really took me on as a son. He was the father I would have liked to have, and I think he recognized that. He was artistic and very intelligent. He took me to the Saratoga Performing Arts Center and recognized the needs that I had that weren't being met. I've often wondered if one of the reasons he got on the draft board was to keep children he knew out of the war.

While attending Williston I went to a War Resisters' League conference with Frances Crowe and got to see people who had a long-standing

<hr>

*From the song "I Feel Like I'm Fixin' to Die Rag" by Country Joe and the Fish – "And it's one, two, three,/What are we fighting for ?/Don't ask me, I don't give a damn./Next stop is Vietnam./And it's five, six, seven/ Open up the pearly gates./ Well, there ain't no time to wonder why,/Whoopee! we're all gonna die."

†Frances Crowe's interview appears in Chapter Seven, "Those Who Loved, Supported and Counseled."

history with choosing to obey a higher power rather than simply follow-ing orders. What do you do when you're given an order that's not right? Do you just follow it or do you reject it? I concluded that I had an obliga-tion to not follow an order when it's morally bankrupt, when it's against the rules of humanity. Older people introduced me to this essential idea. I think that mentors were sorely missing in the peace movement. There weren't a lot of older people who were saying it's okay to do this - you can follow your heart. I think I was incredibly privileged in that way.

I decided that I was going to get conscientious objector literature dis-played in the college counseling office at Williston, because they had in-formation about signing up for the draft in there. The idea of equal distribution of information came from that conference. It turned out to be an incredibly difficult thing for me to do. I had to negotiate with the head-master, who I'm sure was pro-war. He did everything he could to keep me from being able to do it. In fact, he didn't want me to go to the conference even though my parents had given me permission. I remember breaking down in tears in his office. That's how important it was to me, and he fi-nally relented. Again I experienced the theme of someone having power over me.

When I registered for the draft at eighteen, I strongly considered be-ing a conscientious objector. I thought that that was at least one way that I could live with myself. I had friends who were CO's, who I had gone to Williston with and who hadn't gone to college. But as a result of the in-formation that I had from my friend, John, about the secret wars in Cam-bodia and Laos, I came to the conclusion that, "I don't think I even want to be a CO. I don't want to cooperate with this system at all. I think that it's wrong and I won't recognize its legitimacy by participating. I have to choose something else."

I got a number that was in the two hundreds, but it was irrelevant to me because I was deciding that I was not going to be a part of that system. At the same time, in the spring of 1970 when I was at Hobart College, we succeeded in getting ROTC to leave the campus by non-violently occupy-ing its offices. We had a non-violent community of people who were against the war. We were the coordinators for the Washington, D.C. peace demonstration in the spring of '71 because we had shown the leadership and ability to think reasonably at an earlier demonstration in Washington.

Knowing then, and even more later, what was going on in the Nixon administration to root out the leaders of the anti-war movement, there's no doubt there were functionaries working for the FBI who wanted to know about me. I'll add, just as an aside, we exposed an agent provocateur on our campus – Tommy the Traveler. He was working for the local sheriff's department and for the FBI as one of the many COINTELPRO (Counter Intelligence Program) people who were sent out to destroy the peace movement on college campuses like Kent State and Jackson State.

On our campus he got a naïve freshman to firebomb the ROTC office after we had gotten them off campus. They were going to do this all on May 1st. That's when all the shit happened. That's when Kent State happened. It happened all across the country. They wanted to stop us. It was war strategy. We saw the explosion at the ROTC office happen and we knew who did it. I was actually the one who exposed this guy. My friends all got dragged into the sheriff's department as if they were the ones who had done the firebombing and Tommy the Traveler was seen in the parking lot by one of my friends. I had already been incredibly suspicious of him and had actually tried to get people to turn away from him because he was nuts. He carried a hand grenade around, a training hand grenade, and he would pull the pin and throw it to people as a joke. It just seemed really sick to me. He was claiming to be an SDS regional organizer. That was his cover, and my attitude was that we didn't need outsiders to help us.

It was also in the spring of 1970 when Richard Nixon announced to the world that we had, in fact, made some incursions into Cambodia. He had that ridiculous picture of himself with rice or something, telling the American people how we had to go in to keep the Communists from their food sources, which I knew was total bullshit.

I decided to send my draft card back to the State Department with the War Resisters' League. I had hoped that thousands and thousands of young men, from college campuses, which obviously were very privileged places, would show how seriously we were opposed to this war. It turned out there were only about a thousand of us who did it in the entire country, which was kind of depressing, but John Mitchell refused to accept the draft cards when they were sent to him. I thought of it as the war of rejections. We were rejecting the system and he was rejecting us. I believe that they went on display at various colleges that spring.

I had made my decision because I felt identified with the people we were killing. I felt terribly conflicted about even being in college while others were being sent off to war. I left college after my sophomore year.

There were a number of other things that were going on for me at this point. One was the onset of narcolepsy, which severely interrupted my ability to succeed as a student. Another was having PTSD from being beaten as a child by my father. I was trying to come to terms with that in a different way, but there was the backdrop of the Vietnam War constantly in my face re-traumatizing me because Richard Nixon – my father wouldn't let us call him Tricky Dick; we could call him the president in the house – was more of the same. My dad was completely pro-war. All of his investments in the stock market were in the war machine. My mother was basically a pacifist, but she never spoke out. Certainly we were raised as pacifists. I was always taught not to start a fight. I was taught to love, to cooperate. I was taught to tell the truth. I knew my mother did not feel the same way as my father, but she could not have spoken up against him.

I never really thought about what might happen next after sending in the card. I was twenty-years-old and I was incredibly distracted by other psychological processes. I think that when you're the victim of abuse, your talents and light are incredibly compromised. The drama of war acted as a constant reminder of my own abuse. I definitely knew I could go to jail for sending in the card. I was not going to flee the country. I could have worked against the war in Canada, but I felt that I had an obligation in the same way as any young person who joins the military because they love their country and they want to protect it.

I never got my card back. That was my way of being a soldier. I definitely felt very clear about that, and I knew that I could come back to western Massachusetts and be with Quakers, with older people and with a community of people who would be working tirelessly to end the war, which is what I did. I dropped out and I came here and did exactly that until the war ended.

So at any point, I could have gone to jail. It wasn't what I wanted to do, but I would have gone to jail. That's how I would have followed my conscience. As I said in the beginning, I was incredibly caught up in fairness. I knew there were people who were going to war, because they had no privilege. They had no out, and I could not live with that double standard. That was also one of the reasons why I left college. I wasn't looking forward to going to jail. I was scared shitless by the prospect. I knew it would probably wreck my life, but I also knew I could die if I went to war. I have to add that I didn't believe I had a future. This is something that comes as a result of abuse also.

I had cousins who were in Vietnam. They'd been raised in a military family and went. They had always presented for me a real image of what it meant to be a real man. They seemed to have that talent of getting around in the world and using power in that way. I found it very appealing as a young person and I felt very conflicted by it. I was fucked up.

When you're raised up in a family where the love and caring that's supposed to protect you is not there... I honestly felt that I knew a little bit of what it was like to be at war, because I was being attacked. My own father was terrorizing me. I couldn't anticipate when I would get beaten and these were not small situations. These were beatings, brutal beatings. I really didn't think ahead. I couldn't even frankly imagine graduating from college. I didn't know what I was going to do. There were a lot of people who were saying, because of the ecological situation, that everything was doomed. I heard a radical environmentalist, Paul Erhlich, speak at our college, and he said, "My wife and I don't even have insurance policies." There was a lot of that word out there. "We're on the edge of apocalypse." Not apocalypse, but annihilation. That certainly fit with me. It felt like wow, shit, that's what my life has felt like.

In a war like World War II, where there was a compelling need to do the right thing, there were people who were putting their lives on the line because others were having their lives taken from them by fascists. Was it a just war? Could there be a just war? I am willing to think about that idea, because I think that it would be facile and ignorant of me not to think about what you do when confronted with genocide, for example. What do you do? I think I would have been an ambulance driver. e.e cummings had become one of my heroes and as a pacifist during World War I, that was how he served.

Was it fair that people had the option to work the system and get out? Everyone potentially had that option, but some of us were exposed to that information and supported by family and community in a different way. I was certainly not supported by my family to make the choices I did. I never talked with my father about whether or not he wanted me to go to war. I think he would have had to admit that he didn't want me to die.

After his own experience in World War II, he was clearly traumatized. He came back with Post-Traumatic Stress Disorder. I lived with a man who was PTSD all the time, who was agoraphobic and self-medicated with alcohol. I have come to understand that at least a good part of the driving force in his need to be in control was how much his life was not in control in the war. He was a captain, responsible for other people's lives. He never talked about the war. In my whole life, I remember him once or twice talking about it and convulsing and crying and not being able to even tell me the stories of what he had participated in.

Given that this story is in part about the draft lottery, to say that it was the luck of the draw that I was not prosecuted for sending my draft card to the State Department has a certain ironic sound to it, doesn't it? As I think about the period of time in which our cards were sent back, Spring 1970, even just a few of the U. S. government's activities may account for why our protest was treated in the way it was. There had been an organized plan to disrupt the peaceful student protests of the Vietnam War which had culminated in, to name just three examples, the firebombing of Hobart's empty ROTC building (a month-long peaceful student occupation of that office had already resulted in the Corps moving to an off-campus location) and the shootings of unarmed students at Kent and Jackson State. The Kent State protest, which resulted in the slaying of four students by the National Guard, was triggered by Nixon's admission that the U.S. had invaded Cambodia to win "the just peace we desire," although we had been involved in secret wars in both Cambodia and Laos for some time. Also, let's not forget that in November of 1969 the largest anti-war demonstration this country had known, occurred in Washington D.C. After the meeting in New Haven that called for a national student strike, early May saw students striking on campuses all over the country.

In this context a protest of 1,000 men gains perspective. I had been told that Attorney General John Mitchell, who would later serve a nineteen-month jail term for his involvement in Watergate, refused to accept the delivery of the 1,000 draft cards. Perhaps not prosecuting the protesters was part of a strategy to diminish the impact.

Leaving college one year later to actively participate in anti-war organizing in western Massachusetts felt like the only choice I had in order to live with myself morally. I could not tolerate staying in school while others were dying in Vietnam. I was also terrified of the prospect of going to jail and did not stop worrying about that for many years. In the years leading up to my entrance to the University of Massachusetts in 1980, however, I felt that I had conducted myself in a way consistent with the words of Bob Dylan when he sang, "but to live outside the law you must be honest." As a student in the University Without Walls at UMass, I pursued a self-directed degree in Human Services and graduated cum laude in the spring of 1985, fifteen years after sending my draft card back to the U.S. State Department. I plan, sometime in the future, to discover, under the Freedom of Information Act, whether the FBI gathered information about me during those anti-war years.

What's the song? "It's always the poor who go to war." That's Kurt Weill. We know that. Privileged people for the most part find ways out. Look at Michael Moore (in *Fahrenheit 9/11*) asking senators would your son go and the aide was looking at him, like what are you nuts? What kind of a question is that? There it is.

Randy Kehler

Randy grew up in Scarsdale, New York. He is sixty-six and lives in Colrain, Massachusetts, with his wife, Betsy Corner. Four years ago they began sharing their house with three friends in a community living arrangement they are all hoping will continue to last for many years. Randy has devoted most of his adult life to public policy organizing and advocacy on a range of issues including renewable energy, nuclear disarmament, and money in politics. In his late fifties, Randy took what he refers to as a "working sabbatical" during which he was employed for five years as a home healthcare aide, helping to take care of elderly folks in local communities where he lives. He says, "It was very rewarding, very satisfying work." Since then he has moved back into the public arena with a project he has initiated called "Promoting Active Nonviolence," which he says has involved a range of approaches to doing just that. These include speaking in high schools and colleges, organizing a documentary film series, leading community seminars, and helping to coordinate a local grassroots campaign to retire an aged nuclear power plant ten miles from his home. Randy and Betsy have a daughter who lives with her husband a few miles down the road.

When I think about what led me down the path I took with respect to the Vietnam War and draft, the first thing that comes to mind is what happened during my time at Exeter where I spent my last two high school years. What I witnessed we would now call psychological torture. I had a Jewish roommate, and some classmates of ours teased him unmercifully. He was teasable, but what got them was that he was Jewish and wouldn't admit it. "You're Jewish. We know you're Jewish, David." They would do little things like turn his dresser drawers upside down and stand over him while he was studying. When he would finally ask them to leave the room, one of them would say, "Why, David? We're not bothering you, David..." and they'd just keep standing there.

I would witness these mistreatments. One time when he had had enough, he decided to keep them from entering by pushing the door shut and he yelled, "Stay out, dammit! Stay out of here!" When I heard that, I jumped up and braced my body against the door to help him, at which point they all charged the door and came straight in, breaking my leg in the process. After that it seemed like I became their Enemy Number One.

I was on crutches all that winter, but I had taken a stand, and from that point on they laid off him and came after me – everything from dirty looks to tripping me up on my crutches.

The reason I think this incident was important is because for the first time in my life I was no longer part of the "in crowd"; the so-called "most popular" group or clique that everyone else looks up to. All the time I was growing up and going to school in Scarsdale, New York, that's the group that I was part of. But at Exeter, the guys who'd been going after my room-mate were in the "in crowd," which meant that I was now part of the out-crowd. I remained part of the out-crowd for the rest of my two years, which gave me a whole new perspective.

While I was at Exeter, one other related event happened that I'll never forget. It was a Sunday morning talk during all-school chapel by a very impressive and eloquent African-American man named Reverend James Robinson, who was the founder of a program called "Crossroads Africa." I think it was a kind of exchange program. The one thing I remember that he said was something that's never left me. It was something like, "Don't ever ignore the voices of those on the margins, those left out, the misfits. They have a lot to teach us because in some ways they see things more clearly than we do. We need to listen to them." I realized when he said that, that many of the Exeter students I had become friends with were those people he was talking about, and I knew that what he was saying was true. That may have been the beginning of my learning to challenge a lot of the conventional assumptions and ideas peddled by governments and other sorts of "in crowds."

My father was born in 1900 and was politically identified with the Republican Party. My mother was eighteen years younger. She identified more as a moderate Democrat. Peace was never a topic of family discussions. War was never a topic. I'd never even heard of the word "non-violence." What suddenly and totally unexpectedly changed everything for me was what happened during the summer of '63 when I had just turned nineteen. It was after my freshman year at Harvard and I was working at one of the early McDonald's restaurants in Mamaroneck, New York. It was a summer job. One evening I was on my way to an outdoor jazz concert at Lewisohn Stadium in Harlem. I was supposed to meet this friend of mine, George Fine, whom I had met at a Shakespeare play in Connecticut a few weeks earlier and who lived in Harlem with his elderly Jewish mother.

I got off the train from Scarsdale at the 125th St. Station and as I was walking down 125th St. I came upon a huge street rally. Everyone was listening to this powerful speech by an obviously very skillful African-American orator. I had heard recordings of Malcolm X and was fascinated, though also somewhat frightened by his speeches. I thought this might be him, but I had no way of knowing. I stopped at the edge of the crowd to listen, but I wasn't there for more than a few minutes when I felt some hands on my shoulders. I turned around and saw these three young black guys who were starting to gently pull me back away from the crowd. One of them said, "You'd better get out of here before you get hurt. This is a dangerous place for a white man. C'mon, come with us."

Without thinking I followed them around the edge of the crowd, into a doorway and up a couple flights of stairs to a big room where a bunch of other black men and women were busy folding paper, stuffing envelopes and doing other things like that. It turned out this was the Harlem office of CORE [Congress of Racial Equality] and they were putting out a big mailing about the upcoming "March on Washington," which I had never even heard of, for later that summer. They were very friendly and asked me if I wanted to help. I said, "Sure," and to make a long story short, I ended up spending the whole evening there, skipping the jazz concert altogether. I also spent quite a bit of time over the next month or so raising money in Scarsdale to help pay for buses from Harlem to Washington for the march. A couple of times I went back to the Harlem CORE Office to help with other mailings and things.

Of course, I wanted to go on the march myself, and I did. A little after midnight on August 27, I got on one of the CORE buses, right there on 125th Street in front of the CORE office and it was on that bus where another amazing thing happened that had a big influence on my later life. When I boarded the bus and looked around for a seat, the only one I could find that was empty was near the front next to an elderly white guy. He was the only other white person on the bus. As soon as I sat down next to him he handed me a small, soft-cover, spiral-bound book that turned out to be a calendar put out by the War Resisters' League. They're still putting out those calendars, by the way. Each page had a photograph and a short biography of a different person and he had the book opened to a particular page. He said, "Read this," and I did. It was the story of a guy named Max Sandin who had fled Russia in the early 1900s so he wouldn't have to fight in the czar's armies. His mother had told him that killing was wrong. Somehow he got to the United States, but before long he was drafted to fight in the U.S. Army during World War I. When he refused, he was sentenced to many, many years and possibly life in prison.*

The man I was reading about, Sandin, was let out of prison soon after the war ended, but by then it was 1919 and the federal income tax had been passed, and Sandin refused to pay it because he knew part of it would go to pay for war. The government came after him for that and seized his money and possessions. Some years later, when World War II broke out, he refused to register, even though he was too old for the army. They came after him again! Here I was sitting on this nearly dark bus in Harlem just after midnight, using the little overhead light to read this story about this really stalwart "pacifist" – a word that, by the way, I don't think I had ever heard before. I didn't know what to think. When I handed the book back to the old man, he looked at me and said with this thick Russian accent, "I am Max Sandin."

Mr. Sandin and I talked a lot on the way down to Washington and also on the way back. I asked him all sorts of questions about his life and what it meant to be a pacifist – including the typical dumb question, "What would you do if someone were about to stab your mother with a knife and you had a gun. Wouldn't you shoot him?" I was sure he would say that he wouldn't, but instead he just looked at me with this really sincere, intent look and said, "I can't tell you what I *would do*. All I can tell you is what I *have done*." I will never forget that. I thought to myself, "If there's anyone whose consistent life history allows him to say with confidence what he'd do in a situation like that, it's Max Sandin. Yet this man has so much honesty and integrity that he refuses to pretend that he knows what he'd do in some hypothetical situation." That response that he gave has been a model for me all my life.

When I got back to Harvard for my sophomore year, I was feeling pretty alienated from the whole elite, Ivy League scene, so I spent the year getting ready to take a year off, as part of a volunteer teaching program in East Africa. This was another big eye-opener for me, spending fifteen months in a refugee camp for Rwandans in western Tanzania. Seeing what

*Some World War I resisters did get life sentences and a few were even sentenced to death, though soon after the war was over all of these sentences were commuted.

life was like, how people lived in a Third World country and realizing that the majority of people in the world didn't live like Americans was pretty incredible for a nineteen-year-old Scarsdale/Harvard kid.

I also had my eyes opened as to some of the dubious things my country was up to in the rest of the world. This came about in part due to an incident, in which I met up with some young refugees from the Congo. They had had to flee into Tanzania because, they told me, their villages had been napalmed by unmarked C.I.A. planes.* These were being used to put down a rebellion in the Congo's mineral-rich Katanga province, where their brilliant leader, Patrice Lumumba, had been assassinated with C.I.A. assistance.

When I got back to Harvard, a friend of mine with whom I'd been in Africa, and I started a group called "Letters for Peace." It was more his initiative than mine, but its purpose was to flood legislative offices with letters saying, "Stop the war in Vietnam." It was my first effort to protest the war. I think what led me there was what I read in the paper and the photographs. There was a barrage of images – pictures of the Saigon police chief shooting the man in the head, of our soldiers being wounded. There were a bunch of things that I was starting to read, and I felt from what I could understand that there was no justification for the war, for this murderous way of "fighting communism." I felt the whole thing was morally wrong, and that's where I was coming from. I remember being very angry with Harvard because you couldn't criticize anything on moral grounds, and you couldn't show any emotion. Things had to be carefully, analytically, and academically dissected. That was the atmosphere. And yet there was this rise of an anti-war movement on campus. I don't remember that I took a very active part in any protests at Harvard. I would attend and would stand there as one of the crowd. I certainly wasn't one of the organizers or one of the leaders. I think I was intimidated by the anger and the fury of the anti-war students, and I had a hard time with that energy.

Somehow, though, it seemed wrong to me to be sitting in college with a 2-S student deferment. At the time I had started an after-school program in Roxbury, the heavily African-American section of Boston. I lived there, in Roxbury, the summer after my junior year and my whole senior year, and the summer after my senior year. I remember one of the things that

---

*This was later confirmed by the U.S. government in documents released under the Freedom of Information Act.

really struck me. One day I was sitting on this stoop. I had already noticed that there were a lot of young black men in Roxbury who were going off to war. This young girl who knew me came up to me and said, "Hey, Randy, how come you don't have to go?" It was like a dagger in my chest.

After that I felt like my draft card was burning a hole in my pocket. I began to be aware of the connection between having a draft card and the war itself. I began experiencing a sense of complicity and at some point I knew I would have to do something about it. During my senior year, I noticed somebody was circulating a petition among Harvard students which committed the signers to a stand of non-compliance and non-coop-eration with the draft. If you signed it, it meant you were actively refus-ing to go and refusing to cooperate. In addition, you were openly encouraging others to take the same stand, all of which was against the law. I thought, "Oh, boy, I don't know if I can sign this." It was a risk I hadn't thought about. I read down the list of those who had already signed it and out of all Harvard's undergraduate and graduate students there were only about fifty names. I don't think I recognized any of them, except one – my cousin, Tim Wright's. That really caught my attention and I thought, "Well, if Tim can do this, I guess I can do it." Tim is the son of my father's sister, Aunt Betty, who married Bob Wright, the son of Frank Lloyd Wright, so Tim is Frank Lloyd Wright's grandson. I really looked up to Tim. We didn't see each other that often, but I really respected him. I'd been close to sign-ing the petition anyway, but when I saw his name, that was it; I took the plunge.

Nothing ever came of it for either of us, at least as far as I know. Af-ter I graduated I headed off to California and Stanford on a government fel-lowship to study at the Graduate School of Education. It was then that I sent my draft card back to the draft board. That would have been in the fall of '67. I remember holding the card at the opening of the big metal mail-box with my arm in it before letting it go. I thought as soon as I let it go there would be an arm grabbing me by the back of my neck and that would be the end. At Stanford there was a very active anti-war movement. I think it might have been their example that influenced me, but I did this during the first week of school.

I knew there were several other options. One was a CO, one was Canada and one was a deferment. But I had a deferment. I was 1-Y. It's al-most a 4-F. Before I had gone to Africa they made me take a physical because

I was leaving the country. I was prepared to be in the military at that point, but I flunked the physical for sleepwalking. It really surprised me, since I had been a sleepwalker all of my life. They just asked me. They had a long list of questions: have you had this, and this. You're sitting there in your underwear in the Boston Army Base and this shrink is asking me all of these questions and he got to sleepwalking and I said, "Yes." He asked, "When did you last walk?" I said, "Last night." He said, "Would you mind telling me about that?" So I told him. "I was in the upper bunk and I was dreaming about Africa. I dreamt a lion was at the mouth of my tent, because I'd just heard a story the night before from somebody who had come back from this area and there were lions. In fact there had been a man-eating lion. So I grabbed my pillow, which I thought was a club and I clobbered the overhead light and I had all these cuts and scabs and things." The guy said, "Let's stop this interview. I can't possibly classify you as 1-A."

I felt that I would never get a CO. I didn't belong to a traditional peace church. I said to my draft board, "I don't know what I would have done in a past war. I don't know what I would do in a future war. The only war that I am old enough to have experienced is this war and I know I cannot cooperate with this war. It is wrong." I knew that wasn't going to get me a CO. I also felt that, had they given me a CO, I'd have been compromising with the system. The CO status was part of the same system. It was a pressure relief valve for the system to get all of these moral, ethical young men out of the way. The non-cooperation position just made total sense to me.

Canada was a different thing. That could be a form of non-cooperation, but I thought that would be much harder. I thought, I might never come back to the country and my family and I thought, "Goddammit, this is *my* country, too. Who are they to chase me out of my country? *They're* the ones that are wrecking the country." For me the emphasis wasn't, "I just want to go to jail." For me the emphasis was, "I will not cooperate." If I cooperate, I am just one more person being silenced. I thought, it won't stop until people stop cooperating. I had been reading Gandhi and his concept of non-violence, and how it is based on not cooperating, and the notion that people in power only hold power as long as others are cooperative and submissive. All of that made sense to me, and I was shored up by the movement of the Resistance, the War Resisters League, and the other peace groups with whom I had daily contact. There was just tremendous support for that position.

Nothing happened for some time as a result of my action. As soon as I got to Stanford, I knew I shouldn't have come. I'd had it up to here with elite institutions. When I first got to Stanford I was introduced to the Mid-Peninsula Free University. I was drawn to this whole phenomenon of free universities, especially on the West Coast, which consisted of anyone being able to take a course or give a course for a ten dollar registration fee. They met off-campus in people's houses. You could take a course in astrophysics or candle-making or story-telling. Anything really. Their catalogue was much, much bigger than Stanford's. And I thought, this is what education is about. This is what it should be like. I paged through and saw a course being taught by Joan Baez, Ira Sandperl, and Roy Kepler. It turns out they were old buddies. They were giving a course on Gandhi. It sounded like it would be interesting. I wasn't a fan of Joan Baez's music – though I became a fan later – but I got into this course. Right away they said, "There's a big demonstration coming up October 16 in Oakland and members of this seminar are invited to take part in this action." I had been there less than a month and there I was participating in a demonstration where they were blocking the buses carrying army inductees, and again I thought, "This is way ahead of me." At the same time, I was so impressed with the whole spirit of it. It was very different from the angry protests at Harvard. People were singing and non-violently blocking something from happening. I hadn't been planning to risk arrest, but I just felt so moved I couldn't help joining in.

I got arrested, and I went to jail for ten days during which I was recruited by Roy Kepler who asked, "How would you like to come work for the War Resisters League?" At that point I didn't know much about the War Resisters League, but after hearing his explanation, I was totally ready to join. I thought, this is what I want to do with my life *right now*. I felt so fortunate. On top of the experience, they would pay me one hundred and fifty dollars a month! Roy gave me a car to use, and several guys in jail started raising money for the hundred and fifty a month right there in the jail.

What really got me was that while most of the three hundred or so people arrested that day were young like myself, there was a pretty large contingent of older folks, the equivalent of us now, and the core of them had been World War II CO's. I hadn't known anybody who had resisted during World War II. And they all had families and good jobs – one was a landscape gardener and another worked for Sierra Club books. What I saw was that you could have a family and do good work and not give up your principles and still put them on the line and go to jail. I thought, this opens whole new vistas of what my life could be like. I also realized that there was this large community of people that, if I did go to jail for turning in my draft card, I would be held and supported by, which I was. I came out of jail, having come to the West Coast knowing nobody, and within a few weeks I was immersed in this wonderful, wide, diverse community of thousands of people – a movement – that felt so good to be a part of. That was the greatest thing, the greatest turn my life could take.

I don't remember if I told my parents about this whole arrest incident, though I was the type who told my parents everything. My older brother once told me, "You'll get yourself in so much trouble. You don't have to tell them everything." And I said, "If they ask, I am going to tell them." That was my way. Since my parents usually asked me what I was up to, I have a feeling I just told them.

Life was so exciting. Those were the years when we thought, "It's all going to change. This is going to be a different kind of country." We believed it just couldn't go on the way it was. There was also a cultural revolution going on. I lived in a variety of communal households in the Haight-Ashbury section of San Francisco, and our W.R.L. office was there, too, at 833 Haight Street. There were these great potlucks every Friday night at the Unitarian Church, with lots of great singing. It was real community building, and people were taking risks, and participating in demonstrations. We often ended up going to jail, and there was always someone standing right behind us saying, "I'm next." There was a tremendous sense of solidarity, camaraderie and high spirits.

Personally I felt that it was just a matter of time before the government came for me. What they were clearly doing was selective prosecution, so anybody who was a visible organizer was nabbed. The number of draft resisters on the West Coast, especially people who didn't register, was huge. I knew, since I was exceptionally visible, that it was just a question of time. I kept thinking, "Why are they waiting so long? What's going on?" Part of the delay was that my draft board was in Cheyenne, Wyoming, where I worked the summer I was eighteen on a cattle ranch. There was some back and forth thing between the authorities in Cheyenne and San Francisco about my being extradited.

It wasn't until July of 1969 when I was reading a list of the war dead in a demonstration on the steps of the San Francisco Courthouse that something happened. These guys in suits came up to me and said, "We're from the press. Can we interview you? It's kind of noisy out here. Can we step around the corner?" and I said, "Yes." We walked around the corner and they suddenly grabbed me and said, "You're under arrest!" They took out F.B.I. badges, and I asked, "What am I being arrested for?" They said, "You know." And I thought, "Well, is this for harboring AWOL's, or helping deserters get to Canada, or...? It could have been any number of things. They said, "You know." And I said, "I am not going anywhere with you until you tell me." They refused to tell me. I went limp, and they were on me on the ground. A bunch of friends came rushing over to help me and to cover me with their bodies. The F.B.I. men started kicking my friends in the ribs, and one of their guns fell out on the street near the head of a friend of mine. When they started getting brutal with my friends, I said, "Stop, stop. I will go with you. Stop kicking."

After I was arrested they took me into the Federal Building and booked me. At that point I learned I was being indicted for violation of the Selective Service law. I had a number of violations. I was released on my own recognizance and given a date to show up for my trial by a federal judge. The trial date was set for 1970. Initially there were five charges against me, each one carrying a maximum of five years: not carrying a draft card, not giving my current address, not showing up for the physical, not showing up for induction, and one other. Just before my trial, which was held in Cheyenne, they tried to make a deal with me. They said, "We'll drop all of the charges except failure to give your address if you give us the address – and then we'll drop that one." I said, "For one thing, you know my address, but even if you really didn't, I am not cooperating." So I was convicted and sentenced to two years. My father and mother were in attendance. At that point my father was already five years into retirement and was seventy years old, a silver-haired businessman wearing a suit and tie. When I put my father on the stand as a character witness – I was representing myself – he turned to the judge, who was this stern, old codger who had been in World War II as a Judge Advocate General and was said to be the second most powerful man in Wyoming at the time (second to the University of Wyoming football coach), and said to him, "If you want to put somebody in prison, put me in. I am the one who taught my son some of these values, like not killing, and he's just trying to take those values seriously." My mother said something similar. It deeply affected me to have their unconditional support.

My sentence was two years. The judge said, "If you were drafted, you'd be in for two years, so I am going to sentence you to two years. Initially I could've gotten twenty-five years, five for each of the charges against me. When they knocked the charges down to one, I could've gotten five years for just that one. In some places people got five-year sentences. There was a point at which the reality that I was actually going to be in prison for most of two years hit me. It might've been as soon as the sentence was given. The judge gave me a choice of where I wanted to go. To be honest, I think I got off easy from this judge because of my parents. Perhaps he thought, "This is not a wild, crazy guy. He's got respectable parents – a retired businessman father." I think if I had been a lot of other people, I might have received five years, and I would have been in shackles as soon as I was sentenced, and then taken to the prison of the *judge's* choice. But instead he said, "You have a choice of where I send you." I said, "I have a number of friends in Safford, Arizona, and guess I would just as soon go there." So that's where I was assigned. I had two friends there, one of whom was David Harris, Joan Baez's husband, and the other a man named Terry. The judge also asked me, "Do you want to have federal marshals transport you, or do you want to get there under your own steam." I said, "I'll get there under my own steam." He gave me a week.

No one I knew had come out of jail at this point, but I had a few friends who were in prison then, and they were sending letters out. I remember one piece of advice from another resister, which was, "Whatever they sentence you to, count on doing every day of it. Don't let them tell you it's two years but you'll be out in seventeen months with good behavior, because then they will hold that over you at every juncture." There was a World War II guy who had gone to jail, who had become a lawyer despite initially being told he'd never be able to pass the bar examination since he had a felony conviction, but he did. His advice over the phone was, "Don't ask them for anything. Whether it's a pencil to write with or a better bunk to sleep in or extra boots, as soon as you get into that game, they've got you." Basically I knew that the people who were in there were doing just fine.

I was married at the time to a young woman from the War Resister's League named Jane Shulman. We worked at the League office together. One reason we got married when we did was because we thought she could visit more easily if we were married, which turned out not to be true. The marriage did not survive. We got married six months before I went in and divorced six months after I came out. So out of the first three years of marriage, I was in prison for two.

We got to the prison the night before I was to turn myself in. We stayed at a motel nearby. We decided to drive by the prison to see what it looked like at night. It was like a moonscape. It's in the desert on an old Air Force Base. A barren place. It was all lit up with these huge floodlights – totally surreal. I really trembled and I thought, "Oh, my God, this is awful." The next day, in the daylight, it was less scary, but that night...

I saw my two friends the next morning. I remember walking in the door the first day after I did all of the booking. I stepped into the prison yard. David had heard I was coming and came towards me. I yelled, "David!" and I started to give him a hug. He thrust his outstretched hand toward me. We would always hug on the outside, but not there in prison. He was giving me a really clear message to shake hands, which I think was at least as much a reflection of David as it was the prison. David was a very macho sort of guy in some ways. I don't think he wanted anyone there thinking he was gay. Terry, my other friend there, who *was* gay, came up to me and gave me this huge hug and I was glad to hug him.

The second thing I remember may have occurred that first night. There were eight dormitory barracks and I was walking past one of them and this big old guy leaned out the window. He was in his 70s and he said, "Psst, hey you, come here. Are you Randy?" and I said, "Yeah." "Good," he continued, "come here. I've got some things for you. David told me you were coming." Turns out he was an old convict who had been in prison for decades in Alcatraz, San Quentin and Leavenworth, and he was serving the end of a long, long sentence. He was in this minimum custody place because he was going to be released soon. He was very sick – terrible emphysema and asthma. He had befriended David. His name was Earl, and he said, "I've got some toothpaste for you, and a toothbrush. And here's a comb. Here's a little money. You'll need some money. If you need anything just come see me. If you have any problems with anyone, tell me." He protected David and me. He really loved us.

There were three hundred of us. One hundred and fifty were in for the draft, but the majority were Jehovah's Witnesses who had not been organizers or activists on the outside. In fact, we considered them snitches, because they were such goody-two-shoes that, if you broke a rule, they would turn you in. Jehovah's Witnesses didn't believe in fighting, and they didn't cooperate with the military, but for entirely different reasons. For the most part they wouldn't speak to us. They kept to themselves. They had their own Bible readings everyday. The rest of us were smoking dope and arranging work strikes, and these guys were totally different. The other hundred and fifty were either Chicanos, who lived in places like Albuquerque and were in for drugs, or Mexicans who had been caught for border violations.

I did do some organizing and I got sent out of the prison for what I did. This was a minimum custody prison. You could only be there for good behavior. If you violated the rules in any way, you got sent to a medium custody prison in El Paso, Texas called La Tuna, which was a regular looking prison with gun towers and huge walls. If you messed up there you would go to Leavenworth, which had both a military and a civilian prison. The civilian prison is a maximum-security prison like Alcatraz. I never got sent to Leavenworth, but I did get sent to La Tuna for organizing. First I stopped working. They had me initially running the GED program for prisoners. Almost all of them passed and the prison got extra commendations – it was a great feather in their cap. But the assistant warden was impossible for me to work with. He was so arrogant and so demanding. I quit work, and everybody assumed I would be sent out immediately. Everyone else who quit work had been. At least three weeks went by, but it was only when I started organizing a boycott of the dining hall, in support of prisoners at Leavenworth who were on strike, demanding minimum wage for working in prison industries, that the warden finally said, "No, this is going too far."

We had folks who visited us regularly and this Quaker visitor asked the warden why I was sent out. He answered, "It was a bind. We were afraid if we sent him out there might be big trouble and if we didn't there might be big trouble, because he would cause it." I found out later why they thought there would be big trouble if they sent me out. It was because of another of my self-declared protectors, a guy who had been a Hell's Angel on the outside. He had a really mean side. He told me later when we were both in El Tuna, "We put out the word within the prison population and they made sure it got to the guards and wardens, that if you were sent out they would find the dining hall burned down." The warden had then said to this visitor, "But when he started organizing the solidarity strike we had no choice." I didn't care if they sent me out. David had been sent out earlier. The men I most identified with, the most active and the most spirited, had all been sent out by then. And I had heard through the grapevine that you could survive La Tuna. My fear quotient was much lower even though the guards said, "If you get sent out there, the prisoners there aren't like here. They hate draft resisters." It totally wasn't true. They were just trying to scare me.

We were able to get newspapers inside. I didn't feel as though I could do anything to oppose the war beyond being in prison. Whoever knew that I was in prison would hopefully think more about what they could do on the outside while I was on the inside. My focus was really on the conditions in prison and I wasn't trying to carry on the anti-war movement from prison. I was in solidarity with my fellow prisoners and aghast at the kind of treatment we were receiving, which was agonizing, to say the least, as well as arbitrary and capricious. I ran into a person who works as a civilian worker at the Franklin Country Jail [the jail in nearby Greenfield, Massachusetts] just last week and I asked her what the conditions were like there. She responded, "It's horrible. It's run by little boys in men's bodies. Immature, socially inept little boys." That's pretty much how it was at Safford and La Tuna.

I eventually non-cooperated at La Tuna, but my attitude was, you don't walk in and non-cooperate immediately, because then they will isolate you and you won't get to know any of the prisoners, and you might need to know them. I worked in the carpenter's shop there for six months. I didn't plan on non-cooperating. But the more time I was there and aware of the conditions of the place, the more I thought, I didn't want to be helping them to run the prison, which is what you are doing if you go along. After those six months, I finally wrote the warden a letter with a long list of reasons why I thought the prison was not being run properly and I ended up being stuck in the hole for three weeks down in the basement with numerous prisoners in other cells who were yelling and screaming. I thought, here are some people who are really in pain, but after three weeks they moved me to a real cell in a cell block for people being punished, just not as severely as the ones in the hole.

For the last ten months of my sentence I was in a two-man cell – nine feet by six feet, or fifty-four square feet – where we lived, washed our clothes and everything else we needed to do to survive. We got outside for an hour a day. My cellmate was also non-cooperating and it turns out he was a draft resister friend of mine whose name was Tod. There were eight hundred people in that prison and during most of my time there were only three of us draft resisters. One was David who got out before I did. The other was Tod, a UCLA football star and brilliant student who had not only turned his draft card in, but also poured blood on draft files. Tod was an angry man whose mother had died when he was a teenager. Tod and I spent the last ten months together in the little cell. I did yoga and when we got out for an hour a day, we walked around this tiny prison yard. I could read. I could write. I could receive books and I had a guitar.

My whole first year in prison, maybe even my first year and a half, in most ways I enjoyed. People thought I was crazy for feeling that way. I never had a boring moment. People think, what do you do, you sit and rot. Longer-term prisoners learn to sleep eighteen hours a day. They train themselves. But I had so many projects going. I was translating for the Spanish language newspaper run by the inmates. I was teaching yoga at one point when I was not locked up. I was involved in organizing. But the last six months it really began to wear on me. I was really ready to get out. I was getting less and less patient and more and more angry at the way everybody was being treated. I just started biding my time. It was clear that my marriage was completely falling apart. My diary had been confiscated and I went on a hunger strike for eight days. Finally the warden himself gave it back to me. I had been writing about the prison and the conditions. I said to him, "Everything I said here is true." He said, "Here on page so and so you're quoting me as saying, 'The prisoners need to be controlled because they cannot control themselves.'" So I answered, "Didn't you say that?" I would meet with him fairly often and he would tell me things like this. He said, "No, I didn't say that. What I said was...", and then he said the same thing in different words... I had been writing letters saying, "Where else could a kid from Scarsdale, Exeter and Harvard get to meet the people I am meeting, get to know them and like them and hear their stories. This is such an education."

During my time at La Tuna they had had the first strike in the forty-year history of the prison. I had tried to organize a strike and all the old-timers said it wouldn't happen. The reason they believed that, they said, was because fifty percent of the prison population was Mexican and since they were getting "three squares" a day with a roof over their heads, why would they make trouble? But the truth was, most of these guys were finishing up long sentences and they didn't want *anybody* to rock the boat. All of a sudden there was a strike and the prison was shut down. And who was behind the strike? The Mexicans and Chicanos. I was accused of having organized it even though I had been behind bars for months. They knew that I had been the translator for the Spanish language newspaper, which was run by the most radical Mexicans and Chicanos. I had virtually nothing to do with it, but I was honored. During the strike I didn't even get to go out of my cell because they were so sure I was a ringleader. What a compliment to be not let out for an hour for being suspected of organizing the first prison strike in forty years. One guard said to me, "You're the most dangerous man we have here." And I asked, "Why's that?" "Because you are friends with everyone, which allows you to bring people together." The more they could keep the different groups at each other's throats, the more control they had. I think part of the reason I wasn't given a harder time was that the warden liked me, even though I gave him a really hard time. He came into the job as a liberal. He was going to treat people like human beings and he did do a few small things to make some changes.

My parents came to visit me once. They'd been scared to death and felt better after seeing that I was essentially O.K., but I stopped having visitors the last several months at LaTuna. It felt too hard – the dissonance between the inside and then out in the prison visiting area. There were so many restrictions. You couldn't hug and kiss. You were constantly watched. It was humiliating. You had to be strip-searched to go out and strip-searched to come back in. They'd look up your asshole. It was awful. They wouldn't do that to visitors. They'd pat the visitors down, which I thought was humiliating enough. No, they did it to us, the prisoners. But then to be on the outside talking was so unreal. And it was very wrenching to go back in. I told people that I was getting out within the year, so people stopped coming. It was just too hard.

I tried to write a book about the whole prison experience when I got out. I got about ninety percent done and a friend of mine told a publisher in New York about it and the president of the company there called me and asked to see the manuscript. He asked me to come to New York to talk about it. He said, "It's a very beautiful story, but tell me, weren't you ever raped?" I said, "No." "Were you ever beaten?" And again, I said, "No." But you must have seen beatings." I said, "They happened, but I didn't see any." "What about race riots?" "No, there weren't any race riots where I was." He said, "You know this is far too gentle a story for today's shouting book world. It just won't sell, besides which the Berrigans* have already told this story."

So I got out and went back to the Bay Area and things seemed changed. I felt like I had been on the Moon or Mars for two years. Or maybe it was that I was coming back to the Moon and now the familiar seemed unfamiliar. I felt such distance between me and everybody. It's probably like what vets feel coming back from war. How can anyone of us understand what they've been through and they know that. I tried to tell people stories about my experience and prison life, but it wasn't until Tod got out a few weeks later that I felt able to really communicate with someone again – somebody who knows, who I can talk to, who speaks the same language. The experience had left such a deep impression on me. Many things felt alienating. Driving an automobile was suddenly one of the scariest things in my life. People ride around in these little metal boxes at sixty-miles-an-hour passing in opposite directions within a few feet from one another. Also, I remember one time walking around a department store and I thought, I could steal anything here. No one is watching me. In prison you're so used to being watched and suspected. You're not trusted to do anything. So here I was on the outside and I felt this impulse to steal because I was not being watched. Of course, I didn't.

I went to a demonstration soon after I got out. I saw the police throwing down this friend of mine in the street. My impulse was to rush out and jump on the police. I caught myself and said, "Whoa. You've got to leave." I don't think I came out of prison calm, as much as I would like to think I did. I think I had a lot of anger bottled up inside me. Despite the meditation and yoga I'd been doing in prison, when I got out I had a hard time relating, knowing how to fit in. I eventually found my way through the re-entry period and got into the anti-war movement again.

I got out in December of 1971 and tried to see if my marriage could work, but it really didn't. For the first half of 1972 I lived in California and then I spent that summer with my parents in Maryland. During the fall of

---

*Daniel and Phil Berrigan were brothers, Jesuit priests and anti-war activists who committed several acts of civil disobedience, were arrested, served time in jail and wrote about their experiences.

'72, a woman friend, Judy Rubinstein, and I worked in New Jersey with Tom Hayden and Jane Fonda as part of the Indochina Peace Campaign, trying to dump Nixon and elect McGovern so the war would end. That winter, Judy and I went to Mexico where I wanted to write a book about my prison experience using my diaries. We bought an old van, set up a desk and typewriter in the back of the van and traveled around Mexico. While Judy was scouting out each new town or village, I would sit back there and write.

I have not a shred of regret about what I did. If faced with the same circumstances today I would do the same thing. I would refuse to cooperate. I learned that prison is do-able. It's not fun, but it's awfully educational. I often recommend only half-jokingly that if you really want to understand not only how prisons work, but also how the larger society works, spend some time in one. Prisons are truly a microcosm of the whole society. Everything is just more up front and stark. I am glad I did what I did and served my time. I never felt in any serious way that any doors were closed to me as a result of being in prison, although you are told that would happen. At first I wasn't allowed to have a driver's license in Massachusetts. I had to apply for one because I was a felon, but I got it. Even now, if I go visit someone in jail, I have to get special permission from the warden because I am a convicted felon. As far as jobs are concerned, no work that I have ever wanted to do has been blocked. In fact, it has probably opened doors because people have respect for someone who takes what they regard as a principled stand.

I have said a number of times and most recently in several talks that I have given, that I am not aware of any abrupt changes in my life. It seems like a slowly curving arc. There are moments that push me a little further in the direction that I was already going, but nothing sudden. One thing led to another. I put one foot in front of the other all the way. I didn't wake up suddenly and have this new awareness that I didn't have yesterday. Maybe if I hadn't met this person or that one that curve would have straightened out. This period was an extremely formative part of my life. In the period of ten years I went from being a very sheltered, insider, Boy Scout type from Scarsdale, New York to being a war resister. I was invited to give a talk some years ago at Exeter and I entitled it, "How I Happened to go from Exeter to Harvard to Federal Prison." It should have been, "From Scarsdale to Exeter to Harvard to Federal Prison to the War Resister's League."

Do I feel I made conscious choices along the way? The truth of the matter is that that moment at Exeter with which I began this story, when those students attacked my roommate, wasn't a premeditated choice to join in solidarity with him. It was a spontaneous, almost unconscious choice, which is a choice of a different kind. Once you start to do that, the impulse to do it is there forever. I also had this Gandhian notion of cooperation and non-cooperation, obedience and non-obedience. It includes an analysis of what allows war and despotism and tyranny to happen. David Harris had this phrase he used to say, "What we live in is a system of 'participatory totalitarianism.' We are party to our own oppression." I believe that.

I think this is probably the first time in telling any of this story that I started with the incident at Exeter. I identify that as the first really significant turning point that comes to mind. It reminds me that I could have been an insider. I look at my sister who went to all the same kind of insider schools and ended up working for the U.S. Treasury Department, the World Bank and the I.M.F. [International Monetary Fund]. She was surrounded by people who had a certain way of looking at the world and I was surrounded by a very different group of people and for a long time that made all the difference in the world in the way each of us chose to live our lives.

Jim Thornley

Jim grew up outside of Philadelphia, but moved to California during his junior year in high school. He is sixty-two years old and lives in Wendell, Massachusetts. He works as a self-employed salesman. For his job, he travels extensively.

My story begins when I turned eighteen in May of 1965. I was living in Pasadena, California. My father said right after my eighteenth birthday, "We have to get down to the draft board and register you." I didn't have a second thought about it. I just got in the car, went down there, and registered. I was a typical high school student. I had no political consciousness at all. I followed my parents' cues and didn't give anything much thought. Soon after registering I graduated, and at a graduation party I met some people in a band. They asked me to join them. We played all that summer of '65. Also that summer the Watts Riots happened, the first of the more modern riots that occurred in cities across the country in the '60s. This, and the music, brought my consciousness to a more political level.

That fall I attended Pasadena City College. I stayed in the band, but I ended up not feeling as much a part of the school culture as I had hoped. I ended up hanging out with my good friends in the band and with the art students, which meant I soon became part of the more turned-on culture, the hippies. I started letting my hair grow and taking LSD and smoking dope.

It was at this time that I started hearing more about Vietnam, and what was happening over there. All of a sudden there were Buddhists burning themselves in the streets. It started to fit more into a pattern for me, and I began to think something was really going wrong over there, but I had my 2-S deferment. By the fall of '66, the war kept expanding. I kept reading. I began to realize the war was really based on lies.

In the fall of '67 I met a woman, Carolyn, with whom I fell in love. It was all the things that young love was supposed to be, even meeting in past lives. I was just gone. It seemed like she was the same. By that time I was thinking school was irrelevant, and I was much more politically attuned. I basically dropped out after that semester. I got a full-time job, so I could save up some money. I bought an old '49 Ford Woody and made it into a little camper. I got married to this wonderful woman in June of 1968, and we drove away that night.

I always had this romantic thing. I had read *On The Road*, and I had wanderlust. I figured I'd learn more from traveling around the country and getting odd jobs, than what I was doing in school. I was also aware I had a student deferment and that was definitely discriminatory. The thing is it was all really personal for me. The music was a revelation for me. We'd go hear all these great groups. It was just wonderful and fascinating and opened all new worlds for me: the civil rights movement, the riots, and the formation of the Black Panthers. It was so exciting.

I had my first physical just before we got married. I had lost my student deferment, so as soon as they reclassified me as 1-A, they called me for a physical. My parents were pretty religious. I had gone to Sunday School and church. I had met an amazing person through the church, Charles McLain, and he steered me a little bit into community service. I ended up with a job in east L.A. at a teen club. We took kids off the streets. I worked there during the summer and probably for another six months. Then I got called for the physical. I remember being prodded into a room, and people all standing there in their underwear, shoulder to shoulder.

That same afternoon there was a meeting scheduled with these kids I was working with. I was feeling alienated by everything at the draft board. I started mooing and making noises like a cow, because we were standing like cattle. After all the blood tests and the coughing they gave us a test where you had to write stuff. I remember during that test I started letting everything get to me, and I felt like I very easily could have just let everything explode inside me. However, I had this little thing in the back of my head that said I had this responsibility, that I had to be at this meeting with these kids. So I put a clamp on my feelings and emotions, got through the tests, and went to this meeting.

Then there was Carolyn. I thought she was my other half and that we'd be together for life. My decisions didn't have much to do with politics, though that factored in. I knew the war was a big lie. It was just ridiculous that we were over in this little country supposedly stopping communism from spreading all over the rest of the world. Even that becomes personal. What do a people let themselves be submitted to? It comes down to personal responsibility, and over that year or so, from before I met Carolyn to when I went to that first physical, I decided I was going to just live my life and ignore the people who were really doing something completely illegal, and really horrible in the world.

I started getting letters from the draft board, and I didn't respond. The F.B.I started calling my parents' house. They actually came by their house, because that was the address the draft board had for me. They asked my parents questions about me. My mother called and said, "These really nice gentlemen came by, and they want you to call, and here's their number." And I said, "Mom..." The authorities didn't know where I was, and I ended up doing a lot of traveling.

My folks were not politically in tune. My dad went to college and basically adopted his parents' political views – Republican and conservative. He worked hard his whole life and my mom stayed home and raised the three kids. So when things started happening for me, I could tell my parents weren't pleased I'd grown my hair long, wasn't going to school, and was hanging out with hippies as part of the music scene. I'm sure my dad worried about me. I know he was disappointed and he expressed that.

A little background will help to understand my story. I was born in New Jersey, and when I was four my dad moved us to a little town called Flourtown, Pennsylvania, just outside the city limits of Philadelphia. In the middle of my junior year of high school, my dad got a job transfer. On a Friday I was in school in Pennsylvania, and that Monday I went to school in California. It was a big change. The high school in Pasadena was one of the biggest in the country. I was just overwhelmed. The guys in the band became the first close friends I made there, and it was after I had graduated. If my dad had not gotten that job in Pasadena, I would have remained in that small town consciousness, gone off to some college somewhere, maybe worked harder to get good grades. Truthfully, I don't know what track I would have taken.

After getting married, Carolyn and I ended up on Cape Cod for the summer and that fall we lived in Reading, Pennsylvania where a friend of mine from my Pennsylvania high school lived. Carolyn and I both got jobs in a factory. I worked fifty-six hours a week, and Carolyn worked fifty. We were there for about four months, saved a bunch of money, and moved back to the Cape, were we lived for the winter of '68–'69 off the money we'd saved.

We moved around. The F.B.I. started coming, and they mailed me this brown envelope when I was working in Reading. My parents forwarded it to me. When I got it, Carolyn and I did a little ceremony. I never opened it. We just burned it. I then got another form from the draft board, and I let all my emotions spill out. I took India ink and wrote in large letters, "You people are evil, wrong and criminal and I'm not going to have anything to do with you. Also I'm not at my parents' house, so leave my parents alone." I mailed it back to the draft board.

Carolyn was worried. She expressed it sometimes, but in my mind I had it all down. I'm not dealing with those people. They're evil, and I want to stay away from them as much as possible. I don't want them in my consciousness. She basically went along with it and accepted it. But that was part of my failing, that I did not take into consideration her feelings and her understanding of what might happen. Neither of us knew that at the time.

We spent the next winter [1968-1969] at the Cape. Then I got a job in Cambridge and we lived in Somerville in a triple-decker. Carolyn had a job in a factory, and I got a job working for a restaurant in Harvard Square called Barney's Eating and Drinking Place. One day I got off work and heard all this noise, and it was the students at Harvard chanting and marching. It was when they went on strike to protest the war.

Every day I would go back to the apartment. I'd get back from the restaurant at about three o'clock, and I just remember feeling completely exhausted. I would sleep for two or three hours, and then I would be O.K. I remember I went to some clinic and asked the doctor, "What's going on?" We talked for a while. I told him what was happening with the draft and he said, "There you are."

We left Cambridge and went back onto the Cape to my grandparents' beach house for the summer. We then jumped in the Woody and started back across the country, and on the way we happened to hear about this big concert that was going on so we went to Woodstock. That was pretty cool. We got back to California, and I got a job there, and I started feeling off again. It wasn't just feeling exhausted: I started having very typical paranoid flashes. Everything would be fine and all of a sudden …I got a job as a gardener's helper at Cal Tech. I'd be doing outside work with a shovel and a rake, and all of a sudden there'd be something moving out of my peripheral vision. In that instant I would "see" a rat, and then I'd catch myself, laugh, and forget about it. However, I had a pretty good idea that this was also about the draft.

Some of my friends started saying, "You've got to think about your draft status. Something is going to happen." Carolyn was pushing me a little bit, too. I didn't know what was going to happen, but there were definitely warning signs out there. Soon the F.B.I. came. What they first did was come to the job site. They always made sure they came during work hours, not at lunch break. First they went to the boss and asked, "Hey, who is this guy? Is he working for you?" In the fifties, the boss would immediately come down and say, "You're fired. We don't want anything to do with you." But this was the sixties, and my boss didn't say anything.

The next thing they did was they came to interview me. They took me off the job. There were two F.B.I. guys and they asked me, "Have you been getting mail?" I said, "Yeah, I get lots of junk mail." Then they came in again during work times and talked to every person I worked with. They took them all off the job at different times and different days in order to interrupt the work as much as possible. One day at lunch one of the old Mexican guys came up to me and said, "Jim, the F.B.I. came today, and they interviewed me, and they asked me what you said at lunch, and what you talked about, and whether you were political. I told them you were a good guy. Don't worry."

I kept having those paranoid flashes. I was just trying to live my life. As for leaving, it was my country. I was born here. I'm here, and they're wrong, and I'm just saying no. I had a meeting with some guy, and he said, "They're going to come get you. They will come get you and they will put you in jail." And I said, "If that's what's going to happen, that's just what's going to happen. There's no alternative. I'm not running. I'm not hiding." I wasn't really active in the sense that I got involved heavily in the anti-war movement. Obviously I was not for the war, but I never joined any group. It was just very personal for me.

But this is where I feel I sowed the seeds of the destruction of my relationship with Carolyn. I was insensitive to Carolyn's feelings about what was going on. We'd talk about it, and we'd express it, but my conviction was so strong, in a sense, like my love was so strong.

There really was no choice for me, especially after the invasion of Cambodia and Kent State. We'd saved some money, so we could travel again. I had a friend who joined VISTA and was living in Tennessee, and we planned on visiting him. But the F.B.I. came again and handed me a brown envelope. They didn't say this is your draft notice, but there were two of them, so they had their witness that I had received the letter. After work that day I was driving around in a truck and I jumped out and threw the letter down the sewer.

The third time they came they said, "You are to report for induction into the Armed Services on April the 1, 1970." I didn't go, of course. Some time in May there was a knock on the door, and it was the two F.B.I. guys who had been coming to visit me. They said, "You're coming with us." Carolyn came down and started crying, and they took me away. They didn't put the cuffs on me, but they put me in the back of the car, and we rode down to the L.A. County Jail. I was in there for a week. I was under $10,000 bond, because they thought I'd been running and hiding. When they realized I hadn't been, they let me out on my own recognizance.

When I got home my friends started saying, "Maybe you should think about Canada," and "Maybe you should apply for a CO." My lawyer said, "Usually there's some sort of thing in your file that we can work up, because they have all of these arcane laws, and most of the time they don't even follow them themselves, and we can try to get you out on some kind of technicality. However, your file has practically nothing in it, because you just ignored everything." I was probably pretty much a CO, but applying for it didn't make much sense to me. For one thing, I knew they weren't going to go for it, but also it just seemed like a way out, and it wasn't my way. I had to stand up and say, "You guys are wrong. This ain't happening. I'm not doing it. 'Suppose they gave a war and nobody came.' Sorry buddy, I'm not going to go kill people for you. Not in this war..."

My lawyer said, "Why don't you write down your feelings, and we'll submit that." So I wrote down my feelings and I have no record of that. Another interesting thing happened, though. Since I had grown up in the church in a little community in Pennsylvania, I probably had forty or fifty letters of recommendation from people like my minister from my childhood and my fifth grade teacher. All these people, plus my aunts and uncles were saying, "This guy is a good guy." All that was irrelevant, however, but it was a good effort. Basically what it came down to was, since the start of the Nixon administration, no one had been allowed to apply for a CO after they'd been indicted. So that was out the window.

So I went home to Carolyn. She accepted everything, because she was part of me, and I was part of her. I know that she was freaked out. Finally on August 3, 1970, I went to court. The judge had graduated from Annapolis. He had been giving out stiff sentences to draft resisters. I think the letters of recommendation swayed him a little bit. I think I was the first person to get just two years from him. He said, "If I let you walk out of here, will you go and report for induction?" I said, "No, I won't." So he said, "I sentence you to two years in prison." He then asked, "Do you need a week to go tighten up your affairs?" And I said, "Nope." So they remanded me over to the side of the dock. I remember my dad came up to me. He was really emotional. The marshal stood up and said, "Who is this?" but my dad ignored him and came over and shook my hand. I was really surprised that he had come around to the point he had. They led me out of the courtroom, and I had handcuffs on, and I remember Carolyn walking toward the hall crying.

I was in the L.A. County Jail for another week. Then I got shipped up to Lompoc Federal Correctional Institution in Lompoc, CA, which is right next to Vandenberg Air Force Base. Cement, steel, wires, big towers.

I remember walking out of L.A. County Jail all chained to these other six guys, all of us with chains around our waists, chains on our wrists and on our feet all attached together, having to back onto the bus so we could get on and sit down in seats next to each other. There were guys with shotguns standing around. It was definitely surreal. Then we got off the bus, and I remember all the guys yelling from inside the prison, "Hey, sweetheart." They cut our hair really short, and we shaved, and that was it. Everybody there got a haircut every two weeks. We shaved every day. There was no such thing as a phone call. As a matter of fact, when I went in, they said I could write to my wife, to my family and to one male friend. I could receive letters from the same people and that was it, but I could also get visits from those people. That was the only communication allowed.

When you arrive, they give you a battery of psychological tests, and they assign you to a liaison officer. I went to see him within the first couple of days. He sat me down, and we sat there for a couple of minutes. He then looked up at me and said, "You probably had long hair on the outside, didn't you?" I said, "Yeah." And he went on and said, "I hate you, and I hate your kind. I think you got off really easy. In fact the five year maximum was not enough for you, and you should have been in here for a lot longer than that." This is the guy, Mr. Morris, my liaison officer, who I'm supposed to deal with, and who's supposed to approve my visits and everything!

Out of the twelve hundred and fifty prisoners, there might have been twenty draft people there. One of them ended up being a really good friend of mine. He was an amazing guy. He was a surfer before he was busted. He would get up before it was light and go out and surf all day. He was just one with the waves. He didn't join groups. He just wanted to surf. He would say things like, "After you're in the water for twelve hours, your skin starts doing this weird stuff." He became my best friend "inside," the one I could relate to the most.

One of the others was a biker. He was building a bike, and they sent him his draft notice. When they came to get him, he said, "I'm just building my bike." But then he said, "O.K. I'll go take my physical," and they said, "No, you can't go, because you have an attempted murder on your record." He had evidently driven by some house and shot into it. He thought nobody was home. He was a real loner, but what was really crazy was they arrested him for not coming into the army to kill people. And then they were ready to throw him into jail, and he said, "O.K., I'll go," and they said, "No, you can't go. You're not moral enough to go. You tried to kill somebody."

Every two weeks Carolyn would come up to visit on a Saturday. When she'd wake up that morning, she'd be ill, and after she left the prison she'd be ill, because it was so intense for her. I had been ripped out of her life. One of the mornings she was going to come visit me she had gotten sick, physically sick. She ended up getting strep and it advanced from her throat to her nose and ears. She had a very serious case, got quarantined in the house, and lost thirty pounds. She was sick for about two months.

I got turned down for parole, which I had expected. When my parents came to visit, I told them. They shared the fact that I was going to be gone for fifteen more months when they visited Carolyn where she was staying at the beginning of her illness. Basically she just lost it. Eventually she was able to go to bed that night, and when she woke up the next morning, she had decided to emotionally cut me out of her life to save herself. That was it for her. I didn't know that at the time. It being the '60s, and me being that young idealist, thinking that our lives were entwined forever, I had been telling her, "Look, I'm in jail. You just go enjoy yourself. Live your life, and then when I get out, we'll just have that much more to talk about and to experience." I didn't realize at the time that that night was it for her. Later on she told me that the very next morning, once she had cut me off emotionally, she started to feel better.

I didn't see her for three months, because she was still so sick she couldn't come. When she finally got well enough to come see me, we met in the jail's visiting room. They open the door on your side and all the way across the room is your visitor, standing there waiting for you to come in. That day the door opened, and she's across this room. She wasn't a big person, but she'd lost thirty pounds. I could see her shoulder bones and her elbow bones, and I said, "Holy shit." She came up and we were talking, and she said, "You got yourself in here..."

Right then I began to understand that something had changed, but I also denied it. What happened was, first I was getting two letters a week, and then I would get one a week. Then she met some guy and moved to Colorado with him, and I'd get one letter every two weeks. Then, all of a sudden, I didn't hear from her for six weeks. It's not something you can ignore, but in my mind I was saying, "No, no, we're still together, and it's just the way things are right now."

When I got out, I think Carolyn's parents had to convince her to come home and pick me up. Of course, they didn't know that she was living with this other guy while she was still married to me. She came back from Colorado. Evidently it had weighed on her that she had certain obligations. This other couple came with Carolyn, a Christian couple, and I got in the car. I had been in jail this whole time, and the couple said, "Where do you want to go?" Carolyn said, "I'm hungry." So we went to a restaurant. It was just extraordinary, all orange seats, and plants, and women, and children, and people. I was overwhelmed after being in this institution and wearing khaki. I also knew right away that something was way wrong between me and Carolyn.

What happened next was really the crux of the whole story. For the next two weeks, we lived in her parents' house, and I knew I was no longer her partner. I just knew. It was the most intense time of my life, more intense than all the jail stuff. It was just so extraordinary to have half your mind leave. I actually got to be clairvoyant. I saw everything before it was happening. Carolyn was totally freaking out, too. She's a wonderful, amazing person, but after two weeks it was all getting to her and she started to become ill again. It was way too much for her to handle. It was lying in bed at night and not touching each other. She said, "I'm starting to get sick again." We were planning on moving into a friend's house, and I had a job, so I said, "Tomorrow, just drop me off at the job, and I'll get my clothes and take them down to the house, and that will be it."

The next morning as she was driving me to the job site, I felt totally blown away. She was all excited, though, and that totally blew my mind more. She's happy to get rid of me! This woman was my other half. Of course, it was a relief for her. She didn't want to deal with all of the agony and pain she had already gone through. So she dropped me off, and that was it.

For the next nine months I think I slept maybe two hours a night. I was traveling eighty, ninety miles-an-hour in my mind, and I was smoking marijuana all the time. I would go to bed about one in the morning, get up at three, and get out of bed. I don't have any blame or anger towards Carolyn. It was truly what *I* did. It was my choice. I left her. That's the way she looks at it. I understand that, because I did. It was my decision.

The whole effect of the jail experience was those two weeks, and that is what has affected my whole life. It changed my life completely. I have no idea what would have happened, had I not gone to jail. What would've happened if I'd gone to Canada or what would have happened with this or that or the other...I can't even imagine. I've never had a doubt I needed to do what I did. But that's what tore us apart. Right there...I went to jail, but it was my choice.

The fact is I went through an emotional crisis when Carolyn left. Of course, it had a role to play in each of the relationships I've had in the time since, both in the formation and the ending of them. Having been hurt so badly when Carolyn left me, I kept finding women who really needed someone to fix things for them. What I thought, mostly unconsciously, was if I stayed around long enough, and helped them recover from the wounds they'd received growing up, they would never leave me like Carolyn did. If I became so important to them by helping them become more content and happy, they would need me, and I would be protected from being so hurt again. Unfortunately, it was not an approach that worked. My current partner, with whom I share a place in Wendell, seems to be right there on the surface, and it's a good thing.

I know of only one time that my having served time in jail caused me to be denied a job, but I didn't care if I got the job or not. I applied to do tree work in the city of Pasadena, California, and I did real well in the physical part, and am quite capable of the Civil Service exam and did well enough on that; in fact, they told me I did well, but I didn't get the job. Otherwise, I've always managed to just live. I haven't really had jobs. I've worked for myself, firewood, tree work, yard clean-ups, and then being a traveling salesman pretty much full time since 1979.

After President Ford came in, Jan, a very good friend of mine, kept bugging me to apply for a pardon. And I'd answer him, "Why should I apply for a pardon? I didn't do anything wrong. Pardon them, not me." Finally he called me up one day and said, "If I have you over for dinner, I'll do everything. I'll write the letter. I'll run everything by you. I won't write anything that you don't want me to write." I said, "Jan, if you feel that strongly about it, I'll do it." So I went over his house, had dinner, and he wrote some letters. I didn't ask for a pardon, but he wrote the letter, and we sent it out, and this is what I finally got:

> President of the United States of America, Gerald R. Ford, has this day granted unto Robert J. Thornley, a full pardon and designated, directed and empowered the Attorney General as his representative to sign this grant of executive clemency to the above who was convicted on June 23, 1970 of an offense against the United States in the United States District Court for the Southern District of California.

When I look back over the whole story, it almost feels like everything that happened the way it did was defined in me beforehand. I have these emotional things that come up. I cry at inappropriate times; it's like a form of PTSD. I carry those things. I don't engage a lot. I can be really friendly, and I have really good friends, because that's what life's about. But at the same time, it's really personal for me. There's a certain strength in that. I knew who I was then, and I know who I am now. I also know what I'm not. My story is what it is. I don't like to use the word proud, but it sort of gives me strength.

CHAPTER FIVE

THOSE WHO FOUND WAYS TO BEAT THE DRAFT

THE TESTIMONIES IN THIS CHAPTER WERE THE IMPETUS FOR THIS BOOK. Since most of my friends and acquaintances at the time were men who faced the same dilemma as I did, they were the stories I heard first, and the ones that remained most readily available to me. In the immediate aftermath of the Armed Forces Entrance and Examining Station (AFEES) physical of a friend, I would hear his story, and I soon understood that extraordinary efforts were being put forth to "beat the draft." The stories themselves were one thing, but once told and retold, they began to take on the aura of legend. They soon merged with other stories and were embroidered until they created their own genre, a weird hybrid of cynicism, melodrama and black comedy.

The archetype is Arlo Guthrie's "Alice's Restaurant."[1] Several men mention the song's and film's influence on their decision and/or behavior surrounding the draft. That such responses could be publicly avowed, even if not socially sanctioned, is evidence of the animosity this particular war aroused. It also reflects the determination on the part of those involved to avoid the war. But it is past time to separate fact from myth. Each man who shared his experience with me was invariably plunged back into the gritty particulars and realities of the turmoil that surrounded his choice to find some way, any way, out.

Prior to the lottery, many men explored both legal and illegal means to escape service. The war was escalating, and more bodies would be needed. Men graduating from high school with no further education planned, men doing poorly in college, or men finishing college knew they'd soon be reclassified 1-A and would, most likely, be drafted. If those men supported the war or were willing to serve, regardless of the government's policies in Southeast Asia, then the decision was straightforward. If the draftee was either morally or politically opposed to the war and had no readily deferrable condition, then social class and access to doctors, lawyers and therapists could very well become factors.

The amount of research into ways to "beat" the draft, and the planning undertaken before the AFEES physical, depended on an individual's circumstances. For those who chose to ignore, repress or deny the possibility of serving, little preparation would occur. For those who felt the draft as an immediate and pressing threat well in advance of its arrival, the planning could be long-range, intense, and elaborate, with numerous avenues investigated and pursued. The responses of family and friends varied as well and, as the following stories illuminate, had a variety of effects on the men involved. But most importantly, it was access to information, money, and a cohort of like-minded souls that empowered so many men to imaginatively attempt to game the system.

I made the decision to move beyond including only the testimonies of those who were affected by the lottery – as was true for me – to those whose lives were irrevocably changed by the draft itself. As this project unfolded, I came to see that the draft – both pre- and post-lottery – was the essential piece in the story. Yes, there were those for whom the lottery provided an instant escape route, but more significantly, it was the draft and not the lottery that required a response. Even many of those who became exempt due to a high lottery number prepared themselves in advance of the lottery with tactics or strategies that would increase the likelihood of never having to take, or of failing, the physical. That some men enlisted to avoid what they believed would be a certain tour in Vietnam if they waited to be drafted is indicative of the power the draft had to affect lives.

After the first lottery in December 1969, a divide opened between those who confronted the draft and those whose luck had exempted them. Previous to the lottery, the Army was disproportionately composed of economically disadvantaged men (and women) and people of color, since so many men, almost all white, were finding loopholes partly as a result of their social standing. The lottery had been intended to level the playing field. Indeed, in the late '60s and early '70s the lottery did contribute to a slightly more balanced fighting force, but as the following stories make clear, the loopholes were still there; the advantaged still took advantage of the "privileges" wealth afforded, and a disproportionate number of poor people still served.

But the divide did not have the effect of suppressing the ever-growing protest movement. Many men felt an on-going sense of responsibility to participate in the anti-war efforts regardless of their number, since what had inspired them in the first place, before the lottery, was a sense of the immorality and futility of the war.

Once again a few words about the difficulty of choosing which testimonies to include, as well as the challenge of determining when to stop interviewing: I could well have edited an entire book composed of the sorts of testimonies you will find in this chapter. Each story is compelling and illuminates both the common experience of the times and the idiosyncratic circumstances of the individual; each reveals the trauma of the draft, regardless of the individual outcome. These stories occurred across the country, and the home town draft boards represented herein reveal a cross section of the groups of local men and women established to deal with this draft. My hope is that men who read these stories will be inspired to come forth with their own. For this purpose, as well as to make the connections all too rarely seen in the media between the wars in Iraq and Afghanistan and the Vietnam War, I have created a blog (www.iraqandvietnamwarstories.com/blog). It has already received considerable attention, but as men and women read these testimonies, perhaps they will choose to share theirs.

In the meantime the narratives that follow will suffice to indicate at least part of the range of possible experiences.

Andrew Magee

Andrew grew up in Springfield, Massachusetts. He currently lives in the
Walter Szalvo House in Northampton, Massachusetts. He is retired. He takes
great pleasure in observing nature, particularly birds. He also enjoys illustrat-
ing, and painting, as well as being with friends and doing "high physical
activity." An artist as well as a bird researcher, Andrew has also occasionally
hung up a shingle and done re-evaluation counseling.

My consciousness about Vietnam, and what was taking place there,
really increased in 1965, while in my last of five high schools. It was a co-
ed high school, which mostly New York City Jewish kids attended. It was
a progressive boarding school in the Berkshires, Windsor Mountain. I was
there on a full scholarship. Between all the moving and the divorcing, there
would be periods during which I would drop out. It was very difficult at
times, but this last school was a solution I liked a lot.

I had been living in Springfield, Massachusetts, and in Ridgefield,
Connecticut, where I had participated in these bird-breeding surveys from
the time I was sixteen. The dedication and single-mindedness involved in
these surveys helped me get into this last high school. My education there
was free because of my family's poverty. I was basically a drop out with a
horrible record, but Windsor Mountain admissions folks were intelligent
enough to see past my grades. The school grew me up from a psychological age of about two to my chronological age of twenty when I left. I still
have my best friend from that period. I had my first straight and gay lov-
ers there as well, including a teacher, which today would be a no-no, but
for me was a yes-yes.

Windsor Mountain opened my eyes. I went from a small town, problematic, WASP family background into a larger, and more urbane, more
interesting world. Many members of the faculty were refugees from Europe, and there were American blacks, so a lot of fascinating things were
happening. Both my parents were white Protestants, coming from extremely different places, and rebelling against their own personal histories.
My mother was lower middle class, and a fundamentalist preacher's daughter – Assembly of God. She was rebelling like hell before I ever got there.
My father was post-Civil War, *nouveau riche*, industrial class, Episcopalian,
boarding school. Like my mother, he was also rebelling. There was a lot of

searching and misfiring and, as a result, loose attachment to some essential things.

They met when my mother was posing nude for some art classes down in the Quadrangle in Springfield. They were both Bohemian rebels, experimenting sexually as well as culturally. My father had a boyfriend whom he lived with for eight years before he married my mother. He was his life-long "best friend," a very bright guy. After my father and his male lover each got married, the two couples were a literary and Bohemian force. At the time I didn't know all of the details.

My father was marvelously theatrical, but he was also tight-lipped. Along with the positives of being their child, there were a lot of negatives, because my parents were just so different, which resulted in instability for me in terms of having a firm place in society.

During World War II my father got a deferment based on some of his inherited wealth. He had a little factory going, so he looked good on paper, and he managed to convince the draft board the plastic hammers he made were "important for the war effort." The whole place burned down, or was set on fire, towards the end of the war. My father proceeded then to rapidly lose his money during my early years, causing us to be on welfare when I was a child.

My parents were basically isolationists and were against going into the war. I remember my mother saying afterwards she was grateful some of their Jewish friends still stayed in touch, given the Holocaust had occurred, and my parents hadn't considered that aspect of the war in taking their isolationist position. They did not possess political consciousnesses. Their idea was, "Don't get involved," and "We don't fit in anywhere," and "We're just white New Englanders, so therefore we're Republicans," until John F. Kennedy came along, and they saw he was bright enough, and different enough, that they could support him.

The whole thing about my time at Windsor Mountain is I opened up emotionally. My childhood had left me shut down. I had even been doing some hustling in the streets for cash, but doubtless also for affection. At this school I had my first on-going and real relationships. I let down my defenses and allowed myself to enter the stream of life. As I said, I arrived at two psychologically and left at my chronological age, but in reality you can never really make up for that kind of loss. Still I did a damned good job. A few of us, including a guy from Calcutta who was my art teacher, a

Swedish gypsy, a refugee from Hitler married to a secular German Jewish physics teacher, a Prague Jewish intellectual who was the head of the school, a Czech Catholic with a peasant background, my Russian teacher, an angry Black man and the wife of a faculty guy really bonded. There was so much intelligence and goodwill, and also the feeling of folks having "been around the block", especially the Hitler refugee. It gave our interactions a certain poignancy. The school included black scholarship students, so the civil rights movement of the '60s contributed to this intensity. The mood was oozing political liberalism, not in the shallow political sense, but in our beings, our core values. Bobby Kennedy was shot. Martin Luther King was shot. Kids were experimenting wonderfully, and then very poorly, in drugs. It was a moving time, and there was a touch of intellectual and "Red Diaper Baby" socialism. We were pro-Alger Hiss, who was a friend of the school. It was wild.

I ended up going to Reed College in Oregon, the only place I applied, and a place I had been encouraged to consider by teachers at Windsor Mountain. It proved to be a very poor fit, especially coming from a place I truly loved and appreciated so deeply.

By sophomore year I was facing the lottery. I knew there was a chance I would not be going in, because a lot of the higher numbers were not being taken. Plus I was weird and getting older. I wasn't moldable, and everyone knew or would find out. I had not thought much about the draft, though it did influence my decision to stay at Reed, even if I hated being there. I knew I couldn't lose my full scholarship or I would not be able to attend.

I did some draft counseling in Massachusetts when I returned home for the summer of 1969. I threw my draft card away at a rally. I also knew one of the top students at Windsor Mountain had refused induction after receiving counseling, and he got fucked up the ass in prison with the guards standing by. There was no way I was taking that route. Just in case I got a low number, I compiled a dossier at Reed of why I couldn't possibly go: flat feet, queer, bad eyes, psychologically maladjusted, whatever. I didn't care about how I got out. I knew I wouldn't be a soldier, and I would do or say whatever it took to get out.

I approached the lottery with some confidence about escaping service, but I was also very nervous. The pressure to not get off the Dean's List, to not lose my scholarship, to get into the subject area I wanted, to have enough money to live on was always on my mind. The night of the lottery I was flipping hamburgers in the college cafeteria. This ditzy, tiny, frenetic, hyper New York Jewish girl barged into where I was working and was talking non-stop about the lottery. I had chosen not to watch. I didn't want to know!

She kept asking, "What's your birthday? What's your birthday?" I answered rather dryly, "September 14". She went apoplectic, jumping up and down, screaming, pointing her finger at me, and yelling, "That's it! That's it! That's number 1!" Of course, I was midway between, "Bad joke. Fuck off," and "Jesus, is this possible…" Right away I flipped it all over to, "Well, this is not a scene to fuck around with. This is real." And it felt even more incredibly real than if my number had been 17 or 38, even though it wasn't really. There definitely was no leeway. My number 1 was right there. No thinking, "Maybe they won't get to me." But all I said was, "That's interesting."

My father had been embarrassed when I was a high school drop-out, and embarrassed that I had been on a full scholarship. In the midst of all of this lottery craziness, I got the Watson Fellowship (at the time a six thousand dollar travel study grant to pursue the course of study proposed by the recipient in his/her application) and I called to tell him of my good fortune in being chosen. He was unable to grasp the significance of the award, and the honor it bestowed on me. Knowing him, he was probably even a little jealous. He acted a little embarrassed on the phone when I told him I'd won. He had no ability to congratulate me, and neither did my mom. Neither of them had ever even imagined coming to see me in school. No doubt they didn't want me to go into the service, and no one who knew me could see me going, because I was too old, too knowing. I don't blame them. It's way beyond that. They did the best they could.

I knew I needed to stay at Reed. They were taking care of me financially while I was flipping burgers. When I graduated in the spring of '72, I came back to Springfield, Massachusetts, and really wanted to go on my travel study year to India and Kenya. In applying for the grant, I had set myself up as a sort of Thoreau, the American Transcendentalist, who was involved deeply in the reverberations of nature. Ever since I was two years old, getting out in nature had always been my outlet.

However, I was still waiting for the Selective Service folks to set a date for my physical, and the Watson Fellowship people weren't releasing the money until they got the official word I was clear. My best friend and I decided we were going to go to Mexico hitchhiking. We went to Guatemala where I saw one hundred and seventy-five new birds! The culture, the geography and the Indian presence were all extraordinary

Somehow I felt free to do this for three months. Then I came back, and the draft notice came: "Show up downtown..." I went, and it was a crappy, upstairs little room, filled with guys who were younger than me since I was now twenty-four. I was nervous and riveted at the same time. I wasn't scared shitless, because deep down I knew I was not going anywhere.

Before they had everyone strip down to their underwear, they put me in a separate room. I guess reading the queer part of my dossier made them think I was going to get this big erection seeing all these young nubile guys naked. It was just such a foolish gesture. That alone definitely showed me how incompatible we, the military and me, would have been with one another. Maybe they were actually doing the civilized thing of trying not to embarrass me, but I was already grinning inside because the whole thing felt so stupid. I knew I wasn't going to get a hard-on through my underwear. That's insane. But they separated me, and I thought, "This is good. They're taking notice of some of the material in my file." It was the first indication.

Eventually they got me in a room with a shrink, a dry, typical white psychiatrist, who was thumbing through the thick bunch of pages about me. He finally looked at me like a little, dried-up owl and said very simply, "You really don't want to go, do you?" I very rapidly and easily responded, "No, I really don't want to go." He stayed silent for maybe thirty or forty seconds, and I stayed silent. Plainly he was doing his psych eval and observation of me, so I decided to offer a bit of perspective, and I said, "If I were to go, it would be very difficult for me, and it would be a tremendous, small but tremendous, waste of the taxpayers' money." I thought this might be enough to give him the picture I would do whatever it took to avoid this draft. I'd sit down, I'd throw up, I'd strip. Whatever, and it wasn't going to be pretty. If they were going to fuck around with me, what a waste it would be. How unnecessary for all of us. And I was being thoughtful of the U.S. and its taxpayers. What more could they expect of me?

He thought about that short, simple statement I had made for another thirty seconds, and then he said, "You are disqualified." That was it. I dressed, left, walked by some arcade in downtown Springfield, and picked up a postcard, one of those that squeak. It was a very effeminate, royal looking Afghan hound that did this insane squeak. The combination of the picture and the squeak somehow became my victory dance. I paid the buck and pressed it all the way home.

I felt elation and relief. I also, in some measure, felt pissed off that I had to use subterfuge and weirdness, but I was definitely in the Ken Kesey school of saying, "Fuck you," and walking away, rather than the other school of, "Do the right thing and get fucked in the ass a hundred times, and you'll go to heaven."

Looking back now what astonishes me is there has been so much growth and change in our culture, but there is still, as much as ever if not more, this level of problematic "Who are we?" and "How are we dealing with the issues?" That Pogo cartoon that says, "We met the enemy and he is us," is still going on. It is also tremendously sad, because the Vietnam era was a formative one. However, it just happens to be that way for our generation. The internalized ways in which we have been hurt by that war is our story, and important stories are always moving and often sad. The reality is so wild and so inconsistent, so filled with total paradoxes: resolution and the lack of resolution, desperation and peace. For better or worse, if you have as much power as the U.S. has, psychological, advertising, industrial, mechanical, consumer, spiritual, the balance between use and misuse is bound to be sobering.

Rob Zucker

Robert Zucker, MA, LCSW, grew up on Long Island in New York. He is the author of The Journey Through Grief and Loss: Helping Yourself and Your Child When Grief Is Shared *(St. Martin's Press, 2009). He is a grief counselor, hospice bereavement coordinator, national trainer and consultant, and writer on the subject of loss, grief and resilience. He is married with two grown children and resides in Fredericksburg, Virginia.* (www.robertzucker.com)

I entered college in 1968. I was very involved in the anti-war movement, as were my parents. When I was in high school, I was president of a peace group. We went to demonstrations and organized demonstrations, and it was all very much a part of my family process as well. My oldest brother was very involved in the civil rights movement. My father was a pacifist in World War II. He was actually a draft resister.

When I was very young, six or seven, I remember the day clearly, when my father took me into a little bathroom off his and my mother's bedroom. He said he needed to tell me something very important, but that I should not tell what he was going to tell me to any of my friends. He explained he was a pacifist, that he believed all wars were immoral, that he was a conscientious objector during World War II, and that he hoped my brothers and I would never fight in any war. It was really a mixed message. It was something he seemed to take pride in, but he also was conveying there was something shameful, or dangerous, or risky about others knowing. I'm not sure how he understood it himself, because he rarely spoke to us about his choice, and about its implications for him as a Jew. He told me that he refused to carry a gun, and was put in a medic unit where he worked with physicians. He didn't go overseas and had it pretty safe, I think. Dad died when I was twenty-three so I can't clarify these things any further.

Given this history, it's not surprising that my father became extremely active in the anti-war movement during the Vietnam War. It was like a coming out for him, and he was totally out there. We grew up on Long Island, New York, where he was an accountant by profession. When the war escalated, he ran for comptroller as a member of the United For Peace Party. It was a very public thing, giving speeches, producing campaign literature. He also became very involved in draft counseling. The Long Island Draft Information and Counseling Service was the name of the organization he worked with. It became very important to many men and was staffed entirely by volunteers. My dad also had a call-in draft counseling show on WBAI. He counseled thousands of kids. They'd come to our house and he got many, many people out of the draft. He was extremely devoted, but sadly we have no concrete records of his actual work. Recently my mother ran into one of the men he had counseled – amazingly after all these years – and I ended up speaking with him, because I wanted to hear his memories of my dad. He had great things to say about him, really fond memories.

My mother was a member of a group called Women's Strike for Peace. She was chapter leader for that organization in our area. My oldest brother was a CO. He was two years older than I was, so I really watched him go through this. Mark applied for CO status in 1966, and it was amazing to see the process because this was relatively early in the war. He was very involved in the peace movement. He was a draft counselor with my dad. He was also involved in the civil rights movement. So there was a long history of activism in his story and they eventually granted him CO status, but they did a full F.B.I. investigation. They really went to great lengths. They interviewed people throughout our neighborhood. Two F.B.I. guys actually came to our house. They knocked on our door and had their badges; they came in and sat down with the family. We had heard all kinds of clicks on our phones indicating to us that we were under surveillance. It turned out our phone definitely had been tapped, probably for many years. It was quite a time.

Knowing this, when my dad did draft counseling, he was very, very careful about not stepping over the line in terms of confidentiality, or saying things that could be misconstrued. For example, he would always say, "These are some things a person could do," as opposed to saying, "This is what you should do." He was very knowledgeable about the draft law, constantly reading up on any changes, and he was getting reports all the time about the draft and the war. He was able to also refer people to psychiatrists and physicians who wrote "helpful" letters for people. He was part of a whole anti-draft network. However, everyone was being extremely careful, because they were very much at risk.

Now, about the draft and my experience…I remember feeling the lottery was intended to give an illusion of being more inclusive. However, it was very clear it wasn't, because some people had ways of getting out, of getting deferments, while others did not. I think the actual effect was it created a lot of activism. A lot of people who were wishy-washy, who didn't seem to have a strong opinion about the war, seemed to formulate an opinion very quickly when they realized they personally might be at risk.

I lived in a big dorm where I went to school, which was SUNY New Paltz, and I remember the night of that first lottery drawing. Many of us were sitting in a large room in our dorm basement. There was a very intense atmosphere, filled with anxiety. I received a very low number. It was 32. The people with higher numbers were really happy, and we who got lower numbers were very upset. It was a very weird dynamic. What the lottery really did was divide the group incredibly, in a way that would never have happened otherwise. I remember feeling that way at the time.

Somehow, though, I wasn't personally scared that night or afterwards, because I felt that the context I was in was all about resistance. I felt like, okay, here we go. I don't know what I'm going to do specifically, but I know I am going to do something to get out. I knew intrinsically I was not going to go to Vietnam. I knew if worst came to worse, I would go to Canada. I was in college, and college was still a deferment, so I clearly wasn't going to be called up the very next day. It was almost exciting, because there was something I had to do now, a decision I had to make soon.

So what did I decide? Actually, I dropped out of school right after the shootings at Kent State in 1970. I was very into the band I was playing with, and I wanted to devote my time to playing music. I wasn't going to let the draft determine what I was going to do with my life. I was still politically involved, but I was focused on my music. It was a big deal, playing in this band, and we were going to strike out and move to Colorado.

As far as dealing with the draft, my dad was very helpful. Educationally, he was very worried. He was convinced that I would never go back to school and was basically very negative about the whole thing. However, he really stepped up to the plate to help me deal with the draft. He advised that rather than just waiting to be called up, I should initiate the process in my own time frame. I guess that was a good idea. So I wrote to my draft board and requested a physical exam, and a date was set date for October. Then my father and I together devised a plan. He arranged for me to see a psychiatrist. We chatted briefly and he wrote a letter on my behalf. The diagnosis was "psychoneurotic," which means absolutely nothing. I don't know why he did that, or whether that diagnosis would get anybody out or not, but that's what he gave me.

I also should say I applied for CO status first and was refused, so I decided, screw it. I had really wanted to be a CO, but in retrospect, my oldest brother had some really tough times during his CO service. So, by the time my attempt was rejected, I felt somewhat relieved. I still was pissed at being turned down and couldn't see how or why I didn't get the CO status. It just didn't make sense.

One of the really amazing coincidences was that, Carl, the sax player in my band, was called for his physical on the same day I was. Carl did not have a big problem that day. He was very fat, and we assumed correctly that he was going to get out because of his weight. But Carl ended up being my witness, because I was about to put on an intense act in order to get myself rejected. I had done a lot of theater, and I decided that I would create a completely unacceptable character they would never want in their midst. My dad, always enjoyed my acting, and, once he knew what I was planning to do, was totally behind me. His one piece of acting advice was to never break character, because people would be scrutinizing me throughout the day.

For me, this was the performance of my lifetime, so I knew I had to go for it full force. My costume was this Royal Canadian Mounted Police heavy, heavy lambs' wool winter coat, and a big Russian fur hat, chosen because it would be very inappropriate to wear, especially on such a warm October morning. I looked really bizarre. I also pretended to be extremely disoriented. My character was confused, always saying the wrong thing, doing the wrong thing, getting in the way, and just generally being a bumbler.

The morning of the physical my dad dropped me off in Hempstead, Long Island, one block away from the draft board office, where I would take a bus to Brooklyn for my physical. I'm bumbling, and I'm waiting outside the draft building, and many others, of all political stripes, are also there waiting. Many of them see me as some sort of weirdo. And I was. People were laughing at me, talking about me. So I wandered into the lobby of the draft board itself, even though we were asked to stay outside. Then I started wandering into the office area where all their desks were. I started walking around, and sitting at desks, and rummaging through drawers, and really just stepping over the line. Eventually someone, maybe a secretary, saw me and kindly ushered me out.

Meanwhile, other recruits were saying things. Some were trying to support me, to sort of join with me in solidarity; some maybe to spy, to check me out a little bit, or just smile. But I could not let on. I had to be totally in character. I realized later that I was definitely influenced by having seen Arlo Guthrie's over-the-top performance in *Alice's Restaurant*. How could I not have been? The balls it took for me to do what I was doing definitely came from watching Arlo. (Arlo Guthrie pretended he was psychotic and desperately wanted to, "Kill, kill, kill," if he could *please, please* be drafted...).

Eventually I got on the bus, and nobody wanted to sit with me, of course. So I'm sitting alone, not talking to anybody. When we got to our destination, some guy comes onto the bus and starts shouting, "Get out of the bus! Go over here," et cetera. He is very young, but still the classic "tough sergeant." Everybody files out except for me. I stay on the bus until someone finds me still sitting in there twiddling my thumbs. He says impatiently, "What are you doing here? Get out of here! You are supposed to be inside." My father had said to me, "Every opportunity you get, you must tell people you want to see the psychiatrist and show them your letter from the psychiatrist. It doesn't matter where or who, use the letter." So, this is my first opportunity to say, "Please, I would like you to see my file, my letter from my psychiatrist." His response is, "Get out of here! Now is not the time!"

He pushes me out the bus door and I start wandering around the parking lot. I can't seem to find my way in. After wandering for some time, someone finds me in the parking lot and directs me into the building. When I get inside, I suddenly drop my file and all my papers and they scatter all over the hallway. I start crawling around trying with great difficulty to pick up my precious papers until someone ushers me into a large classroom where I join my bus mates. There are two men in uniform up front glaring at me as I enter. Everybody in the room stares at me and I hear some giggling. I'm looking really anxious, trying to figure out where I am and what I should do next. A sergeant in the room seems to quickly calculate that I would be the perfect foil for his cruel jokes. He starts referring to me as the jerk, which was really cruel, since, of course, I could have been someone who truly was incompetent as I appeared to be.

I find my seat in the classroom, with great difficulty, and suddenly, it seems, everyone's getting up out of their seats and leaving the room. So I follow them. As we file in. another tough guy in uniform stands in front of the room and explains that he's giving us an intelligence test. I sit in the back. He then shouts out in military fashion that each man in the last seat of every row must come up, get the correct number of pencils for every-body in his particular row, and pass them out to the men. This is very hard for me to understand because it involves coordination and counting. I can't seem to figure it all out, which becomes is a big joke; everyone's laughing. So someone else gets the pencils and distributes them for my row.

So I just sit there, and get stuck on the first question on the test. It's multiple-choice, and I just can't figure it out. After several minutes, I break my pencil by pushing on the page with the pencil tip. Papers are collected, and we all have to sit there in silence as the men in uniform grade each test. One of them struts to the front of the room and says, "I want you men to know that any idiot could pass this test, and everyone of you passed ex-cept for three morons here with us this morning." And then, he says, "Ev-eryone can leave except for..." and with a snarl he announces the names of the three morons.

They all get up and start to leave, and the three of us who failed the test are called up front so everyone can see us as they leave. We just stand there, and I decide to become very agitated. I am expressing my embarrass-ment for failing the intelligence test, and I am hurt by what that man said about me. The test administrator next says to us, "You assholes are going to take this test again, and we're watching you. Either you're faking this or you're too damn stupid." At this point, I feign panic, because I think, "Oh my God, I have to do it again?" I start to cry, and I just lose it. As I am going through this "anxiety attack," another official wearing a suit and holding a flip chart happens to be walking down the hall and sees me freaking out. He comes over and, in a critical tone, asks the sergeant, "What's going on here?" It is instantly clear this guy cares about me. He looks at me and is really concerned. He puts his arm around me and says, "You can skip the test, son. Just come along with me."

He takes me into another room and asks softly, "What's the matter?" He is being very supportive, very sweet, and I say something like, "I am so upset because I failed the test. What will that mean?" He responds, "You don't have to take the test. Just come right here. We'll get you right into the physi-cal exam area." Meanwhile I keep asking if he will read my letter and take me to the psychiatrist. No one would look at my psychiatrist letter. He says, "We'll look at it later, don't you worry about that now, son."

Now I'm in the place where you have to walk around in your shorts and take all the tests. First I take the hearing test. I have to raise my right hand if I hear the sound in one ear, and my left if I hear it in the other, and two hands if I hear it in both ears. I just can't do this; it's too confusing for me. "Which hand for what?" I ask. They throw me out of the room. They can't deal with me. I guess they are passing me on.

That sweet man with the flip chart periodically checks in on me. He totally believes me. This is really remarkable. Other people are very angry with me, while some of my fellow draftees keep saying, "Great job." Obviously I can't acknowledge their praise. It is all very surreal.

The last part of the physical, the most humiliating, is in this little anteroom where this guy has to examine our private parts. As I wait to go in, I hear him barking out rhythmically, over and over again, "Stand over there. Pull down your shorts. Spread your legs. Cough." I decide that this is going to be my opportunity to really perform. I walk in and he shouts the same orders, "Stand over here. Pull down your shorts..." So I interrupt him and say, "Wait a minute, sir. I don't think I understand you. Do you want me to pull down my shorts first, or do I spread my legs and then pull down my shorts?" He will not flinch. He repeats himself. "Stand over there! Pull down your shorts!! Spread your legs!!! Cough!!!!" But I am still quite confused. "Do you want me to spread my legs over here and cough over there before I take off my shorts, sir?" "Stand over there!! Pull down your shorts!!! Spread your legs!!!! Cough!!!!!" Finally, he just loses it and starts screaming at me. "Get the fuck out of here!"

After this strange encounter, I find myself ushered into the final line-up where you get stamped with your draft status. I'm thinking to myself, "uh oh, no one has seen my letter." Well, I have made it this far with my performance, but I am still pretty worried because my dad had made the point very clearly that I had to get someone to see my letter and I had to see the psychiatrist. So while on line I keep muttering out loud, "I want to see the psychiatrist." But no one took me there. So I say to myself, "Screw it, I'm not going to see a psychiatrist and maybe what I did was good enough. I'm just going to have to see what happens." This is the moment of truth. It is my turn. Some guy grabs my papers and I see him stamp 4-F. I look at it. It is unbelievable. It is like getting an Oscar. Suddenly I totally break character. I start laughing. I take off my hat right there in front of everybody. I just figure I have my 4-F; they can't take it away from me now. This is my deferment. I am not sure even now whether I should have done that or not, but I did. And then, I'm telling you, the whole place started applauding me. It was unreal. It was like this whole community that had been watching me all day suddenly saw me for who I was, beneath my role. It's really moving when you think about it. I felt like a celebrity on the bus ride home, and later when I got back home we had a big celebration. Everyone was really, really happy.

A few years ago, I started to think about that performance, and wonder if I was proud of it or not. Most of the time, I was, especially during the war. It was, after all, my war story. After getting deferred, however, I wasn't as much of an activist as I had been. I was playing in my band and doing more personal stuff. In retrospect, I wish I had considered my 4-F as a challenge to become even more active against the war. In a way, I was being pretty selfish.

Years ago, when I used to tell the story, it was funny and friends would say, "Wow, that's a great story." But then there came a period when it didn't seem as relevant because, of course, life goes on. It was no longer as clear to me how my war story fit into my life. After all, the times had changed so much. For example, and for good reason, there is now much more respect and concern for Vietnam vets. In the '60s, we were pretty oblivious to what it must have been like to have fought in the war and return to a public that didn't seem to care about them. Many of us were more focused on the Vietnamese experience; being napalmed and having their villages destroyed. So I feel like the picture is not that clear anymore, and I wonder how people will hear my story today; will they understand it? I guess that's why this book is important; these stories are a part of our history.

When I look back, obviously my experience with the draft was quite emotional. I also feel grateful I was able to do it my way and for the support of my parents. I'm really grateful that I wasn't in a family where the assumption was that you go "because it's the law," or even worse, in a family that was *for* the war. That was really a gift. It allowed me to have the freedom to find my own path. There was a war going on, and, as a kid, I wanted to decide how to relate to it myself. But that's part of the confusion now as I look back on what happened to me, and what happened to those who did serve.

I admire people who went to jail. I admire people who really risked everything. It defined their lives. I, on the other hand, just did what felt good to me. I was not going to go to jail. I knew that. I'd already decided if my act didn't work, I'd leave the country. I didn't know what it would mean, but I had that as my out. I was not going into the Army, let alone to Vietnam. If I had failed, if I had received a 1-A instead of a 4-F, I knew there was going to be a time period before they called me up. I knew I would have time to generate whatever energy it would take to figure out what I had to do next, and my parents would help me. I really didn't think about how serious it was. I was just focused on, "This is what I'm going to do, and it's going to work." I was so sure of that, I didn't even bother to rehearse my act. At that time, I didn't feel anything but good about it.

Recently I was on a business trip to Arizona. A soldier on the plane sat next to me and I struck up a conversation with him. He was a black guy and he seemed very well educated. It turns out he'd just been to Iraq. The essence of the conversation was that he had briefly come back because a buddy of his was killed, and he wanted to express his condolences to the family. He had gotten a temporary release from Iraq to come back home to visit them. It was a friend he had known before the war, too.

He explained to me that he had been separated from his own family at a young age, and this friend's family had taken him in and raised him. They became like a second family to him. Now, their son had died, and he was going to comfort them. He proceeded to tell me the story of what happened to his friend. They were going somewhere in a caravan and were attacked. He told me he saw his friend get blown up, right before his eyes. Obviously, he said, it could just as easily have been him. We were both practically in tears. My heart went out to this kid sitting beside me. He wasn't talking politics, and I wasn't talking politics. He was just talking about his pain. I thought to myself, how different I was at his age.

Guy Sussman

Guy is sixty-five and was born in Plainfield, New Jersey. He is semi-retired, having run a business and lived in New York City for thirty years. After selling the business he became a computer programmer, and, at fifty-five, when the tech bubble burst, he was out of work. He had been in retailing, so he did not see himself going back to work for seven dollars an hour. He moved to Northampton, Massachusetts, where he felt he could be as easily unemployed as in New York. He's divorced and has a daughter, thirty-eight, who lives in California.

When I graduated from high school in 1963 in Plainfield, New Jersey, I was part of the post-war generation that grew up in the glow and glory of the good fight of World War II. You'd watch movie actors like John Wayne and Kirk Douglas mowing down the enemy by the hundreds with tears in your eyes. I think that profoundly influenced me.

I went to Rutgers University in the fall of 1963. Up to that time I still felt a deep-seated sense of patriotism, but as I progressed through college, I gradually became aware of what was really going on. Freshman year at Rutgers there were civil rights demonstrations organized on campus by SNCC (Student Non-violent Coordinating Committee). SDS (Students for a Democratic Society) was also protesting many things on campus and nationally, especially related to the war in Vietnam.

During my junior year of high school, a friend who was a year older came up to me and said, "There's this great program, the Naval Reserves. You go to meetings once a week in your senior year, get a year off of your naval active duty service and only spend two years in active duty. You get all sorts of benefits, and then go to college for free."

When I told my mother I was interested, she had a hissy fit. Normally she was the typical kind of Jewish mother who did not want to deny me things I wanted to do, but she just exploded with, "A Jewish boy going into the Navy?" In retrospect, of course, had I done it, I would have been out by '66. I probably would have spent time in a very safe zone. My brother-in-law, who's my same age, did that. He was on an aircraft carrier in communications and tells me today that when he looks back on that time period in his life, he didn't know what was going on in Vietnam. They would load the planes with bombs and they went off and came back and he wasn't thinking about what happened in between.

I was aware of Southeast Asia. I didn't quite understand exactly what was going on there. There were protests, people in orange robes, I think, but I didn't have a color TV then. I remember in high school seeing the monks burning themselves, but I didn't understand what they were protesting with these incredibly extreme actions.

College for me was about studying, getting drunk, and going to demonstrations. Between my freshman and sophomore year, I decided I was going to grow my hair long. It wasn't about my wanting to be a hippie. It had more to do with folk music and Bob Dylan. My senior year in high school I saw Bob Dylan in Atlantic City and saw him again during my freshman year in the Rutgers gym. By then he was very much into protest songs and songs of peace and pacifism. Some of what he was singing about affected me and I came back in September with my hair pretty long. Before that I had a real crew cut. I think growing my hair like I did was symbolic of a loosening up of my values. It was the summer of '64 and I didn't even know the word "hippie," but I was really moving in that direction.

When I returned for my junior year I knew there was something happening and Rutgers was one of the first schools to have a teach-in, the first of which I didn't attend. There was a history professor at the University by the name of Eugene Genovese who was very outspoken about our role in the war. It was an all-night teach-in and it also included another history professor, Warren Susman, who spoke passionately against U.S. involvement in Vietnam. I remember one of the quotes from Genovese who was a Marxist Socialist. He said, "Being a Marxist-Socialist I do not fear a Vietcong victory in South Vietnam. I welcome it." The controversy his remarks sparked resulted in Genovese having to resign from Rutgers.

I had a draft card, of course, but I never thought about it. Sometime around these events on campus I had the realization that there was a personal threat to me involving my draft status and that there was a moral issue about this war. It was also around this same time that I took my first acid trip and started smoking marijuana. There weren't a lot of kids on campus doing that at the time. I kept it a secret. You'd put rugs against the bottom of the door so the smoke didn't get into the hallway. Most of the other students didn't know what marijuana smelled like, but the cops did. The drug experimentation was certainly a good distraction and could take me away from the reality of the moment. However, by the spring of my junior year, which was '66, I had a definite understanding that, if the war wasn't over, I would graduate a year later and be drafted.

At this point I became aware that there were groups forming that were aiding people and educating them on how to get out of the draft. I started finding out about all the loopholes. Of course, there was still the hope the war would end, but that was really a flight from reality. As time progressed, I got more and more fearful of what might happen to me. I also got more angry and acted out a lot more. I smoked a lot more dope, dressed more wildly, and my grades went down. I shifted my major because I wasn't studying. I had been a physics major, and in the middle of my junior year I was just getting C's, and that wasn't good enough. I switched to German, because I could graduate in German without prolonging my stay at Rutgers. There was this sickening anger inside me, and I know now it was all about the draft and the war.

The first thing I actually considered was joining one of the services, either the Navy or the Air Force. Towards the end of my junior year I went to the local Air Force recruiters' office because somebody in my fraternity had joined. I walked in there, and the recruiter was an asshole, a real GI Joe. He saw that I didn't have that crazy-ass spirit, so he said, "You have to go to the recruiter in your hometown." I guess he figured I wasn't really Air Force material. I walked right upstairs and went into the Navy recruiter's office. He also knew immediately where I was coming from, that I wasn't enthusiastic about military service, and I was just looking for an alterative to possibly finding myself in the Army. For me, at this point, it was really about self-preservation.

I began looking into a lot of options like becoming a conscientious objector. I was afraid of jail. I didn't really feel I was a pacifist. I'm a little guy and if somebody backs me into a corner, I'm not going to say, "Peace and happiness." I hate the idea of having to fight, but if it comes down to it, I'm going to turn around, and I'm going to go after somebody who threatens to harm me.

By 1967 attending graduate school could give you one additional year of deferment so I decided to go to graduate school. I registered for graduate work in German at New York University. After one week I realized it was very expensive and very difficult. I just said, "Screw it. I'm going to travel to Germany." The exchange rate was four marks to the dollar, which made it very cheap to live there. I could live there for eight months for seven hundred and fifty dollars. I attended school and made friends there, all the while learning more German. I had decided at that point to throw caution to the wind and accept whatever happened. It turned out I got a graduate deferment. I was surprised about that. My draft board gave me a deferment for that year.

There was a lot of social activism in Europe in 1967. I was in Munich when Paris was shut down. There were a lot of demonstrations going on in Germany that I participated in. There was a good deal of protesting against American imperialism. There was also a strong worker's movement for better conditions for workers – shorter work weeks and more pay and benefits.

There was another big event that had occurred before my time in Germany that had a major effect on my family – the victory by Israel in the 6-Day War. The war happened in June 1967. I was sitting at home watching Americans getting shot up in Vietnam on TV. At the same time, especially in the Jewish community, of course, there was this rabid kind of militaristic ecstasy as Israel vanquished all of those Arab countries. My father was particularly delighted. I had just graduated college and for me this set up a great conflict. I remember trying to say, "There are other issues here, Dad." He looked at me with this rage in his eyes, and my mom, who was extraordinarily active in the Jewish community, was silent and clearly perplexed.

My dad was very unaware of what was going on in Vietnam. He just saw it as another nuisance that the Marines would take care of. He was a very hard-working guy. My relationship with him was never close, but when I finished college he wanted me to come into his business. That was the Jewish thing to do. I was his only son. So we had this real kind of crisis talk. I said, "Look, this is ridiculous. If I start working for you, I'm not going to be there for very long before I get drafted, so there's no point."

I think he began to get it. In that same conversation about me working for him we began to talk about how I could possibly get out of the draft and he said, "Well, maybe I know somebody on the draft board." My dad and I actually had a moment of closeness then, because I asked him, "How did you feel during World War II?" My father was born in 1911, so in December of 1941, he was thirty years old and he married. He had a business that was just getting started, a young wife, and my sister, who was born in October of 1941.

Pearl Harbor was bombed when she was a few weeks old, and every three months he got reclassified. I remember seeing these reclassifications in a drawer and seeing food tokens my mom would get to buy butter and sugar. He told me, even with two kids and a business, he was ultimately drafted in 1945, two days before they dropped the bomb on Hiroshima. He was actually inducted into the Army, and after they dropped the second bomb, he was discharged. Technically he was in the service for a couple of days. So his response to my question was, "I was worried, but I got up one morning, I got into the shower, and I thought, 'If I get drafted I'll close the shop. I'll lock the door and I'll go.' After that I didn't worry any more." After he told me this I said, "Well, dad, if you felt that way, I can really respect you," and we hugged, really hugged in a genuine loving way. There was a real connection there because there was a common experience: fear of war, fear of having to fight in a war.

While I was in Germany having the experiences I mentioned, I was also keeping up with the regulations about the draft that were changing in America. Sweden wasn't far away, but I knew that once you went to Sweden, you couldn't travel in Western Europe because you'd be a deserter. You could get arrested. They were arresting people who didn't report for physicals. I kept my eyes open and renewed my application to VISTA (Volunteers in Service to America*) since working in the program guaranteed a deferment for the year you served.

I had decided to go see a doctor about my teeth before I went to Germany, since I knew you could get out if you had braces on. The doctor was conflicted because he didn't know how to deal with my situation. In the end he said, "Look, you're going to have to have these four teeth pulled out. It's probably going to change the shape of your jaw. It might exaggerate the size of your nose because your teeth are crowded." I was looking at myself in the mirror while he was talking and I said, "My teeth are crooked, I know that, but I like the way I look!" It was going to take two years and cost five thousand dollars! I didn't like the idea of doing this type of disfigurement to myself, so when I was in Germany, I realized that if I could get into VISTA, okay, I'd get another year's deferment.

In June 1968, I landed in New York, and within days, I was in a VISTA training program in Eugene, Oregon. Who was in the training program with me? Religious goody two-shoes, some older people who were looking for things to do, some women and a lot of guys my age who were looking to get out of the Army. I ended up working in a rural area with white

---

*VISTA was begun during the Kennedy administration as a domestic Peace Corps.

people and Native Americans. This was definitely a rich experience. Here I am, a Jewish kid in the middle of America in a county that is probably as big as all of northern New Jersey, with a population of 20,000 people. I found out later there were two other Jews in the whole county.

While I was in VISTA, I remember going up to Vancouver, British Columbia. I got in contact with the American ex-patriots up there who were helping people immigrate to Canada. There was a point system. I educated myself about what you had to do to get in. I was always collecting information, and keeping myself aware of what the law was and how it affected me. In the middle of my VISTA service I was classified 1-A. I had to get VISTA to write a letter to the draft board, but even with that, I had to go for a physical. I reported to a draft board in Oregon, which was across the river from where I was working.

I passed the physical, but I was still in VISTA, so I was safe until August of 1969. While I was finishing up my service, things were getting more violent in the protest movement against the war. I remember coming back home after VISTA and going to some demonstrations. I remember getting gassed by these National Guard troops. I also remember some extremist types who were talking about forming affinity groups during the demonstration, getting arrested, getting into the Fort Dix stockade, and liberating it. The anger and frustration had really grown so much. Young people were now acting out in that very angry way that demonstrates how far you're prepared to go to express your displeasure with something like the war.

I got out of VISTA and arrived home around Labor Day of 1969. I was at the end of my rope. Time was running out. I knew I was not going to go into the Army. Still I was scared shitless. When the first draft lottery approached in December of 1969, somehow I knew I was going to get a low lottery number, so I didn't sit up and watch the television. I didn't buy the newspaper the next day either. I never even did the research to find out what my number was until about six months ago, when I went online. I was born on April 18, and I think my number was 135.* I didn't like the idea of the lottery, and I didn't like the idea of the draft. I'm not a pacifist, and I think everybody should do service for their country. That was one of two things I realized in the '60s as we were protesting: number one, if this had been World War II, I'd have felt differently, and, number two, there's no reason why white, middle class, educated people should not go.

---

*It was actually 90.

There's one other reason why I didn't want to watch the lottery or know my number. I had a very dear friend from college whom I'm still very close to who was in graduate school. He has his own story, so I won't give his name. We'll call him Ralph. In September of '69, as I was driving from Washington State to my home in New Jersey, I stopped off to see him and his new wife. I said, "Ralph, what are you doing about the service?" He was very reluctant to tell me exactly how he got classified, so his wife told me instead. She told me about Anita Stevens. "She's a shrink who's writing these letters for people to use in getting out of the draft." I then asked, "Do you want to give me her name?" and he said, "Yes, I'll give you her name."

As the lottery approached, I was so fearful that I called Dr. Stevens up to make an appointment even before I got my number. What if she died or stopped doing this? When I went to see her, sometime before the lottery, she interviewed me for about ten minutes, wrote out this letter, and handed it to me. I think it cost one hundred-fifty or two hundred dollars. Things went along, the lottery came, and I got drafted. When I got the letter telling me to report for a physical in May 1970, I called up Anita Stevens and asked her, "Can you reissue a new letter that's more up to date?" She said, "We need to conduct a new interview." Now the price was five hundred dollars, so from the fall of '69 to the spring of '70 the price had essentially doubled.

I again went to her personal office in a Park Avenue apartment. I walked in and her regular patients were there. This time I was directed to a different floor in the same building. I sat in the waiting room, which was filled with a bunch of guys just like me. She didn't even see anybody. She had a fleet of psychiatrists interviewing us. There was another room with IBM electric typewriters. I would say at least five typists were in there, just typing letters. I walked out of there with the letter and really felt sick to my stomach. Even while I was going through this experience, I was realizing that it was all about privilege. How many black guys were there? How many poor whites were there? How many guys without an education?

The second letter didn't come soon enough, and I had to get my physical delayed twice. During this time I decided that I would go to my dentist, and I asked him for a note about my teeth. He was very sympathetic. He examined my mouth and said, "You have a partially impacted molar," which was not going to be enough to help me. This gave enough time for the second letter to arrive. I got a call from this Asian-sounding woman at the induction center at about the same time, and she told me they had the letter from Dr. Stevens. My first thought was, "What's going to happen now?" I had heard that Anita Stevens was on the Board of Medical Advisors to determine standards of suitability for induction into the Army. I also recalled seeing a photograph in her office of her standing next to General Hershey, the head of Selective Service. I was definitely confused and worried. I had imagined that the Army had some sort of arrangement with her to allow people like me to quietly get out of serving, because there were problems with discipline in the Army from people who were aware of the anti-war issues before they were drafted. By this point my girlfriend, soon to be my wife and my eventual ex-wife, was living with me, and I had a Volkswagen bus. I remember saying to her, "Look, if I pass this, I'm going to walk out of there. I'm not going to be sworn in. I'll drive straight to Canada." That was it.

I went to Newark for the physical, and I was walking around naked with a folder in my hand. It came time for the psych eval. This guy walked into the room and said, "So what's your problem?" He was a little bit nasty, and I was very deferential and acted very scared. I said as little as possible, and I remember him writing very fast. I said, "You know, I have a few problems." He said, "So you saw Dr. Stevens." My response was to again say, "Well, I have some problems." As I try to piece this together I think I was directed to him. I think he was acting nasty, so as to make sure that I didn't have that kind of arrogant swagger of someone who knew they were going to get out. I sensed he was in on whatever it was going to take to get me out.

After that interview I was very quietly taken away from the general group, walked around the periphery of the building, and brought to this door where the Asian woman who had called me on the phone was sitting at a desk. I was told I had flunked, but as I left I remember thinking, "Now somebody else will be stepping into my boots. The Army will take them since they don't have me." My girlfriend was there when I came out, I got into the VW bus, told her "I failed," and that was the end of it. They didn't want me, and that's how I got out of the service.

My Dad did not concern himself with what happened to me at the physical, but my mom was very much in favor of it. She's the one who gave me the five hundred dollars for the second letter, and she was relieved when I got out. What mother wants her son to be killed? Nevertheless, it was a pretty shameful, embarrassing, cowardly thing to do thinking back on it. There was definitely a quiet sense of relief, but there was also a lot of regret and guilt and sadness. And I suppose anger at the fact that there were still guys over there dying.

For me that whole draft experience was a big part of the real story of the '60s. It's the one that you're really reluctant to tell when you see young people who look back to the '60s and say, "Oh, you're from the '60s. That was a great time." No, it was a fucked up time, man. Guys were getting their heads bashed in. Guys were getting killed. Where's the romance in that? And how different would my life, our lives, have been without that war and the draft hanging over our heads? I would have played around more. I wouldn't have gotten married as quickly, but then again that would mean I wouldn't have had my lovely daughter. I think I would have stayed in Germany much longer. I liked it there. I liked living there. It was cheap and I made lots of friends there. My German was getting very good. I was getting relaxed and comfortable at it. Munich is a very pretty city. I definitely would have stayed there longer.

There's a very interesting twist to all of this. A few months later, a friend of mine who was a lawyer called me up and said, "Listen, I have a friend who wants to get out of the draft. Can you help him?" I agreed to put him in touch with Dr. Stevens, because most people were afraid to get involved in something so obviously illegal. After all, the letter included such false statements as, I was a danger to myself and others; that I had homosexual tendencies; and that I had delusions of grandeur. The response to this kind of fabrication was to keep quiet about what was going on, to keep this exit tool a secret. Nevertheless I gave the information requested.

So this friend of a friend of mine goes to Anita Stevens' office and is met by her skinny little hyperactive office manager who asks him how he heard of Anita Stevens. Afraid to give him a truthful answer and blow my cover, he replies that he heard of her on the radio. I was told that this manager nearly jumped out of his skin.

A couple of months ago, my friend Ralph, the one who told me about Dr. Stevens, and I decided to do a Google search to try to find out whatever happened to her. He works with Vietnam War era veterans. We couldn't find anything that led us to her. I really think her story should be outed. That's another untold story about the war and the draft. What I really want to express with this opportunity to reflect on my life in those times is that, for guys like me who went through this, when you ask, "How did you get out of the service?" I either say, "Well, I'd rather not say," or I say, "Well, I'm a little bit ashamed of it. I'd rather not talk about it," or I say, " Well, I saw a friendly doctor." I sense the same reluctance with other people like myself who, when they give you some vague response, are indicating the direction they took, but they're also saying, "Don't ask me any more questions about it," and there's a mutual respect for that. There's a kind of understanding.

Even before this interview, Guy was obviously thinking long and hard about what had happened to him during this period in his life. He had also recently seen the film, Sir, No Sir, *a documentary by David Zeiger that is described below in the website summary:*

> In the 1960s an anti-war movement emerged that altered the course of history. This movement didn't take place on college campuses, but in barracks and on aircraft carriers. It flourished in army stockades, navy brigs and in the dingy towns that surround military bases. It penetrated elite military colleges like West Point. And it spread throughout the battlefields of Vietnam. It was a movement no one expected, least of all those in it. Hundreds went to prison and thousands into exile. And by 1971 it had, in the words of one colonel, infested the entire armed services. Yet today few people know about the GI movement against the war in Vietnam.

After viewing Zeiger's film, Guy was moved to write to him. He summarized his experience with the draft and ended with this statement about the film's effects:

> Finally, David, I want to say that it's my sense that many men like me quietly and shamefully availed themselves of this dark process...I don't think there are ten people in the world who know that I got out of the draft this way. Meeting others of my age who avoided the draft, the subject of, "How did you get out?" often comes up. All too frequently the mutual responses are vague and imprecise – as if to quietly acknowledge a secret we'd both rather not discuss. This is literally an untold and unspoken story motivated by courageous, mutinous soldiers and grasped at by a desperate, frightened and educated few. I wish you could incorporate stories like mine into your film as a curious incidental phenomenon of the Vietnam soldier rebellion.
>
> The actions of the mutinous soldiers documented in the film inspired me at the time to refuse to serve and shamed me for my cowardly method of resistance.

Bob Brown

Bob Brown was raised in Hartford. He is sixty-four years old. He has been working at the University of Connecticut for thirty-nine years. For the first fifteen years he was an assistant to the director of the Upward Bound Program at the Storrs campus. Upward Bound is a program for inner city high school students who are college-bound. Since 1986 he's been at the West Hartford campus of the University of Connecticut. He's program manager for student support services. He runs an educational opportunity program for high school grads from low-income, first-generation-in-college families. The university gives them the opportunity to matriculate as long as they go to a six-week, pre-collegiate rigorous academic program in the summer. The only stipulation is that the students start out during the summer and do well in their classes. Bob's program then supports them with a lot of academic counseling, career counseling and, most essentially, personal counseling. He officially retired on July 1, 2009, but has been rehired on four separate contracts since the program clearly is not fully prepared for his departure.

Bob is remarried and has two grown children from a first marriage. Both participated in Upward Bound in Storrs. He lives in Bloomfield, Connecticut, which is a very diverse community, approximately a third of which are people of color.

I graduated from Hartford Public High School in June of 1964. I hadn't applied to any colleges. I never received any proper advising or counseling in high school. What triggered me even thinking about college was a conversation with a co-worker at the A&P where I had my first full-time job after graduation. There was this black woman that I was working with. She was a cashier. After I had only been there a short period of time, she told me that I needed to go to college. So I actually went back to Hartford Public High School to do a post-graduate year. Sometime in the fall of '64 I decided to apply to Central Connecticut State University. Tuition was only one hundred dollars a semester. I had it in my mind to become a French interpreter and then a French teacher, but while there I became involved in the politics of Central as well as in national and world politics. I soon decided that being a French interpreter or teacher was not really what I wanted to be, so I switched to elementary education.

In the meantime, there were things going on at Central in terms of racial discrimination that I became involved with. These were issues affecting a lot of minority students in predominantly white institutions, so we started a student organization. Ironically, I was not on campus on the day that there was a takeover of the administration building by the black students who felt Central Connecticut was responsible for certain injustices they were experiencing. There were instances I had witnessed and experienced in the classroom where instructors made racist remarks. Some of us who weren't involved in the takeover got wind of what was going on and supported those inside the building by picketing outside. Those inside were arrested. Prior to this a bunch of us had gotten together to form a singing group. Some of us had sung before at our local churches, but many of us hadn't really sung with other people. We got into a competition at the college, and we sang that religious song, "Oh, Happy Day." We won first prize! The couple of hundred dollars we received ended up being used to help pay for the legal costs for some of the people who had to go to court.

At the same time as all of this was going on at Central, the word was going around that there was a possibility college students might be drafted. I ended up getting married in '67 during my sophomore year, and we had just begun to have babies. However, because of all the talk, even though I was married and a father, I was a little nervous just like everyone else. I was really concerned about this whole idea of the draft, and then the next thing we heard was that there was going to be a lottery.

I came from a large family: I was number five out of nine children. We lived in a low-income housing project in Hartford, and I was the only one who had had the opportunity to go to college. My parents were very supportive of me, both financially and spiritually, and they did everything they could to make sure that I had what I needed as I tried to fulfill my wishes and further my education. They watched all the protesting against the war that was going on, and they felt a lot of concern. Coming from a place like the projects in Hartford, we all were painfully aware of the injustices in this country regarding how a lot of blacks were being mistreated. I knew some people were saying, "Hell, no, I won't go," but I also knew a person had to come up with some strategies to answer the question: "If I am drafted, what will I do?"

For me it wasn't just about Vietnam; I felt that the whole system was unjust. I was asking myself, "Why should I go and defend the flag when the flag wasn't defending me here in this country?" I did not feel Vietnam was a place for me to become involved when I didn't even get the respect and the rights I felt I deserved in this country. There were so few of us who had the opportunity to really think about college, and maybe, through our own pushing, to actually make the right moves to get there. The reason the blacks at schools like Central banded together and formed organizations was because we needed someone to "watch our backs." Then throw in the whole idea of the Vietnam War and, we wondered, what was going to happen to us?

By the night of the lottery, I had a plan. If I got a low number, since I was married and had two children, my first approach was going to be to come up with a hardship argument. Plan B, if the hardship defense didn't work, was to flee with my family to Canada. I knew I wasn't going to Vietnam no matter what happened. My folks were with me on the two plans. I am pretty sure if it turned out I had to leave the country, they would have supported me financially to the extent they were able.

For the friends of mine who didn't have the opportunity to go to college, everything about the draft and Vietnam was different. Some volunteered to go into the military. Some who were drafted went to Vietnam and only their bodies came back. Others came back, but their minds were completely messed up, or they had lost parts of their bodies because of bombings. Many of them unfortunately became mental cases, or drug addicts, or got into trouble with the law and ended up going to prison. I spoke to those who returned and, based on what I heard and saw, I wasn't buying into the whole propaganda about how we were fighting to stop the spread of communism. Instead I became much more aware of such lines as, "There were no Vietcong calling me nigger..."

There was also so much division in the country about the war. There were many protests against the war, and soldiers definitely were hearing about some of this because that was thrown at them as well. It was devastating for some of the friends I spoke with to know, "Here I am in a foreign land trying to defend my country, and my own people back home are against the war I am fighting." That was part of why some of the men who I knew were screwed up; they experienced a mental breakdown due, first of all, to having gone there. But there was more to it than that: it was also due to being scared, seeing friends killed or wounded, doing and watching horrible things being done to the civilians and, if you were lucky, making it back, only to face no jobs, no money and no respect – especially if you were black. It was just a horrible situation, and the country was in complete turmoil.

As for the lottery, I can recall sitting nervously with a bunch of friends at the college, both black and white, waiting to see how our birthdays were going to come up. Every time a number was chosen from that rotating bin, all of us were breathing heavily, wondering what the hell was going to happen, whose number was going to come up next. My number was 227. It was a very uneasy feeling afterwards, since I did not know what it was going to mean. I was not able to sleep well for days, because I realized I would just be waiting, and I didn't know how far along they were in Hartford with the numbers. I felt a lot of anxiety, uneasiness, and sweated a lot. I was distracted from the books and the studying.

Somehow, with the help and support of those who cared about me, I managed to take things one day at a time. I kept trying to do enough to get by in college, but at the same time I was always worried about what direction I would end up going, if I heard from the U.S. Army telling me, "O.K., it's your time to go." College classmates were getting letters telling them when and where to report for their physicals, and I remember wondering when in the hell would I be getting mine. I was fortunate enough not to get one of those letters, but still it was a very uneasy time. I felt a lot of empathy for those who had to go and really didn't want to.

Of course, we all knew there were a lot of blacks getting drafted and being sent to Vietnam, when middle and upper class whites were getting out or not getting called in the first place. Their parents had either money or influence or both. We were very aware of this, and it was a terrible feeling to see that there it was again – racism. That was definitely a big issue in the community: the number and percentage of blacks being drafted and going into the military. We wanted to know the truth about how is it we're a certain percentage of the population, but a much higher percentage of us are fighting this white man's war. So given the way the whole system was set up, the lottery didn't help makes things less unfair and unjust.

I definitely asked myself whether the real reason I didn't want to go was fear or my belief that it was an immoral war. I supported Martin Luther King and Gandhi in terms of using peaceful means to bring about social change. That had a big influence on my thinking and my feelings about the war. It was the idea that every effort should be made to resolve things peacefully and not automatically to go to war.

I had seen examples of inequality from my earliest years. I was born in '46, and the situation that confronted my family was that a low-income housing project was just opened, and even though the entire neighborhood was white, they only allowed blacks to move in. That was when you began to see major white flight. Even though I was very young, I knew what was happening was pretty rotten. But one of the things that was always good about my folks was they always bent over backwards to help people out and, despite the fact that we lived in a low income housing project and that there were eleven of us counting my parents, with four bedrooms, there was always room for someone else. There were many families my folks helped out both financially as well as bringing them into our home.

After all of us got older and started moving out, my folks took in foster children, even adopting a couple of the kids. I know I picked up on their kindness, because I actually was supposed to go into teaching. It turned out I wasn't so keen on going into teaching, but I wanted to help people out. That's when I discovered a position at the University of Connecticut with Upward Bound. Financially, I would have been better off going into business someplace, but I decided that was not what I really wanted. Job satisfaction was most important to me and here it is, going on thirty-six years and I'm still here. I can honestly say the money isn't the greatest, but in terms of job satisfaction, seeing so many people come through this program, and the great things that have gone on for them, has been very gratifying for me.

There have been situations where I was working with students who were contemplating the military, and I told them to remember to read that fine print. I didn't try to persuade them one way or the other, even though truthfully I was persuasive with my advice to get an education. The military was saying all these grandiose things to young people to entice them to go into the service, and once they got in, it was basically, "We got you!" and it was tough for them to get out. I leaned toward advising them to stay in school, and I did tell them, based on my Vietnam War awareness about the service, that the military isn't always telling you the truth. That realization, and the feelings that went along with it, have affected me in terms of how I worked with students from back when I first began at the university in the '70s until the present.

It's hard looking back on those days. Thinking about all the turmoil in the country, and the many people who didn't make it through, brings back a lot of the anxiety and sadness. What do you do? Today I am still involved in some peace groups, and my beliefs about finding peaceful ways to resolve conflict haven't really changed. Obviously a lot of the work is related to what is going on today in America, but the memories of those days during the Vietnam War will never fade. They will always be there.

George Laye

George is originally from Havre de Grace, Maryland. He is sixty-eight, divorced and has been living in the Berkshires for thirty-nine years. He's done a variety of things, from being a carpenter to being on the road as a road manager. He is currently director of the Guthrie Center in Great Barrington, Massachusetts. George met Arlo Guthrie in the late sixties and has been a close family friend ever since. He is the godfather of Arlo's children. Here is a brief description of the Guthrie Center:

Alice's Restaurant isn't around anymore. But, as the song says, "Alice didn't live in a restaurant. She lived in the church nearby the restaurant..." And the old Trinity Church, where Alice once lived and where the saga began has become home to The Guthrie Center and The Guthrie Foundation.

Arlo Guthrie, wanting to provide a place to bring together individuals for spiritual service, as well as cultural and educational exchange, founded the Guthrie Center, an Interfaith Church, in 1991. The Trinity Church where the song "The Alice's Restaurant Massacree" began, and where the movie "Alice's Restaurant" was filmed, continues to service the local and international community.

I was a senior in high school, and I had turned eighteen in March of 1960. The recruiters came into our high school in April, and they were talking to us about the Army, and about what we would need to do to register for the draft. I raised my hand and asked, "What do you mean 'register for the draft?'" They told me when you turn eighteen you register for the draft. I said, "Oh, well, no one told me anything about this. I'm eighteen."

"You're eighteen now?" they asked, and suddenly stood at attention like it was very serious. I was very naïve; I didn't know registering was so serious. They pulled me out of school within a matter of minutes and took me to go register for the draft that day. It was just a month or two since I turned eighteen, and they were telling me about penalties and jail time for failing to register. It was unbelievable. I thought they were just joking around with us, but they were not joking. I guess I was the only one who had turned eighteen by that point. What really sticks in my mind is that these guys were deadly serious.

I was still living at home. I was preparing to go to college. I was going to go to a satellite school of William and Mary down in Richmond, Virginia.

My parents wanted me to attend college, because they didn't get the chance and I should. My dad had been in World War II and, of course, he had had to register for the draft, but I guess my folks didn't realize I also had to register. They weren't anti-war. They were "regular Joes."

I began college that fall of 1960 at the William and Mary satellite. I went one year and then flunked out. I wasn't ready for college. I dropped out, worked for a year, and then went back to school. This time I chose a school in Baltimore. That's where I discovered folk music. I got a job working at the Blue Dog Cellar. I worked there as a waiter and whatever else they needed from '62 through '63.

I was again exempt from the draft when I returned to school, and that was one of the reasons I went back. I stayed in college another semester before deciding to move to New York City. I was out of school and 1-A again in 1963. I worked as a road manager for a new group that was put together at the Blue Dog. We shared an apartment, and I worked in a department store to make ends meet. I hated it. I was freezing all winter, and I was poor.

While I was working at the Blue Dog, I met a black gospel folk rock duo called "Joe and Eddie." They had a couple of hit songs, and we became really good friends. One time they said, "You gotta come to LA." I read the *New York Times* every day at lunch and at one point I saw a big ad that they were going to be in town. Within two days, I had joined them and was living in Hollywood. By this point it's mid-'64, and I recall my mom calling me from Maryland and saying, "You have a letter."

Of course, it was a letter from the Selective Service. She opened it while we were on the phone, and it said something about court and a physical, so I said, "Mom, send it out here right away!" She did. I then called the Selective Service in California and told them I'd moved. They basically said, no problem, and they would just re-register me in California. I was petrified. I said, "Oh, Jesus. I'm 1-A. I have no deferments. I'm going to go. What am I going to do?" Oh, man, I was panicked. The war had really started by then, and it was all we were talking about. I had been saying this war is crazy, but I had done nothing to protect myself. I was scared.

I got hold of some friends right away. I wasn't drafted yet. I was re-registered in California, so I had more time to think this situation through. I got together with a buddy of mine and told him, "I'm going to get drafted. What the hell am I going to do?" By that point I had gotten my draft notice.

He said, "You know there's this guy we hear about through the grapevine. He's an attorney and very sympathetic to the cause. He's giving a free clinic that gives legal advice to guys in your situation."

I got hold of this guy, and he said, "Well, here's the deal. You could have done some kind of a psychiatric thing if you'd been seeing me for a few months, but you can't just let them feel like, "Oh, you've gotten drafted, and all of a sudden you're seeing a shrink?" I guess I was one of those guys who thought it could never happen to me because I had known about it and hadn't done anything, but the fact was when I'd dropped out of school, and nothing had happened, I ended up believing nothing would happen. Now that it had, I only had so much time.

I had my draft notice, and there was a date. My counselor said, "Here's what you have to do. When you go for the physical, there are a lot of different avenues you can explore. One is the hearing test. If you fail the hearing test, you're not going in the army. It's that simple. You'll be put in this little chamber, and they'll put headphones on you and give you a button. Then they'll say, 'Tell us when you hear the sound in the earphones.' Meanwhile you'll count, 'One thousand one, one thousand two,' but you've got to be consistent. You have to have the same results each time." Another one he told me about was, "When the guy in front of you has his blood drawn, start holding your breath. You'll pass out as soon as they jab you with the needle."

Each strategy was to make you look weak, not fit. You could tell them, "I can't pee," or "I don't have to pee." You could sit down in line. He told me not to get physical with anyone, but you could say you're tired or you have a headache. He told me not to be too much of an asshole; just be natural. There was a place on the form that asks, "Are you homosexual?" The counselor suggested that I should check "yes," and then scratch it out with my fingernail and check "no." That was intended to make them wonder what was going on. If one tactic didn't work, try the next one.

By this point I was getting very nervous. People were throwing a party for several of us facing the draft at my friend's house in the Valley. We decided we were going to get really stoned and really drunk. We would not sleep all night and be totally exhausted the next morning when we went in to downtown L.A. I wasn't much of a druggie, though I smoked marijuana regularly. I tried everything else that night. You have to wonder how I stayed alive.

I went downtown the next day. When we got there all the peace movement folks were out in front. We took all their flyers and pamphlets. Of course, the military folks took all of these hand-outs from us as soon as we arrived. They wouldn't let us take them inside.

I really didn't believe in the war. I was still a young kid and I was afraid, but I didn't believe in the bullshit and I knew I wasn't going to go. I had faith in myself. I remember the first room I was in and I remember seeing all these guys and thinking, "Man, these guys have nothing to do with me." We had nothing in common. These guys really wanted to be there. Of course, I quickly found out I was in the wrong room. I was in the room with the guys who had enlisted. These guys were Army guys, and talking about how they were going to do this and that when they got in and went to Vietnam. I raised my hand, and the officer in charge said, "You're not supposed to be here. This is for enlistees."

He took me to another room, and that's when I saw *my* people. None of us wanted to be there, so at least I had someone to talk to until the processing started. I spent the rest of the day in my underwear feeling humiliated. The hearing test was first. I kept my composure, and I thought, "I can do this." All I had to do was fail this test, and I could go home. It was just like they said. There was the button you held, and then counted to whatever you counted to, and pushed. You had to do a couple of different things at different pitches. I got through it, and I came out, and there was an Army guy standing there. He sent me right back to the test area again. You had to do it three times if you failed the first time. They wanted to see if you failed in a consistent way. The third time I was thinking, "All I need is one more time, and I can do it." When I came out after the third time, there was another guy standing there by the door who said, "That's close enough. You passed." I was just beside myself.

The next part I remember is I was sitting down in line. We're just hundreds of guys in line in endless hallways with different colored lines, blue lines and red lines that you had to follow. Everyone was standing, but I sat down in the line, and this guy came up and screamed at me. He screamed at me so loud, he scared me. He was yelling, "Get up. What are you doing? Who the hell are you?" I said, "I have a headache, and if I sit down my headache will go away." I was trying not to be arrogant. I wasn't trying to piss him off. I was just trying to say, "Look, I've got a headache and this is what helps it." He screamed at me again to stand up, and I said, "No, I'm not in the Army.

At the end of the day you'll tell me to stand up, and I'll probably have to, but now I'm sitting." They didn't force me to stand.

Then we went into the room to do the blood test, and I held my breath, and I swear to God, as soon as they put the needle in, I was gone. I had no idea it would work like that. The next thing I remember was I was lying on a bed. It didn't stop them from taking blood.

They sent me to the shrink because of the homosexual thing, since I had tried that angle, too. I had filled out the form, and they had a question. The shrink asked me, "What does this mean?" I had written I was homosexual, then crossed it out, so he asked, and I won't ever forget this, "Are you a homosexual now?" I said, "Well, if I was a homosexual now, I would be coming onto you, wouldn't I?" That's all I could think to say. I didn't know how their system worked. I'd never been to a shrink before, and I certainly didn't ask to see one.

Next I got sent to an officer, and he asked, "Do you have any outstanding warrants?" I hadn't heard anything about this from anyone I had spoken to before. They hadn't advised me about that at the attorney's, but the way he said it made me think he knew I'd been busted recently for hitchhiking. I hadn't been hitching on the sidewalk; I was on the street and so I'd gotten arrested. I didn't have it taken care of yet, but I knew it was coming, and I was prepared to deal with it. The officer said I needed to make a phone call to a friend, and it needed to be on a conference call, because he would be on another line. I had to have a friend verify they would take care of this warrant by the time of my induction. They got the phones out and said, "O.K., call your friend." I said, "Well, I don't have any friends." He asked, "How long have you been living here," and I answered, "Oh, four years." I said, "I don't know anybody, I haven't met anybody." I was desperate, so I thought I'd play with it. They kept insisting, but I kept saying I didn't know anybody and that I had no friends. I stuck with it. They said, "Well, you're not going anywhere until this is taken care of." Next thing I know, I'm walking out of that fucking place. All those guys out back were getting on the buses, and I felt like I had just been let out of jail. Even just thinking about it is affecting me again right now.

I went down to a funky little diner somewhere in downtown L.A. I couldn't talk to my friends. I couldn't call anybody. I'll never forget what happened during that physical. I ordered the chicken salad sandwich with a glass of milk, and I savored every bite and sip, and then I called my friend. I said, "Come and get me out of here." I couldn't believe it.

I didn't call my family. I had a very close and wonderful relationship with my family, but they were of another school of thought. They wouldn't have understood it. They might have looked at me as a draft dodger. They knew it wasn't World War II, so they didn't want me going to war, but they wanted me out on a college deferment. They weren't well-read enough to understand what was really going on over there; they just didn't want their son going off to die in *this* war. I kept thinking that if this *had* been World War II, I would have joined just like my dad did.

When I saw those men getting on those buses, I knew that if I hadn't gotten off on the warrant, I would have had to have another alternative. I wasn't going. I had thought about Canada or jail. We were all talking about it. Jesus, I didn't want to go to jail, and I really didn't have any idea about going to Canada. I had only one more tactic in mind if the warrant thing hadn't happened, and I had passed the physical. I was thinking about it as the day of the physical wore on, since I didn't know there was going to be a warrant question. It was something the counselors had told us about being clumsy once you got to boot camp. I was just going to have to fuck up there. I had nothing else left. It was just the grace of God, and the part of my mind that allowed me to think of how to handle that circumstance when it arrived, that kept me sane. It was desperation at that point. Getting kicked out of boot camp was the last option.

Within two months I received a letter from the Army, which said: "Dear Mr. Laye, Your records have been misplaced. Please call the Selective Service." I put it right in the fireplace. I knew I was supposed to take care of that warrant. They said after I took care of it, they'd talk to me and re-do my physical, but I felt a tremendous sense of success and relief. If I had called a friend like they told me, I could have been on one of those buses and might very well have ended up in Vietnam. The amazing thing was it was all about this warrant. Hitchhiking got me out of the fucking Army. The only bad thing was I should have written a song about it [an allusion to his friend, Arlo Guthrie's "Alice's Restaurant" ballad.]

The truth is that physical was one of the milestones of my life, and it's still with me. It actually feels like it was yesterday when I think about it. I'm choked up talking about it, and I can still see those buses there. I can't find words for it. It was amazing, and it had a big impact on my life. For years I was always looking over my shoulder, waiting for them to come after me. I was always waiting for the next letter. I kept thinking, "It's the Army. They're going to find me." I didn't feel free at all when I was burning that letter. It was just, "Fuck you. This is my next move. You've had yours, now this is mine. You've lost the shit, and it's just unbelievable. I hope you really lost it." It was many years before I stopped worrying. It wasn't that I was paranoid all the time, but I kept wondering, "Is there a statute of limitations? Are they going to catch up with me and say, 'You did this, and your ass is going to jail?' You can't do this to the United States.'" There were still more years of the war, and it was always in the back of my head. I got married, I moved back east, but it was always with me.

There's still the sense of relief. I have no regrets about not getting drafted. I didn't believe in the war in Vietnam. I don't believe in the wars in Iraq or Afghanistan, and I probably would do the same thing again, if I were that age now and there was another draft. Again, if it were World War II, I probably would have joined. It's that simple.

As I tell my story I realize I really haven't shared it with hardly anyone. I told my wife when it was all happening. Sharing it now makes me wonder what has kept me from telling my friends. I don't know why I haven't chosen to. Maybe there's something inside me that still feels the need to protect myself from being caught. It feels good to talk about it, to get it off my chest this way.

I really didn't think about it at the time, but I am now also aware that someone else went in my shoes. I got out this way, and another man went. That seems kind of selfish, now that I think of it. But I know I'd do the same thing if it were happening again now. I wouldn't go to Iraq or Afghanistan. Self-preservation is a huge thing.

Roger Wallace

Roger grew up in Springfield, Massachusetts. He now lives in Amherst with his wife. His older daughter also lives in Amherst with his four grandchildren and his younger daughter is a doctoral student at Yale. He teaches sixth grade at Fort River Elementary School, where he has been employed for thirty-six years. He met his wife, a social worker, at Clark University. He believes living in Amherst enables him "to live on multiple islands – as an African American, a male teacher in an elementary school, a Christian, a member of Town Meeting and a coach."

I grew up in Springfield, Massachusetts, in an apartment in Reed Village, across the street from Oak Grove Cemetery. It was public housing, and quite a few servicemen lived there, mostly from Westover Air Force Base in Chicopee. For me, being in the service was a cool thing. Those who lived in public housing, and whose husbands were in the service, drove cool cars. It was an opportunity to leave the neighborhood. Someone's father would take me to air shows, since my father was absent; my parents divorced when I was two. The military wasn't a scary thing for any of us growing up. It was also "peace time," after the Korean War, and soldiers came home on leave and hung out with us kids.

During my high school years, I was lucky enough to get a scholarship through the ABC (A Better Chance) Program to Wilbraham Academy. I was a little on the young side, with an August birthday. I had to register for the draft in 1969. I remember going to the post office in Springfield that summer, after graduating from Wilbraham. In retrospect, filling out that card didn't mean a thing.

By 1969 Clark University was already a hotbed of activity. There were undercover F.B.I. guys posing as students and assistant professors. We knew who they were, and I think they knew we knew. But for me what really mattered was the plight of the African American in this country. I didn't think at the time about the statistics of how many soldiers were African-American, or whether this war was, according to the Black Panther leadership, a methodology of genocide for blacks, particularly males, of course. I knew I had a future. I was willing to use the student exemption, because I was actually doing something – getting an education.

I was at Clark when they closed the school down in 1970 to protest the war. By this point I believed the war was unjust. Muhammad Ali had said, "No Vietcong has ever called me nigger." I was a history and economics major, and I had my political science classes. I followed the war in my living room or the dorm room. I got to see it, and it was scary, and I developed a different view of the military. It became a killing machine. It wasn't the Blue Angels, or the other Air Force stunt flyers any more. It was a lot more than that, and I was scared.

The day I got my number we were all sitting in my college dorm room. We were listening to the radio, and people made a variety of noises when their numbers came up. August 20 came up and I got the number 69. I said, "This is a good thing. 69 in '69. It's going to be O.K." At that moment, I had not yet seen the terrors of war in a way that made me think, "Oh, my God, that could be me." So I never gave it a bit of thought other than that's my number. There were about fifteen of us, black and white, mostly basketball players since I played for Clark. We made it not a celebration, but a reality. I remember this man Dave, who was legally blind and wasn't going anywhere, but he was included, and we wanted him with us. He said, "Guys, we're adults now. That means two things. Number one, I don't want you guys to go. And number two, you may have to go." We all just got quiet.

I did not have a phone in my room. My mom had the dorm phone number. Of course, she had to be first to call. "Roger, your number is 69." And I said, "Mom, back up. I am just eighteen and if I go..." She just stopped me in mid-sentence. I had told her there were FBI guys at Clark, since it was such a radical place. She then asked, "When are you coming home?" I told her, "Mom, I'm coming home. I've got exams. Please don't worry about it."

I got home, and we immediately went to my grandmother's house where we discussed all of this. I remember my grandmother was just sitting in her chair and my grandfather was sitting in his swivel chair. I don't know why we didn't have this conversation at home, but we had it there, a conversation about what I could do now that I had this low number. I said, "Mom, I think I'm grown." To say that to a mother who is a black woman, well you better *know* you're grown, there's no such thing as "thinking." She said, "You'll always be my baby." And I responded, "But I am your grown baby and if I have to go, I will."

In church Reverend Fullilove, a contemporary of Dr. King, did a prayer. A lot of us were back from college and attending the Third Baptist Church in Springfield. There was a prayer service, and several mothers came to the altar and prayed. Some were reluctant, but my grandmother was a deaconess, which meant, "Get your butt up and pray..." They prayed for their sons' safety, but it was not an anti-war statement. There is another important thing to be mindful about in terms of the political structure, and the black people who lived in the country back then. We were going to prove ourselves worthy. Unfortunately we didn't realize there was nothing to be proven: we were already worthy.

Then I saw the atrocities, and I didn't want to go. It was quite clear in my heart and mind, but I didn't talk about it. If I was going to be inducted, then I was going to run. Did I make any plans? No. This is a man who read every Harriet Tubman story. I knew where the North Star was. If I wanted to run, I would run, and I wouldn't tell anyone until I got where I was going. But it never came to that. My wife knew I was willing to face leaving if that became necessary, but plans did not have to be made until that time and we didn't talk about it much. I also learned about being a conscientious objector. I might have gone that route. It would have been very hard for me to leave the country. I'm a family guy, and don't give up connections very well. I believe I probably wouldn't have just run. I was prepared to, but fortunately there were other avenues.

And, of course, there was a whole other social movement going on. There were the riots in '65. You had Detroit exploding. You had King walking through Chicago and being stoned in '66. People still called me nigger in the streets of Worcester away from campus. I had to decide what I was going to do. I chose to become part of an anti-war group at Clark. They had these pamphlets printed up and I had to drop them off at the homes I was assigned in places like Paxton. They had never seen a black person in Paxton, let alone one passing out leaflets, but I went. It seemed like the people knew we were coming.

The leaflets were well done. They were generic. They contained questions like: "Think about what this war means." "Are we saving the world?" "Should our boys be dying?" "Will Communism in Vietnam affect you?" I got tongue-lashings like you would not believe. The first was from some retired servicemen. I did something I didn't think I had the capacity to do at the time. I just sat and listened to these men. They talked about

World War II. We had received a little training because our leaders anticipated that we would encounter resistance. This was an opportunity, as I
saw it, to dialogue about what their war meant to them. Being a history
major I was very aware, so when they started talking I said, "Yes, and this
is what you were fighting about. There were concentration camps...There
was Pearl Harbor, but do you realize that Japanese Americans were locked
up in camps like Manzanar* in California and they had done nothing? They
owned shops." Sometimes the light would go on.

Other times one of the men I was addressing would say, "But they
were our enemy." And I'd answer him, "Here you are, a white American,
and me a Black American, talking about whether we should be fighting this
war. You say, "Yes," and I say, "I'm not sure," but I want you to think about
these things." Here I was talking to white folks in Paxton, Massachusetts.
I got an education. There were some wars worth fighting, and it did get me
to think and ask myself, "Is this one of those?"

Those are the good stories. There are the stories of people saying,
"Don't be putting that stuff on my porch! Boy, you better leave out of here."
And they meant "boy" in the sense of "Nigger, you better be getting off my
steps." But it was O.K., because interspersed every now and then I made a
good connection.

What was the hardest, though, was when you came to a house where
someone was serving. I would just sit with the person, and it would come
up. "My son is there." And I would say, "Then we need to talk. You need
to tell me what you're feeling." And they would. Sometimes they felt the
war was just, and sometimes they didn't. But I would say, "I need to put
these flyers down and listen to your story." It was at that moment that I
realized whatever I was going to be and do in life had to be along these
lines, something where I could stop at any point and hear someone's real
story. Now you can do that being a lawyer, which I thought I was going
to train to do, or you can do it as a teacher. There are other professions as
well, but I loved kids. It was at that moment, sitting on a porch with one
of those mothers, that I had this realization. She would say, "I'm glad my
husband isn't home, because he would hurt you." And I would say, "I know,
but may I come back? I would like to talk more with you, because I need
to learn."

---

*Manzanar is most widely known as the site of one of ten camps where over
110,000 Japanese Americans were imprisoned during World War II.

I didn't have a car. My friend would drive me out there and he would drive me back. Sometimes the husband would be there the next time. We'd bring sodas and I would say, "Would you like a soda? We came out here as people against the war, but we need to learn about how it is affecting people." People respected that. The man bristled, but he went in, got his military hat, put it on and said, "You're going to listen to me. I served and my son is serving." And I said, "Tell me what it means." I was against the war, but I was one of those people who were not against the military. They follow orders; right, wrong or indifferent. I was willing to say to them, "I don't share your point of view, but I do understand your son is doing the work he has been ordered to do, and I respect that."

At that moment, my canvassing work changed. I had been doing in-the-city canvassing, but the anti-war group on campus wanted me to work outside the city, I guess because I was a good listener. I was very quiet. I asked a lot of questions. I still felt it was important to be against the war, but I wanted to link up with those people who had an investment there. It was one of the things I worked out for myself. It enabled me to talk to people who had never talked to a black person in their entire life, but who talked to me, and I was thankful for that. I listened and I learned.

And I got lucky. I didn't graduate from Clark until '73 and, after those four years with my student deferment, they stopped calling people. I didn't have to face either the physical or the tough decision. All of the angst I felt about what I might have to do disappeared, and I became a person who thought globally, but acted locally. When I knew I wasn't going, I asked myself, "What the heck are you going to do now?" The only thing I could think about doing was helping people, and I was determined to make a difference in the lives of the people I touched. I decided I wanted to be a teacher, and that's what I did. My life has become one in which I try to teach the children in my classroom alternative methods of dealing with conflict.

In my friendship world, I had people who came back from Vietnam, and later, in my professional life, I met people who served. In my family, my wife's brother served, but the things he did and the atrocities he saw, he kept to himself. In my adult life I have met people who flew over Vietnam and dropped bombs. One of the gentlemen I met was one of the perfecters of Agent Orange, a chemical engineer. He and I never talked about what happened, but I work with his wife. He didn't have to connect the dots for me. I did it for myself. I think I know what that meant for him. I never pressed it. If you were not there, if you did not serve... All of those I encountered talked about the emotional scars they felt – not why, but because they were there. I did not want to push them, and I didn't really want to know.

When I was fifty-two, I learned that a man I'd known for years was a pilot in the military. We were sitting together at an anniversary party, when two of the men said they'd both served in the military during Vietnam. The one who flew planes realized he'd flown over the terrain where the other was stationed. They told stories, and they allowed us to listen. The rest of us became silent, because we hadn't been there, and they were letting us in. For me, that's all I really needed. I was no longer curious about the atrocities. There were enough atrocities that I, as an African-American male, as a black person in this country, as a person related to those in Africa and the things that happened there, I didn't need to know all the details. I chose not to ask. These people I heard stories from were kind, church-going, and family-oriented, with a part of their lives that was painful, scary, and had left emotional scars. Those are theirs. They belong to them. When they choose to share them, I'm willing to listen. It reminds me that when I was eighteen years old, I did some good things. I sat on steps, and listened to people, and didn't act like I knew it all, and didn't act like I knew what it was like to make the "supreme sacrifice" of having my son or my daughter going to war. I am proud of that ability to listen, and to listen without adding a word. People don't do that enough.

What I have learned from all this, and what I know now as I look at our modern day conflicts, is that people make the sacrifice; governments make the commitment but people make the sacrifice. On a moment-by-moment level that's very hard to understand for those of us who haven't been sent, who haven't gone. I don't really understand it. I have only shared in it, because people have told me.

Being in a place that is predominantly white, there is a certain degradation that black people feel as a result of white privilege. Some people say, "But I am Jewish." And I respond, "If you are walking down the street, some people might not identify you that way, but when I am walking down the street, I *am* black." I have been walking down the streets of Amherst, Massachusetts at two in the afternoon and had someone roll down their window and say, "Hey, nigger..." I've had parents in the school where I teach who wondered if I could academically challenge their eleven and twelve year olds. It means that the war I fight is not one of blood and guts and guns and bombs, but one for personal respect and dignity.

I have my own respect and dignity, but being a member of the Amherst teaching community...black folks have to be better than whites to be accepted. We have got to be better. That's the war we fight. There have been twenty-some years here where I have been the only African American male teacher in the whole entire elementary school system. That's a war. That's a war for recognition, and it's a war that I have to fight. It was the man on the steps in Paxton who taught me how to fight it. He put aside whatever negative opinions he had about blacks, so he could tell me about the pain of war in a way I could understand. As I've said, sometimes you just sit and you listen and you're willing to share.

When you are eighteen, nineteen, or twenty, you're stupid. My daughter is twenty-one. Her opinions are so strong, and so directed, and she is so sure she's right. And yet, in Paxton, I got the blessing that, for a few minutes, I realized I might not be right, I better listen to this man. That moment changed my whole life. I can never forget it. And when I started to tell about it now, I almost decided not to, because I didn't want anybody else to know – that there is honor in serving. That man had served in war and his son was serving and there was a link between them. It didn't matter whether the war was just or not. Those two men were linked and I had never thought about the honor in men serving. In much the same way I was going to be the first person in my family to graduate college and this man was going to serve like his father had served and there was honor in that. I realized the son was achieving a goal that he wanted to accomplish to please his father in the same way I was pleasing my family by going to college. It was the same. For me this realization is the keynote. It is the story. One of those men in Paxton asked me, "Did your father serve?" And I answered him, "My father left when I was two years old so I never really got his story, but you can tell me yours."

Art Carrington

Art was raised in New Jersey. He is the owner of a tennis academy in Amherst, Massachusetts. He is a former tennis pro who played on the tour and was one of only a very few African Americans, along with Arthur Ashe competing on an international level. He has been married to Suzanne since 1967 and they have one son, Arthur Lex Carrington III ,who is a professional tennis coach. He and Suzanne also have three grandchildren.

I was teaching high school in Elizabeth, New Jersey in 1969-1970 in what they called an "inner city school." That gave me a deferment. At the end of the school year I notified the district that I wasn't going to be returning so immediately my name went to the draft board. I wanted to be a tennis pro. I wanted to teach tennis, live the life of tennis.

I grew up on picket lines, you understand. I saw Malcolm X when I was eight or nine years old. My aunt lived on 129th Street and Lenox Avenue in Harlem. I went to Malcolm X's funeral. My father was a Tuskegee Airman* so I was brought up with an active civil rights scene right in my home. He was a brick mason by trade, but he was a black leader, too. When he was young he couldn't be in the brick masonry union because of his race, so he was active in getting the first trade unions opened to blacks in New Jersey. Once it finally happened he was very involved in the union. My mother worked in a recreation department. She graduated from college at 50, got a masters degree, retired as a guidance counselor, and then taught school in Elizabeth. The bottom line is, even though my father was in World War II, he and my mother were both against the Vietnam War.

My brother, even though he is younger, faced the draft first, because he left school to travel and go to Europe. He found a way to beat it. He put tracks in his arm. He knew you got to scam these dudes into believing that you're going to be counterproductive. It doesn't make any difference, pick what you want to, but it's got to be something like drugs, being gay, black

---

*Tuskegee Airmen were the first African-American military aviators in the United States armed forces. During World War II, African Americans in many U.S. states still were subject to Jim Crow laws. The American military was racially segregated, as was much of the federal government. The Tuskegee Airmen were subject to racial discrimination, both within and outside the Army. Despite these adversities, they flew with distinction. They were particularly successful in their missions as bomber escorts in Europe.

militancy, Islam, something. Nobody ever got down on him for doing this because nobody knew what he was doing.

I went to Dr. Kaplan, the Jewish doctor in our neighborhood who had been my doctor since I was a baby and charged us $5 a visit in the early days. I wanted him to write me a letter saying I had smoked marijuana, so I could get their attention when I got called to go for my physical. I scared him with this request. I told him, "Man, you been knowin' me since I was born. You got to give me a note just like you givin' to all these white boys. I know what's goin' on. I meet these guys in the tennis world. I can't go over there." I wanted to be presenting to the draft board that I was part of the counterculture, that if they took me it was going to cost them and this letter would help make that case. His son was on the draft board and I figured he'd know the in's and out's, but I had definitely scared him. He said, "Art, you've got to sign so you never hold me responsible." But it turned out he wouldn't do it even with me signing off, so I had to go to someone else. I found another doctor who would.

My parents knew I was trying to get out of 'Nam. I chose to go to Hampton (Hampton Institute, a historically black college in Virginia). Large white schools had recruited me and I counted them out. I wanted to be at a black college. That gave me a deferment for four years, but I was on my own. My parents weren't even an issue with me and the draft.

As soon as I left the teaching job I had taken after graduating from Hampton, I immediately got a letter from the draft board calling me for a physical. I went up to the Elizabeth board and they bus you over to Newark. Everybody comes in there like a herd of cattle. First you go in and take some mental tests. I went in and flunked everything. From the very beginning I told the guys, "You don't have anything down here for my race." I thought, "I'll show them I'm an original maniac." I started acting weirdly in the room when they gave us the first test. My intention was to not cooperate at all with this process. I went in there and everybody white got busted. I had to just portray another dude. This was all about survival. From the time I started the first test, I told the dude, "I'm a college graduate. I'm going to be flunking everything. There's nothing I'm cooperating with here. What you going to do about that category."

I went from one station to another. I was harassing, if I could. What were they going to do, beat me up in there? I tried to convince them they didn't want someone like me in the military. "You can waste your time with me, because you'll have to rehabilitate me. Get somebody else that's 'fresh'."

I remember the first doctor I saw. Nice guy. He was like the fathers of guys I went to high school and played tennis with. He was Jewish and he was trying to rap to me. I knew where he was coming from, but at the same time I had to portray this image that I needed to get me out of the situation I was in. He was trying to tell me that my people needed young guys like me – young, educated, college material. I told him, "You don't know a fucking thing about me, what I'm like, and you don't know my people either. So just be the doctor here and shut the fuck up about who I am and who my people are." I was trying to do whatever I needed to do, present however I needed to present to get out of this – whether it was him suspecting that I was doing drugs or whatever was necessary. He was trying to speak to me and get personal with me and I couldn't let that happen. His way of supporting me was to send me to the next level, not to get mad and keep me in the system, but to somehow say, "I really do believe that you have something that needs to be dealt with." It reminds me of something I recently read. It said, "Nature unaided fails." He was my aid.

What happened next was he wrote me up to the psychiatrist. Once you get pulled out like that, you've got the best chance to be pulled out of the numbers game. That's what I needed. I needed him to send me to someone else. The psychiatrist was a black dude who knew my athletic director at Hampton College, my tennis coach – he knew everybody. He was part of the black intelligentsia that knew all of my mentors. Getting to him was my out. It was now just a question of how we were going to classify my "out." The truth is I had no idea I would be sent to a black man. When I got into his office it switched the game up. He knew the doctor sent me. He knew I was coming. I never thought this was luck. It all reinforces my spirituality in terms of how life is and what is meant to be. It was all written. I was just playing a part that was already scripted without even knowing it.

So I was out. I didn't have to go over there and the why didn't matter. I was not going to have to die over there in Vietnam. Muhammed Ali wasn't going and if I hadn't gotten out the way I did, I would have found another way, because I didn't see myself going. My father had to be a laborer, a brick mason; nobody was giving us no reparations for this. What would I be doing going to fight in some war for a country that treated us this way? Nobody paid any attention to what happened to me. I told folks I got a 4-F. I wasn't embarrassed. I came from a different environment and I didn't really talk about it. This is the first time I am talking about what really happened. But if someone asks how I end up standing here today I have to tell them that the story is about me going up against the system like I did with the draft board. Being able to travel around the world with tennis and being able to go to college was me beating the system. My motivation for my son to be a world class junior tennis player was for me to beat the same USTA (United States Tennis Association) that denied us because we were black. What I felt was defiance.

So then why didn't I just become a tennis pro when I got out? Tennis was secondary. I couldn't mentally just accept playing tennis all the time with a bunch of white kids at freaking country clubs. I rejected that part of myself. It was very hard for me to overcome that rejection of being successful at something that was so far away from the other experience of being black. I used what I needed to use from that experience, the same thing my white counterparts used to get out of that situation. "Doctor, give me a letter because I heard white boys were getting letters."

Then there was this guy, Billy Morton, from Cleveland, Ohio. He was my doubles partner at Hampton. I met him when I was fourteen years old in 1962. He won the National Black eighteen-and-under junior championship. I was in the final of the sixteen-and-unders and Arthur Ashe won the men's title that year. He was the best black after Arthur Ashe and then I came on over the next couple of years and passed him. He left Central State University in Ohio where he'd started college and got drafted by the Army when he dropped out of school for the semester. He went to Vietnam, did his time and then got out and I hooked him up at Hampton where I went. He went there and played number one and he and I would travel around on the amateur circuit and when we were traveling he would tell me all of these Vietnam stories. He told me that when he first got to 'Nam the high-up officers had him just for tennis. All he did was play tennis. The underlying racism snatched him from there out into the field. So he would tell me what it was like to walk out there and see someone who was killed and hung up there with a penis in his mouth. He told me how low war took men. When I think about these crimes that they say that our men are doing in Iraq, all I can think about is the stuff he would tell me about how when you are out there in battle it takes you to the lowest state a man can go to.

Billy and I were driving through Biloxi, Mississippi and I was driving a 1973 gold Eldorado with the white wall tires. We were wearing gold chains, big panama hats and we were going from Tallahassee, Florida across I-10 over to Houston. We got to Biloxi and the highway stopped and the road took us down into this hick town. We looked over and there was a state trooper. We see him see us and I've got this Eldorado and we're on cruise control and these dudes roll up on us. My boy Billy leans over and says, "What in the fuck are you harrassin' us for? Listen, we got cruise control. We weren't speedin'. I just came back from Vietnam fightin' the fuckin' war. What in the fuck are you fuckin' with us for?" And the dude said, "Go ahead." This is why I say it was all spiritually guided.

Frank Marotta

Frank is originally from Medford, Massachusetts. He is a psychotherapist re-
siding in Northampton. His wife, Carolyn Hicks is a psychologist. He has a
twenty-five-year-old son, Philip, who is presently at Columbia University get-
ting his master's degree in social work. Frank joined several other townspeople
in arranging for a special counting machine to be placed in the window of a
local business that would track the various dead and wounded in the War in
Iraq – American soldiers, Iraqi soldiers and civilians.

I grew up in Medford in a very roughneck suburb and during the mid-
'60s there were many fights in school. It was always very confusing for me.
I felt that if I was to have an affiliation with one group I was going to have
to show some kind of hostility to everyone else and I was very uncomfort-
able choosing either a violent approach to relationships or to staying isolated. Instead I found a girlfriend and she became a kind of haven for me.

I did not want to go to college so I worked for General Electric. Little
by little the Vietnam War began to seep in. I was not attuned to the news and
in many ways my high school experience had not been touched by the war
since those around me were too busy fighting their own local wars against
one another. At G.E. though, those in vehement opposition to the growing
anti-war movement surrounded me. We were working in a place that was
profiting from the war. Regularly I'd be hearing, "We need to kill the bastards. We need to just drop atomic bombs on those darn demonstrators!"
Listening to all this stuff I'd be thinking, "Hey, they're talking about a peer
group that I am no longer part of." It aroused my interest in that peer group.

In the meantime I was racing cars and dealing with my girlfriend and
then along came pot. My old friends from high school and the neighborhood were smoking pot so I joined in. We listened to a lot of music. I think
it was through the music that I was able to get a little space from the adult
male crowd that I depended on in my work circumstance. The music was
the way that things opened up for me. I really listened to the words to these
songs. It soon became clear to me that the road to hell or to enlightenment
was the words. There were the Beatles, Janis Joplin, Jimi Hendrix, Crosby,
Stills, Nash, and Young, and Dylan. My God, Dylan was really like taking
a hallucinogenic drug all by itself. We started to go to Harvard Square to
hear some of these performers and that became a vehicle for a dawning of
consciousness.

At the same time I started to think that my job was not going to be my way of life. It just couldn't be. I couldn't bear it. I had two uncles who were white-collar workers there. There was a lot of expectation that I would follow this newly solidifying family tradition. I began to let my two uncles know how disillusioned I was becoming and one of them told me, "At least finish the apprenticeship." I had this friend in the work environment who was also becoming disillusioned and he took vocational aptitude and interest testing at Boston University. It sounded encouraging to me so I signed up for it. I spent my vacation week taking these tests. While I awaited the results, stuck like I was at G.E., my self-esteem was plummeting. It was just amazing how I would lie awake fantasizing over what freeing things I would discover when the test results came in. I fantasized that if they discovered who I *really* was, they'd solve my problem by kicking me right out of G.E!

Finally the day came for me to go in and get the results, which indicated my interests lay in fields like psychology! At some point I had to say, "Can you start over again, this doesn't sound like it relates to me. I don't recall that section. I must have been imagining things when I answered." What I was thinking was, "You can't be talking to *me*." He assured me the results were real, suggesting, "Why don't you take a course at the college level. See what happens?" He was commiserating with me that the gap between what the testing indicated and what I was doing was large. I could feel my mind opening up to bigger things.

In the summer of '69, I decided to take two courses at Tufts, but the first thing I did was give my notice. I stayed employed for a while on the night shift. In retrospect, this was very decisive, because now I was utterly cut off from my old friends and suddenly in with all these new people. My old friends came awake at night and raced cars on the weekend, but I had to be at work at night.

I was called up in late '67. My girlfriend, who was normally quite soft-spoken, was on my side. Even before I went on the bus that morning she was saying things like, "Resist. Don't do what they want." I went to the physical and it felt like a wake up call. At six o'clock in the morning two old ladies gave me some tokens and I was put on a bus of people my age. We were being herded to this examination center. I was furious, but my feelings stayed deeply buried. I couldn't stand up and say what I wanted to say. I wanted to stand in the front of the bus and say to everybody, "Look around! Two old ladies and some fat guy driving the bus are controlling us, and we can't take matters into our own hands? Do you *want* to go fight in some war? Do you even want to be physically prodded and messed with? Let's say, 'Stop!' We can't allow this to happen." I could hear all this in my head, but I did not have the courage or the trust in my sense of reality to say it out loud. I wanted to say, "We can not only disable this bus, but we can totally destroy the draft center. Then there'll be no records. There'll be no nothing. They won't even know our names. We can do that. We have enormous power in our hands, but we're just being herded like cows to the slaughter!"

I wanted to say something, but I couldn't. There were only two things I *could* do. On the written stuff, I said I slept with my mother and that I urinated in the bed at night all the time. Then, when they asked, "Is there anything we don't know about you?" I said in desperation, "Yes, I have a broken knee that I got in a skiing accident two years ago." In fact, I *had* been in a skiing accident, but the x-ray showed I had only *twisted* the knee. I qualified to be seen a second time.

A period of time went by before I was called for a re-examination. By this time my anger was turning into action. My girlfriend was decisive in this, because she got me hooked up with her minister. After he and I talked for a while, he suggested, "If you want to do something to educate people, I have this room in the church house you can use." So two things started to come together. One was the beginning of a support network, and the other involved going back to my family physician. I explained my situation to him and he said to come back the following week. I went back a week later and, handing me an x-ray, he said, "Use this." I went to my reexamination and they asked, "Do you have any further information to add concerning your broken knee?" I said, "Here's the x-ray."

Soon after I received a card in the mail, telling me I was now classified 1-Y because of my injury. I remember how I felt when I got classified this way. I didn't feel that I was participating in a crime. Not at all. I felt like I was *refusing* to participate in a crime – the war. I felt the same feeling I have now about the war in Iraq: rage. At the time all my strong feelings were being channeled and fed by the draft, leading me to draft resistance.

So the 1-Y got me out, but my whole psyche had been affected by this experience with being drafted and going to my physical. I decided I had to get involved and began working at a draft resistance center. There were three other guys and me, with the minister in the background. With the help of the American Friends Service Committee, we started to get educated. These guys would come at night and lecture us on a whole range of things to implement straight-ahead resistance: conscientious objector status, emigration, hardship status, and how to get a medical disability.

Somehow, given these strange twists of fate, I was becoming a draft counselor. It wasn't because I had an informed political position. I didn't really even know what Vietnam was. I didn't know why we were there. I didn't know why communism was bad or democracy was good. I didn't give a damn. I didn't care. I didn't study it. I didn't want to know anything about it. I was not interested in it. What I *did* know was that many people were being taken from their lives against their will. They were being sent into battle and they were being killed and at this point even some of my friends were coming back dead. The whole thing just kept feeding an outrage at this visceral, direct level. There was nothing intellectual about it. I had friends who were saying, "I'm going to war and that's great." A guy named Kevin went to the Marines. Ray and Dennis went to the Army. I would try to push them, but we just couldn't talk. I would ask them, "Why would you want to do that?" "To kill Gooks," they'd respond with all this empty bravado. They were no more politically oriented or geographically knowledgeable than I was. No, it was some kind of machismo thing they were salivating over. That only struck me as stupid and ignorant. I feel exactly the same way now as I did then, and want to scream: "Don't you know that guns kill? What do you think you're playing?"

There's this woman in the Moore film, *Fahrenheit 9/11*, who sends her kid to war and then is shocked when he dies. I can't understand this. And then she comes out the other side saying the government took her son? No. Wrong. The government didn't take her son. Of course, they took him, they're happy to put him up as a target, but *she* gave them her son. Can anyone ever come to grips with that? She gave her son.

So, I was trying to talk to people, to help them see all this. We were setting up draft meetings, not just waiting for people to come to us. We were trying to go out and get people to *not go* in any way, to *not* do this! The more my own friends came back paraplegic or killed, the clearer the need for resisting the war became to me. Such unnecessary death was so hard to watch. These guys and I had smoked together and listened to music. We hung around and got big guys to buy beer for us and commiserated over hurts. We talked of the future. We complained about each other's parents, our own parents. We really felt that we understood each other as no one else understood us.

I remember my friend, Jimmy and his desolation. He was paralyzed from the waist down. He was in a wheelchair and on so many drugs he often could hardly recognize us. Then, when his senses cleared, he killed himself. I can't begin to tell you the rage that I felt and still feel over the loss of Jimmy and all the others. Not just now because we're talking about it. I feel it these days a lot. I go to the websites of the Iraq War casualties and look at the body counts on a daily basis. It's just dominating my thoughts all the time.

I have not yet gone to the Wall in Washington, but I'm going to at some point I know. My son, Phillip, and I went to Washington, walked around, and did everything, everything *but* that. I wasn't ready. I did go to Vietnam though, somewhat fortuitously but very determinedly nonetheless, because my wife Carolyn's brother was an engineer for a company working in Vietnam in the late '60s. So he was there, really literally walking in the park, when the first fighting broke out. He heard the pop and snap of bones and the whole thing. His company was doing supplemental engineering projects, transportation and communication systems for the military. Now he lives in Singapore. After Carolyn and I got married some twenty years ago, we went to Singapore to visit him and then about ten years ago now, we all went to Vietnam together to where his company has offices. We drove around and went to all these different places.

I spent a lot of time standing by myself on the sidewalk trying to comprehend, trying to grasp. Occasionally, I would see, in the crowd in Saigon, a deranged American face flit through. There are people there who got lost and can't find their way back. They were spirits almost. They were tangible ghosts of the whole fiasco. Our son, Philip, went back a third time and went to Hanoi as well as Saigon. He spent a lot of time absorbing the culture and when he returned he asked me, "Why were we at war? What was that about?"

And I can't fathom it. Throughout Vietnam now, you will see an extraordinarily high number of women. Where are the men? You cannot forget that there was a war, and that will not be forgotten for a long time. I can't say how many generations it is going to take. However, amazingly, there was no animosity towards us. People would be so kind. They'd come up and speak to us, those who could, and through my sister-in-law's interpretation, we could speak to each other. I try to explain it to myself and the best I can do is that in the scenario we experienced, as is much the case now in Iraq, there was a kind of cultural pride that got caught up in massive government-based, abstract clashes of ideology. That cultural belongingness is a vehicle through which the larger ideological positions can take up the populace and then the government can say, "Here's a gun. Here are some rations. Here's a target. You're shooting for your country, your identity, your culture." It's not really about fighting other human beings in this presentation. They never had human beings as the target. They had the defense of an ideology as the target.

Getting back to Vietnam in the '60s... The lottery system took the wind out of our draft counseling sails. The middle population – the less strong, the less enraged, were willing to accept the crapshoot that was the lottery, especially since by 1970 and 1971 the tide was turning and fewer people were being drafted. The tide was turning in many ways, politically, militarily, economically, so the opposition to the draft and to the war dissipated.

CHAPTER SIX

THOSE WHO CHOSE CONSCIENTIOUS OBJECTION

AS THIS PROJECT EVOLVED, I CAME TO UNDERSTAND how large an issue conscientious objection was in terms of this war. Some men knew from the first moment the draft became real for them that they would seek to become conscientious objectors. Others found the issues surrounding the war deeply affected their moral development and helped create a growing belief in pacifism; still others approached CO status as yet another strategy in their efforts to avoid the draft. Regardless of individual motivations, this status was more ardently pursued during the Vietnam War than during any other war in our history, and, as always, a successful application entailed many hurdles, often involved numerous allies, and invariably was a source of stress and struggle.

The evolution of conscientious objector status is checkered. It parallels in many ways the evolution of this country's conceptions of war, morality, religion and personal choice. To more fully appreciate both the Vietnam-era laws governing application for conscientious objector status, and the political and social climate surrounding conscientious objection during the Vietnam War, we must look again at the past.

Whether one believes that conscientious objection is a fundamental right available to all citizens, or a freedom given to only a select few deemed worthy by a panel of chosen governmental representatives, for those who *are* chosen, it undeniably grants freedom from the most basic, and potentially most dangerous, of duties: the defense of one's country. Over time legal definitions of this status have expanded. They now include more categories of exemption, as well as additional alternative methods to meet the obligations of citizenship, all of which have led to an expansion of the definition of national service.[2] The route to this destination has been long and circuitous.

Records of the first resistance to service go back to 1658 in the province of Maryland. Richard Keene, a pacifist, refused militia training and was fined and "abused by the sheriff" for "refusing to be a soldier."[3] Keene's experience seems aberrant, since from their beginnings, the American colonies permitted members of pacifist religions, the Mennonites and Brethren originating in the rural German Anabaptist tradition, and Quakers of urban, well-educated English stock, to be exempt from the draft. The requirement for such exemptions was the payment of a fee (commutation), and no colony ever forced those who objected on religious grounds to bear arms if they paid.[4]

During the Revolutionary War, the three religions experienced different treatment. Mennonites and Brethren were able to purchase exemptions from serving in the military, while Quakers were obliged to pay fines or even lose their property for their refusal to participate in the war. Over time the moral integrity of these objectors earned them some measure of grudging respect and acceptance, but the framers of the Constitution made no provision for these groups and their pacifist views.[5]

It wasn't until the Civil War, several generations later, that conscientious objection first achieved legal recognition. The same three groups composed the objectors, but their ranks now included the Seventh Day Adventists, most of whom were members of the urban working class. During the war, treatment of objectors varied, from relative leniency in the North to harsher penalties in the South.

The draft law in the North was revised in 1864 in part as a result of the protests against the draft, including the New York City Draft Riots and similar protests in Boston, Newark, Toledo, and Troy, New York. The Quakers added their voices in objection to the commutation fees that allowed wealthy men to exclude themselves from service by paying the government to hire a replacement. The result was the first law in U.S. history that recognized conscientious objection for members of the "peace" churches and made provisions for them to perform alternative service. It also afforded those whose beliefs prohibited them from any form of service with an exemption from service. Commutation was eliminated for these men.[6] The law provided further that objectors drafted into military service "be considered non-combatants." It became government policy, thanks to Lincoln, to assign such noncombatants to duty in hospitals or in educating freed slaves. For the first time, a *de facto* mode of alternate civilian service introduced civic content into conscientious objection. This was a sea change in terms of the meaning of national service in America.[7]

The World War I draft law exempted from combat service, but not military service, only those conscripts who came from traditional peace churches. CO status was created as an accommodation with two main criteria a would-be Objector *had* to satisfy: (1) the objection had to apply to all wars in all forms; and (2) the objection had to be based on "religious belief and training." Those who belonged to religious groups who did not have a traditional anti-war stance and opposed war for political reasons, or simply refused any form of service, were either forced to serve, or court-martialed and sentenced to military camps or prisons. Five hundred men were court-martialed. Seventeen received death sentences, and one hundred forty-two were sentenced to life in prison. Although the death sentences were not carried out and the life terms were reduced, these men were commonly subjected to physical abuse by their guards including cold showers, solitary confinement, poor rations and cruel punishment. One objector who refused to wear a uniform, died from pneumonia in prison, and his body, dressed in a uniform, was sent home to his parents.[8]

In the end, 65,000 registrants sought CO status during World War I. Only four thousand managed to receive CO status and do alternative service. Most did medical work in the army, but some ended up doing menial labor in and around military encampments. The American Friends Service Committee, a Quaker organization founded during World War I in response to the draft and its injustices, succeeded in pressuring the military authorities to make local and limited adjustments to alternative service, but what emerged fell far short of the standards for alternative service set by Lincoln some fifty years before.[9]

More changes occurred for conscientious objectors in both the peacetime conscription law of 1940 and the draft legislation of World War II. No longer did a man have to belong to a strictly pacifist group, although religious motives were still required. There were now three categories of objectors: noncombatant soldiers, who, though unwilling to fight in combat, are willing to serve in other military roles; absolutists, who refuse to cooperate in any way with the conscription system or to participate in alternative activities, even if unrelated to the war effort; and alternativists, who refuse any military service, but accept alternative civilian work as directed by the government.[10]

The first category, with 25,000 men, was the largest. The military set up special basic training courses in which "1-A-O's," as they were known from their draft board designations,[11] were neither trained in, nor required to carry weapons. Most served in the medical corps, where they often performed extremely hazardous work. Some were killed in combat areas. One received the Congressional Medal of Honor.

Conscientious objectors in uniform, willing to perform noncombatant roles, cause little problem for the system and easily meet the standards of the citizen soldier.[12] On the other hand, absolutists disrupted the system and were sent to jail. About six thousand men were sentenced to prison terms of up to five years. About three-quarters were Jehovah's Witnesses, whose claims for blanket exemptions as ministers have never been recognized by the government.[13] Roughly one thousand were radical pacifists, affiliated with the War Resisters League, the Catholic Worker movement, or the Socialist party. Still others were Black Muslims protesting the racism still so prevalent in society, and in a Jim Crow army, and refusing to fight in what they viewed as a "white man's war."[14]

Alternativists came under the provision of the draft law that allowed conscientious objectors to be assigned "to work of national importance under civilian direction." The lessons of World War I regarding the need to provide alternative service options had been learned, and as a result, the authorities decided that those CO's willing to do alternative service would not be sent to prison or forced to serve in the military. What resulted was the Civilian Public Service (CPS). Five hundred objectors volunteered to be human guinea pigs in government-sponsored medical experiments on diet, endurance, and the transmission and control of malaria, hookworm, typhus, and infectious hepatitis. Two thousand were assigned work in asylums and mental wards, which brought a surge of humane treatment into working with the mentally ill.[15]

Twelve thousand alternativists served in CPS camps located in rural areas, where participants performed conservation work without receiving pay. They had to depend on their own savings, if they had any (the country was still recovering from its worst depression), family, or religious groups. Their wives and children were thus on their own, which provoked great anger and resentment among objectors. As for the CPS camps, the Selective Service officials were the administrators, but the peace churches ran them, providing food, clothing and medical care along with supervision. The Agriculture or Interior Department supervised the conservation work.

Most camps tended to be religiously homogeneous. The Quaker camps were more tolerant and, as a result, attracted non-traditional "peace" church objectors as well. However, perhaps because of their diversity, these camps were more likely to experience frustration and demoralization caused by the harshness of the work, the conditions, and the lack of compensation. The names of those who committed offenses against camp rules were reported to the Selective Service and could be prosecuted in a civil court.[16]

In 1943 the government set up several of its own camps for conscientious objectors who did not want to serve or could not adapt to the regimen of the church camps. From the outset these camps had many problems. Those assigned to work at the government camps were as frustrated as those in the Quaker camps. Here are the words of one of those who worked in a camp, Igal Rodenko, who was interviewed for the Southern Oral History Program Collection on April 11, 1974:

> In the camps, they said they would ask the CO's to prove their sincerity by supporting themselves... and they asked all of us to pay thirty dollars a month for our board and keep. Many of the campers worked, but there were, from the very beginning, dissidents. It started perhaps, or was highlighted by a group of Union Theological students, led by Dave Dellinger and George Houser and a few others, who refused to register in the very beginning, when the draft was signed, the day that people were asked to register. They were looked on as absolute freaks. As we got deeper into the war, we began to realize – we being a very small number of less church types in the CO camps – that the camps were set up, not because the government values conscience and respects it, but... because the government recognized that the CO's were a bunch of troublemakers and dissidents, and even if they could force them into the army, they would be more trouble than they were worth, and the camp system was a means of getting us out of circulation. They had rules that you could do your alternative service, but you had to be at least fifty miles away from any place you had ever lived in. So you wouldn't be a focus for anti-war activity of any kind.[16]

Clearly, then, the efforts of the CPS, which at first seemed to be a major step forward for conscientious objection compared to the mistreatment applied to them during World War I, ended with mixed results. In fact, by the end of the war, many religious CO's came to feel that the CPS had been a "major capitulation by the pacifist establishment to the state."[17]

The more radical objectors also came to see the CPS camps as closer to being prisons than works camps. "Management of conscientious-objection camps by pacifist churches was an unhappy experience that future administrations would try to avoid."[18]

Despite the problems encountered by CO's during World War II, increased clarity emerged regarding the relationship between conscientious objection and national service. World War II pointed up the difference, from a civic standpoint, between the alternativist and the evader, deserter, and absolutist. When given the opportunity, these objectors were able to fulfill their civic obligations. For the first time in American history, the government, its citizenry, and the CO's themselves accepted that certain forms of civilian national service could be acceptable substitutes for military service.[19]

Next came the Korean War. The draft was definitely not popular, but evasion occurred at no greater rate than it had during World War II. This may have been the result of the special treatment accorded college students. The Universal Military Training and Service Act of 1951 set up a two-fold criterion for student deferment: class standing and performance on a college qualifying test. Although the final decision regarding classification was left to the local draft board, deferments were granted liberally. The number of those applying as conscientious objectors was proportionate to the number that applied in World War II, and they were treated similarly. Objectors were classified 1-0 if opposed to all military service and 1-A-0 if opposed only to combat service. 1-A-0 men were considered essentially part of class 1-A and no numbers are available, but 1-0 men "were the ones who posed the problem."[20]

By June 1951 amendments to the Selective Service Act required all 1-0 registrants to perform twenty-four months of civilian work "contributing to the national health, safety or interest." The local draft board determined both those who received CO status and what their assignment would be. The only legally acceptable criterion was still religious training and belief. "Rational, political and philosophical objections" were not recognized, though that was destined to change. For a variety of reasons, there were far more CO registrants than there were jobs, though as in World Wars I and II, many refused to accept any work assignment.[21]

Hospitals and mental institutions offered the most jobs between 1951 and 1965. The CPS camps were abolished. One-and-a-half percent of inductees during the Korean War were exempted as CO's whereas just fifteen hundredths of one percent received that status during World War II.

With the Vietnam War, the number of men applying for CO status increased dramatically. 170,000 exemptions were given between 1965 and 1970. The percentage of CO's soared from eight percent of inductions in 1967 to forty-three percent by 1971.[22] The extraordinary increase in applications and exemptions granted, starting in 1965, has a number of causes. First and foremost was the war itself. Unpopular from the outset and then made more so by the draft, the Vietnam War became the focal point of the anger and frustration of a generation. Those applying for conscientious objector status received support from mainline religious groups as well as anti-war and anti-draft groups. Seeking ways out was made legitimate as never before. Then there were two Supreme Court decisions that significantly changed the possibilities. In the Seeger (1965) and Welsh (1970) decisions, secular ethical beliefs were allowed to be included in the criteria for CO status. This essentially opened the floodgates. Not only did the numbers of those applying for CO status prior to induction expand exponentially, but also 17,500 members of the armed services applied for non-combatant status or discharge as CO's between 1965 and 1973.

Another radical effort to remove one's self from the possibility of combat due to conscience arose during Vietnam. Two cases, one involving a serving officer, Captain Howard B. Levy, and the other, a draftee, David Mitchell, attempted to make use of the Nuremberg defense – that either performing duties or being drafted would place one in the position of very possibly having to carry out criminal orders. The assumption of this defense was that the Vietnam War was itself illegal and immoral. Levy was asked to train Special Forces [Green Beret] medics in dermatology, and he believed that his teaching would be "prostituted" by the Green Berets who would, in his opinion, commit war crimes upon arriving in Vietnam. He argued that the government could not constitutionally place a soldier against his will in substantial jeopardy of becoming implicated in committing war crimes. However, the law officer in charge of the case ended up ruling that none of the evidence pertaining to government policy and the actions of individual soldiers in Vietnam was admissible.[23]

David Mitchell refused to fill out draft forms or report for induction. His defense team focused on the Nuremberg theme of personal accountability in the face of criminal orders. Mitchell was neither a pacifist nor a conscientious objector; he was a staunch resister. Here are his words in a letter of February 10, 1964, in response to a notice listing verifying certificates required for deferment:

> I realize that I could employ means to gain exemption from induction, but this does not interest me. My purpose is not to be classified quietly within the draft system, but rather to oppose the draft. While classification might suit some sort of individual 'convenience,' my acceptance of classification would be a negation of my social responsibility. I oppose the draft, not as something wrong for just me or wrong for only certain people, but as something wrong for the peace and survival of the world. Selective Service is the criminal in this case as can be judged by American militarism throughout the world – from Cuba to Panama to South Vietnam, and by our basing of policies on nuclear war. I refuse to cooperate in any way which would support the continuance of such activities. I certainly wouldn't have worked in a Nazi concentration camp just because I would not have to tend the ovens or the gas, but could be a guard or a clerk. Rather, as I am doing with the draft and the militarism it contributes to, I would have dissociated from such wrong and worked against it.[24]

Mitchell's case resonated through the legal system. He was eventually sentenced to two years in prison, which he served. His and Levy's stories reverberate to this day. Take the case of Ehren Watada. Like Mitchell and Levy in the 1960s, Watada is not a pacifist. He offered to go to Afghanistan, but refused to go to Iraq for the same reason Mitchell refused to go to Vietnam, not because of an objection to all wars, but because of a conviction that war crimes were being committed in this particular war, giving rise to an obligation, under the principles declared at Nuremburg, to refuse military service."[25] His case has received considerable attention and has had a circuitous route through the military justice system. The harshest part of the eight-year sentence he faced was a direct result of what was termed "conduct unbecoming an officer," namely his public comments regarding his objections to the war in Iraq. In early 2009, after an initial mistrial and a second court martial hearing, both in 2007, the case was dropped.[26]

The story of conscientious objection is still being written. The draft ended in 1973 and an all-volunteer army fought the Persian Gulf War in 1990-1991; nevertheless, between fifteen hundred and two thousand soldiers applied for discharge as CO's. Those affected struggled with a system that had no place to put them and with the harassment of their fellow soldiers and commanding officers. Only one hundred eleven were granted CO status before the leadership ended the option. This resulted in twenty-five hundred soldiers going to prison, according to Bill Gavlin, from the Center on Conscience and War, quoting a report from the *Boston Globe*. Reports have emerged from Camp LeJeune in North Carolina that some of those seeking CO status were "beaten, harassed and treated horribly."[27]

And the beat goes on...During the Iraq War many have sought CO status as well. To succeed in getting CO status, soldiers must demonstrate that their beliefs about war have changed since they enlisted. Soldiers who have this change of heart fall into three main groups. The first contains, according to J. E. McNeil from the Center on Conscience and War, "those who go into the military understanding war and are willing to accept it. But then something happens during their service and they are no longer OK with war."The second contains people who have "sought out spiritual growth and have come to believe that God doesn't want them to participate in war."[28] The third, and biggest, group, she says, is made up of young people who join the military in their late teens. The drafting of these recruits is often referred to as "the poverty draft," because military recruiters deliberately target poor youth, both in urban centers and in areas of rural poverty. These recruits are often poor whites, blacks, or Hispanics, who either have limited employment opportunities or are looking for a way to fund their college education. They make up the fastest-growing group of COs, as well as the biggest.[29] A friend who works on the GI Rights Hotline in support of those questioning their service, has observed that it's these "poverty draft" soldiers who most often go into the military believing they understand what war is about, and so are willing to accept it. However, as they actually experience the killing and other acts involved, something changes for them, and they no longer feel the same way about taking part.

I have been following the recent case of Andrew Shepherd on my blog (www.vietnamandiraqwarstories.com/blog/2009/06/01/a-heroic-story-were-not-hearing-about/). He is seeking asylum in Germany after having received orders to deploy to Iraq. Here are the words of Elsa Rassbach from an interview she conducted with Shepherd entitled, "Soldier Seeking Asylum: 'I Want to Be Able to Atone'":

> Shepherd argues that there are strong reasons, arising from Germany's history, for Germany to grant him asylum: the

Nuremberg Principles and the Constitution of the Federal Republic of Germany that has provisions written in the spirit of Nuremberg. In 2005 the highest German administrative court upheld a German military officer's right to refuse orders in 2003 to provide software that might have been used by the U.S. for logistics during the invasion of Iraq.

Shepherd's case is of significance in part because of the strategic importance of the bases in Germany for the U.S. wars in the Middle East. Outside of Iraq and Afghanistan, the U.S. has far more bases in Germany than in any other country; 68,000 U.S. troops are stationed at U.S. bases throughout southern Germany. Approximately 80% of the soldiers and supplies to the war zones are routed through Germany, which also hosts the Pentagon's commands for Africa (AFRICOM) and for Europe and the former Soviet Union (EUCOM).[30]

Here are his own words about why he is pursuing this course of action:

It is my sincere belief that the United States has gone too far. In Iraq alone 1.3 million people have died so far, and that includes American soldiers as well. We've attacked several countries over the past eight or nine years: Afghanistan, Syria, Pakistan, Iraq, and some places in the Sudan. All over the world, we're just destroying property and killing people, all based on lies. And I feel like that I have to do everything I can to help put an end to this. I feel guilty enough for having taken a part in this war for almost five years. I want to be able to atone for that.[31]

Shepherd's case is still pending.

It is perhaps ironic, yet best, to end this introduction to the voices of the men who chose to take this route during the Vietnam War with the words of the president responsible for the beginning of the escalation of the war, John Kennedy. In a letter to a Navy friend, he wrote: "War will exist until the distant day when the conscientious objector enjoys the same reputation and prestige as the warrior does today." It is safe to say that as we anticipate this "distant day" the tension that exists between the freedom-of-conscience principle and the citizen-soldier tradition of America will continue to define the evolution of conscientious objection in America.

Jim Henle

Jim grew up in Arlington, Virginia, and now lives in Northampton, Massachusetts, with his Filipina wife whom he met while serving in the Peace Corps. He has one grown son. He has been teaching mathematics at Smith College for many years. He does all his local commuting on an ancient bicycle and is a Charlie Chaplin look-alike.

I graduated from Dartmouth in 1968. I wanted to attend graduate school, but I knew the Selective Service System would allow me one year and no more. I wasn't married, had no kids, and had no idea what I was going to do about the draft. I had a very strong idea about what I wanted to do with my career, however. I wanted to be a mathematician and teacher, so graduate school was my immediate goal.

I decided to postpone graduate work rather than have it interrupted. I thought maybe I would have more control over my life if I joined the Peace Corps. It was not in lieu of military service. It was a deferment. If I joined the Peace Corps, that gave me two years for the situation to change. I applied to the Peace Corps, was accepted, and went to the Philippines. I also applied to graduate school. When I was accepted, I asked that the acceptance be deferred, and it was. I was told I had to reapply, but that was only a formality.

I was totally opposed to the war in Vietnam. I had been opposed for at least two years. The United States had no business killing people in Vietnam, and I didn't want to be a part of that. I got involved in the protest movement at Dartmouth, but very tangentially. I demonstrated a couple of times. Part of the Peace Corps process involves an FBI background check and I was clean, though I would say I was accidentally clean rather than intentionally.

The Peace Corps program I applied for was teaching high school mathematics, but when I got to the Philippines, I was actually appointed to a college, which was a wonderful experience. I had good friends among the Filipino students and close friends among the faculty. It was also a branch of the main university, and the students were very politically aware. While I was there, there were student strikes and demonstrations. However, these actions did not relate to me on a personal level; the signs they held were all against American policy, not against me or against Americans as individuals. While there's a certain amount of violence in the Philippines, and they can't seem to have an election without killing a few people, Philippine culture is a very warm and friendly one. I think the Philippines as a nation sent troops to Vietnam only at the urging of the United States.

I heard about the lottery in the Philippines. I believe my number was 123. It seemed like an abstract thing at the time. I don't know how my fellow volunteers reacted, because I didn't spend time with them. That's not the way the Peace Corps is set up. You go there to be part of a community of Filipinos, not Americans.

I got married in the Philippines, and my wife, a Filipina, was pregnant by the time we were leaving. We arrived in the States in the summer of '70, and our son was born in August. Now, at this point, fatherhood deferments had ended.* However, my life experience up until that point was that basically nothing terrible happened to me, or to people I was close to. That only happened to other people, so, in terms of the draft, I felt things were going to work out okay for me. Unfortunately that did not turn out to be the case for a high school classmate of mine, who ended up dying in Vietnam.

Nevertheless, Vietnam certainly affected my life. I was a pretty aggressive person intellectually in those days. Only something as significant as the draft could have deflected me from graduate school, since there was no longer a deferment for attending a graduate degree program. When I went to my physical, I was really hoping for a 4-F. I had a grandfather who was not allowed to fight in World War I because of flat feet. I had very flat feet, but the Army had moved beyond that, and flat feet did not work. During my physical there was a loose cannon of a doctor who, with every other individual, said, "Ah, something wrong with your heart. You need more tests." I wasn't the every other one. I passed my physical.

The next thing was I thought I might get a hardship deferment, since my wife was not a citizen. She was a new mother, not used to American society, and she would suffer extensively if I were taken away. The appeal went to the Arlington, Virginia, draft board, since that's where I grew up. They had no sympathy, which was not surprising, given the Virginia laws

---

*The Family Exemption was officially ended in April 1970.

against miscegenation, marriage between races, had only been taken off the books a year or two before we were married.*

I had begun thinking through the issues and was coming to the belief that war itself was wrong, not just the Vietnamese war. Killing people is not a good way of settling problems, and is not justified. However, I had no religious basis for this view. I was raised without any religion, and I couldn't claim much intellectual lineage for my pacifism either. My father had fought in World War II. Fortunately for me, however, the Supreme Court then ruled a person didn't have to have a religious background for one's pacifism.† As I no longer needed a religious basis, I applied for status as a conscientious objector. My local board turned me down. I appealed. I had heard that you could shift the appeal from the state where you grew up or where you were registered to the state where you were living. I was in graduate school in Massachusetts and the state had a different attitude toward the war. My understanding was that the head of the Massachusetts Selective Service was eventually forced out, whereupon he immediately went into private practice counseling draftees.

So I shifted my appeal from Virginia to Massachusetts. I also went to a lawyer who was in business drawing up appeals. He helped me with the appeal, and I won conscientious objector status. Of course, with my draft number being 123, I was still called up. That happened in the spring of '71 and so I had to find an alternative service job that was acceptable. At one time the local board would find a job for you; that's probably what happened in World War II and the Korean War. By the time the Vietnam War rolled around, there were more CO's than before. Also, it was a tight employment market, so it was not easy to find jobs for people. It became up to us to find our jobs. I thought teaching would be fun, but I found out that teaching in a public school was not acceptable, because public school teachers were paid too much. It was actually considered too plush a job.

Loving v. Virginia, 388 U.S. 1 (1967), was a landmark civil rights case in which the U. S. Supreme Court, by a 9-0 vote, declared Virginia's anti-miscegenation statute unconstitutional ending all race-based legal restrictions on marriage in the United States. Source: http://en.wikipedia.org/wiki/Loving_v._Virginia

†In *Welsh v. United States* (1970), the Supreme Court held that a man could claim conscientious objector status based on the "depth and fervency" of his beliefs, even if they were not religious in character. Source: http://www.answers.com/topic/conscientious-objector

I began looking for jobs at private schools. My parents knew people involved in a private school in Alexandria, Virginia, the Burgundy Farm Country Day School, the first integrated school in Virginia. I'd done a summer job there. They ran a nature summer camp, and I had worked for one summer driving the school bus and dumping garbage, so they knew me. I also was a math major with a year of graduate school and some teaching experience, so they hired me. As for my being a CO in that community, it was not an issue with anybody. The school, the community, and northern Virginia were all fairly liberal. The local draft board was another story. During my original interview for the CO they wanted to know what I would do if my mother was raped. My answer didn't convince them I was sincere. They wouldn't have been convinced that anyone was. Pacifism wasn't going to fly with them.

My relationship with my parents while I was working through all these issues was complex. During my last years at Dartmouth, I had emotional arguments with my mother about Vietnam. She felt the war was the right thing to do, and we were saving Vietnam from communism. My father felt the same way about the war as my mother, but was just delighted his son had these passionate views and was speaking so forcefully. Whenever I tried to argue with him, the argument petered out, because he was quite content that I had my views and he had his.

When push came to shove, however, my parents were always in my corner. By the early '70s, they had begun to realize the war was not working out. They saw I was passionately against the war, and they certainly didn't want me to serve. I never had any feeling from them that there was anything wrong with applying for CO status. In fact, they were helpful in finding me my CO job.

I think both of my parents would have been unhappy had I chosen to go to jail, and I think they might have been unhappy if I had chosen to go to Canada. My own personal view is I don't deserve any blame for being a CO, but I don't deserve as much credit as the people who went to jail. Going to Canada had about the same moral significance as being a CO, but going to jail had a far greater moral weight.

The people who went to jail, those were the people who are truly admirable. There should be a monument in Washington to the people who went to jail. By becoming a CO, I didn't hinder the war effort in the slightest, and what happened might have been that one more individual, who didn't have the education and the resources I had, went to Vietnam. Those who chose to go to jail made a dramatic point, and they made a great sacrifice. The only guy I know who did that was a fellow math major at Dartmouth. He was a brilliant guy with a very intuitive mind, and he wasn't the same when he got out of jail.

As for me, if I had not gotten the CO, I didn't have a plan. I'd thought about going to Canada. I really don't know what I would have done. I don't want to know. There are certain things you don't want to know about yourself. What was my level of cowardice? Going to Canada? Could I have knuckled under and been drafted? Maybe Canada would have happened. Maybe there would have been some way of going back into the Peace Corps and deferring longer. My wife would have preferred the Canada option. She wanted us together and that would have been the simplest way. I don't know. As I've said, I just had this faith that really bad things wouldn't happen to me.

I'm a mathematician. I'm in fact a logician. As I think about these issues in this interview, it matters a great deal to me that my positions are consistent and rational. Am I still a pacifist? Am I still opposed to war? What about the first Iraq war in which we were in some sense punishing an aggressor? What about the bombing in Kosovo? What about World War II? The answer is: Yes, I am still a pacifist.

In regard to how I would react to an attack on my mother, I'm not opposed to the rule of law. I think we need protection from criminals, and that protection has to be measured and appropriate. So you must have policemen, and occasionally they will have to use force, and even violence, to protect human life. And on the world scene the same is true. What we need is essentially a world government. We need a world in which there are laws governing how a country behaves, and there is an international police force, which would of necessity be an army that can enforce the will of the world, one way or the other. How this world government is ever going to appear, I don't know

It has been a pleasure for me to revisit these memories. I think this is an exquisitely interesting time in the life of our country. The issues I have been talking about are coming back right now. Long ago we should have been fleshing out these things, but it was so emotional back then. People have said the battle, the intellectual battle, the emotional battle, over this was replayed in the impeachment of Clinton, and I believe that. The hatred of that man by the conservatives can only be explained by historical events going back to the '60s and Vietnam and how they affected us all.

Peter Jessop

Peter is from Connecticut. Sixty years old, he's a contractor who runs a business in Amherst, Massachusetts, called Integrity Development and Construction. It is a company that employs from seven to twenty-five people depending on the job and season. He is married and has a daughter, now twenty-five. He and his wife live in an intentional community, one designed to foster a greater sense of interconnection in the place they live. He is also involved in local politics as chair of the Community Preservation Act committee and as a member of the Amherst Housing Authority.

I grew up in a white, lower-middle class environment. My father owned a laundromat in a small town, Guilford, Connecticut, right outside New Haven. During my junior and senior years of high school I began to become aware that not everybody lived like my family, not everybody had the same options. I did some community work in New Haven through my church. I began to look beyond the boundaries of what was going on politically in this country and to think about where I fit in.

I remember having several spirited discussions during my senior year in high school about the war in Vietnam. Most of the discussions were about the politics of the war, the history of Vietnam, whether it was appropriate for us to be there given the role the French had played. My friends and I structured the conversation around a political point of view, not paying too much attention to the carnage, or the generalized immorality of organized warfare as a way to solve problems.

I graduated high school in 1968 and applied to college. I had done well academically, because I was pretty good at playing the game. My father had graduated from college. My mother had not, but there was definitely an expectation I would go on in school. I applied to a bunch of places and ended up going to Trinity College in Hartford.

The summer between high school graduation and college, I worked for the United Church of Christ, which is a traditional Protestant denomination. I worked at a summer camp for kids affiliated with the church. It was there that I met my friend, John Bach, who was the director of the camp's waterfront, and his father, who was the minister in the town. John had been at Wesleyan University, and had left after his first or second year. He was in the process of refusing induction into the service. John was the first person I knew up close that was suggesting there was some other way of approaching this war rather than doing what was required.

We got very close that summer. He was a couple of years older than me, but there were still a lot of similarities as far as what we were thinking about. His words and actions began to affect some of my thinking. I turned eighteen that June, and I had to register for the draft. I was going to school, so I had a student deferment for at least my first year, but as a result of my involvement with John, I was convinced I wasn't going to go into the military. I wasn't going to bear arms to do somebody else's political bidding. While it was during that summer that the idea grew inside me of wanting to find a way out, an avenue to express this refusal, deep down I realized it had always been my position.

John's basic stance was you don't cooperate at all with these older fuckers. This is the beast that needs to be spoken to, and filing for a CO, in John's eyes, would have been cooperation. I think at that point, as I look back at this now, it brings me to tears to remember how much the burden of those decisions weighed on me. It was a lot to be carrying inside, that question of where I was fitting in, and the politics of my country, and what was being done in my name with my money. In the end, it was more than I could bear to not make a decision and do something.

I arrived at Trinity, having come off of this summer of work in this church conference, and having lots of discussions. Certainly my relationship with John was indicative of another path than the one I was embarking upon. I knew about the possibility of being a CO, and the idea of going to Canada, and I knew about staying in school and keeping my 2-S student deferment. The fact is I was never much of a student. I was smart, and I knew what to do to get through if I needed to, but I was an experiential sort of guy and I liked to *do* things as a way to learn. I'm sure if there hadn't been a draft, I would have done something else immediately after I got out of high school rather than head off to college.

So it was a combination of saying to myself, "What the fuck am I doing here in college? This is stupid," coupled with what was going on politically in the country. Meanwhile I was just muddling my way through Trinity, and along came the lottery. It was December 1, 1969, which would have been the middle of my sophomore year. Somewhere along the line, I wrote my draft board, which was in New Haven, because the small town where I grew up was just outside the city. I told them I intended to apply for status as a conscientious objector. I did it on someone's suggestion to let them have that on file, even if I hadn't filled out the paperwork yet.

I was listening to the lottery in a North Campus dorm with a bunch of other guys, and I drew 85. I remember the energy generally being subdued. I just don't remember people yelling, "340! Yes!" Maybe it was a sigh of relief on everybody's part to at least know where we stood and what we were doing. My reaction at that point was, "Okay. 85. That helps clarify my situation. Now I know." I didn't have a sense of, "Ah, shit, I missed it." As far as I was concerned, there was no mourning for the people on the low number end, and no celebration for the people on the high number end. To me it was, "This is fucked. This whole concept is fucked. What we're doing is fucked."

At some point during my sophomore year, I decided I was going to leave school. My initial decision was to refuse induction, since I knew with my number I would be drafted. That was my original path. If I had gotten, say 360, I would have left school and might have done other things. There was a certain amount of fatalism with 85. I look back and say, "Yeah, I needed to take that stance," so of course, I got a low number. Other people who didn't care one way or the other, and were determined to stay in school, got high numbers.

I knew there was a consequence to leaving school. I couldn't have stayed in school anyway though, because I wasn't doing that well academically. I wasn't doing anything really. In the spring of 1970, we didn't go to class at all. We were shutting the school down, and going to Washington, and doing everything we could to stop the war.

I stayed at Trinity through the spring. I told my parents I was leaving school, and I probably would get drafted, and at that point my intent was to refuse induction. They were pretty freaked out. My dad had served in the military in World War II. He had enlisted, like a lot of guys did. He wasn't a gung-ho military dad, but he was pretty mainstream in some of his thinking. My mom was a little bit more liberal and understood a little more about where I was coming from, but of course they were still freaked out. It's not a happy thing where you say, "Great, my son's going to go to prison." They weren't upset that I wasn't supporting the war; it was a fear of what was going to happen to me when I refused to serve.

So I dropped out of school. I was pretty clear about what I was doing. I was getting some support from the Central Committee for Conscientious Objectors, so I had a sense of what might lie ahead. I had filled out my CO form. For some time I had just planned to refuse induction, but at some point I began to think through what my options were, and I eventually came around to thinking it was better for me to apply for CO status, and to cooperate to that degree. I struggled with that, but my avenue was pretty clear. I wasn't going to be inducted. That wasn't an option.

I also wasn't going to go to Canada. I knew people who did that, but for me that would have been cowardly. I don't say that with any judgment at all about what anybody did. I really don't have judgments about people who enlisted, who were drafted, who went to Canada. All the choices were horrible. I know people who served in Vietnam, and I'd never ever judge them for that. I appreciate the pain that they went through, then and since, and I know it was a horrible experience for them, so I appreciate them. For me personally, going to Canada would have been not taking the stand I needed to take for myself, to say "I don't believe in this!" That was the primary thing. I wanted to stay in this country. The whole bit about I could have never come back, never see my family, wasn't the issue. If I had felt that was the right thing for me, I would have been across the border in five minutes. I wasn't operating on the system of not wanting to leave. If it felt right, I would have done it. It just wasn't true for me.

So the choices then became either apply for a CO or refuse induction. On one level it was now my concern that I hadn't applied for the CO immediately after my registration for the draft, but on a deeper level I wasn't really concerned about it because I wasn't going anyway. Once I made the decision to apply for a CO, I was actually okay about that. I felt a little disappointed in myself that I hadn't maintained the kind of rigorous, in-your-face, up yours relationship with my government I felt might have been called for at that point. There was a little bit of a sense of disappointment in myself that I hadn't carried that through, coupled with the feeling I was doing the best that I could. "Jesus, I'm nineteen years old, after all! I'm making decisions about how I am going to approach this thing. Pretty amazing!" I look at kids now who are eighteen and nineteen and think it was incredible that I was able to function at that level and to make such life-affecting decisions. It was a lot to think through, a lot to feel your way through. Of course, I didn't actually experience the feelings, because you weren't really supposed to feel anything about this kind of thing. It wasn't that we weren't a little bit afraid, or mad, or sad, but it was something that was supposed to stay fairly intellectual. Women that I was around would generally support me, like "Okay, that makes sense," but it was more support of men by men. It felt like a guy thing. It was sort of like, I'll never understand pregnancy. I see what women go through, but I'll never have any internal experience of that, and, so far at least, women will never have to deal with the draft. I'm not wishing it, but that's why it felt to me like something other men would be more likely to understand.

I left college at the end of my sophomore year. That summer I worked as a counselor for kids from Cleveland in an Upward Bound program a friend of mine was running. Later, I worked washing dishes for a little while. I was in the process of receiving my 1-A status and filling out the forms for my CO status. Basically I had to write an essay. Then I went to Europe for a couple of months with a friend. We were backpacking, just trying to squeeze all this in around what was happening with the draft.

My application for status as a CO was rejected by my draft board. I was classified as 1-A. I appealed that decision, and in the course of my appeal, I was asked to report for my physical, which I did. I passed with flying colors. I would have been perfect for the military. It never occurred to me to botch that. I knew I would appear before my draft board, would go through the appeal process, and whatever I got was their decision, not mine. My decision was not to serve in the military for reasons of objection of conscience.

I felt generally very peaceful. I felt thrilled to be having a real life response to what was going on. There was a place where I felt like, "Fine, I'm finally in the middle of this. I'm making a decision about what to do, and I'm doing it. I'm no longer just going along and getting along," which is what I had done for so many years. You know, go along, behave, do the right thing in the right order. Finally I just said, "This doesn't work. I want to say something different here. You want to send me here to do this job. I don't want to do this job."

The CO was still my fall-back position at that point. It was never as if, "Oh well, they rejected my appeal. I guess I'll just let myself be drafted." I knew what the results of losing the appeal would be, and I was prepared. Prepared may be too strong a word. I don't know if I could have been prepared. However, I was certainly aware that the possibility at that point was jail time and that would have been the next step. My parents were thrilled when I applied for status as a CO, only because I could try to do something else, rather than spend a couple of years in jail. I think they were happy about that and at least a little bit supportive.

At that point I was out of school, and I was out of touch. I didn't have a lot of contact with people who were doing what I was doing. I was in contact with John Bach, and we were writing. John was very supportive, and I found that to be useful, although there was always a little bit of tension in me about, "Am I as courageous as he is? Am I doing enough?" His was a very high standard. Finally I decided I didn't need to meet that standard. I only needed to meet my own standard: applying for status as a CO.

For my appeal, I stood in front of my draft board. I don't remember the faces. I remember them being white, and I remember them being men and suited. I had a guy I knew with me, the minister in the church I grew up in. I didn't know him well, but I'd had a long discussion with him. He agreed to accompany me to the appeal; I think you could take one person there with you. I was nervous about how I was going to do. I hadn't done a lot of prep work with anybody, but I re-read everything I'd written.

There were two things that struck me about the experience. One was that conscientious objector status is for those who know how to read and write well. I was really aware of that. Writing the essay was like writing a thesis. How do you explain your beliefs? The other was this sense that it didn't matter what they decided. There was a certain amount of strength in that for me. They asked me lots of questions. There was one similar to the "What if your sister is being raped?" question. In the end I remember saying, "Basically it doesn't matter what you do here today. I don't intend to serve in the military." I remember adding, "I don't mean that as a threat. I don't mean that necessarily to influence your decision. I just mean to tell you that I have no intention of being inducted into the Armed Forces, so I appreciate your time here today." I remember trying to be relatively straightforward about it and not expressing anger, which I certainly could have tapped into. I simply said that I had chosen this path, and if they didn't experience the sincerity in my voice, then that's their decision. I remember leaving there thinking, "Okay, that piece is done now. I can stop worrying about that piece and start looking for the next one."

Three weeks later I received my new CO status, my 1-O. When I got that, I was pleased. I was not excited, I was not happy. I was not mad. I remember being relieved that now it was really clear what the next piece of my future would be: I wasn't going to have to serve against my will and, at least at this point, I wasn't going to have to go to jail. I respected hugely the people who went to prison. I appreciated everyone else's decision about the draft, but I really *respected* guys who went to jail. They really had my admiration. I felt like that was really courageous, and also a really clean statement. In the end, that didn't work for me. I might have had to work it, and I certainly felt prepared to do that. If that had been the next step, I would have dealt with it, but I was relieved to know my path could go this other route. I have no problem with public service. I think that's a great thing. I think everyone should do a few years of mandatory service work. I didn't mind that at all.

When I had first dropped out of school, I had gone down to Puerto Rico for four months and worked at a hospital as a male maid, so for my alternative service, I got myself a job there. If you provide your draft board with a work situation they could live with, they were usually fine with that. I applied to this hospital in Puerto Rico, and they approved it. I went there in late fall of '71 to start work. I worked there for two years and made $305 per month, which was enough to live on. I had a little house in the country, and I worked forty hours a week. I gave people bed baths, and transported people to x-ray, and did whatever nursing activities were required. In the middle of my time, at the one-year point, a colonel came out to San Juan and spent ten minutes with me to make sure I was still there. It was an odd conversation. He came out to see me and found me at work, and he said "Hmmm" and I said, "Hmmm," and that was my one check-in. That was all that they did.

Some Puerto Ricans have done very well in the military. That was a path of great stability and advancement for them in the '50s, '60s and '70s. There was a great military presence in Puerto Rico. Generally I would say people there were puzzled by my decision. There wasn't really a category for what I had chosen. I had to explain to people if you object to fighting in the war, you could do two years of alternative service. Most people's response was, "Hmmm? What? How does that work?" As U.S. citizens they could be drafted, or they could enlist, and those were the only things that people did. I wasn't connected to a network of people who were doing anything like what I was doing in response to the draft and the war. I wasn't involved in intense politics there. My recollection was generally people were understanding, if not completely approving.

I ended up staying in Puerto Rico for another year after that. I taught school over there, first and second grade. My Spanish was really quite good. Many of my friends were Puerto Rican, and I ended up taking several classes at the college in town. I really could have stayed, but instead I came home and finished my degree. Sometime after I returned I began to think, "What the hell did I come back to the States for?" partly because I was thinking America would never be my home. I realized, though, that I'll always belong here, and I would have never really fit in completely in Puerto Rico, so I stayed.

I've continued to be fairly cynical about the U.S. government and what it's doing. The last thirty or so years have been horrible. There's no connection between national priorities, and what we do locally. How did we get up to the point where we spend two hundred billion in Iraq and nobody says shit? Where do we think that money's coming from? So I guess I continue to look at things through filters that were formed by the Vietnam era experience of reading through the lies, and the bullshit, and Nixon's crap. It made me pretty cynical, even about guys like John Kerry, who was probably pretty good, but I'm sure he had his bit of bullshit, too. I think because many of us of draft age had our asses in a sling back then, it was easier for us to think about taking a stand, and we were more likely to be active about it.

A few months ago [2006] I participated as part of a mock draft board down in Amherst for people who were counseling about the potential for another draft. I got to interview Elias Sanchez [a local youth activist] as a potential draft board guy. It was amazing to hear his responses, and to think about how to "nail" him. It was also amazing on another level to hear the answers and responses of an unformed eighteen year old. Mine must have been just as muddled. Still it was sweet to be around so many men who were there supporting Elias and thinking about resistance or conscientious objection as a possibility.

Because I was white, male, and educated, I could fill out the paperwork for the CO. Because I was articulate, I could go to my draft board and have it be possible for those guys to look at me and see I could possibly be their son. That's huge, as opposed to what some young black man would face. What's *he* going to say? What's *he* going to do?

I haven't talked through this whole process before. Some of the tears I shed this morning were from an appreciation of who I was at that point in my life, and the amount of inner fortitude it took to stand up for something at that age and say, "I don't believe in this. I'm not going to do it and you can't make me." The whole experience was something I think I carried for years. It had a huge impact on me.

Part of me also mourns the loss of the feelings I had at certain points in the process of becoming a CO, when I experienced a sense of real personal power I have rarely felt since. There were a couple of times, especially during the spring of 1970, when the college was on strike, where I remember speaking to audiences about what our country might be doing differently. I felt a great sense of being able to influence people's thinking, and to be charismatic based on my beliefs, my personal integrity, and my personal power. I don't know if I had any influence on people, but I felt like this was truth speaking to power in ways that have become much more difficult to do. I think about going up there and talking about how we were sending our draft cards back to Washington, and feeling that sense of personal power inside on a very deep level, with a passion about what I was saying that might have had an affect on other people's actions. Sadly, I don't feel that way these days. It was just the clarity of that time period and being able to have this clear focus; it just seems more muddled now about whether to do this or that. There's a place where I miss some of that crystal clear vision. Now it's like, "Should I put the money in the 401K?" Life has continued to evolve, and some of my needs have changed. It's confusing to learn I want to be a certain kind of person in one way, and also a certain kind of person in another way.

Tom Gardner

Tom was born in New Orleans and spent time growing up in Virginia, Panama, Florida, New Jersey, and North Carolina. He now lives in Amherst, Massachusetts. He moved there to go to the University of Massachusetts where he received a doctorate in communication in 2005. He helped develop the Media Education Foundation, the nation's leading producer and distributor of educational videos on media and culture. He currently teaches communication law, public relations, and journalism at Westfield State University in the communication department. He is the author of The Media Rhetoric of Law and Order: How ABC Framed the Mumia Abu-Jamal Story *(Mellen Press, 2010). He's been married since 1994 and has two children, ages fourteen and twenty-eight.*

My story starts with growing up in the Navy, which means that for many of my early years I wanted to be in the Navy. I just loved the uniforms and the ships and moving around from place to place. I became a competitive swimmer in high school, so I was going to go to the Naval Academy and be on the swim team and then be in the officer corps. When I was younger, I wanted to be in the underwater demolition team or UDT, the forerunner of today's Navy SEALS.

That was my dream – to serve in some capacity. I began to shift around '64, my senior year in high school, to wanting to work on world problems through diplomacy rather than military approaches, to go into the State Department instead. I was quite inspired by John F. Kennedy and the idea of the Peace Corps. I think it was probably the rhetoric of the Kennedy years about peace that got me thinking that there are better ways to build a stable world than the military solution.

My dad was probably the most unmilitary military person I've ever met. He was a small town dentist who happened to be wearing a uniform. He joined to serve in World War II and stayed for thirty years. He loved to read, especially history, and he was actually somewhat of a liberal, especially for someone who was raised in western Kentucky. His dad was the only dentist in a small town. My mom was from a less educated, large family, and she had worked for my father as a dental assistant. Her dad died when I was a child, so I never knew him. One way to describe the two different strands of my family is that, when the Klan tried to organize in the

'20s or so, my father's father, the judge and the sheriff rounded up a couple of these guys and told them if they came back into town they would ride them out of town on a rail. On my mother's side, when the Klan rallied, she and her sisters went out and sang at the rally. On the one hand, they probably didn't know much about the Klan; they would just go sing whenever they were invited. On the other hand, their parents didn't tell them not to. At the last family reunion I went to I probed a bit, but nobody really knew or wanted to talk about the Klan or her father's possible sympathies. Her family was also very religious, as Southern Baptists. Reunions were about singing hymns and eating.

The Navy was desegregated by the middle '50s, so people swam in the same pools, but the Florida town we were in was still segregated. I knew some of the black kids on the base. We would be able to swim together or play ball, but they then got on a different bus and drove off to a different school. This always seemed unfair to me. Here's an example of what I mean. A friend and I wanted to go sit in the balcony when we went to the movie theater in town since that is where we usually sat at the Navy base theater. We got our tickets and went around to the balcony section, but of course at that time the balcony area was for "colored only" so the owner called the sheriff, thinking we were staging a civil rights protest. In reality we were just unaware little kids that didn't know any better. That was unconsciously my first civil rights act.

We then moved to New Jersey and I went to Haddon Heights High School, which was about one third African American. I found myself more drawn in some ways to the black kids than the white because they seemed more southern. They were sort of interested in me because I was the only southerner in the school. Those were the years when I lost my southern accent. It was the time when all the things were going on in the South and my accent was really a source of both shame and insecurity. But I made black friends, and some of my white friends wouldn't come to my parties because I invited my black friends. I learned that racism isn't just a southern phenomenon.

I went to the University of Virginia in 1964. I decided not to go to the Naval Academy because I got a letter from the swimming coach there that looked like it was written by a fourth grader. I was leaning towards a diplomatic career, which I would commence after spending two years in the Peace Corps. There were a lot of people in the State Department who came from the University of Virginia. It was a good plan, but a funny thing happened on the way to the State Department – actually not so funny. It was called the War in Vietnam.

Soon after I got to the University of Virginia, I got involved in a civil rights organization that was formed by students and I got exposed to different ideas about Vietnam. At first I argued against taking a position opposing the war. I was one of the new civil rights liberals who claimed we shouldn't oppose the war because it might hurt the fight for civil rights. I would tell my fellow student activists that we had to stop the "communist threat." I was a successful debater in high school, so I thought I made some pretty good arguments. I expected to win these debates, but I was losing some arguments. That bothered me. I went to the library and got every book on Vietnam they had. I came to realize that the reason I was losing the debates was because I was on the wrong side. In fact, U.S. policy couldn't be worse.

I think for a lot of us in our generation we really had come to believe in these ideals: that America was a beacon of freedom; that our vision of being an American inspired a lot of us to be involved citizens and activists. Kennedy certainly contributed to this. But what was happening with Vietnam was that a lot of us were torn between this ideal of our country's supposed support for democracy and the fact that Eisenhower, in his book, *Mandate for Change*, said Ho Chi Minh would have won eighty percent of the vote had elections been held in 1956. The U.S. instead cancelled the elections and installed its own dictators in the South. Before that, the U.S. had supported the French who colonized Vietnam. France had said they would support independence after World War II, but instead, with U.S. support, they reasserted control. We were undermining democracy, not defending it, through our own imperialistic ambitions and Cold War hysteria. I think that the contrast between the ideals that we were taught – the words – and the reality that we learned as we found out more about what was really happening in foreign policy is what drove a lot of our activism and, eventually for many, a sort of militancy. People were really pissed off; we had been lied to by the older generation.

Meanwhile, in Mississippi, people were being burned out of their homes for trying to register to vote. We took up a collection on campus at U.Va. and sent down a van of supplies. By the spring of '65 I was active enough that I went down to the march from Selma to Montgomery. That was a turning point for me. A group of us, black and white college students, formed an organization to work in southern Virginia, called the Virginia Students Civil Rights Committee (VSCRC). John Lewis (then SNCC chairman, now a U.S. Congressman) came up to speak at our conference. He had just been beaten in Selma and he still had a bandage on his head. I remember thinking that if he could do that, then I could get on the train and go down to Montgomery. I was also inspired by a southern history professor, Paul Gaston, a native of Fairhope, Alabama, who talked to us in his melodious Alabama accent of the southern tragedy of racism and of his own involvement in local civil rights efforts.

The Southern Student Organizing Committee (SSOC), which was an outgrowth of white southern students working with SNCC (Student Non-Violent Coordinating Committee) was formed in 1964 to foster civil rights work on campuses. Through VSCRC and SSOC, I was in touch with black and white southern activists from all around the South. By this time I was also doing teach-ins on Vietnam so by the end of my freshman year I was pretty active.

My mom was not happy with any of these developments and I'm sure she was pressuring my father to do something about it. He was more quietly supportive, but he wanted me to focus more on my college education. I sent out a survey to the entire college faculty about issues affecting freedom, and the dean of students called my father and told him that this is the kind of thing his son was doing. My dad made the obligatory call saying, "You have to stop doing all this stuff or we're cutting the money off." I told him I felt I was doing the right thing, and if he disagreed then he would just have to decide what to do about the money. I called his bluff and he didn't cut me off. He told me years later that he had to try that for my own good, but that he was proud of what I had done.

I was a full-time activist during my second year. During the spring semester before I dropped out, I took an international relations course and instead of answering any of the questions on the final I wrote this scathing attack on the professor's mistaken notions about Vietnam and the supposed monolithic world communist threat. He gave me an "F", which I later chose to write about in my application to the Kennedy School at Harvard in 1984. I believe that "F", or possibly my comical account of it, may have helped my application. I decided to drop out of the University of Virginia in '66, and I joined the civil rights organization in Southside Virginia full-time. Several people had dropped out and were working full time in different counties in voter registration. The draft, of course, was in full swing by this point, so dropping out of school and losing my student deferment meant facing off against the selective service in a very real way. That was the first practical decision I had to make about the draft – whether I would stay in school just to avoid the draft or do what I really believed I needed to be doing.

I knew if I got drafted I would refuse. I knew that meant either prison or Canada and I would not be able to do the work I wanted to do. It was a combination of a calculated risk, a moral choice and an adolescent rebellion all mixed together. The adolescent rebellion part was, "Damn it! I'm not going to let these old bastards tell me what to do." The moral choice was one of simply wanting to do the right thing. The practical aspect was really beginning to look at the people like a friend of mine, David Nolan, who actually had dropped out. He had managed to elude the draft somehow. There were others out there who were trying to deal with this. Dropping out of college in spite of losing my student deferment, wasn't really making a final choice. It was deciding that for now I was not going to let them tell me what to do. I didn't know what I would do if push came to shove.

My dad was a pretty laid back guy. He didn't try a lot after that first phone call to tell me what to do. He was disappointed I was dropping out of school, but he also said since I wasn't doing a good job of it, maybe it was best to drop it and then get back in school soon. In '65 when I was doing all that reading about the war we had a lot of conversations about what the war was about. I sent him all the titles of the books I read. He read a lot of the books, and he became opposed to the war. He was commander of the Fourth Dental Company at Camp Lejeune, North Carolina, which was a major staging base for the 2nd Marine Division. So occasionally they would have a junior information officer do a little briefing for the dental company staff and tell them about the history of Vietnam and why we were there. After the presentation, my dad would step up and say, "I think your history is pretty good up until 1948, but after that there are just a few things I want to take issue with you about." He would then give the Bernard Fall* version of the war's history. He had definitely come around.

---

*Bernard B. Fall was a scholar, historian, writer, and humanitarian whose life's work was the study of the people and country of Vietnam. At the time of his death in 1967 he was one of this country's leading authorities on Vietnam. His was the first, most insightful and powerful voice warning Americans that the war in Vietnam was an unwinnable war. His warnings were ignored.

My mom didn't really get any of this. She was worried for my safety. She had been upset that I had black friends when I was in high school. Her upbringing hadn't prepared her for that. My falling out with her happened about then, about my senior year in high school. There were topics I just had to avoid when I went home; it was too contentious. That was a rough spell because we had been very close as I was growing up. We did patch things up though in the late 1970's before she died.

When I dropped out of school, I got some financial support for the civil rights work I was doing from the Student Religious Liberal program of the Unitarian Universalist Service Committee. I had started to convert to Unitarianism while I was in Charlottesville. The summer I joined VSCRC staff, we were all getting about eight to twelve dollars per week for living expenses, but since I was also being sponsored by the Unitarian Church I had $25 a week, which, of course, I put into the general pool.

Back when they tried to desegregate Virginia's schools, the state government launched what was called "massive resistance" where they closed the public schools and set up private schools for whites, while black students were out of luck without schools. Some alternative "Freedom Schools" were set up to fill the gap for black children. A lot of people came down from the North to teach. There was a young man in Prince Edward County, next to Charlotte County where I was working, whose case was referred to me, because I knew about draft counseling. His name was Charles. He was eligible for the draft even though he was still in high school, because he had been denied a public education for several years. He was older than he would normally be, so the draft board said, "Oh, you don't qualify for a student deferment any more. You're past nineteen." He was working full time. He was the sole supporter of his family. His father was older and disabled, and he had younger siblings. He was in school and the only reason he was not attending school was because the state had closed them. I thought this was ridiculous, so I actually contacted Senator Ted Kennedy's office, and to his credit they responded. I wasn't in his constituency, but because he'd gone to the University of Virginia's Law School, I thought I could make a connection with him. He called up Lewis Hershey, who was the head of Selective Service, and said something to the effect of, "This is a ridiculous case. Do I have to bring this up in a hearing or can we take care of this?" Charles got his deferment.

This situation was symptomatic of what was wrong with the draft. Almost all southern draft boards were all white and they were looking for cannon fodder. If they had to choose between sending the mill owner's son who they went hunting and fishing with or sending another black kid, guess who they would send. Statistical analyses done over the Vietnam years show this to be a pattern in southern draft boards, not just an isolated case here and there.

After working in the civil rights group I joined the staff of the National Student Association's (NSA) Southern Students Human Relations Project. Although I was being paid by NSA, I was working about as much for the Southern Student Organizing Committee. I was based in Atlanta. I had been doing some research regarding racism in the Selective Service System. SNCC people knew I was doing this kind of work. They got a call from a guy who was challenging his induction order on the basis of his race and they asked me if I could go help him. I talked to him on the phone. He was interested in things like how another black man, Rob Williams, had gotten out of the country and how to form a legal challenge against the draft system. So I went up to Greensboro, North Carolina, where he was going to be tried and I got in touch with the Law Center on Constitutional Rights. They had too many cases, so they couldn't do anything for him. Instead, I worked with them to discover what motions could be filed to delay the trial.

I started doing research on the draft board. I went to the court and wrote motions and gave them to the defendant so he could file these motions, and while I was doing that, two other draft cases came up. One concerned this young guy from Ramseur, North Carolina who'd had no contact with the anti-draft movement and didn't explain why he didn't want to submit to the draft. I talked to him and his father during one of the breaks, and his dad's comments reflected the anti-federal government perspective you see in the mountains: "What right do the feds have to take my son and have him go halfway around the world and kill people who ain't done nothing to us?" I asked the young man how he came to his position on the draft, and he said, "I took a course at Appalachian State and I read a book by Albert Camus and it got me to thinking."

When we returned to the courtroom, I kept sitting as a protest when the judge entered the courtroom. When the judge said, "Will you rise?" I said, "No." When they recessed for lunch, the bailiff came over to me and asked me what I was doing there. I explained that I was assisting another defendant, and I said I'd be back for the afternoon session. He told me to stay right there. He got my name and the judge came back in before the lunch period ended. The judge read out an order that said I was guilty of disrupting the order and decorum of the court and obstructing the administration of justice. He sentenced me to thirty days in jail for criminal contempt. A federal marshal whisked me out of the courtroom. I didn't even have a chance to give a little speech about why I refused to stand.

It was shocking, and I felt pretty stupid. I was in the movement and I was used to people being arrested, but usually you do it for the publicity and you're not alone, and here I was alone in Greensboro, North Carolina. I was taken to the county jail in Winston-Salem. I was in a pretty benign situation, with a bunch of bootleggers, mountain guys from North Carolina, but I heard lots of prison stories and helped them write letters home.

It was while I was in jail that I made my decision that I would do what it took to avoid going to prison for five years. Being confined is a powerful teacher. Those bars close behind you, and you know you can't go anywhere. My sense was I was a pretty good organizer, writer, and speaker. To be languishing in prison for five years while the war was going on and people were being slaughtered and the civil rights movement was going on, it just felt like a waste. I definitely had doubts about how hard it would be for me to maintain my sanity in prison. I understood the non-cooperator position, and I respected the people who chose prison over violating their principles against war. I also could see that you had to be fully convinced that that was the right thing to do – to go to prison. If you weren't fully committed to that choice, it would be much harder to lose your freedom.

My decision may also have been influenced by the fact that three other people were up on draft charges that week in the Greensboro federal court; two others were sentenced that day and nobody, except their families, seemed to notice. I later reported the sentencing of the young man from Ramseur to Peacemakers, a group that put out a list of draft resisters in prison so people could write them letters. Years later I got a letter from him thanking me because he'd gotten all those supportive letters from people.

I felt like I needed to be out, organizing. The other thing that happened was there were only three books I could get into the jail past the censors: the Bible, the *Last Temptation of Christ* by Kazantzakis - they thought it was a good Christian book - and the House Armed Services Committee hearings on the Selective Service System. This is where I learned about channeling. Hershey's testimony verified that the SSS was using the draft to channel people into occupations that business leaders thought were important. Being in an occupation vital to national security gave you a deferment from the draft, so they were essentially using the threat of death or prison to channel people into certain civilian jobs. For the southern conservative anti-government mentality this seemed like a perspective on the draft that might really hit home. I could imagine even some of my more conservative relatives getting upset about that level of government interference in people's lives. So I wanted to get out there and organize about this. I later wrote a pamphlet for SSOC about the channeling function of the SSS.

A friend from American Friends Service Committee (AFSC) got the judge to let me back into the courtroom to apologize. My dilemma was how to word the apology. The judge asked me if I knew I would be going to jail for remaining seated and I didn't, so I didn't realize the consequences. The judge then asked if I was aware of the consequences and I said, "No, sir. I wasn't aware that in this country... " Before I got going, my friend yanked me down and said, "What I think he meant to say was, no he wasn't aware," and, of course, the judge understood what was going on and basically said, "Okay, that's good enough for me." He let me out right before Christmas, after serving eighteen days of my sentence.

Before being released I had been on a hunger strike to protest the conditions in the jail. It was incredibly cramped. Bars closed us in so tightly that all we could do for exercise was push-ups and pacing. Then they brought in a chaplain and he preached to us "sinners." I preached back to him about who the real sinners were in this society. One of my cellmates said, "You sure are good with words." So I ended up helping some of them write letters to their girlfriends apologizing for getting arrested.

When I got out of jail and returned home, my father arranged for me to have a conversation with a Navy chaplain. The chaplain told me God wanted me to go to Vietnam and fight for my country. I wasn't convinced. My mom got upset and left in the first five minutes, but my dad sat in on it. I preferred the theology of my uncle G.O. on my mother's side, a long-time Southern Baptist preacher, who wrote me a letter of support.

When I got out, I worked with David Nolan and Nancy Hodes to organize a project of southern "peace tours." We organized our first tour in Florida and later expanded them across the South. Three of us would go around to colleges and talk to the students about myths about Vietnam and China and the flaws in U.S. foreign policy. We'd spend two or three days at each campus. We'd show films. We'd provide draft counseling. We'd speak to classes and help organize any marches that might take place. We often faced threats and, in many cases, our visit prompted a free speech battle to open up the campus to its first critical discussion of the war.

Just before the Florida Peace Tour, I had a meeting with the NSA vice-president for national affairs. He said I had to stop all of the anti-war, anti-draft activity. He told me it was not what we were supposed to be doing. He said if we persisted, the NSA staff would lose their occupational deferments. This was quite clearly a way that they used these occupational deferments to silence people. They gave occupational deferments to the officers of the NSA, because the Association, unbeknownst to members and most of us on staff, was working internationally as a front for the Central Intelligence Agency. I don't know how much this guy knew about that at the time.

I left the NSA staff. I was asked to stay on a little bit longer by some researchers who wanted more information about the NSA/CIA nexus, but I couldn't help them. My only contact with NSA's questionable, covert international work was when NSA wanted me to arrange for some Bolivian student leaders who were touring the U.S. to meet with SNCC organizers. They would bring these guys in, these leftists, and they would show them around to the civil rights movement, enabling the NSA staff to identify the more militant leftists among the visiting students. As we now know, leftist students were targeted for murder and disappearance by the repressive regimes the U.S. was supporting. The SNCC people were suspicious of the NSA, so I didn't set up the meeting.

I didn't announce a public resignation for a while because another guy on staff and I were going to announce our resignations together and publicly condemn the NSA/CIA connection. Instead, while I was still down in Florida on the peace tour, I read a news column where my compatriot on staff resigned and did an interview with Drew Pearson. He got to publicly condemn the NSA-CIA collaboration, so I just sent in my resignation.

By this point, I'd decided that I would try to change my draft status to conscientious objector. When I was still on the NSA staff I'd gone to a non-cooperators conference in New York, hosted by long-time pacifist leader A. J. Muste.* All these people, who were very inspiring, were taking this morally pure position, and I signed on to the first "We Won't Go" statement, which said we would refuse any cooperation with the Selective Service System. I wrote a letter to my draft board saying I would not co-operate in any way. I held on to it for a few weeks before walking to the mailbox and dropping it in. Even when I dropped that letter in the mail, I continued to have second thoughts about whether I would remain a full non-cooperator and risk prison.

When I finally got my order to report for a physical, I knew that a bunch of people were doing all kinds of things to get out - not signing the loyalty oath, pricking their finger and dropping blood in their urine, etc... I didn't do any of these things, though I do recall a futile discussion with a sergeant about why the defunct Abraham Lincoln Brigade was on the subversive organizations list. He said he didn't know and it didn't matter whether I signed it or not. I passed the physical. I was supposed to report for induction on December 14 of '67 which was right when I was in jail on the contempt citation, so I wrote to my draft board and said, "I can't report for induction because I'm in jail for helping someone refuse the draft," thinking, okay, maybe that will work. They just gave me a new order to report for induction. So then I filed for CO. I was denied by the local Board and then later given the CO status by the Kentucky Appeals Board (the same appeals board that was ordered by the Supreme Court in 1971 to grant Muhammed Ali's CO status). One of the local draft board guys told my dad, "We've never seen anyone like him. We don't know what to do with him."

My draft board was in Kentucky, because when you move around with the Navy you have one permanent address, which was my dad's hometown of Bardwell, Kentucky. I actually didn't have a hearing; they denied it on the basis of the application just to send it up to the appeal board.

---

*A. J. Muste was a pacifist, anti-war activist and a leader of the labor and civil rights movements whose personal integrity won him a rare universal respect. In 1939, when war clouds over Europe became darker by the hour, *Time* magazine called Abraham Johannes Muste "the Number One U.S. Pacifist." The designation was certainly appropriate and he wore the label proudly. From World War I until his death in 1967 at the height of the Vietnam War, Muste stood out in the struggle against war and social injustice in the United States.

My dad was generally supportive of my applying for CO; he certainly thought it was better than prison. He would often say, "You know, people think military people are for war, but many military people are those most against the war. We are the ones who have to fight it, not the politicians who get us into it." I recently found a copy of the letter my dad wrote to my draft board attesting to the sincerity of my beliefs and in support of my CO application.

I went to a meeting in '67 in Bratislava, Czechoslovakia with the North Vietnamese and members of the National Liberation Front of South Vietnam, about two dozen Vietnamese and thirty or so civil rights and anti-war activists from the U.S. My dad helped finance the trip, accepting my argument that we can't end a war if we don't listen to the other side and our government's not doing that. Months later, he got called in by the Commanding Officer at the Albany, Georgia. Naval Air Station, where he was stationed, and told that his son was either a communist or a comm-symp (communist sympathizer). What evidence did they use? He said my girlfriend's parents were communistic. My friend had lived in China as a child when her father taught there, and she wasn't actually my girlfriend. Then they said that the communist party paid for my trip, and my dad said, "Of course, the communist party didn't pay for his trip, I did." The C.O. just closed the folder and said, "That'll be all, Captain Gardner." My dad was a prosthetics specialist and they desperately needed them in the Navy, so they weren't going to kick him out.

I decided to go back to the University of Virginia in 1969, and I then applied for a student deferment. My first semester there I was working with some students to start a Virginia Research Institute studying poverty in Charlottesville. For my alternative service I wrote to the draft board and told them of this local non-profit organization, and billed it as the most benign alternative service project possible, so I got it accepted. The board sent a letter to the president of the Virginia Research Institute appointing me to work there as my alternative service. Really, it enabled me to keep organizing.

The FBI kept following me around, as they did with a lot of civil rights and peace activists. When I got my FBI files later, I learned that they looked at my tax returns to see if they could find something illegal and use that to turn me into an informer. They also asked my draft board for my CO application, but my draft board refused to give it to them. There is an interesting memo in my FBI file from the agent in Charlottesville. He says I am involved in student politics and constitutionally protected activity and suggests that I should be removed from the Priority One status that required full-time surveillance. Perhaps he had joined the FBI to fight crime. There is a terse memo back, signed by J. Edgar Hoover saying I was still a threat to national security and to keep filing his reports on me under the existing classification. I have that one framed.

Basically, I was able to negotiate my way around the draft so I could continue to do what I loved to do. I went back to college not because of the draft, but because I really felt like it was something I wanted to do. I really wanted to learn and understand more about the way the world and society worked in order to change it, and I decided to do it there because U.Va. had good professors. Then I got my alternative service doing exactly what I wanted to do and kept on organizing.

I recently reread a chapter I wrote in a book called *We Won't Go* edited by Alice Lynd (Beacon Press, 1968). The chapter was called "Manpower Unchannelled." It was basically describing my experience with the draft and the whole channeling policy I read about when I was in jail. Reading that, it really struck me that we were just eighteen to twenty-two then, the age of my students today. The instant maturity you're expected to acquire when you turn eighteen is astounding. It was then; it is now. It was a challenge at that age to sort out these philosophical questions about whether doing something which is moral, but may be less effective is, in fact, the morally correct action if it isn't effective at stopping the war. That was a big leap for me, because I was so impressed initially with the ethical purity of the moralistic absolutist position on the draft. It was probably a good thing I was sent to jail for contempt. I should thank the judge. After a few more arrests I became fairly skeptical about the political value of spending time in jail (though I do respect the need for civil disobedience in certain circumstances). I remember taking a position during a sit-in at U.Va. to protest the war and racism that we had had enough of going to jail; we came in and made our point, let's march out of here victorious. And that is what we did.

I am still very much anti-war. My mixed experience of growing up in the military, then working in the South and nationally against the war, makes for a very deep emotional well. I read these news stories today about a twenty-three-year-old sergeant, with a three year old, killed in Iraq or Afghanistan. These guys are like many of my students. They are from a working-class background, working through school, maybe signing up with the National Guard or military to get help financing their education. They had beautiful futures ahead of them. The Bush administration tried to suppress the casualty stories in the very compliant national media, but when these local guys come home in coffins, there is no way to suppress the local news stories. It is such a tragedy, every one of them. I had friends who went to Vietnam and died, kids I knew from high school and guys I got to know lifeguarding on the Marine base. I also know Vietnamese who lost friends and family members. It was tragic then, too – on both sides of the trenches.

Now I see teaching as a really important part of the work of fostering alternative and critical ways of thinking. Media literacy is an important part of that as well. Teaching citizens to critically examine what they see and hear in the news media seems essential to avoiding war in the future. I have also seen my work with the Media Education Foundation and the Men's Resource Center for Change in trying to redefine masculinity away from the cultural norms of violence and domination as part of that work.

Many of us who went through the movements and the wars of the sixties and seventies are feeling like we haven't done enough. I certainly do. We want to connect with that energy and passion and feeling of success we had then. This is not how it was supposed to turn out. The frat boys who threw snowballs or worse at us back in the '60s, or just ignored politics and partied through school, were not supposed to run the country when we all grew up. We were going to change everything, and yet look how we repeat the worse kinds of tragedies. Trying to understand this is what got me back to finish my degree at U.Va., and later to get a master's in journalism at Georgia, and a Masters in Public Administration at Harvard's Kennedy School and then a doctorate at UMass. I wanted to learn more about the press and public opinion and how to stop our varied spirals to disaster. I just hope our generation will hook up with the younger generation and stay engaged in trying to change things. We really have no other choice, do we?

Paul Richmond

Paul grew up outside of Buffalo, New York. He now lives in Wendell, Massachusetts with his partner and stepson. He is fifty-eight-years-old. For twenty years he was a performance artist working in public schools across the country on programs to assist students in making informed choices about tobacco, drugs and self-awareness. He did this with the use of juggling, humor and by involving students in the arts. He has been a community activist for over thirty years and has helped start food coops and men's groups. He is presently working to create a digital library for educational leaders who then create "schools" for all students with different learning styles while developing a sense of the joy in learning. He is also a spoken word poet who delights in bringing poetry to children and grown-ups through sharing his own work and organizing events to enable fellow poets to share theirs.

I graduated high school in 1969. I went to Woodstock that summer. I was living in Cheektowaga, a suburb of Buffalo, where you could feel pretty isolated. Buying record albums, listening to the radio and watching the scenes on TV of the civil rights movement and the war were my windows to seeing there was something happening in the outside world. I would hear about things through the University of Buffalo and learn from older sisters and brothers of friends, but my family lived in a pretty non-political environment.

I had an early sense that something was not as it was being told. When I was in junior high school President Kennedy was assassinated. I remember being with relatives at one of my uncle's houses when Oswald got shot. We were watching it on TV. People said, "Oh, now we're never going to know what really happened or who did it." Up until that time I had never heard any adults around me implying that America was not totally truthful or that there was something else going on. I was always presented with the reality that we were the ones who upheld truth and justice and the Russians were the evil people.

In high school there was definitely a pecking order. I went out for sports, but soon quit because the jocks at my school were pretty heavy duty in terms of who was the top rooster and who was on the bottom. I wasn't necessarily on the lowest rung, but when they got tired of picking on the people that they picked on every day, I was among those on the next rung.

There would be days when they would knock my books down or push me into the bathroom to give me a couple of punches. Later my dealings with the military had me feeling like I was dealing with the same sort of guys.

October of my first year in college I turned eighteen. I went to the post office and registered for the draft. I remember thinking, "Do I want to do this or not?" and "What do I want to do?" but I never really thought it through completely. I received my lottery number before I graduated high school. It was 78. I realized that at some point I was going to have to deal with whether I would go or not. I had gotten into college, which gave me a deferment. I went to Morrisville State College of Agriculture and Technology because it had contacted me. The school was low on enrollment and asked if I'd go. I wasn't that interested in school. It didn't really make much sense to me and I didn't do that well in school so I didn't think that I could even go to college. When this college approached me, I decided I would go and then sort of fell into the idea that I had a college deferment.

Morrisville State was a very small two-year school in central New York. It had never really opened up its campus to outside influences, but the year I started there were a lot of people from New York City. Some were Vietnam vets. The people from New York were organizing demonstrations. The school was really down on them and there wasn't even that much activity because they were such a small group. This was a farming community and they were pretty freaked out by this new student body with so many who smoked pot, did a variety of other drugs and went back to New York City on the weekends to see concerts and demonstrations. The school had primarily been kids from the area who rode their horses and their snowmobiles and joined fraternities and threw tables through windows while being drunk.

During the year I attended I was heavily influenced by the political activity. We used to go up to Syracuse because that's where a lot of the concerts and demonstrations took place. The music, the protest songs, questioning authority and questioning the war were my motivations for being there.

The fact is I didn't do that well in that college. The program wasn't really what I wanted. Plus there I was seeing all these fraternity guys getting drunk and beating up on each other and I wasn't really into that. I took a leave of absence, not quite realizing that as an eighteen-year-old I was going to lose my draft deferment. I left Morrisville in May, moved back in with my parents and was instantly classified 1-A by my draft board. By that September I was drafted.

Buffalo had a number of FM radio stations, which were basically guys who showed up with their record albums and played them. There were no commercials and late at night there was nothing else happening. They could say whatever they wanted to say and these guys talked about all kinds of interesting stuff. One night this one guy asked, "Is anybody in Buffalo having trouble or not knowing what you're going to do about the draft? Here's a phone number you can call and they'll give you counseling."

I actually called those guys after I realized that I was 1-A. On the phone they asked me a bunch of questions. Buffalo, like so many cities then and now, was very segregated and they told me about a cafe in a predominantly black area. I was supposed to wear something of a certain color and go to this café. They would then know to approach me. It all seemed rather bizarre and I don't know why I trusted them, but I went to the café and sat there for about forty minutes. These guys were there in a booth where I couldn't see them. I didn't know who they were. They were just watching me and waiting to see if anybody was coming in after me. Eventually they walked over to my table and asked if I was who I was and sat down. We had about a three-hour conversation during which they asked me why I called them and what did I think I wanted to do and what were my beliefs. They were definitely checking me out.

At this time in Buffalo there were two different major groups dealing with the draft and fighting the war. One group took the position that the American government was acting illegally and that the Vietnam War was illegal. They were basically saying, "We don't recognize what the government is doing. We don't have to recognize our 1-A status." They took sanctuary in churches and when the FBI and police came to drag them out, they fought back and tried to escape. One of their members was Bruce Byers, with whom I became friends years later. Bruce escaped the draft by leaving for Canada and then he went to Switzerland. Sometime in the mid-'70s he made a big decision to come back across the bridge from Canada with a number of vets to say, "Here I am. Here's what's happened to me." He told stories of those who had fled, about people becoming alcoholics and feeling abandoned once they fled to Canada.

The people I met in the café were part of the second group. It was run by two aspiring lawyers who had the support of volunteers they had pulled together who wanted to battle the draft and stop the war. They had convinced the local Quakers who owned a house into letting them use the living rooms and basement for their meetings. They had been there for at least five years before I showed up, compiling, filing, and putting people through a mock version of a CO hearing, getting information, and creating documentation of the whole process. Their main role was to help men seeking support around being drafted. They felt that if they could fight the system with as many people as possible saying no, then they could possibly slow it down and hopefully stop it. Their tactic was to do everything possible to delay the process as long as possible for anyone being called into the military. They also encouraged you to work on applying for CO status and helped in whatever way they could so you might win your case. In the end, if you were still facing having to go in, they offered help getting you into Canada if that's what you wanted.

What struck me about going to these guys was that from the very beginning they never *told* me anything. Years later when I had gotten very political, I was running into all sorts of people, the Marxists and the Maoists and who knows what and everybody had their own rap and analysis of the system. But these guys weren't anything like that at all. These guys were very much about asking, "What do you believe and how will you stand up for those beliefs?" They would give you a sheet of paper and half an hour to write down what you believe. Then all they would do is take your sheet of paper and read it aloud. They didn't give you any comments. They read it back to you and asked you, "Is that what you wanted to say?" No one had really done something like that through all my years of school, or anywhere else for that matter, so until that moment I had no real sense that I could write about my beliefs or that I'd ever questioned being a Catholic and whether I actually believed in God or not."

They told me right off, "What we're offering you is free. It's donations only if you can afford to. We're going to help you. You have to follow our lead in relation to writing letters to the military." It was about a two and a half year process. At the beginning they told me, "You have to show up for your induction. You have to be there at 7:30. Make sure you're there on time. Stand up to the line and when they ask you to take the oath, say no. Then you haven't broken any laws. Be prepared for all the harassment and then we'll work on the letters for you once you leave that situation." It essentially boiled down to, "Here you are. Here's where you're at legally. You've gotten this notice to report. You have to deal with that first. We'll deal with what needs to happen next when the time comes. Otherwise these are your choices to make." My other options were to go in or get arrested for not showing up. They were very good at explaining all my options and then letting me decide. I really welcomed this. It's definitely a big part of why I'm doing the work I'm doing now. It's what I'd been yearning for most of my life, that dialogue. My dad and I had some of this kind of dialogue, but it was mostly my grandfather who always wanted to talk and always wanted me to talk and would always ask me things."

My family was pretty divided in terms of values, politics and attitudes. One side lived in Buffalo and the other in Washington, D.C. The Buffalo side was Polish and working class and had bought into the Polish stereotype that they were dumb workers. They worked like mules and they were shocked when they made management. The Washington crowd was a typical Jewish family. They assumed you were going to get an education and, of course, you would get better jobs than your parents and, of course, you would be thinking and, of course, you would be reading. Reading was the Polish family's aversion. For them if you didn't know who the Bills (Buffalo's professional football team) quarterback was, there was something wrong with you. That was their major concern in life. For me this was a vast difference, and for the two weeks every summer that I spent in D.C., I got this insight that things could be different. It was during these vacation times with my Washington family that I began to realize that there was another kind of reality I could think about being part of.

By the time I hooked up with the draft counselors at the Quaker meetinghouse I was questioning a lot. Being at Woodstock was powerful, too. I didn't do anything bizarre. I didn't do any drugs. I was high from the experience, a contact high. Even if many people felt that the West Coast and hippie scene were dying, it finally hit where we lived in a big way. Being there I got that we were somehow part of a much bigger picture. Our minds were expanded.

This was now the background for what was unfolding for me personally. When I had arrived at college the year before, things started happening, like smoking pot and listening to the Vietnam vets' stories, which had made the war more real. But nobody had really pushed me to take a position I had to defend. I hadn't been pressed. When I was actually drafted and the military was forcing me to decide, "Okay, you're going to pull this trigger and you're going to do this act," I was now facing and addressing the real realities of killing and of war. The people who were working with me were really creating a format for that to happen, for me to look at my belief system and myself as it was evolving.

The other big influence was really the military personnel. Every experience I had with the military made me realize these were the same type of guys that I had dodged during high school. There was this gut, visceral reaction – why would I sign up with these guys regardless of the war? Why would I turn my power over to them and be out of control with these guys who I thought were dangerous? Watching them interact with me at the induction center I realized they could have convinced more people if they had consulted with a psychologist, because the approach they were using completely turned me off. They were acting like such assholes that it just strengthened my conviction that I would never join them. They were basically just saying we were all losers and yelling in our faces like all the classic movies.

Another factor was that by 1971 the system had experienced enough people going to drug stores and drinking concoctions and pretending to hear things and cutting off toes in order to get out, that they changed the procedures. When I got there, if you implied anything like you were sick or anything like that, MP's would just come in and take you off. They would take you somewhere and you would be held for a week to see if you still had those symptoms or whether you had done something to yourself so you just had the symptoms that day. They were not taking any bullshit. I remember a couple of guys were acting like they couldn't hear and they just dragged them off. They kept telling me that I didn't know what I was doing, that I was going to get into a lot of trouble and that I must want to spend a lot of time in prison. I never actually felt like I was this defiant person. I was fairly meek, but I knew I had to say no. Otherwise I was going. So I said no, and then it was just dealing with the after-effects of that. I was pushed into this room with a psychologist to try to ply me and get me to say I was just chicken shit and I had to say no to him a couple of times, too. Finally they just gave me a sheet of paper and said, "O.K, you'll be seeing the police," and, "You've made a big mistake."

I went back to my support guys who never pressured me. They gave me the opportunity to see that someone could help me. Their actions towards me were so much more humane than what I had experienced with the military. I didn't really know who they were personally, but I knew that I'd much rather spend my time with them than with those other guys. At the induction center people were standing up and being defiant. It was like a classroom out of control. I realized these military personnel didn't have a clue and didn't care. They were just trying to use force and the fear of power. My political awareness of the lies about what we were doing in Vietnam had also become stronger as I was doing this. I had a growing awareness that this was not a war for anything that made any sense.

When I got to the "safehouse," as always there were two guys there. One guy was always in the kitchen, which had been transformed into a law office. There were zillions of military books and he sat at a desk. He was always rifling through things. The other guy helped set up counselors who were in the other rooms. When they saw me they said, "So you said, 'No'. Great." It was always expressed that you were making these decisions. They didn't want anyone to think that later on you could turn around and say, "You told me to..." or "Why did I do this?" That atmosphere was really empowering. I had already gone through this thing with my parents about wanting to move out of the house and them responding with, "Why are you moving, you're not married yet?" These interactions were definitely not empowering in the sense of me not feeling like I was an adult. My parents thought I was just going to fight going for a while and eventually I was going to sign up because that's just how it goes and I'd come around. My father kept having hopes that I would go into the Navy and do what he did because he felt, why sleep in a ditch when you can have a bed. You'd be done in four years and you wouldn't really have to shoot anyone.

When I came into the "safehouse" after the induction center experience, one of the guys said, "Okay, this is going to be the format. Anytime you receive a letter from the military you come here immediately. When you come into this room, from now on you'll be given paper. After I read the letter, I'm going to tell you what to write to deal with what they sent you." I would write down what he said after he looked up info in the various law books. Then I'd write my name and anything else I needed to write. One of them would read it over and make sure it was legal and then I had to send it registered mail so the military would have to sign for it. You sent nothing unless it was by registered mail so they can't read it and then send you something else and screw over the process." I would say that I sent out, without exaggeration, thirty registered letters or more.

I also received support for filing as a conscientious objector. First I was told, "We're going to give you some time so you can think about what you want to say." They informed me of the various procedures and they gave me the papers. There were five questions. They told me to go home and answer them. There were questions like, Do you believe in god? What is your definition of who is the supreme being? Why do you think you can't kill? It was probably eight months to a yearlong process where I went back every week or every two weeks and handed these papers in. They would read them out loud to me. I would sit there and say yes or no. That started the process in which I got mail from the military telling me things like, "What you wrote in section three makes section four void," etc. ...I would bring the letter into the kitchen and the guy would say, "Yes, but section six brings it back to life," and I would send them back a letter explaining everything they had misinterpreted.

That went on for two and half years. What was really interesting was that by the time I got done I had really bought into what I was writing. This was actually the closest I'd ever come to trying to formulate my beliefs and answer questions like how I would stop a rapist who was trying to rape my mother and what I would do to not kill him.

By this point I had forced them to give me a trial for getting a CO. All the letters I wrote were giving me as much time as possible, but the time was up now and I had to go face my trial. I went through two weeks of intense preparation for the hearing. The counselors had sent so many people through the process that they knew what went on and they asked people to reenact what went on in the hearing room.

I went to these really bizarre meetings that went on at midnight in their basement. You stayed up in the kitchen and all the people who were ready to go to trial went down one by one. Downstairs there were five people, several counselors and others who had already had the experience of being at one of the draft board hearings, sitting around a table acting like the military. It was definitely an attempt to knock you out of your comfort zone, to make you scared, to have you want to punch them out. There were several observers to keep things balanced because people did get kind of pissed off. When that happened the observers made the "actors" stop and remind us they were trying to prepare us for what was going to go on. They said the hearing board was going to try to get us to react. Then they'd say, "See, you are violent. You're not a CO."

Next I had to ask my father to be my witness and that's where it got really tricky. My father was a door-to-door salesman so taking off a day or even a few hours was a big deal. I don't think the boss realized where he was going. He said, "Well, why don't you just let it go. I can't believe you're doing this." Something about my mother's involvement in all this came up last September at my brother's wedding and it was something that I never knew. My mother told me that two military guys came to the house at two different times during my appeal process to talk to me and she didn't let them in. After she told me, I asked her why she had never let me know about this before. She said, "I didn't like them and I didn't like how they were being. You were home, but I told them you weren't home or you hadn't gotten up yet." This shocked me since she never said this during the time I was going through the process to give me any support. I found this out thirty-five years later.

My father hemmed and hawed about coming with me. I told him that I had to show up at 8:00 and my hearing was scheduled for 9:15. He asked, "How long is this supposed to last? What's going to happen? When can I get out?" I said, "I don't know. We may have to wait." Sure enough, when we got there, there were fifty other guys all with trials. We were scheduled in blocks of fifteen minutes with six hearings supposedly being held in each fifteen-minute slot. The reality was I was scheduled for 9:15 and I didn't finally get in there until six at night.

We waited in a really long hallway. It was very cinematic - the long hallway with two doors on the other end. We were all sitting in a row looking down the hallway. One of the doors would open up a crack and someone's name would be called out and that was all you'd hear. The person would wander down there. The doors would close. Every once in a while all these alarms would go off, some M.P.s would rush in, the doors would be flung open and you'd see some guy being dragged out yelling, "Motherfuckers!" and grabbing the flag on his way out. The doors would slam shut and then it would be incredibly quiet until the doors would open and another name would be called.

They told us we couldn't leave to get lunch because one of us could be called at any point. We sat there for nine hours. My father kept saying, "Listen, I need to go. I need to keep working," but he stayed there. Finally when it was my turn, unbelievably, he was supposed to be my witness and they wouldn't let him in. I went in and told them, "My witness is outside." One of them said, "Oh, he isn't supposed to come in now," to which I said, "Well, then how is he supposed to be my witness?"

I sat down. There were four men and a stenographer and one of the men asked me a question. I started to answer the question and, as I was mid-sentence, the fellow to the right of the first guy asked me another question. I stopped and started to answer him. The first guy said, "You're not answering my question?" I said, "I was, but then he asked me another one." The first man said, "You don't want to answer my question?" He then knocked the papers I had brought to the floor. I had been practicing for this sort of intimidation for two weeks in rehearsals for the big event, so in some way this seemed very comical to me. I remember saying to myself, "So these are the guys who say they're the military. They run the country and they are acting like they actually want to talk to me about my involvement, yet this is how they're treating me, and this is how they're acting. This is really adolescent. It has nothing to do with anything. They don't really care." This gave me the major strength of feeling, "I'm not giving in to you guys. I mean this is ridiculous. I can't believe the country's run this way and that this is how the military does things."

After waiting almost nine hours, the whole hearing lasted about seven minutes. I was told to leave. They called my father in. He was in for about a minute and a half. He came out and I asked him what they asked and he said, "They just wanted to know whether you believed what you believed. I said yes, those are his beliefs and that's all I could tell them."

Within a very short time I got the notice that my appeal was rejected. I was 1-A again. My support people told me I next needed to get the transcript of my hearing. Before that though, they said I needed to sit down and write down the questions I had been asked, what I answered and how they responded. I wrote everything down the way I remembered it and then went to get my transcript. It didn't look anything like what I had written down. One, they didn't even really give me a hearing. Two, there was nothing in the transcript about what actually went on. It even indicated that I said other things than I actually said. It was one more piece in their efforts to get me into this threatened position where they could say, "O.K. You're going to go to jail, so you might as well sign up now." The process had gone on for two and a half years and I had lost. Through the verdict they had finally said, "We're not giving you any more chances to appeal."

I went back to my support guys and this is what I liked about these guys that really came through at the end. They thanked me and said, "You've done what we hoped for by being a part of saying no, and slowing down the system. Now here are your options..." They said I could sign up, of course, but what was great about these guys was there was no judgment about it. If I felt I wanted to sign up it was up to me. My other choice was a tough one, no romancing about it. I could be on the run and possibly end up in jail. They then said, "If you want to go to Canada, we can help you, but it's a bit tricky. We'll give you a week to decide. You can't take much more time because they'll be coming after you. You'll need some money and some clothes and you'll be blindfolded. You won't see the people who will take you. This is how it'll happen so let us know."

I went home and that night at dinner my father was trying to tell me that I should join the Navy while I was trying to figure out whether I was going to pack up and go to Canada and what I would take with me? This was the point I had come to. I then looked over at the TV screen where there was a news flash. Nixon came on and said, "We're moving to the next lottery." The reason that was revealed later was that my year there had been thousands of people who were saying no.

Essentially that meant that they were taking everyone who had been 1-A for a year and who they couldn't get to go in and making them 1-H. They were hoping they could come back to us and fuck us over after the war, but for now all the people out there like me got a 1-H. Two days later I got the classification in the mail, 1-H. My whole life changed. I didn't have to go to Canada. That next lottery went to somewhere around 225, a long way from 125, which had been the highest. They now just moved past people who said no and took anyone who said yes. They needed guys there.

I felt like I was given a new life. I had never done anything for two-and-a-half years in my life that was so concentrated, but all of a sudden I had to switch over my daily activities. I had been constantly writing and doing work for my draft case. I then started to go to summer school and night school. I wanted to do something to make a change.

While at the University of Buffalo I found a situation that mirrored what happened for me at the "safe house." I started teaching at College F! The college was one of thirteen "colleges" at the University of Buffalo. College F was almost a total replication of the Quaker Meetinghouse. It was a place where people used that format to educate students by asking, "Why do you want to learn this? What does it matter to you that you learn this?"

We did some important things in College F – alternative newspapers, cooperative businesses were started and supported, demonstrations were organized, and political classes were taught. We focused attention on environmental pollution, fighting nuclear power and starting free schools. It was never easy, but it felt important and it was all about working to create a change in the society.

These thirteen colleges that College F was a part of came about due to incredible street battles that then forced the university to give the students and faculty at that time, 1969, their desire for classes on issues important to the times. Thirteen big pink trailers were put on campus for these groups to set up classes. The battles had won the right for these colleges to hire who they wanted to teach their classes. The University could no longer say, "We don't have any blacks," or "We don't have any women who have PhD's so we can't have women's studies and black studies." Now these colleges could hire the people that they wanted to hire to teach the courses they wanted to offer with the hope that in a few years there would be people with Ph.D.'s in women studies, African-American studies, etc.

That's how I got to teach. I was brought into those colleges that were given this mandate, which was a great victory. There had been enough counter-cultural force that many of the university officials had to address the demands. Not surprisingly, once they had allowed these colleges to come into being, the University attempted to quiet things down and get the various colleges entangled in budget fights. But for me, once I met the people working in this alternative setting, I felt at home and started using what had happened to me – the encounter with the counselors, their approach, my experience with the draft board – in my teaching.

With so much going on all around me, much of which I was participating in, I really believed there would be a major change in American culture. I experimented in communes and different living arrangements, but then suddenly the rest of the world went what felt like backwards. I remember being really depressed by "Saturday Night Fever" and disco. I had a lot of friends who went into major depressions and became druggies just to drown their disappointment that what they thought was changing wasn't. It was different for me. Maybe it was my own constitution or some of my experiences with those draft counselors and their continual optimism about battling the system and that it was nothing new, but I realized that this was an ongoing struggle and that people were fighting for a long time.

The next thing for me was being exposed to the Wobblies* and World War II veterans, civil rights activists and old Communist Party members. Through interactions with these people, it became apparent that things

---

*The Industrial Workers of the World (IWW or the Wobblies) is an international union. The IWW contends that all workers should be united as a class and that the wage system should be abolished. The origin of the nickname "Wobblies" is uncertain. One of the IWW's most important contributions to the labor movement and broader push towards social justice was that, when founded, it was the only American union, besides the Knights of Labor, to welcome all workers including women, immigrants, and African Americans into the same organization. (http://en.wikipedia.org/wiki/Industrial_Workers_of_the_World)

changed over much longer periods of time. What I learned from these older organizers was, "You may never see the change, but don't let that discourage you from working each day for it."

When I look back on the draft and the lottery, it was apparent that if you separate and divide folks it's easier to conquer. It's hard to say to one of your friends who had number 325 and wasn't going to be drafted, "Help me out," because they were just laughing, "Hahaha, I'm home free." The whole experience put us in this general lottery mentality where, "Life is a game. I won and you lost so stop crying. Suck it up and deal with that you didn't win like a man." But it didn't necessarily happen that way. I don't think everyone just thought about it as, "Oh no, I wasn't lucky enough to get a higher number so I think I'll just go." More and more people started to say no. This meant people with high lottery numbers started to be called. I think that's what started this even bigger challenge for the system, because more people started to realize, "I'm not safe with 150," or "I'm not safe with 175." " I'm not even safe with 225 – okay, now what's going on here?" And at the same time more and more stuff started to come out in the news about what was happening and what wasn't happening – with the draft, the War and the culture itself.

I would say I was lucky coming of age when I did. The battle we don't see happening against the War in Iraq was happening then because there was the support of rebellion. You knew there were others around even if you didn't realize how many. Then there were all of the contradictions – being taught that America is the best place in the world and then learning what was being done in the name of democracy. You found yourself asking, "What's behind the curtain?" When the Vietnam vets started to come back and say, "Guys, I wouldn't go," their information gave many of us the incentive to resist.

Talking about this part of my past is actually encouraging to me. It makes me see where I came from and what I continue to value and work for as I try to hold to my beliefs. I really appreciate those people who influenced me to take a stand and to be true to myself. Remembering them helps me remember to ask myself, "O.K., what am I doing for young people to encourage them, as one individual to another individual." I know that when I talk to people it can have an effect, even though it's played down that you can have any effect. When the story I have just told comes out maybe it will inspire other people to see what I have seen and it will give them courage to be fighting back and creating anew.

CHAPTER SEVEN

THOSE WHO LOVED, SUPPORTED AND COUNSELED

MY TEMPTATION IN COMPILING THIS BOOK was to focus my attention solely on the men who faced the draft, since their stories directly reveal the impact of our government's policies and practices during the Vietnam War on their individual lives. But in reality, countless others – those who cared about the men themselves – were also affected, before, during, and after whatever ordeal their men faced.

Once again, this category includes a great variety of stories. I considered a whole section covering the experience of parents, since their role in many instances was singular, whether it included active support for or staunch opposition to their son's choices. No doubt a book could be written that delves deeply into the conflicts, hardships, and struggles that afflicted many families during these difficult times. In addition, there would be stories of parents who supported sons and daughters who chose to serve their country, and whose parenting challenges pertaining to the war began only after their adult child returned.

Those whose stories do appear in this section cover a variety of roles that people played during this period. Wives who accompanied their husbands to Canada are here. A draft counselor shares her experiences. A woman who felt that the draft and lottery could never be fair if women were exempted reveals her connection to both through a man she loved. I have once again revealed just the iceberg's tip, yet in each oral history so much is exposed about what this war and its draft did to change people's lives.

The interviews I conducted for this chapter brought back many memories for those whose stories you are about to read. Consistently I was reminded that loving, supporting, and counseling took commitment and a willing suspension of one's own needs in order to meet those of the man or men whose lives were being changed by the war. This took its toll – on marriages, on friendships, and on parent-child relationships. Much of this has been depicted in earlier interviews. It felt very important to give those whose presences contributed to the men's stories an opportunity to tell their own.

Diane Clancy

Diane Clancy graduated from Trinity College in Hartford in 1971. She lives in Greenfield, Massachusetts, where she is an artist and an activist who suffers from several debilitating chronic illnesses. She has raised a daughter alone and now shares her life with a woman who is a photographer.

I felt very mixed about the draft lottery. I was glad it leveled the playing field a little by making all men more equally vulnerable instead of some being more vulnerable because of their race, class, and/or educational opportunity. However, I was also outraged that many men serving in Vietnam really never had the same opportunities for an education or to somehow avoid the draft, as the people I was going to school with.

I was also both angry and relieved that as a woman I didn't have to face the draft myself. I didn't like preferential treatment for women, but I was also relieved I didn't have to face the same decisions about whether to go to jail, to Canada or to serve, that some of the men I knew were facing. It felt like a privilege, similar to the privilege that white, upper class men had before the lottery. I also felt deprived – because I couldn't make the same dramatic statements and choices that men could. I didn't have a draft card, so I couldn't choose to burn it. I didn't get the opportunity to speak and make choices from the same moral pulpit. So in some ways I felt left out.

If I had been drafted, I would have tried to be a conscientious objector: war was and remains against my values. I think we need to do a lot more diplomatic work towards peaceful resolution. Look at the Danish in World War II: nonviolence can be a powerful tool. Unfortunately I don't know whether the U.S. wants to live in harmony with others rather than make others follow our will.

At the time of the war, I was also scared. The draft put some of the men I loved into the vulnerable position of either having to go to Canada, to jail or to serve in a war they didn't believe in. If they served, they also faced the awful reality of fighting, killing innocent civilians, and potential disability or death. We were demonstrating a lot and trying to convince people to put pressure on the government to stop the war.

Many of my friends went for conscientious objector status, because I went to a school, which was largely anti-war, pro-community building, and for building bridges across differences. That's why it's important for me to say also that, even though my friends and I were against the war, we weren't angry at the troops; we wanted to work *with* them. I never saw disrespect toward soldiers. I had a friend whose husband had served in Vietnam, and he and I talked quite a lot. Listening to what he'd seen and experienced saddened me. However, I understood how grateful he was to have someone who hadn't served want to hear about what he'd been through, and what his thoughts and feelings were. I treasured this time.

Part of the reason I was so angry about the draft was that my male friends were considered old enough to be drafted, sent to war, and even killed, but not considered old enough to vote. They weren't considered mature enough to help make decisions and elect those that were sending them over to Vietnam. You can see that even though I didn't serve, and couldn't have because of my health, as I later realized, I took the draft very personally – that my peer group, people my age, were being sent to war, especially without voting rights!*

I paid a lot of attention to the lottery numbers of the men in my life. The results were really important to me. I knew my boyfriend and many of my friends would apply for conscientious objector status if their numbers were low – or would go to Canada. But I worried terribly about my younger brother because I didn't know what he would do.

It became very important for me to know what my number would have been. Even if I wouldn't be drafted, it still made me feel a little bit more connected to the whole process instead of just being on the outside of it all. The night of the first lottery in 1969 was very nerve-racking for me.

We all gathered together in a public area in the school and watched as they drew the numbers. I felt like a fraud because my neck wasn't on the line, but I was still horrified knowing that this would greatly impact thousands of lives. It turned out that those I was closest to either had high numbers, were conscientious objectors, or had health problems that they hoped would eventually cause them to receive a 4-F. My boyfriend had a pretty low number, but he expected to be 4-F. My brother had a high number so, in a sense, I was protected from the full effect that some had. I was relieved and guilty.

---

*In 1971, the 26th Amendment was ratified, giving everyone over the age of 18 the right to vote. The Amendment was passed in large part because of the letter-writing and peaceful protest efforts of a large number of college students – young women and men facing conscription. Ratification was accomplished in four months – the shortest period of time of any constitutional amendment in U.S. history.

I did know some men who had low numbers and because I was so politically active I knew evaders and resisters. Most of the time when I was with one or more of these men, I was also with other people so I trusted someone would be there who would know what to do if the police went after one of these men.

There was a scary moment for me when I was giving a draft evader a long ride. The tires had very low treads on the used car I had bought. I was on the way to get new tires and the police stopped me because of the tires. I was absolutely terrified that the police would ask to see the draft card or identification of the person I was with. I kept practicing the name I was supposed to call him as we drove. I knew him by his real name and by the name on his documents. I wanted to make sure I did it right. Also, I kept trying to decide what to do if they caught him – what was the appropriate, responsible action? Fortunately, they never checked, but I still remember how frightened I felt as we sat there on the side of the road.

Another time, my boyfriend and I had borrowed my mom's car for a long trip. The car was having problems and we had to go slowly on an interstate as we were figuring out how to get off to get the car fixed. The police pulled us over as suspicious. It was again terrifying to me. He had his draft card, but apparently they stopped us because they thought we were members of the Weather Underground, a group that was willing to use violence to end the War in Vietnam. Thankfully the police realized we were harmless.

Another thing about the lottery for me was that I became very aware of a division resulting from that night of the drawing of numbers. It was horrible sitting there as the men I cared about were divided into different groups: those all of a sudden at enormous risk with low numbers, those who were safe with high numbers and those with mid-risk from medium numbers. I imagined the insecurity for the mid-risk – it was still unknown whether they would be called. I ended up feeling very isolated and alone – it was like before we were all in this together and we weren't together any more – just individuals now.

As for the anti-war movement, the lottery changed things some for me. I could feel a different heaviness or lightness from those with different numbers. But many of us were very passionate about stopping the war – it had little or nothing to do with serving or not serving. Also there were certainly many people active in the anti-war movement that were too old to draft or even serve. Maybe some people didn't care as much about the war if they weren't at risk of being drafted – but they weren't the ones who were very active in the movement.

Then there were the effects of the war on those who served. I got to know men who returned from Vietnam with invisible scars – psychological wounds. I participated in several arenas in which I saw close up the toll the war took on the souls of these men. At the V.A. I administered tests to returning vets and through talking to them and debriefing them, I saw how alienated they felt, surrounded by professionals who had no appreciation for what they had been through. Many had turned to drugs and alcohol as a response to the violence they'd witnessed. I think the dissonance between their post-war lives back home and what they had been living through in Vietnam was too much to bear.

I encountered many of these same and similarly desperate vets through support groups for those with substance abuse problems. I saw the intensity of their anger and felt it was at a different level than others in the circle. For too many of them there was a tragic lack of self-control and the places they went with drugs and alcohol were so self-destructive. Inevitably, for those trying to stay in a marriage or raise children, this rage was destructive to those around them. In my mind the internal pain these men were dealing with from what they had witnessed and participated in was so extreme that drugs and alcohol were used in ultimately dangerous ways to numb the intense feelings inside them. Normal social restraint was just not there for these men. Many of them were trying really hard to do the right thing, to be responsible, but there was a lion inside them, an enormous pile of anger and violence, which never healed and would come out in rage. Layered onto this was the enormous difference between World War II vets and Vietnam vets. The former felt they had done something to be really proud of – stopping the Nazis and restoring democracy to Europe. Many Vietnam vets felt that what they did in the war was wrong and the results were guilt and shame.

The fact is that in the '60s I certainly thought women should be drafted if men were. To me, it was a part of women's independence, which meant having to take the bad with the good. Now I believe in compulsory national service for everyone. I think it's good for everyone to serve in some way. Definitely women, too! I think it's possible that so many people crossing paths and working together with such a mix of race, class, gender, and sexual identity (yes, gay people should serve!) and ability (I think it makes sense for disabled people to serve, too, with accommodations) would truly help people accept difference more. There would have to be training and supervision so that societal norms weren't played out and so this form of service to promote peace and economic prosperity, not war, would be a responsible, educational experience for everyone involved. But lots of good work could get done...and the society would change for the better. And maybe with everyone having a stake we'd be in less of a hurry to go to war.

Frances Crowe

Frances is ninety years old and has been an activist for over fifty years. She lives in Northampton, Massachusetts. She has three children and five grand-children. She continues to protest against war and is now organizing against the Wars in Iraq and Afghanistan.

Prior to the escalation of the Vietnam War, I was a full-time mother, housewife, and homemaker with three kids, two of whom were adolescent boys. The kitchen seemed always to be filled with young men after school talking about what they were going to do about the draft. After hearing their stories, I decided I would go to the Central Committee for Conscientious Objectors, to take a week's draft counseling training course. I came back and visited some draft centers, such as one in Cambridge, one in New Haven, and several others, but I didn't get to see what I considered draft counseling. I saw angry young men, mostly resister types, "conducting interviews." What they were really doing was telling other men about their (mostly illegal) options, such as how they could throw protein in their urine samples to indicate kidney problems, gain or lose weight, or see a psychiatrist. These crazy, demonizing things were very disturbing to me.

I came back and went to the University of Massachusetts School of Education for a course in group counseling. I decided to take what I called the feminist approach to draft counseling, i.e. to do groups, similar to the consciousness-raising groups of the women's movement. We had a home with a large lower floor where I could have a draft-counseling center. I decided that Tuesday and Thursday afternoons, and Friday nights, I would do groups from two to five o'clock and seven to ten. I went to our local paper, the *Daily Hampshire Gazette*, to see about putting an ad in announcing my groups. Their immediate response was it would be illegal to print that. I asked them to check with their lawyers; after all, all I was doing was telling draftees about their legal options under Selective Service. The lawyers affirmed my right to put my ad in, but they ran it as a little ad in the classifieds. "Young Men, are You Conscientiously Opposed to Participation in War in Any Form? If so, come to a draft information session." Nobody came.

Now remember, this was before there were Xerox machines. I had a big, old mimeograph machine. It was very hard to cut stencils and grind out copies; nevertheless, I prepared flyers. In those days students at the five colleges in our area weren't allowed to have cars, and there was no bus service between the schools. So everybody hitchhiked. I decided the thing I should do was to drive back and forth between the colleges in our area, Amherst and Northampton, picking up hitchhikers and giving them the flyers with information about the counseling sessions. The first Monday morning I went out, I managed to fill up the station wagon with young men going to Amherst. As soon as they got in the car, I asked them," What are you going to do about the draft?" Oh, they had crazy ideas about going to Canada or Sweden, failing physicals, or cutting off part of their trigger finger. I talked fast and drove slowly. Then I gave them stenciled maps to my house, with an invitation to my first draft counseling session, the following Tuesday at two o'clock.

I did that all day, and by Tuesday afternoon, I had a roomful. There were people *in* the military, people trying to decide how to *not* go into the military, or whether they would let themselves be drafted. There were girlfriends, mothers, wives, even at one point, a father of a potential draftee who was chairman of the Holyoke Draft Board, who came because he really wanted to understand the law. I was prepared for that: I had all the legal books, had studied the draft law carefully, and had even subscribed to the *Law Reporter*.

My fellow draft counselors and I had great success with people in the military. The only outward difference between them and the others was the way their hair was cut! In fact, we worked with the first CO in the Air Force: a pilot flying out of Thailand and bombing Vietnam. He was home on leave when our Women Against the War group blockaded the entrance to Westover Air Force Base. We dressed as Vietnamese women while this pilot, back in the States, was serving at the base. He had been given an M-16 and put on guard duty. He later told us that he had been struck by our group of women kneeling there in front of the gate, many of us crying. While we had been leafleting there for over three years, the day he observed us happened to be International Women's Day. Inspired by the Vietnamese poetry we'd been reading aloud, we spontaneously just got down on our knees to honor all the Vietnamese women affected by the terrible war and to block the gate. He said that suddenly he had a vision of the people he had bombed in Vietnam. He wasn't aware of all his conflicting emotions at the time, but that night, while he was watching "West Side Story" with his wife, he started crying and he couldn't stop.

The next day he was ordered back to Thailand. He thought very seriously, and decided he could never bomb again. He went to see the Air Force chaplain, and I heard on the radio later that week that he refused an order to bomb and was going to be court-martialed in Westover. He was from Danbury. On the same radio piece, I heard his mother say, "My son is not a CO. He would have fought in World War II." I raced to the phone and began the process of trying to call his mother in Danbury even though I only had his last name. Fortunately I got her on the third try. When I asked for her son, she said he was in Thailand. I told her, "Then I want to talk to you. Your son does *not* have to say what he would have done in World War II! That's something he will never know. He only needs to say how he feels about *this* war. I want to send him some material." So she gave me his APO (Army Post Office) address, and I immediately ran downstairs, got all my best copies of things, and sent them to him. Luckily, he got the package just as he was getting on the plane to come home, so he called me when he arrived at Westover. We got together, and he got the help he needed. Now he's a lawyer doing really good anti-death penalty work. Of course, there were many others. This is just one of the stories I could tell you.

In addition to working with this pilot, we'd also begun counseling high school drop-outs from some depressed communities in our area such as Chicopee. It was all word-of-mouth. One would hear about the sessions, and soon they would bring others. That meant we were fortunate to have a very diverse group of people. We had Amherst College students with Chicopee youth. The Amherst College students were often very articulate, but out of touch with their feelings. The Chicopee youth were really in touch with their feelings, but lacked the competence to express them. They helped one another, and out of that came a support network.

Some of the most difficult sessions involved those who were serving. There was one who was AWOL and we helped him talk about what he needed to do. I didn't consider myself a military counselor, so I sent these men off to get military counseling to help them sort through the issues. I remember at one point he turned himself in to go back to apply for a CO discharge, and of course, we helped him and others with the letters of reference. We had certain ministers in town who we knew would be willing to talk to these people and help them search their conscience if they felt they were sincere. Then they'd write them a letter of support. He told us later that at one point he was standing there in this wooden barracks some place down south and he refused to put on his uniform. He had only his underpants on. They threw a gun at him that he was supposed to catch and he didn't catch it. At that moment he knew he was a conscientious objector. He later said, "The group was with me." They tested him and he used his feelings of solidarity to withstand their pressure tactics.

We also had one young man who was totally out of the system. He was a drop-out living out in the woods in Chicopee. He had trouble expressing himself, but he was a very good wood carver. Encouraged by the group, the way he decided to express himself was to use his art. He made this beautiful box. On the first side of it was Gandhi, on the second, Martin Luther King, on the third, Dorothy Day, and on the fourth, César Chávez. All four of these people were his non-violent heroes and he took that into the draft board to show them. Of course, their first reaction was that there was a bomb in it, which still makes me laugh. He got his CO!

There were others who joined us for the meetings including mothers and fathers whose sons were confronting the draft. Some were very skeptical at first. "What are you doing?" "Who are you?" "What's this all about?" But we were just right out there with our efforts to support their sons. We were honest and trusting, and soon they trusted us. It was a wonderful open process.

I was very glad to see parents coming. I feel parents have the responsibility to really level with their kids about what *they* feel about participating or not participating in war, rather than saying, "It's your life. You have to decide." I also believe that parents are responsible for promoting their children's moral and philosophical lives. I have a son, Tom, who was away at a farm high school in Vermont when he first began thinking about the draft. He was trying to be very objective about the idea of conscientious objection; with his mother so deeply involved in encouraging this approach, he was a little skeptical. Eventually he said, "I think I'm going to go into the Army and find out for myself what it's really like." My husband and I were very concerned about this approach, so I called him and said, "Tom, you've got to come home and spend a day with us. We'll talk this through, because we feel this is not you. Come on a Wednesday when I don't have a group. We'll take the phone off the hook, I won't answer the door, and we'll be there totally for you." He came, and we talked all day. We really talked it through, and at the end of the day he said, "I will apply for a CO but I'll do so on environmental grounds. I am doing so to help protect the earth. War damages the planet, and animal life, and endangers species," so he applied for his CO on those grounds.

He stressed to us that he was not a Quaker as we were, but he grew up around the Quaker faith and we sensed it was that belief system that he tapped into. Then Tom got a number that didn't put him at risk, and I was very glad for him. However, soon after he learned his high number, he said, "That was really important what you did, having me come down and us talking things through for the whole day. If I had waited to get drafted or volunteered it would have been a big mistake." So I think parents should be encouraged to get actively involved, and I was very glad that our counseling sessions provided an opportunity for that to happen.

When people first arrived at the draft counseling sessions, I had them fill out a form with their name and address, their draft status, whether they qualified for any physical exemptions, and if there were other exemptions for which they thought they might be eligible. I kept those forms, so if they happened to be on vacation when they heard about a change in the draft law, they could call me, and I could look at their record and say, "Yes, I think you should do this" or "No, I don't think this change applies to you."

Once the forms were filled out, I invited everyone to sit in a circle. We went around the circle, with each young man telling his particular story. As we went around the circle, they gained confidence by hearing one another. They could identify. "Yes, that's the way I feel." We asked them questions such as, "What's the basis of your belief and where does it come from?" and "What do you think are the seeds in your background for these ideas of conscience?" They shared stories. One told about how he had accidentally killed a squirrel with a bb gun when he was young and shared his emotional response to taking a squirrel's life. Another would tell about a book he had read, such as *Johnny's Got His Gun*.* I showed slideshows such as Don Luce's "Remember Vietnam,"† which really helped them get

---

Johnny's Got His Gun is an anti-war novel written by American novelist and screenwriter Dalton Trumbo. It was written in 1938, published in 1939, and adapted into a film by the author in 1971. It tells the story of Joe Bonham, a young soldier serving in World War I, who wakes up in a hospital bed after being caught in the blast of an exploding artillery shell. He gradually realizes he has lost his arms, legs, and face, but that his mind functions perfectly, leaving him a prisoner in his own body. His wish is to be put in a glass tube and taken around the country to show people the true horrors of war.

†This filmstrip made in 1970 by Don Luce, shows the beauty that was Vietnam before the start of the war with the U.S. and its subsequent devastation.

in touch with what was going on there. The slideshow made the viewers think about Vietnam a lot. We talked about similar books, music, and films. Those who weren't familiar with the titles became eager to get their hands on them to see if they were helpful.

They came back week after week, clarifying their thoughts and beliefs. They also began to slowly write their answers to the CO application questions. As new people came in, they were helped by those further along in the process. We went over their applications together as a group. Often people would strengthen their CO responses as they heard ideas others expressed and recognized they felt the same way. We also role-played personal appearances in front of the draft board, so people would feel as prepared as possible.

First we challenged people with the crazy questions draft boards might well ask them, such as, "What would you do if someone tried to attack your grandmother?" And then we coached them to respond, "That's not war and my grandmother locks her doors. She doesn't have guns and I don't have a gun." People asked, "What if the draft board says, 'You pay taxes, so you must obey the law?'" We would counsel them to say, "It's illegal to not file a tax form, just like it's illegal for me to go into the Army if I am a CO." So, we were helping by showing them the relevant law.

We based a lot of these role-plays on what members of the group told us after they had been to a draft board hearing. Using their experiences, people in the group took turns being the chairman or members of the board. They loved doing that, and it helped everyone prepare for their own personal appearance.

I had copies of all of the medical regulations, but I really urged them not to take a medical or illegal way out because I said, "It's going to be on your record for the rest of your life. It may influence your health insurance coverage. It may influence a job you want to get if it says you are psychologically unstable. It's hard enough to figure out who we are and if you've got this label of being unstable...There are times when you think well, maybe I am. And I don't think it's a good way to see yourself." I think it was a very positive experience for me and for the young people.

Along with this work, we had coffee and tea, and people would bring cookies or cheese and crackers. We stayed up late, and sometimes it was hard, Friday night particularly, to get them to leave because they had developed into a group. It was a community. Whenever someone who received a 1-0 classification as conscientious objector came back and shared their experience, we celebrated! Those who had been successful kept coming so they could help the others. That first year, '68 through '69, I had 1,776 come for counseling. 1776: it's a wonderful number, don't you think?

We went on for three years until the draft finally stopped. Out of all those who came to the counseling groups, only one person went to prison. He was a non-registrant from New Hampshire and had his trial up there. We all went up to support him. We also wrote to him while he was in prison, and I picked him up when he got out. We didn't forget about him when he was no longer coming to the group: we saw him through his choice. Only one person went into the Army. He went in as a 1-A-0, as a medic, because his brother was in Vietnam. Everybody else ended up as a CO!

We tried to help people who got their CO classification find creative alternative service employment. The law says your alternative service has to be in the national interest and has to force you to disrupt your personal life in some way, usually by moving from your local community. We got churches and non-profit organizations to sponsor CO's, so they could work for alternative schools, health care centers, food banks, and shelters. Many worked in hospitals.

I frequently run into people in all walks of life who say, "I came to your draft counseling sessions, and that was the turning point of my life. Facing the draft, figuring out who I was and where I wanted to go with my life and why, and seeing that I had a conscience that I could follow and take control of my life – that changed my life forever!" Our "graduates" are all doing wonderful things now, such as being a principal of a high school or working on all kinds of very interesting and useful alternative things.

This was confirmed for me a few years ago when I got an honorary degree at UMass at their graduation. Afterwards, one of the people ran up to me and said, "Jesus Christ! I can't believe you're still here doing this stuff. I was one of your CO's. My son is one of today's graduates, and I'm just so happy you're here!" Similarly last winter someone who had seen something on the Internet about me immediately emailed, saying, "I want to see you. I was one of your early people when I was a student at UMass." He came to visit on his way through town with his wife and children and we had a lovely time. I learned he had become very active in the U.S.-China People's Friendship Association, going to China and participating in talks. Now he's an immigration lawyer in New York City, working with Chinese immigrants. He clearly felt proud of what he was doing. That pleased me, because always the most important thing about our work with all those we counseled about the draft was that they ended up feeling good about their decision and themselves.

The lottery changed things for sure. We were no longer doing draft counseling, but there were more calls from men asking about their eligibility for CO status. I would always be saying, "Look at the law. Read the law. You are qualified." I told them, "The government doesn't want anyone who is conscientiously opposed to the war. If you fit that description, you are actually violating the law if you go in." I shared with them a landmark case during World War II, which involved a man named Dan Seeger. He was not religious, but he held a moral, ethical, and philosophical objection to participation in war. He declared his beliefs with the same degree of intensity as one would if the appeal were based on a religious belief. His lawyers challenged his conviction all the way up to the Supreme Court. Unfortunately it was a long time before the Supreme Court heard that case: it was about a World War II soldier and the decision only came down in the early '60s! Dan was actually in prison when the Supreme Court finally ruled on his behalf. It essentially said if a person holds a moral, ethical, and philosophical objection to war, belief in a supreme being is not essential.

That decision in Dan Seeger's case was really a *pivotal* turning point in the understanding of what defined a conscientious objector. I keep stressing that, and have even printed a letter explaining the role of this case, because most people don't understand its significance. There was a family who lived not far from me that had three sons. The local draft board had turned down the oldest one's application for CO on the grounds that it wasn't religiously based, and as a result, he had gone to Canada. When his younger brothers finally gained an understanding of the law, they said, "Our brother shouldn't have been denied. There was no reason for him to have to refuse induction." We brought him back from Canada and the government dropped the indictment against him.

An important part of the draft information work I did here was monitoring our local draft board. They met on Monday nights, and I would go down Tuesday mornings, when they posted the draft meeting minutes, to be sure they were drafting people in the right order and weren't skipping over people who had political connections. We monitored them closely, and when they knew we were monitoring them, it made a difference. I even parked out in front of the draft board. I would park there and observe who went in for a personal appearance and who came out. I could check to see how honest the draft board was being, but it took that kind of vigilance, and I think most draft counseling centers didn't put that kind of energy into it. We also kept records on draft boards outside of our local area. I knew the draft boards in New Jersey, Vermont, New Hampshire, and even places like Long Island. With that information we were better able to be of service and that's what we were all about.

I didn't care if I was taking risks, because I, too, was acting on my conscience. I knew the government watched me. They even sent someone into one of our sessions, who was very bumbling with a tape recorder, and I knew he had a wig on. So I said, "Look, take off your wig. It's too hot in here. Put your tape recorder away." And he bumbled and fled. Having the sessions at my house wasn't always easy. My neighbors objected to all the motorcycles, and the kids coming in with jeans torn at the knees, and my having so many people coming to my house. One Friday night, in fact, there were seventy-nine of us, and we had to break up into small groups all over the house and yard.

Our neighbors may have taken note, but there was no media coverage of what we were doing. Now as we've been counseling soldiers about their choices in Iraq and Afghanistan, there's a little bit. Recently our local newspaper let me tell the story of my work in the late '60's, but one local article is obviously not enough. Unfortunately, people are still so socialized into an artificial patriotism that any talk of not wanting to fight for the U.S., regardless of the nature of the war, is considered totally un-American. The advertising and propaganda that promote this feeling is just so unrelenting that people become fearful and their minds are totally paralyzed. Only people like Amy Goodman and her show, "Democracy Now", are breaking through the awful misinformation and inertia, trying to wake people up. People need to pay attention and listen. That's why I want to tell people what the law actually is, and give them the GI Rights Hotline number where they can get help, so we don't have to have other soldiers committing suicide like the one that happened in a nearby town!

Diane Bowman

Diane is a partner of Dreeszen & Associates, a consulting firm for non-profit arts groups with her husband, Craig Dreeszen, whose interview is in Chapter Three, "Those Who Left." They have a twenty-three-year-old daughter who lives and works in Oakland, CA. Diane's passion is ballroom dancing, in particular the Argentine tango.

I grew up in Lincoln, Nebraska. My father was a professor of geography at the University of Nebraska. We traveled every other summer to vacation in New Hampshire. The other summers we traveled all over the US camping at national and state parks. My mother went back to get her master's degree in the early '60s and then taught at Lincoln High School.

I went to the University of Nebraska in Lincoln for a year and a half. I had a hard time at the university, because it was so large and I lived at home. It was expected of me to go to college, but in those days it was more to find a husband than to have a career.

There was a march to the capital against the Vietnam War and I had my picture in the newspaper. I remember when my mother saw it and saw how sad I looked, she said that college was supposed to be a fun time in your life. For me it wasn't. I didn't really know what I wanted to study. When I dropped out of college I worked as a sales clerk as a temporary thing to make some money. My career goal at that point was to be an airline stewardess so I could travel and see the world.

Craig had already made the decision to leave the country before I met him. He and a group of friends had even decided where to go in Canada. It was a live-off-the-land thing. My sister and her boyfriend were part of this group.

It was a very emotional time. My parents had already threatened my sister that if she left for Canada, they would disown her. I didn't have to go through that. My parents were off at their summer home in New Hampshire when I left home. I just wrote them a letter saying I was going to visit Craig and my sister and friends in Canada. Later, I wrote to say I wasn't coming home. I didn't have to deal with my parents' disappointment in me.

I knew Craig left the country because he was trying to get out of the draft and avoid going to Vietnam. He had tried to imagine going and he couldn't. He used to joke about it being the only lottery he'd ever won. I don't really remember the lottery itself, but knew people who "won." Some of them got out for health reasons, like having asthma. I remember one friend pretended to be gay, which got him out of the draft.

I got a phone call from Craig a month-and-a-half after he left asking me to join him. I had already made my decision to go – for the adventure and because I had fallen in love with Craig. It was such a wonderful thing to find love. At the time I don't think I really thought it all through in the sense that we were going to get married and live together forever. I was going off on an adventure.

I hitchhiked to Canada with another man who was joining the group, but not dodging the draft. We met up with the group in Vancouver kind of miraculously. We had a phone number, but no address of where they were staying. It ended up being the wrong phone number. The ride we got left us off right as Craig and his friends were crossing the street in this big city to go to a Chinese restaurant. To me it was like fate, that I was really meant to be with this person.

We traveled around British Columbia looking for property to buy and found it was very expensive. The group continued to get smaller. One couple, who had the most money to buy property, left and went back to Nebraska. Finally it was my sister and her boyfriend and Craig and me. We realized that we couldn't really afford any place we were looking at in British Columbia.

We met some people who had just been to northwestern Ontario. They told us how cheap the land was up there. We didn't really know much except there was as much water as land and it got down to nearly forty below in the winter. It was finally a matter of money that made us go. I loved canoeing, so the thought of a bunch of lakes to explore was wonderful, and it was actually closer to Nebraska for when we did come back and visit.

The four of us went east and we bought 140 acres with a very old cabin on it. After we got there my sister ran out of money and went back to Nebraska. Her boyfriend stayed to help us dig a well and build an outhouse. Then he went back to Nebraska, too. Craig and I spent the first winter just the two of us living in one room of the cabin.

We hadn't gotten the property until the beginning of September, which meant we didn't have much time for getting wood to heat our cabin. I remember neighbors coming to check up on us that winter. They were worried that we were going to freeze to death! We didn't have electricity and had a hard time getting our truck started. It was a question of survival. We couldn't even get our car started without electricity. Most people plug their cars in to start them in the winter. Craig would light a kindling fire on a metal shovel and put it under the truck. I was afraid he was going to blow up the truck and himself. He did all kinds of things to get the truck started to get to work. He carried the battery in each night and put it by the stove. Sometimes he would drain the oil and warm it. Then when the car wouldn't start, he'd have to take the battery in a wheelbarrow three quarters of a mile to a neighbor to have it charged.

The hardest times of all were before I had a job and Craig had a shift work job that changed every week or every other week. I was home alone in one tiny room of a small cabin. I started learning crafts, like candle-making and macramé. I'd never been alone in my life. I developed a love of nature and went for hikes in the woods and later learned cross-country skiing. Craig was always so tired with the shift work job. I remember try-ing to have conversations with him when we were going to bed, and he would be falling asleep and I would say, "This is really important to me," but he was so tired we couldn't talk. Growing up I had shared a bedroom with one of my sisters, and we always talked before falling asleep at night. I was very lonely that first winter in Canada in spite of being in love. I missed my parents, sisters and girlfriends terribly.

My first job interview was at a bank. I did fine on the interview and they were ready to hire me. Then they asked about my being from the United States and wanted to know why my parents had decided to move to Canada, as I was only twenty. When I told them I was living with my boyfriend, they wouldn't hire me. Consequently, at my second job inter-view I said I was living with my sister, which was partly true. She and her boyfriend joined us the second year.

Once we were in Canada I didn't think about the war. For two years we didn't have electricity, so we didn't have a TV or even a radio to get news. It was hard that Craig couldn't go back to visit relatives. Most of our neighbors knew Craig was a draft dodger, because we were in such a small community. We were half an hour away from Dryden, a town of seven thousand. It was a five-hour drive west to Winnipeg and a five-hour drive east to Thunder Bay, the nearest cities.

I remember the first winter having a flat tire and a woman in a truck stopped to ask if we needed help. I grew up in a city and was surprised that a woman by herself would stop to help strangers. Maybe it was the harshness of where we were or maybe it was because it was so rural.

We found it odd that neighbors would show up after dinner unannounced, although we didn't have a phone. It was certainly a different way of life than I had growing up in a city. At first we didn't know why people stayed so long, but we finally realized that they were waiting to be served tea. We had a wood cook stove so it took us a while to boil water. We learned to get the fire started as soon as they arrived.

Our neighbors just accepted us. Nobody mentioned anything about us evading the war. Craig would talk about chain saws and things the men were interested in like hunting. Most of the neighbors hunted for deer and went fishing. Most of the local women had children so they talked about their children. I think the people who we became the closest to were transient people, people who were there and then went on to somewhere else. We didn't get any bad reactions. People seemed to be very understanding. We encountered other Americans who lived in that region, but I don't think they were running from the draft. They were just there as part of the "back to the land movement," but they were also trying to get away from the craziness of the war.

My parents came to visit us in Canada after we were married. We were married two years after we moved there. I don't remember them ever asking us to come back. I do remember my father saying it was quite bizarre that we were picking some place to move to and we didn't have jobs. In his generation, the way he grew up, you would move to where the job was, but he never had a conversation with Craig about his draft dodging. They knew that the Vietnam War was different than World War II. My dad's problem with what we had chosen to do was that he believed you don't leave the country when it becomes tough.

We were labeled immigrants and I remember thinking at one point about becoming Canadian, but I didn't want to give up my U.S. citizenship. Later on, when we were living in Toronto, we met a guy who was a lawyer who claimed you could be a dual citizen, but I think we were just too nervous that we wouldn't be able to come back to the U.S.

For eleven years we lived on a one hundred forty-acre farm. We were building a house and we had a woodworking business. We started out building canoes and then we started making wooden toys, which were easy to ship. We shipped them to about sixty stores throughout Canada.

When President Carter granted amnesty to draft dodgers, Craig could have moved back to the U.S., but we were wrapped up in our business. What was wonderful was that we could come back to visit. It's hard to be away from family and not be able to visit. One time, before the amnesty was granted, Craig and I went back to visit his family in Nebraska. I remember his parents being quite nervous that somebody would recognize him and report him, but he wanted to visit his grandmother. She was getting older. I remember being very, very nervous at the border because our truck was in Craig's name and not mine. He was pretending to be somebody else with somebody else's I.D. and they kept questioning us as to why we had this truck. They didn't have computers then. Nowadays this wouldn't have been possible to do. They didn't go inside to look at a list of draft dodgers. They were just at the window of the car questioning us.

We weren't thinking about moving back. I didn't start thinking about it until we moved to Toronto. When I held my mother's hand as she died in 1982, I started thinking about having a child. I think that made me want to move back to the U.S. I also wanted to finish college. We moved to Northampton, Massachusetts in December 1983. We left Dryden, Ontario when it was 40 below zero with a 24-foot U-Haul truck and arrived in Massachusetts in a terrible ice storm with cars driving 30 miles an hour on Interstate 90 and lots of vehicles off the road. That was quite a journey! We bought a house in Florence, Massachusetts in 1985 and spent two years renovating it. Our daughter was born in 1987 and I graduated Smith College in 1996.

It was very hard to leave our rural home because we had made friends there. We had a beautiful property and a house that we built. It was also hard leaving the country. We had wildlife all around us. There were deer, moose, and bears and we could hear the wolves cry. It was easier for me to leave Toronto because I wasn't a city person.

There was also a part of me that never really felt at home in Canada and was sensitive to the jokes about Americans. Part of the time, I just felt like I didn't belong there. It was not that the people weren't welcoming. I just wanted to come back to my roots in New England and the island that I loved.

So it was not hard to come back to the U.S. When I went up to Canada it was for an adventure. I think the harshness of the climate made us not want to stay in Canada, but it was also my wanting to be near my parents' summer home in New Hampshire. When we returned, people here were accepting. I don't remember any judgment made against us for having left the country. People liked hearing about our experience in Canada. Nobody took issue with Craig being a draft dodger.

We went back to Canada where we'd lived in the country when our daughter was five. As much as I missed it, I didn't really want to move back. It was just so isolated. It was fun to see people and I was amazed at my memory and my ability to remember all these people's names.

I remember meeting a man in Northampton who had gone to fight the war in Vietnam. At one point when we were sharing our stories, he said how hard it was for him to come back home at the end of the war. He didn't come back as a hero from a war the way he imagined. Instead some people asked him whether he'd killed women and children, too. I had no idea the anti-war movement would prompt some people to be so mean. I don't think he would have judged Craig. I think he was more upset about how nobody thought he was doing the right thing.

The adventure in Canada took me out of Nebraska and away from my family. The harshness of where we lived in Northwestern Ontario, and the fact that we didn't have running water for nine years didn't make me want to be a mother and to deal with diapers. It was losing my Mom that made me decide to become a mother.

Most of our Canadian experience was positive and we learned a lot about surviving. It was a truly wonderful adventure. I have great stories of canoeing up close to a moose swimming in the water, of camping alone in the woods in the snow and having a wolf sniffing around my tent. Perhaps the harshness of two years without electricity and nine years without running water having to use an outhouse at forty below zero and haul buckets of water from a well made our love grow strong. Craig and I are still in love after all these years.

Libby Holtzman

Libby grew up in California. She was the director of the Faculty and Staff Assistance Program at the University of Massachusetts in Amherst, Massachusetts for ten years. On May 2, 2010 she retired from that position. Four years ago she moved from the home she lived in for twenty-eight years to what she originally called a "fishing shack" and now calls a fishing cottage along the banks of the Swift River in Belchertown, MA. Libby was married to Jay Holtzman, whose interview is in Chapter Three, "Those Who Left." Together they had two children while living in Canada.

My story goes back to my father's side of the family. I come from an unusual family to say the least. My father was a nudist when nobody was a nudist. He would set the hills on fire to burn down the weeds and the fire department would come. He would look like Moses in the middle of this fire. We were the "crazy people" of Los Altos, California, which was very difficult for me. I think he was bi-polar. My father owned a bookstore in Palo Alto. It's called Bell's Bookstore, and it's still there. He was a larger-than-life character in many ways. He had been a conscientious objector during World War II. He had Odetta come to our house to do concerts on the patio. He knew Joan Baez and many other well-known people. She would come to the bookstore and my father would talk with her about the peace movement. I lived with him in the summers after my parents divorced when I was four. My mother would leave to teach in the summer sessions of the Smith School of Social Work. I felt very abandoned. I would write letters to her telling her how unhappy I was and asking her to "get me outta here," but she never did.

I graduated high school in 1959 and went to college as a pre-med student in Seattle at the University of Washington. I studied like crazy, and I was the top student in my pre-med class. I applied to the University of Washington, Stanford and UCLA for med school. I got a call from UCLA asking if I wanted to be interviewed in Seattle. I was interviewed by a guy from the University of Washington who said, "You're going to get married. You'll never be able to pay for this…" I didn't get in, and, since he did the interview for UCLA as well, I got axed there, too. Ten years later a woman sued this man for discrimination and she won. My father's response was, "Maybe you just seemed too immature."

My back-up plan was the Peace Corps. I went to Nigeria for two years. I was in love with an African American. He dumped me, and I was devastated. I finally wrote a letter to my father and said, "Please do not tell my mother..." He got the letter, called my mother and started reading it. My mother had the Peace Corps find out if I was O.K. Then she came to Nigeria to save me from this guy who had dumped me.

When I came home my mother asked me to go to a cocktail party with her as her "trophy daughter" who had been in the Peace Corps. I went around talking about the truth, which was, "I don't think we did a hell of a lot for the Nigerians, but they did an enormous amount for us." I also said, "It should be mandatory to participate in the Peace Corps, because you learn so much about the world and about how completely isolated and bigoted we are," and "When we were out traveling most of us pretended we were Canadian." This was not what my mother expected me to be saying.

I moved to New York after the time in the Peace Corps. I got a job in Bedford-Stuyvesant, New York teaching high school reading. While I was doing that, I applied to social work schools and ended up going to Smith College in Northampton, Massachusetts.

After I graduated from Smith, I got a job at Mass General and that's where I remember everything hitting the fan, and my becoming aware of things. I remember watching the news and being absolutely beside myself. I was very strongly anti-war, but it got to be more central in my life after I met Jay. We dated, and then we got married. His military status, being with the Berry Plan, was a huge factor. His fellow residents, who were also with the Berry Plan, formed a group of conscientious objectors and applied for that status. I think all of them except Jay got it. Then the Air Force started to woo him. They said, "We'll send you to this wonderful place in Florida – Elgin Air Force Base – and you'll never have to go to Vietnam." They knew he didn't want to come in and they were saying, "We'll take really good care of you." I remember saying to him, "If you have to do it, do it, but I cannot play the part. I cannot go to some military wives' tea and act like I belong there." I never directly said to him, "You can't do this," but my perception was that I was the driver on almost all of this. If he had not been with me, I think he would have gone in.

He applied for CO and was turned down. We turned down going to Elgin and moved to California from where he appealed the CO decision. We found this really cute place to live next to a large house in this area called Los Trancos. We were just getting ready to move in and we drove to the place. There were all of these fire engines, and it turned out the house next door had burned to the ground. They had saved the little cottage that we were going to move into, but we couldn't move in until they re-wired the place. So we moved in with my mother. We were devastated, and finally my mother said, "Couldn't you just move in with candles and bottled water?" At which point I said, "Jay, we have to find another place."

Meanwhile, Jay's family was hysterical, and his parents were begging him to go into the service. He had to go to Colorado for his appeal hearing. It was just horrible for him. He came back and talked about how they made him sit way down below the judges. We waited...and waited...and waited to receive word of their decision. I kept saying, "Call your lawyer. Something's got to be wrong. The appeal has got to be lost. It has to be behind somebody's desk." Finally Jay convinced his lawyer to do something and, in fact, that's exactly what had happened. It had been lost, and we'd just been sitting there.

I was horrified about America, and felt we should leave. While we'd been waiting on the outcome of Jay's appeal, we applied to be landed immigrants in Canada. When he came back from Denver, appeal rejected, we got ready to go. We ended up moving to Vancouver, where Jay had no trouble finding a job, and I loved the house we were renting. Jay went through far more challenges than I did. I don't know if I have ever told him how impressed I was, and still am. He had to take all his medical boards over again! Because he hadn't been working in his medical specialty, psychiatry, for several years, he had to do another year of psychiatry residency and take the psychiatric boards all over again. He dealt with amazing stuff and very quietly. It wasn't like he was bitching or being some sort of martyr, he just did it. For him, marrying me was his statement. Going to Canada was far less of a statement than his marrying me.

We had some very good friends who were mostly medical people. Our neighborhood was more a metaphor for what Canada was like at that point. There were British, German, Swedish people. However, the friends we had were mostly Canadians, and I don't remember sitting around talking American politics with them. We were Americans, they were not. Mainly, we were very self-contained. I guess we didn't really seek out other people like ourselves who had left.

And I had babies – closer than I would have chosen. My mother came to visit when they were born, but that's different from having family nearby to help on a more day-to-day basis. Not having that support began to make being in Canada feel hard for me. Mothering was difficult for me. One baby was a challenge, but unexpectedly having a second one only fifteen months after the first took everything I had. Yet I felt I couldn't go home to the States, because I might be arrested for "aiding and abetting" a traitor. So, essentially, the main thing I did in Canada was have two children.

I was also confused about how I wanted to live my life as an American in Canada. I didn't want to be looked upon as somebody who had left fleeing her country; I just wanted to be there living my life like everyone else. Yet I was still so involved with the politics going on in America – much more so than when I lived there. I was addicted to the news, and I wanted justice. Also, there was a whole thing of the military trying to lift Jay's medical license on the basis of "moral turpitude." We had to get the ACLU to represent Jay. Meanwhile, the FBI was visiting his parents, saying, "Get your son home!" and Jay's father was suddenly audited by the IRS. Just unbelievable stuff! I was so angry, and I focused my anger on Nixon and the whole Watergate and his being responsible for everything. The day I remember most vividly is the day that Gerald Ford pardoned him. I cried all day. I wasn't thinking about coming back.

It was the amnesty that changed everything. I wanted to come back and Jay didn't. What happened next was really tough. I remember Jay talking about why he didn't want to go back, and my talking about why I did – being able to take the kids to see my dad (he'd visited us once in Canada, and said he thought what Jay was doing was admirable and brave) and the whole family piece. I don't remember exactly how we made the final decision, but I sure remember what happened after we did. Jay had to go to some camp in Indiana. He got ready, and I went to a friend's house with the kids. I was just a wreck, though he was far more of a wreck than I was, understandably. Next thing I know he's back. He had gotten to the border, and they were so nasty to him, because they knew where he was going, he just turned around and decided he wasn't going to go. When he came back, it was horrible, and it feels more horrible now than it felt then. He did what he needed to do, and ultimately we came back to the States, and that was a difficult transition. Eventually Jay got a job at Baystate Medical Center in Springfield, Massachusetts, and we got a house in nearby Belchertown.

As far as coming back is concerned it was all about what I felt being in Canada. I didn't feel like I belonged. You'd hear about all this stuff going on in the States, and I'd think, that's my country. For better or for worse, that's where I come from. I want to explain this, so I am sure it's understood. The bottom line for me in the decision to leave was: I am not Canadian. I could look at Canada and say, "This is a wonderful place. These are sane people. They have really good moral principles that make sense, although they have their own crazy thing with the French situation." I felt, and I even voiced, that I felt more foreign in Canada than I did in Nigeria, because in Nigeria I was an expatriate. In Canada I "passed." I could've been Canadian, but I wasn't Canadian. It was really that, as much as I hated our country, I was a product of it; I am very American, not in terms of politics, but in terms of all the rest of it. It's hard looking back, but you might say I felt grief because I couldn't be Canadian.

As far as either regrets or appreciation for what happened, I really don't think there was a choice. There was no way I could have played the role of the military wife. If Jay had said, "I am going to Elgin Air Force Base," we probably would've gotten a divorce then. (Jay and Libby were divorced years later while living back in the States). I feel bad that I don't think I ever gave Jay enough credit. What he did was amazing, and he did it for me. I certainly would give him that credit now.

I think nobody realizes how absolutely toxic that time period was and how many people were affected, like the fact that Jay's parents had the F.B.I. going to his house on a regular basis and that my brother, who'd been sent to federal prison as a draft resister, essentially went crazy there. I am going to start crying again. And to think that we were going through all of that, and yet the president, Nixon, could get away scot free after all that he had done! I wasn't sure we would survive as a country. But I realize in talking about it that I need to acknowledge what Jay did. I need to write him a letter...

CONCLUSION

AS I FINISHED EDITING THE FINAL INTERVIEW, filled, like all the others, with remarkable twists and turns and moments of deep emotion, both in the living and in the telling, I realized that I have been on a mission. Being able to bring these stories to an audience, and simultaneously launching a website and blog that will give others the opportunity to tell theirs, has proven to be one of the most inspiring and satisfying experiences of my life. Time after time those whose stories are contained herein – and the other thirty I interviewed – let me know that having the opportunity to give testimony has made a real difference in their lives, both in bringing closure to the past and in re-framing its influence on the present. War and the threat of war most assuredly have enormous power to shake a person up, and this particular war, with all of the turmoil that surrounded it both here and in Vietnam, shook people's worlds in unimaginable ways. With these stories and the others I hope will be given voice through the website and blog, the unimaginable can be acknowledged, and understood.

Our country continues to expend enormous energy pretending that the consequences of war are somehow worth it. We are engaged in two wars at present, in two countries far from the homeland, each of which has a culture as foreign to us as was the culture of Vietnam. From one of these, Iraq, we are slowly extricating ourselves, even as in the other, Afghanistan, we have become increasingly embroiled. The latter has an ominous history of almost endless warfare, and more than one recent commentator has written that Afghanistan has become "President Barack Obama's Vietnam."

One of the participants in this book, Tom Gardner, wrote an article entitled, "Healing Old Wounds," in the *Valley Advocate*, a news and arts weekly in western Massachusetts, which touches upon a greater purpose for my work. Although his focus, when writing in 2004, was on the role the candidacy of John Kerry might play in bringing about reconciliation among those affected by the Vietnam War, his key points transcend the politics and the time period. Gardner begins his piece by stating that, "We Baby Boomers have yet to overcome the divisions of the Vietnam era. In fact we are often reluctant to talk about that period." He goes on to describe asking students in his classes at Westfield State College, how many of them had family members who were involved in the war. Two-thirds raise their hands. When he asks how many have had conversations about the war, only one or two hands go up.

Gardner posits that the difficulty for all those who faced the realities or the threat of war is that "the trauma runs deep and silent." But he also points to the role of the media in "painting those who actively opposed the war and those who donned uniforms and hit the rice paddies...into opposing corners." He acknowledges that "there were some bridges built between protesters and troops during the war" and as examples he cites "G.I. coffeehouses, support for conscientious objectors and resisters within the military, [and] banners that read 'Support our Troops. Bring Them Home Now.'" But he also points to the recent damage that's been done by those he dubs the "chicken-hawks" who avoided Vietnam service, but promote and advocate pre-emptive wars in the 21st century and who have re-invigorated the accusations against those who oppose their actions as giving "aid and comfort to the enemy."

The national conversation that Gardner yearns for is one that allows all sides to know, understand, appreciate and respect one another's experience of the Vietnam draft and war. He points out that "the long hairs and others who dared to point out the mistake, dared to dissent from their government's wrong turn at the time...fought against that war...because we loved our country and its values as much as anyone who donned a uniform."

This is yet another and possibly the most important reason I have written this book. These stories can be part of the process of enabling all those who read them to see the humanity in each person's experience, no matter how different they were. Gardner says it as well as it can be expressed: "Breaking through the divisions of the past might just help us avoid future disasters and shorten present ones. But we need to talk – the combat vets and the anti-war activists and the many in-between including the many G.I.'s who came to oppose the Vietnam War." I hope this book can begin to provide such an opportunity.

That's the higher purpose, but then there are the other aspects unique to the Vietnam era, which are brought alive by the testimonies in this book. I was fascinated as story after story plunged me back into a vital and tumultuous time. The ongoing struggle for racial justice led to an increasing awareness of racism in the military (and in filling the ranks of the military);

as well, its lessons, strategies, and tactics informed the anti-war movement and inspired many to join it. Add to that the revolutions in the culture, in terms of music, drug usage, sexual mores, women's liberation, educational reform, co-education, definitions of gender, and we see afresh a time in American history when everything appeared poised on a knife's edge. On the one hand those times engendered a vast sense of hope and promise; on the other, with the assassinations of Kennedy, Malcolm X, King, and Kennedy, and with the spiraling catastrophe of the War, they were often apocalyptic and suffused with a sense of fatalism and despair.

And no one escaped unscathed. Those who loved the men whose lives were on the line suffered with and through them. On the homefront the racial triumphs of the March on Washington, the Selma to Montgomery March, the integration of public places, gave way to riots in virtually every major city when the Reverend Dr. Martin Luther King was killed in Memphis. What enormous spans of emotion the decade encompassed and what a backdrop to the struggles of the men and women who faced the draft! Learning about these events is essential for the generation coming of age today and those destined to do so when the Vietnam generation to which I belong is gone.

Finally, it has been a great honor to be the recipient of these remarkable testimonies. Each represents a commitment on the part of the teller to revisit and relive challenging times as well as to seek a fuller understanding of themselves by doing so. They allowed me to experience the depth and breadth of the effects of the draft and the war, and it has often been overpowering three times – hearing the testimonies, transcribing them, and, finally, editing them. I have been living with these tales for seven years and now I feel, at least, that this portion of my work is done.

But there is much more to do. Please tell anyone you know who might have a story to tell to find someone who will listen. Then invite them to visit the website and blog (http://www.iraqandvietnamwarstories.com/blog) that accompany the book. I am convinced they will find solace there.

AFTERWORD

Victoria Safford has been minister of White Bear Unitarian Universalist Church in Mahtomedi, Minnesota since 1999, following a ten-year ministry in Northampton, Massachusetts and four years as an organizer with the American Friends Service Committee.

> My story is what it is. I don't like to use the word proud,
> but it sort of gives me strength.
>
> – Jim Thornley, in *Called to Serve*

THIS IS WHAT I HAVE COME TO BELIEVE ABOUT HUMAN BEINGS: we require food, water, shelter, air, and stories. Thornley says of his narrative, "It sort of gives me strength," and indeed, his story radiates strength, contagious strength. His story is beautiful, not because it is happy, necessarily, or hopeful or pretty or noble; it is beautiful, and urgent, because it is true. Like the others gathered in this volume, and like countless others we have known and heard – and not heard – for over forty years, Jim Thornley has spoken truth here. He has given his testimony, given his word, and as with so many stories from the terrible years of the war in Vietnam, it strengthens us to hear it told, to hear truth spoken plainly, in an honest, human voice.

We require stories to survive. Something in us needs to speak and to be heard, to forgive (ourselves and others) and to be forgiven, to make meaning from events and loves and losses that at the time may have made no sense to us, to sing and pass along to children old songs that bear old wounds, old dreams, old agony and old, resilient hope. Telling and hearing stories around a campfire, or through a book like this (or maybe collected on a blog, like the one Tom Weiner has set up), we take part in the transmission of truth, which can be so different from anything transmitted on the evening news, officially filtered for public consumption. True stories are wild and unfettered, unfiltered, beautiful, and sometimes unbearably raw.

The telling can be hard, even after decades of so-called "normal" life. The last American troops left Vietnam in 1973, but certain pieces of the truth have remained there ever since, or lain deep within the hearts and silent memories of those who were called to serve, called to leave, called to refuse or resist, those called to answer conscience before country, those called to offer their support. So many of the men and women represented in this book confess at certain points that they have never shared before the stories that they tell here, so painful or confusing are the memories. They call back a time when the world was exploding in southeast Asia and imploding in American living rooms as the lottery cylinders spun like wheels of fortune, dividing friends and communities in sickening, sorrowing, unimagined ways; when young men (many of them boys) were faced with moral choices complex enough to confound theologians and philosophers -and in they end they were condemned for any choice they made. It was a time when the government was lying and people were dying by the thousands for no cause justified by conscience, and the barely latent, ever-present realities of racism and class privilege could be denied no longer in the "indivisible" (now broken) nation fighting endlessly, it seemed, for "liberty and justice for all."

The men speaking in these pages come from vastly different backgrounds, yet many shared a similar experience: they could plainly see, even at the time, that wealth, race, education and social standing divided all too often those who would go to Vietnam from those who would not, those who might really die from those who need not worry. The telling of such things is hard. The telling of shame, fear, loss, ambivalence, anger (even righteous anger) is hard. Raising old memories to the surface is a mighty work. As Peter Jessop puts it in his interview, "As I look back at this now, it brings me to tears to remember how much the burden of those decisions weighed on me. It was a lot to be carrying inside..."

To those who took the risk of speaking here, and to Tom Weiner who extended such a safe and open welcome in his interviews, we can only be deeply grateful, for these stories are a gift, like lost chapters of our common history recovered. These stories are interwoven with our own, no matter our age or our circumstance. They illuminate our own. Truth telling, truth seeking, truth speaking, secret-breaking, brave naming, bearing witness – this is how trust is restored, healing begins, and the sacred connections of communities rewoven. This is how hope carries on.

Here is one example: On a warm spring evening with a light breeze blowing and crickets singing just outside the open windows, thirty teenagers are sitting in a circle in a congregation's social hall. They are tentative and ill at ease, shifting in their seats, mindful that their parents are present, too, in chairs along the walls beyond the circle. It is 2003, several weeks after the commitment of American troops to "Operation Iraqi Freedom," and these families are worried. Suddenly they are filled with questions about those Selective Service registration cards their children must sign on the day they turn eighteen. They want to know what this "Operation" means, whether it's an all-out war or a counter-terrorism action or an invasion of convenience by the "Coalition of the Willing." They want to know how long it's going to last and already they are asking whether there could be a draft. A presenter from the Central Committee on Conscientious Objection has been invited to speak, along with two CO's, one from Vietnam and one from World War II, and veterans from both those wars, and a third who's closer in age to the young people themselves, a man who served proudly in the first Gulf War, but who will not serve in this one. He believes it is a travesty.

The teens are all in high school, juniors and seniors, young men and women for whom the concept of compulsory military service in a conflict they barely comprehend is as remote and impossible an idea as perhaps it was for some of the adults in the room three and four decades ago. Before any of the speakers speak, we give each teen three pieces of paper and a pen and ask them to answer three questions: *What are your beliefs about war (not* this *war – but* any *war, about war in general)? How did you come by your beliefs? In what ways are you living out your beliefs and values right now, in your everyday life?* They are similar to questions a draft board might ask, that draft boards *did* ask, years ago. For a long while, most of them sit without moving, tapping their feet, looking around, checking their phones. These are difficult questions for people so young. Then slowly one begins to write, and they all begin to write, and the room is very quiet. The adults are given paper, too, much to their surprise, and they are asked to answer the same questions. We are all in this together.

Later, in small groups, they share their answers, and still later, each youth is paired with an adult (not from their own family) and these pairs ask and answer questions of each other back and forth, across the gap of generations and experience: *What would you do? What did* you *do? What did you believe then? What do you believe now? What does it mean to you to be an American citizen? What are your fears, and your hopes, for the future, for yourself and for our country?*

At the end of the night, these pairs commit to continuing the conversation in person and by email, and we arrange to keep a file for anyone who wants one, holding their writing, their dreams and fears – their stories – and encouraging revisions as their convictions change and deepen, and their consciences and consciousness expand.

Unlike their counterparts in 1973, or 1963, these young men and women have the gift of time. Their dilemma is theoretical – at least we hope it is, at least for now. But perhaps the most important difference in their circumstance is the circle in which they are held, a circle of community that contains not only the stories of their elders, told in halting, vivid memories like the stories in this book, but also their own stories, chapters only now beginning, and held with great respect. They are not expected to know all the answers to all the hard questions, not required to carry the conscience of the whole country on their young shoulders, nor to be more courageous than they are. They are not expected to be paragons of virtue, or perfect patriots, or exemplars of political resistance. We only hope that they will understand and in time trust the power of their own moral agency, and that they will come to know that conscience is constructed in community, shaped by stories handed down, and stories they themselves will have a hand in writing. We mean for them to know that they are not alone.

The stories in this book are beautiful, however hard. In sharing them so generously, the men and women represented here help shape "the beloved community," stretching backward in time and also reaching forward. When Martin Luther King used that phrase, through the years of the great movement for civil rights that ran concurrent with the catastrophe in Vietnam, he was referring not to a utopian ideal sometime in the future, not to a distant, gauzy goal of peace and justice, but to a way of being right now, an orientation of the human heart.

It is the goal toward which we walk and it is the *way* we walk, with every step. It is a daily practice, a spiritual politics, which requires honesty, humility, courage, self-respect and mutual respect. It demands the hard, hard discipline of speaking one's truth, and granting gracious hospitality to the truth of other people. Beloved community requires all of this and also unrelenting hope, that we can learn from the past, and walk together toward that future in which, at long last, we will study war no more.

APPENDICES

A Vietnam War Timeline

[Note: This timeline is an abbreviated version of the more detailed timeline posted on the Public Broadcasting System's "Vietnam Online" section of "The American Experience."]

1945

Ho Chi Minh Creates Provisional Government: Following the surrender of Japan to Allied forces, Ho Chi Minh and his People's Congress create the National Liberation Committee of Vietnam to form a provisional government. Japan transfers all power to Ho's Vietminh.

Ho Declares Independence of Vietnam

British Forces Land in Saigon, Return Authority to French

First American Dies in Vietnam: Lt. Col. A. Peter Dewey, head of American OSS mission, was killed by Vietminh troops while driving a jeep to the airport. Reports later indicated that his death was due to a case of mistaken identity — he had been mistaken for a Frenchman.

1946

French and Vietminh Reach Accord: France recognizes Vietnam as a "free state" within the French Union. French troops replace Chinese in the North.

Negotiations Between French and Vietminh Breakdown

Indochina War Begins: Following months of steadily deteriorating relations, the Democratic Republic of Vietnam launches its first concerted attack against the French.

1947

Vietminh Move North of Hanoi

Valluy Fails to Defeat Vietminh: French General Etienne Valluy attempts, and fails, to wipe out the Vietminh in one stroke.

1949

Elysee Agreement Signed: Bao Dai and President Vincent Auriol of France sign the Elysee Agreement. As part of the agreement the French pledge to assist in the building of a national anti-Communist army.

1950

Chinese, Soviets Offer Weapons to Vietminh

The United States sends $15 million dollars in military aid to the French for the war in Indochina. Included in the aid package is a military mission and military advisors.

1953

France Grants Laos Full Independence

Vietminh Forces Push into Laos

1954

Battle of Dienbienphu Begins: A force of 40,000 heavily armed Vietminh lay seige to the French garrison at Dienbienphu. Using Chinese artillery to shell the airstrip, the Vietminh make it impossible for French supplies to arrive by air. It soon becomes clear that the French have met their match.

Eisenhower Cites "Domino Theory" Regarding Southeast Asia: Responding to the defeat of the French by the Vietminh at Dienbienphu, President Eisenhower outlines the Domino Theory: "You have a row of dominoes set up. You knock over the first one, and what will happen to the last one is the certainty that it will go over very quickly."

French Defeated at Dien Bien Phu

Geneva Convention Begins: Delegates from nine nations convene in Geneva to start negotiations that will lead to the end of hostilities in Indochina. The idea of partitioning Vietnam is first explored at this forum.

Geneva Convention Agreements Announced: Vietminh General Ta Quang Buu and French General Henri Delteil sign the Agreement on the Cessation of Hostilities in Vietnam. As part of the agreement, a provisional demarcation line is drawn at the 17th parallel, which will divide Vietnam until nationwide elections are held in 1956. The United States does not accept the agreement, neither does the government of Bao Dai.

1955

Diem Rejects Conditions of Geneva Accords, Refuses to Participate in Nationwide Elections

China and Soviet Union Pledge Additional Financial Support to Hanoi

Diem Urged to Negotiate with North: Britain, France, and United States covertly urge Diem to respect Geneva accords and conduct discussions with the North.

Diem Becomes President of Republic of Vietnam: Diem defeats Bao Dai in rigged election and proclaims himself President of Republic of Vietnam.

1956

French Leave Vietnam

US Training South Vietnamese: The U.S. Military Assistance Advisor Group (MAAG) assumes responsibility, from French, for training South Vietnamese forces.

1957

Communist insurgent activity in South Vietnam begins. Guerrillas assassinate more than 400 South Vietnamese officials. Thirty-seven armed companies are organized along the Mekong Delta.

Terrorist Bombings Rock Saigon: Thirteen Americans working for MAAG and US Information Service are wounded in terrorist bombings in Saigon.

1959

Weapons Moving Along Ho Chi Minh Trail: North Vietnam forms Group 559 to begin infiltrating cadres and weapons into South Vietnam via the Ho Chi Minh Trail. The Trail will become a strategic target for future military attacks.

U.S. Servicemen Killed in Guerilla Attack: Major Dale R. Buis and Master Sargeant Chester M. Ovnand become the first Americans to die in the Vietnam War when guerillas strike at Bienhoa

Diem Orders Crackdown on Communists, Dissidents

1960

North Vietnam Imposes Universal Military Conscription

Kennedy Elected President: John F. Kennedy narrowly defeats Richard Nixon for the presidency.

Diem Survives Coup Attempt

Vietcong Formed: Hanoi forms National Liberation Front for South Vietnam. Diem government dubs them "Vietcong."

1961

Battle of Kienhoa Province: 400 guerillas attack village in Kienhoa Province, and are defeated by South Vietnamese troops.

Vice President Johnson Tours Saigon: During a tour of Asian countries, Vice President Lyndon Johnson visits Diem in Saigon. Johnson assures Diem that he is crucial to U.S. objectives in Vietnam and calls him "the Churchill of Asia."

1962

US Military Employs Agent Orange: US Air Force begins using Agent Orange – a defoliant that came in metal orange containers – to expose roads and trails used by Vietcong forces.

Diem Palace Bombed in Coup Attempt

Mansfield Voices Doubt on Vietnam Policy: Senate Majority Leader Mike Mansfield reports back to JFK from Saigon his opinion that Diem had wasted the two billion dollars America had spent there.

1963

Battle of Ap Bac: Vietcong units defeat South Vietnamese Army (ARVN) in Battle of Ap Bac

President Kennedy Assassinated in Dallas: Kennedy's death meant that the problem of how to proceed in Vietnam fell squarely into the lap of his vice president, Lyndon Johnson.

Buddhists Protest Against Diem: Tensions between Buddhists and the Diem government are further strained as Diem, a Catholic, removes Buddhists from several key government positions and replaces them with Catholics. Buddhist monks protest Diem's intolerance for other religions and the measures he takes to silence them. In a show of protest, Buddhist monks start setting themselves on fire in public places.

Diem Overthrown, Murdered: With tacit approval of the United States, operatives within the South Vietnamese military overthrow Diem. He and his brother Nhu are shot and killed in the aftermath.

1964

General Nguyen Khanh Seizes Power in Saigon: In a bloodless coup, General Nguyen Khanh seizes power in Saigon. South Vietnam junta leader, Major General Duong Van Minh, is placed under house arrest, but is allowed to remain as a figurehead chief-of-state.

Gulf of Tonkin Incident: On August 2, three North Vietnamese PT boats allegedly fire torpedoes at the USS Maddox, a destroyer located in the international waters of the Tonkin Gulf, some thirty miles off the coast of North Vietnam. The attack comes after six months of covert U.S. and South Vietnamese naval operations. A second, even more highly disputed attack, is alleged to have taken place on August 4.

Debate on Gulf of Tonkin Resolution: The Gulf of Tonkin Resolution is approved by Congress on August 7 and authorizes President Lyndon Johnson to "take all necessary measures to repel any armed attack against forces of the United States and to prevent further aggression." The resolution passes unanimously in the House, and by a margin of 82-2 in the Senate. The Resolution allows Johnson to wage all out war against North Vietnam without ever securing a formal Declaration of War from Congress.

Vietcong Attack Bienhoa Air Base

LBJ Defeats Goldwater: Lyndon Johnson is elected in a landslide over Republican Barry Goldwater of Arizona. During the campaign, Johnson's position on Vietnam appeared to lean toward de-escalation of US involvement, and sharply contrasted the more militant views held by Goldwater.

1965

Operation "Rolling Thunder" Deployed: Sustained American bombing raids of North Vietnam, dubbed Operation Rolling Thunder, begin in February. The nearly continuous air raids would go on for three years.

Marines Arrive at Danang: The first American combat troops, the 9th Marine Expeditionary Brigade, arrive in Vietnam to defend the U.S. airfield at Danang. Scattered Vietcong gunfire is reported, but no Marines are injured.

Heavy Fighting at Ia Drang Valley: The first conventional battle of the Vietnam war takes place as American forces clash with North Vietnamese units in the Ia Drang Valley. The US 1st Air Cavalry Division employs its newly enhanced technique of aerial reconnaissance to finally defeat the NVA, although heavy casualties are reported on both sides.

U.S. Troop Levels Top 200,000

Vietnam "Teach-In" Broadcast to Nation's Universities: The practice of protesting US policy in Vietnam by holding "teach-ins" at colleges and universities becomes widespread. The first "teach-in" — featuring seminars, rallies, and speeches — takes place at the University of Michigan at Ann Arbor in March. In May, a nationally broadcast "teach-in" reaches students and faculty at over 100 campuses.

1966

B-52s Bomb North Vietnam: In an effort to disrupt movement along the Mugia Pass – the main route used by the NVA to send personnel and supplies through Laos and into South Vietnam — American B-52s bomb North Vietnam for the first time.

South Vietnam Government Troops Take Hue and Danang

LBJ Meets With South Vietnamese Leaders: U.S. President Lyndon Johnson meets with South Vietnamese Premier Nguyen Cao Ky and his military advisors in Honolulu. Johnson promises to continue to help South Vietnam fend off aggression from the North, but adds that the U.S. will be monitoring South Vietnam's efforts to expand democracy and improve economic conditions for its citizens.

Veterans Stage Anti-War Rally: Veterans from World Wars I and II, along with veterans from the Korean war stage a protest rally in New York City. Discharge and separation papers are burned in protest of U.S. involvement in Vietnam.

CORE Cites "Burden On Minorities and Poor" in Vietnam: The Congress of Racial Equality (CORE) issues a report claiming that the U.S. military draft places "a heavy discriminatory burden on minority groups and the poor." The group also calls for a withdrawal of all U.S. troops from Vietnam.

1967

Operation Cedar Falls Begins: In a major ground war effort dubbed Operation Cedar Falls, about 16,000 U.S. and 14,000 South Vietnamese troops set out to destroy Vietcong operations and supply sites near Saigon. A massive system of tunnels is discovered in an area called the Iron Triangle, an apparent headquarters for Vietcong personnel.

Bunker Replaces Cabot Lodge as South Vietnam Ambassador

Martin Luther King Speaks Out Against War: Calling the U.S. "the greatest purveyor of violence in the world," Martin Luther King publicly speaks out against U.S. policy in Vietnam. King later encourages draft evasion and suggests a merger between anti-war and civil rights groups.

Dow Recruiters Driven From Wisconsin Campus: University of Wisconsin students demand that corporate recruiters for Dow Chemical – producers of napalm – not be allowed on campus.

McNamara Calls Bombing Ineffective: Secretary of Defense Robert McNamara, appearing before a Senate subcommittee, testifies that U.S. bombing raids against North Vietnam have not achieved their objectives. McNamara maintains that movement of supplies to South Vietnam has not been reduced, and neither the economy nor the morale of the North Vietnamese has been broken.

1968

January

Sihanouk Allows Pursuit of Vietcong into Cambodia

North Vietnamese Launch Tet Offensive: In a show of military might that catches the U.S. military off guard, North Vietnamese and Vietcong forces sweep down upon several key cities and provinces in South Vietnam, including its capital, Saigon. Within days, American forces turn back the onslaught and recapture most areas. From a military point of view, Tet is a huge defeat for the Communists, but turns out to be a political and psychological victory. The U.S. military's assessment of the war is questioned and the "end of tunnel" seems very far off.

February

Battle for Hue: The Battle for Hue wages for 26 days as U.S. and South Vietnamese forces try to recapture the site seized by the Communists during the Tet Offensive. Previously, a religious retreat in the middle of a war zone, Hue was nearly leveled in a battle that left nearly all of its population homeless. Following the U.S. and ARVN victory, mass graves containing the bodies of thousands of people who had been executed during the Communist occupation are discovered.

Westmoreland Requests 206,000 More Troops

My Lai Massacre: On March 16, the angry and frustrated men of Charlie Company, 11th Brigade, Americal Division entered the village of My Lai. "This is what you've been waiting for – search and destroy – and you've got it," said their superior officers. A short time later the killing began. When news of the atrocities surfaced, it sent shockwaves through the U.S. political establishment, the military's chain of command, and an already divided American public.

March

LBJ Announces He Won't Run: With his popularity plummeting and dismayed by Senator Eugene McCarthy's strong showing in the New Hampshire primary, President Lyndon Johnson stuns the nation and announces that he will not be a candidate for re-election.

April

Martin Luther King Slain in Memphis

May

Paris Peace Talks Begin: Following a lengthy period of debate and discussion, North Vietnamese and American negotiators agree on a location and start date of peace talks. Talks are slated to begin in Paris on May 10 with W. Averell Harriman representing the United States, and former Foreign Minister Xuan Thuy heading the North Vietnamese delegation.

June

Robert Kennedy Assassinated

August

Upheaval at Democratic Convention in Chicago: As the frazzled Democratic party prepares to hold its nominating convention in Chicago, city officials gear up for a deluge of demonstrations. Mayor Richard Daley orders police to crackdown on anti-war protests. As the nation watched on television, the area around the convention erupts in violence.

November

Richard Nixon Elected President: Running on a platform of "law and order," Richard Nixon barely beats out Hubert Humphrey for the presidency. Nixon takes just 43.4 percent of the popular vote, compared to 42.7 percent for Humphrey. Third-party candidate, George Wallace, takes the remaining percentage of votes.

1969

Nixon Begins Secret Bombing of Cambodia: In an effort to destroy Communist supply routes and base camps in Cambodia, President Nixon gives the go-ahead to "Operation Breakfast." The covert bombing of Cambodia, conducted without the knowledge of Congress or the American public, will continue for fourteen months.

Policy of "Vietnamization" Announced: Secretary of Defense Melvin Laird describes a policy of "Vietnamization" when discussing a diminishing role for the U.S. military in Vietnam. The objective of the policy is to shift the burden of defeating the Communists onto the South Vietnamese Army and away from the United States.

Ho Chi Minh Dies at Age 79

News of My Lai Massacre Reaches US: Through the reporting of journalist Seymour Hersh, Americans read for the first time of the atrocities committed by Lt. William Calley and his troops in the village of My Lai. At the time the reports were made public, the Army had already charged Calley with the crime of murder.

Massive Antiwar Demonstration in Washington, D.C.

1970

Sihanouk Ousted in Cambodia: Prince Sihanouk's attempt to maintain Cambodia's neutrality while war raged in neighboring Vietnam forcing him to strike opportunistic alliances with China, and then the United States. Such vacillating weakened his government, leading to a coup orchestrated by his defense minister, Lon Nol.

Kent State Incident: National Guardsmen open fire on a crowd of student antiwar protesters at Ohio's Kent State University, resulting in the death of four students and the wounding of eight others. President Nixon publicly deplores the actions of the Guardsmen, but cautions: "... when dissent turns to violence it invites tragedy." Several of the protesters had been hurling rocks and empty tear gas canisters at the Guardsmen.

Kissinger and Le Duc Begin Secret Talks

Number of US Troops Falls to 280K

1971

Lt. Calley Convicted of Murder

Pentagon Papers Published: A legacy of deception, concerning U.S. policy in Vietnam, on the part of the military and the executive branch is revealed as the New York Times publishes the Pentagon Papers. The Nixon administration, eager to stop leaks of what they consider sensitive information, appeals to the Supreme Court to halt the publication. The Court decides in favor the Times and allows continued publication.

Nixon Announces Plans to Visit China: In a move that troubles the North Vietnamese, President Nixon announces his intention to visit The People's Republic of China. Nixon's gesture toward China is seen by the North Vietnamese as an effort to create discord between themselves and their Chinese allies.

Thieu Re-elected in South Vietnam

1972

Nixon Cuts Troop Levels by 70K: Responding to charges by Democratic presidential candidates that he is not moving fast enough to end U.S. involvement in Vietnam, President Nixon orders troop strength reduced by seventy thousand.

Secret Peace Talks Revealed

B-52s Bomb Hanoi and Haiphong: In an attempt to force North Vietnam to make concessions in the on-going peace talks, the Nixon administration orders heavy bombing of supply dumps and petroleum storage sites in and around Hanoi and Haiphong. The administration makes it clear to the North Vietnamese that no section of Vietnam is off-limits to bombing raids.

Break-In at Watergate Hotel

Kissinger Says "Peace Is At Hand": Henry Kissinger and Le Duc Tho reach agreement in principle on several key measures leading to a cease-fire in Vietnam. Kissinger's view that "peace is at hand," is dimmed somewhat by South Vietnamese President Thieu's opposition to the agreement.

Nixon Wins Reelection

1973

Cease-fire Signed in Paris: A cease-fire agreement that, in the words of Richard Nixon, "brings peace with honor in Vietnam and Southeast Asia," is signed in Paris by Henry Kissinger and Le Duc Tho. The agreement is to go into effect on January 28.

End of Draft Announced

Last American Troops Leave Vietnam

Hearings on Secret Bombings Begin: The Senate Armed Services Committee opens hearing on the U.S. bombing of Cambodia. Allegations are made that the Nixon administration allowed bombing raids to be carried out during what was supposed to be a time when Cambodia's neutrality was officially recognized. As a result of the hearings, Congress orders that all bombing in Cambodia cease effective at midnight, August 14.

Kissinger and Le Duc Tho Win Peace Prize: The Nobel Peace Prize is awarded to Henry Kissinger of the United States and Le Duc Tho of North Vietnam. Kissinger accepts the award, while Tho declines, saying that a true peace does not yet exist in Vietnam.

1974

Thieu Announces Renewal of War

Report Cites Damage to Vietnam Ecology: According to a report issued by The National Academy of Science, use of chemical herbicides during the war caused long-term damage to the ecology of Vietnam. Subsequent inquiries will focus on the connection between certain herbicides, particularly Agent Orange, and widespread reports of cancer, skin disease, and other disorders on the part of individuals exposed to them.

Communists Take Mekong Delta Territory

Nixon Resigns

Communists Plan Major Offensive: With North Vietnamese forces in the South believed to be at their highest levels ever, South Vietnamese leaders gird themselves for an expected Communist offensive of significant proportions.

1975

Communist Forces Capture Phuoc Long Province: The South Vietnamese Army loses twenty planes in a failed effort to defend Phuoc Long, a key province just north of Saigon. North Vietnamese leaders interpret the U.S.'s complete lack of response to the siege as an indication that they could move more aggressively in the South.

Hue Falls to Communists

Communists Take Aim at Saigon: The North Vietnamese initiate the Ho Chi Minh Campaign — a concerted effort to "liberate" Saigon. Under the command of General Dung, the NVA sets out to capture Saigon by late April, in advance of the rainy season.

Ford Calls Vietnam War "Finished": Anticipating the fall of Saigon to Communist forces, U.S. President Gerald Ford, speaking in New Orleans, announces that as far as the U.S. is concerned, the Vietnam War is "finished."

Last Americans Evacuate as Saigon Falls to Communists: South Vietnamese President Duong Van Minh delivers an unconditional surrender to the Communists in the early hours of April 30. North Vietnamese Colonel Bui Tin accepts the surrender and assures Minh that, "...Only the Americans have been beaten. If you are patriots, consider this a moment of joy." As the few remaining Americans evacuate Saigon, the last two U.S. servicemen to die in Vietnam are killed when their helicopter crashes.

DRAFT BOARD CLASSIFICATIONS

The following is a list of Selective Service classifications that could be assigned by draft boards:

I-A Available for military service

I-A-0 Conscientious objector available for noncombatant military service only

I-C Member of the armed forces of the U.S., the Coast and Geodetic Survey, or the Public Health Service

I-D Member of reserve component or student taking military training

I-H Registrant not currently subject to processing for induction

I-0 Conscientious objector available for civilian work contributing to the maintenance of the national health, safety, or interest

I-S Student deferred by statute (High School)

I-Y Registrant available for military service, but qualified for military only in the event of war or national emergency

I-W Conscientious objector performing civilian work contributing to the maintenance of the national health, safety, or interest

II-A Registrant deferred because of civilian occupation (except agriculture or activity in study)

II-C Registrant deferred because of agricultural occupation

II-D Registrant deferred because of study preparing for the ministry

II-S Registrant deferred because of activity in study

III-A Registrant with a child or children; registrant deferred by reason of extreme hardship to dependents

IV-A Registrant who has completed service; sole surviving son

IV-B Official deferred by law

IV-C Alien

IV-D Minister of religion or divinity student

IV-F Registrant not qualified for any military service

IV-G Registrant exempt from service during peace (surviving son or brother)

IV-W Conscientious objector who has completed alternate service contributing to the maintenance of the national health, safety, or interest in lieu of induction into the Armed Forces of the United States

V-A Registrant over the age of liability for military service

A further note from an email in May 2002:

"I noticed that my draft classification was not listed on your site's list of draft board classification - 1SC. It meant that you had exactly six months to get your affairs in order before you would be drafted.

I was 2S until February 1966 when I received my draft notice to report for induction. After talking with my draft board they let me finish my school semester then drafted me. During that period I was issued a draft card with the 1SC designation.

In July of 1966 I was drafted into the US Army. Regards, Tom Olsen, Pvt, USCDCEC, 1966-1968"

RESULTS OF THE FIRST VIETNAM WAR DRAFT LOTTERY HELD DECEMBER 1, 1969

The highest number drafted in this group of men was 195.

Jan 1 305	Feb 1 86	Mar 1 108
Jan 2 159	Feb 2 144	Mar 2 29
Jan 3 251	Feb 3 297	Mar 3 267
Jan 4 215	Feb 4 210	Mar 4 275
Jan 5 101	Feb 5 214	Mar 5 293
Jan 6 224	Feb 6 347	Mar 6 139
Jan 7 306	Feb 7 91	Mar 7 122
Jan 8 199	Feb 8 181	Mar 8 213
Jan 9 194	Feb 9 338	Mar 9 317
Jan 10 325	Feb 10 216	Mar 10 323
Jan 11 329	Feb 11 150	Mar 11 136
Jan 12 221	Feb 12 68	Mar 12 300
Jan 13 318	Feb 13 152	Mar 13 259
Jan 14 238	Feb 14 4	Mar 14 354
Jan 15 17	Feb 15 89	Mar 15 169
Jan 16 121	Feb 16 212	Mar 16 166
Jan 17 235	Feb 17 189	Mar 17 33
Jan 18 140	Feb 18 292	Mar 18 332
Jan 19 58	Feb 19 25	Mar 19 200
Jan 20 280	Feb 20 302	Mar 20 239
Jan 21 186	Feb 21 363	Mar 21 334
Jan 22 337	Feb 22 290	Mar 22 265
Jan 23 118	Feb 23 57	Mar 23 256
Jan 24 59	Feb 24 236	Mar 24 258
Jan 25 52	Feb 25 179	Mar 25 343
Jan 26 92	Feb 26 365	Mar 26 170
Jan 27 355	Feb 27 205	Mar 27 268
Jan 28 77	Feb 28 299	Mar 28 223
Jan 29 349	Feb 29 285	Mar 29 362
Jan 30 164		Mar 30 217
Jan 31 211		Mar 31 30

Apr 1 32	May 1 330	Jun 1 249
Apr 2 271	May 2 298	Jun 2 228
Apr 3 83	May 3 40	Jun 3 301
Apr 4 81	May 4 276	Jun 4 20
Apr 5 269	May 5 364	Jun 5 28
Apr 6 253	May 6 155	Jun 6 110
Apr 7 147	May 7 35	Jun 7 85
Apr 8 312	May 8 321	Jun 8 366
Apr 9 219	May 9 197	Jun 9 335
Apr 10 218	May 10 65	Jun 10 206
Apr 11 14	May 11 37	Jun 11 134
Apr 12 346	May 12 133	Jun 12 272
Apr 13 124	May 13 295	Jun 13 69
Apr 14 231	May 14 178	Jun 14 356
Apr 15 273	May 15 130	Jun 15 180
Apr 16 148	May 16 55	Jun 16 274
Apr 17 260	May 17 112	Jun 17 73
Apr 18 90	May 18 278	Jun 18 341
Apr 19 336	May 19 75	Jun 19 104
Apr 20 345	May 20 183	Jun 20 360
Apr 21 62	May 21 250	Jun 21 60
Apr 22 316	May 22 326	Jun 22 247
Apr 23 252	May 23 319	Jun 23 109
Apr 24 2	May 24 31	Jun 24 358
Apr 25 351	May 25 361	Jun 25 137
Apr 26 340	May 26 357	Jun 26 22
Apr 27 74	May 27 296	Jun 27 64
Apr 28 262	May 28 308	Jun 28 222
Apr 29 191	May 29 226	Jun 29 353
Apr 30 208	May 30 103	Jun 30 209
	May 31 313	

Jul 1 93	Aug 1 111	Sep 1 225
Jul 2 350	Aug 2 45	Sep 2 161
Jul 3 115	Aug 3 261	Sep 3 49
Jul 4 279	Aug 4 145	Sep 4 232
Jul 5 188	Aug 5 54	Sep 5 82
Jul 6 327	Aug 6 114	Sep 6 6
Jul 7 50	Aug 7 168	Sep 7 8
Jul 8 13	Aug 8 48	Sep 8 184
Jul 9 277	Aug 9 106	Sep 9 263
Jul 10 284	Aug 10 21	Sep 10 71
Jul 11 248	Aug 11 324	Sep 11 158
Jul 12 15	Aug 12 142	Sep 12 242
Jul 13 42	Aug 13 307	Sep 13 175
Jul 14 331	Aug 14 198	Sep 14 1
Jul 15 322	Aug 15 102	Sep 15 113
Jul 16 120	Aug 16 44	Sep 16 207
Jul 17 98	Aug 17 154	Sep 17 255
Jul 18 190	Aug 18 141	Sep 18 246
Jul 19 227	Aug 19 311	Sep 19 177
Jul 20 187	Aug 20 344	Sep 20 63
Jul 21 27	Aug 21 291	Sep 21 204
Jul 22 153	Aug 22 339	Sep 22 160
Jul 23 172	Aug 23 116	Sep 23 119
Jul 24 23	Aug 24 36	Sep 24 195
Jul 25 67	Aug 25 286	Sep 25 149
Jul 26 303	Aug 26 245	Sep 26 18
Jul 27 289	Aug 27 352	Sep 27 233
Jul 28 88	Aug 28 167	Sep 28 257
Jul 29 270	Aug 29 61	Sep 29 151
Jul 30 287	Aug 30 333	Sep 30 315
Jul 31 193	Aug 31 11	

Oct 1 359	Nov 1 19	Dec 1 129
Oct 2 125	Nov 2 34	Dec 2 328
Oct 3 244	Nov 3 348	Dec 3 157
Oct 4 202	Nov 4 266	Dec 4 165
Oct 5 24	Nov 5 310	Dec 5 56
Oct 6 87	Nov 6 76	Dec 6 10
Oct 7 234	Nov 7 51	Dec 7 12
Oct 8 283	Nov 8 97	Dec 8 105
Oct 9 342	Nov 9 80	Dec 9 43
Oct 10 220	Nov 10 282	Dec 10 41
Oct 11 237	Nov 11 46	Dec 11 39
Oct 12 72	Nov 12 66	Dec 12 314
Oct 13 138	Nov 13 126	Dec 13 163
Oct 14 294	Nov 14 127	Dec 14 26
Oct 15 171	Nov 15 131	Dec 15 320
Oct 16 254	Nov 16 107	Dec 16 96
Oct 17 288	Nov 17 143	Dec 17 304
Oct 18 5	Nov 18 146	Dec 18 128
Oct 19 241	Nov 19 203	Dec 19 240
Oct 20 192	Nov 20 185	Dec 20 135
Oct 21 243	Nov 21 156	Dec 21 70
Oct 22 117	Nov 22 9	Dec 22 53
Oct 23 201	Nov 23 182	Dec 23 162
Oct 24 196	Nov 24 230	Dec 24 95
Oct 25 176	Nov 25 132	Dec 25 84
Oct 26 7	Nov 26 309	Dec 26 173
Oct 27 264	Nov 27 47	Dec 27 78
Oct 28 94	Nov 28 281	Dec 28 123
Oct 29 229	Nov 29 99	Dec 29 16
Oct 30 38	Nov 30 174	Dec 30 3
Oct 31 79		Dec 31 100

The following news article appeared in newspapers the day after the 1969 draft lottery, December 2, 1969

September 14 'Wins' Draft Lottery
June 8 Brings Up The Rear;
850,000 Affected by Drawing

By Mike Miller

WASHINGTON — The Selective Service System today was notifying the nation's 4,000 draft boards to arrange their files of draft eligible young men for 1970 with those born Sept. 14 at the top of the heap to be called up first. And the official notice sent to state and local Selective Service authorities places those men with June 8 birthdays in 366th position — at the very bottom.

850,000 Involved

That was the start and the finish of last night's long-awaited lottery-by-birthday drawing, which opened with an invocation and closed with a benediction. In between it saw the draft future being determined for an estimated 850,000 young men, many of whom must have been saying their own prayers about the results. For those with birthdays drawn in the upper portion of the lottery list — Apr. 24, Dec. 30, Feb. 14, Oct. 18, Sept. 6, Oct. 26, Sept. 7, Nov. 22 and Dec. 6 round out the top 10 — the uncertainty over their draft status has ended.

Plans Can Be Made

They now know they will be drafted early in the year unless they volunteer first. And those at the bottom know that they will not be drafted and can plan their lives accordingly. For those in the middle or marginal area of the drawing, uncertainty still exists. But they certainly will know definitely by the end of 1970 whether they will be inducted. They would have had a maximum of seven years of uncertainty under the old system of drafting first the oldest available men age 19 through 25. This system expires Jan. 1.

Drawing Low-Key

The lottery was conducted in low key fashion with young men and women representing Selective Service's youth advisory committees in the various states drawing capsules containing slips of paper with the birth dates on them from a water-cooler size glass bowl. Rep. Alexander Pirnie,

New York Republican who drew the first date, was the only person in an official capacity to pull out the capsule. Mr. Pirnie is the senior Republican on the House Armed Service Committee's special subcommittee on the draft.

More Reform Urged

But the use of the young people led to a few public expressions of dissent that while the lottery is commendable, more wide-ranging draft reforms should follow. Three young men expressed such sentiments while a fourth, David L. Fowler representing the District of Columbia, said he had been "notified" not to draw and walked out. Nevertheless, Lt. Gen. Lewis B. Hershey, 76, Selective Service director who has been accused of heavy-handed draft policies, rose and shook Mr. Fowler's hand. About a dozen youthful demonstrators picketed outside, denouncing the draft, the lottery and the Vietnam War, but they failed to interfere with the smooth precision of the drawing.

Following the drawing of dates, including February 29 for men born in a leap year, the young people also drew the 26 letters of the alphabet to determine the order for induction for men registered with the same draft board and having the same birthday. J was drawn first, V last. Thus a man named Jones would be drafted before Vickery under those circumstances. Upon receiving official notice of the lottery's results, local draft boards will arrange their files of registrants accordingly and draft in the order dates were drawn. After a board has filled its draft quota for the year, those men whose birthdays have not been reached will be free of all draft liability except in time of extreme national emergency.

As a general rule, Selective Service expects those with dates drawn in the upper third of the list will be drafted. Those in the middle third are of questionable status and those in the bottom third will not have to serve.

The estimated 850,000, who will be nineteen through twenty-five and classified 1-A or draft eligible as of January 1 are directly affected by last night's drawing. After the first year, only men 19 at the beginning of the year and older men with deferments which have expired will be affected by the annual lotteries.

For men now in the 19-25 pool with college or other deferments, the position their birthdays were drawn will determine their liability in the year their deferments expire. For example, President Nixon's son-in-law, David Eisenhower, apparently will be ripe for drafting when his deferment expires in mid-1970 upon his expected graduation from Amherst College. His birthday, March 31, was drawn 30th. Since men in the 30th position in his draft board probably will already have been drafted by June, David would go to the top of his draft board's list of eligibles.

Neither Gen. Hershey nor any of the other Selective Service officials present moved to cut off the statements of the handful of participants who spoke out. Larry McKibben, the Iowa representative, read a petition he said represented the views of 14 young people. The 14 objected to the barring from the proceedings of Michigan and Alaska delegates who had come to Washington for the occasion, but then reportedly announced they would refuse to draw out birth dates. John M. Bowers of Minnesota said the petition did not represent the views of any of the others.

BIBLIOGRAPHY

"American National Guard: A History of the American Militia since its Beginning," *National Guard Heritage*, 1995/2009 <http://www.desertgold.com/america/1637.html>.

"Arthur Wellesley, First Duke of Wellington." Encyclopædia Britannica. 2009. Encyclopædia Britannica Online. 13 Aug. 2009 <http://www.britannica.com/EBchecked/ topic/639392/ Arthur-Wellesley-1st-duke-of-Wellington>.

Ashton, John. *Social Life in the Reign of Queen Anne.* London: Chatto and Windus, 1882.

"Central Commmittee for Conscientious Objectors" <http://www.objector.org/How_We_Began.html>.

Ehrlich, Judith, Tejada-Flores, Rick.filmmakers, "The Good War and Those Who Refused to Fight It," PBS, January 2002, <http://www.pbs.org/itvs/thegoodwar/story.html>.

"Chronology of Conscription in the U.S. – Colonial Era to 1999", *American History Teacher's Book of Lists*, Dec. 3, 2008 <http://www.teachervision.fen.com/us-history/resource/5669.html>.

Coakley, R.W., Scheips,P.J., Wright, E.J. with Horne, G. and Sandler, Stanley (ed.). "Anti-war Sentiment in the Korean War, 1950-1953," *The Korean War: An Encyclopedia.* New York: Garland Publishing, Inc. 1955.

D'Amato, Anthony A. "War Crimes and Vietnam: The 'Nuremberg Defense' and the Military Service Resister," 57 California Law Review 1055 (1969) <http://anthonydamato.law.northwestern.edu/Adobefiles/A69d-nurembergdef.

Draft Classifications, http:/www.landscaper.netdraft.htm#How's%20your %20%22Luck%20of%20the%20Draw%22?

Ehrlich, Judith, Tejada-Flores, Rick.filmmakers, "The Good War and Those Who Refused to Fight It," PBS, January 2002, <http://www.pbs.org/itvs/thegoodwar/story.html>.

Foner, Eric and Garraty, John.*The Reader's Companion to American History.* Boston: Houghton Mifflin, Co., 1991.

Ford, Gerald. "Remarks Announcing a Program for the Return of Vietnam Era Draft Evaders and Military Deserters," September 16,

1974 <http://www.presidency.ucsb.edu /ws/index.php?pid=4713>.

Greenberg, David. "Rough Draft: The revive-conscription movement has history against it," *Slate* Jan. 23, 2003, 20 July 2009 <http://slate.msn.com/id/2077346/>.

Hummel, Jeffrey Rogers."The American Militia and the Origin of Conscription: A Reassessment," Journal of Libertarian Studies, 15 (Fall 2001). http://www.mises.org/journals/jls/15_4/15_4_2.pdf)

Jennings, David."No Taxes for Freedom," DISCOVERTHENETWORKS, May 2, 2003 <://www.discoverthenetworks.org/groupProfile.asp?grpid=6635>.

"Join the British Army", <http://www.umich.edu/~ece/student projects/soldier/>.

Jordan, Harold. "War Resistance, Amnesty and Exile – Just the Facts", http://www.afsc.org/Youth&Militarism/ht/display/ContentDetails/i/18993

Kohn, Stephen. M., *Jailed for Peace*. Westport, Conn.: Greenwood Press, 1986.

Kusch, Frank. *All American Boys: Draft Dodgers in Canada from the Vietnam War*. Santa Barbara: Praeger Publishers, 2001.

Lynn, Conrad J. "The Case of David Mitchell versus the United States," *Left and Right: A Journal of Libertarian Thought*, Vol. 1, Number 2, Autumn 1965.

Mount, Steve. "Constitutional Topic: Powers of Congress." *USConstitution.net*.30 Nov 2001 <http://www.usconstitution.net/consttop_mlaw.html>.

Moskos, Charles C. *A Call To Civic Service: National Service for Country and Community*. New York: The Free Press, 1988.

O'Brien, Tim.*The Things They Carried*. Boston: Houghton Mifflin, 1990.

"One Discharge for All," *Winter Soldier*, November 1973 <http://vvaw.org/veteran/ article/?id=1079>.

Oral History Interview with Igal Roodenko, April 11, 1974. Interview B-0010. Southern Oral History Program Collection (#4007) in the Southern Oral History Program Collection, Southern Historical Collection, Wilson Library, University of North Carolina at Chapel Hill

Packard, Gabriel. "Iraq: Hundreds of U.S. Soldiers Emerge as Conscientious Objectors," Inter Press Service News Agency <http://ipsnews.net/news.asp?idnews=17584>.

Rassbach, Elsa. interview, "Soldier Seeking Asylum: 'I Want to be Able to Atone", May 28, 2009, <http://www.commondreams.org/headline/2009/05/28-4>.

Raugh, Harold E. *The Victorians at War: An Encyclopedia of British Military History, 1815-1914.* Santa Barbara, CA: ABC- CLIO, Inc., 2004.

Schulzinger, Robert D. *A Time for Peace, The Legacy of the Vietnam War.* Oxford: Oxford University Press, 2006.

"Sept. 14th 'Wins' Draft Lottery, June 8th Brings Up the Rear; 850,000 Affected by the Lottery," http://www.landscaper.net/draft.htm#Sept.%2014%20%27Wins%27%20Draft%20Lottery

Solnit, David. *The Way out of Iraq,* Alternet, 5/9/05 <www.alternet.org/rights/21974/ >.

Sutherland, David. ed. *Guerrillas, Unionists, and Violence on the Confederate Home Front,* Arkansas: The University of Arkansas Press, 1999.

Vietnam War Timeline, http://www.pbs.org/wgbh/amex/vietnam/timeline/index.html

"War Resistance, Anti-Militarism, and Deportation, 1917-1919," *The Emma Goldman Papers,* exhibition coordinator Sally Thomas, 2002 <http://sunsite.berkeley.edu/Goldman/Exhibition>.

Ward, Harry. *Going Down the Hill: Legacies of the American Revolutionary War,* California: Press LLC, 2008.

Whayne, Jennie M.,Deblack, Thomas A., Sabo, George. *Arkansas: A Narrative History.* University of Arkansas Press, 2002.

Whiteclay Chambers II, John."Conscription," *The Oxford Companion to American Military History 2000* <http://www.encyclopedia.com/doc/10126-Conscriptio

ENDNOTES

CHAPTER ONE – The Draft in America: A Brief History

1. Harold E. Raugh, *The Victorians at War: An Encyclopedia of British Military History, 1815-1914,* (Santa Barbara, CA: ABC- CLIO, Inc., 2004), xiv.

2. "Arthur Wellesley, 1st Duke of Wellington." *Encyclopædia Britannica.* 2009. Encyclopædia Britannica Online. 13 Aug. 2009 <http://www.britannica.com/EBchecked/ topic/639392/ Arthur-Wellesley-1st-duke-of-Wellington>.

3. "Join the British Army", <http://www.umich.edu/~ece/student projects/soldier/>.

4. John Ashton, *Social Life in the Reign of Queen Anne,* (London: Chatto and Windus, 1882), 309.

5. "American National Guard: A History of the American Militia since its Beginning," *National Guard Heritage,* 1995/2009 <http://www.desertgold.com/america/1637.html>.

6. David Greenberg, "Rough Draft: The revive-conscription movement has history against it," *Slate* Jan. 23, 2003, 20 July 2009 <http://slate.msn.com/id/2077346/>.

7. "Chronology of Conscription in the U.S. – Colonial Era to 1999", *American History Teacher's Book of Lists,* Dec. 3, 2008 <http://www.teachervision.fen.com/us-history/resource/5669.html>.

8. Harry Ward, *Going Down the Hill: Legacies of the American Revolutionary War,* (Academica Press LLC, 2008), 100.

9. Ibid.

10. Harry Ward, *Going Down the Hill: Legacies of the American Revolutionary War,* (Academica Press LLC, 2008), 100.

11. Ibid.

12. Steve Mount, "Constitutional Topic: Powers of Congress." *USConstitution.net.* 30 Nov 2001 <http://www.usconstitution.net/consttop_mlaw.html>.

13. Charles C. Moskos, *A Call To Civic Service: National Service for Country and Community,* (New York: The Free Press, 1988), 26.

14. Ward, *Going Down the Hill,* 101.

15. Ibid.

16. Ward, *Going Down the Hill,* 101-2.

17. Eric Foner and John Garraty, *The Reader's Companion to American History,* (Boston: Houghton Mifflin, Co., 1991), 216.

18. Ibid.

19. John Whiteclay Chambers II, "Conscription," *The Oxford Companion to American Military History 2000* <http://www.encyclopedia.com/doc/10126-Conscription.html>.

20. Jeffrey Rogers Hummel, "The American Militia and the Origin of Conscription: A Reassessment," *Journal of Libertarian Studies*, 15 (Fall 2001), 29–77. http://www.mises.org/journals/jls/15_4/15_4_2.pdf).

21. "Chronology of Conscription in the U.S. – Colonial Era to 1999", <http://www.teachervision.fen.com/us-history/resource/5669.html>.

22. "Chronology of Conscription in the U.S. – Colonial Era to 1999", *American History Teacher's Book of Lists*, Dec. 3, 2008 <http://www.teachervision.fen.com/us-history/resource/5669.html>.

23. Daniel Sutherland, ed. *Guerrillas, Unionists, and Violence on the Confederate Home Front.* (Arkansas: The University of Arkansas Press, 1999), 24.

24. Foner and Garraty, *The Reader's Companion*, 217.

25. Ibid.

26. Moskos, *A Call To Civic Service: National Service for Country and Community*, 26.

27. "War Resistance, Anti-Militarism, and Deportation, 1917-1919, *The Emma Goldman Papers*, exhibition coordinator Sally Thomas, 2002 <http://sunsite.berkeley.edu/Goldman/Exhibition>.

28. Ibid.

29. Foner and Garraty, *The Reader's Companion to American History*, 217.

30. Moskos, *A Call to Civic Service*, 27.

31. Ibid.

32. Jeannie M. Whayne, Thomas A. Deblack, George Sabo, *Arkansas: A Narrative History*, (University of Arkansas Press, 2002), 297- 8. This story was uncovered by high school students of Sheryl Norwood, a classroom teacher in Arkansas, who created a unit to teach them that draft resistance during World War I – in their home state no less – set the precedent for future efforts to protest war.

33. Daniel G. Jennings, "No Taxes for Freedom," *DISCOVERTHENETWORKS*, May 2, 2003 <http://www.discoverthenetworks.org/groupProfile.asp?grpid=6635>.

34. Foner and Garraty, *Readers Companion to American History*, p. 217. This is precisely what our government did with those serving in Iraq and continues to do with those serving in Afghanistan. In the 2004 presidential campaign, John Kerry claimed that George W. Bush, through employment of such tactics as the Stop-Loss program, the involuntary extension of a service member's active duty service under the enlistment contract in order

to retain them beyond their initial end of term of service date, was conducting a "back door draft."

35. Foner and Garraty, *Readers Companion to American History*, p. 217.

36. Judith Ehrlich, Rick Tejada-Flores, filmmakers, "The Good War and Those Who Refused to Fight It," PBS, January 2002, <http://www.pbs.org/itvs/thegoodwar/story.html>.

37. Ibid.

38. Foner and Garraty, *The Reader's Companion to American History*, 218.

39. "Central Commmittee for Conscientious Objectors" <http://www.objector.org/ How_We_Began.html>.

40. Foner and Garraty, *The Reader's Companion to American History*, 218.

41. There was never an actual declaration of war.

42. "Vietnam War" <http://www.wikianswers/Q/When did the Vietnam War start and end>.

43. Foner and Garraty, *The Reader's Companion to American History*, 218.

44. Ibid.

45. Foner and Garraty, *The Reader's Companion to American History*, 218.

46. Ibid.

47. Harold Jordan, "War Resistance, Amnesty and Exile – Just the Facts", http://www.afsc.org/Youth&Militarism/ht/display/ContentDetails/i/18993.

48. David Solnit, *The Way out of Iraq*, Alternet, 5/9/05 <www.alternet.org/rights/21974>. Actress Jane Fonda, singer Holly Near, actor Donald Sutherland and others participated in the political vaudeville show known as FTA, which toured the country in 1971 and was released as a film in 1972. The acronym FTA supposedly stood for "Free the Army" or "Free the Americans" or "Fun, Travel and Adventure," the name of a popular GI antiwar newspaper published in Ft. Knox, Kentucky; but they were all stand-ins for what came to be the political statement "Fuck the Army."

49. Foner and Garraty, *The Reader's Companion to American History*, 218.

50. Harold Jordan, "War Resistance, Amnesty and Exile – Just the Facts."

51. Ibid.

52. Gerald Ford, "Remarks Announcing a Program for the Return of Vietnam Era Draft Evaders and Military Deserters," September 16, 1974 <http://www.presidency.ucsb.edu /ws/index.php?pid=4713>.

53. Robert D. Schulzinger, *A Time for Peace, The Legacy of the Vietnam War*, (Oxford University Press, 2006), 3 - 4.

54. Ibid.

55. Harold Jordan, "What Happened to Vietnam Era War Resisters?" <http ://www.afsc.org/ Youth&Militarism/ht/display/ContentDetails/i/18993>.

56. "One Discharge for All," *Winter Soldier,* November 1973 <http://vvaw.org/veteran/ article/?id=1079>. There are five classifications for discharge from the military: honorable and the four less-than-honorable categories — general, undesirable, bad conduct and dishonorable.

57. Harold Jordan, "What Happened to Vietnam Era War Resisters?" <http :/ /www.afsc.org/ Youth&Militarism/ht/display/ContentDetails/i/18993>.

58. Ibid.

59. Ibid.

60. Ibid.

61. Moskos, *A Call to Civic Service,* 46.

62. Harold Jordan, "What Happened to Vietnam Era War Resisters?" <http :/ /www.afsc.org/ Youth&Militarism/ht/display/ContentDetails/i/18993>.

CHAPTER THREE – Those Who Left

1. Tim O'Brien, *The Things They Carried.* (Boston: Houghton Mifflin, 1990, 60-61)

2. Ibid. 61-63.

3. Hagan, John, *Northern Passage: American War Resisters in Canada.* (Cambridge: Harvard University Press, 2001)

4. Kusch, Frank. *All American Boys: Draft Dodgers in Canada from the Vietnam War.* (Santa Barbara: Praeger Publishers, 2001.

CHAPTER SIX – Those Who Were Ruled By Conscience

1. Charles C. Moskos, *A Call To Civic Service: National Service for Country and Community,* (New York: The Free Press, 1988), p. 26.

2. Stephen M. Kohn, *Jailed for Peace,* (Westport, Conn.: Greenwood Press, 1986), p.6

3. Moskos, *A Call To Civic Service,* p. 26.

4. Ibid.

5. Eric Foner and John Garraty, *The Reader's Companion to American History,* (Boston: Houghton Mifflin, Co., 1991), p.214.

6. Moskos, *A Call To Civic Service,* pp. 26-27.

7. Foner and Garraty, *The Reader's Companion to American History,* 214.

8. Moskos, *A Call To Civic Service,* 27.

9. Ibid.

10. A simple "1-A" meant the draftee could be assigned anywhere.

11. Moskos, *A Call to Service,* p.27

12. Moskos, *A Call To Civic Service,* 28.

13. Foner and Garraty, *The Reader's Companion to American History*, 215.

14. Ibid.

15. Moskos, *A Call To Civic Service*, 28-29.

16. Oral History Interview with Igal Roodenko, April 11, 1974. Interview B-0010. Southern Oral History Program Collection (#4007) in the Southern Oral History Program Collection, Southern Historical Collection, Wilson Library, University of North Carolina at Chapel Hill.

17. Ibid, 29.

18. Ibid.

19. Moskos, *A Call To Civic Service*, 29.

20. R.W. Coakley, P.J. Scheips, E.J. Wright with G. Horne and Stanley Sandler (ed.), "Anti-war Sentiment in the Korean War, 1950-1953," *The Korean War: An Encyclopedia*, (New York: Garland Publishing, Inc. 1955), 25.

21. Coakley, Scheips, Wright with Horne and Sandler (ed.), "Anti-war Sentiment in the Korean War," 25.

22. Foner and Garraty, *The Reader's Companion to American History*, 218.

23. Anthony A. D'Amato, "War Crimes and Vietnam: The 'Nuremberg Defense' and the Military Service Resister," 57 California Law Review 1055 (1969) <http://anthony damato.law.northwestern.edu/Adobefiles/A69d-nurembergdef.pdf.>.

24. Conrad J. Lynn, "The Case of David Mitchell versus the United States," *Left and Right: A Journal of Libertarian Thought*, Vol. 1, Number 2, Autumn 1965, 15.

25. Lynd Straughton, "Soldiers of Conscience," *The Nation*, Oct. 20, 2006.

26. Ibid.

27. Gabriel Packard, "Iraq: Hundreds of U.S. Soldiers Emerge as Conscientious Objectors," Inter Press Service News Agency <http://ipsnews.net/news.asp/idnews=17584>.

28. Ibid.

29. Ibid.

30. Elsa Rassbach interview, "Soldier Seeking Asylum: 'I Want to be Able to Atone," May 28, 2009, <http://www.commondreams.org/headline/2009/05/28-4>.

31. Ibid.

ACKNOWLEDGEMENTS

My gratitude and appreciation goes to all of the men and women who were willing to share their stories with me. Without their honesty and openness there would be no book. I also want to thank Peter Smith and Seth Shulman who provided much encouragement during various stages of the project. Llan Starkweather has given enormously – his time, his knowledge and his wisdom. For editing assistance I want to pay tribute to the way beyond-the-call efforts of Margaret Lobenstine and Steven Bauer whose devotion to and support of the project and whose hands-on labors helped to make this book what it is. And not only did Tom Gardner share his story and provide some of the inspiration for the conclusion, he also proofread the final manuscript. I want to thank Diane Clancy for her incredible assistance in setting up the website and blog that accompany the book.

I want to also express my deep appreciation to my wife, Susan Dudek and my children, Annabel, Caleb, Madeline and Stefan. whose acceptance of my dedication to the project and whose patience with me for the past seven years during which I not only wrote this book, but taught 6th grade, was immense.